ENGLISHMEN AT SEA

ENGLISHMEN AT SEA

LABOR AND THE NATION AT THE

DAWN OF EMPIRE, 1570–1630

Eleanor Hubbard

Yale

UNIVERSITY PRESS

New Haven & London

Published with assistance from the Mary Cady Tew Memorial Fund and
from the Fund established in memory of Oliver Baty Cunningham,
a distinguished graduate of the Class of 1917, Yale College, Captain,
15th United States Field Artillery, born in Chicago September 17, 1894,
and killed while on active duty near Thiaucourt, France, September 17,
1918, the twenty-fourth anniversary of his birth.

Yale University Press books may be purchased in
quantity for educational, business, or promotional use.
For information, please email sales.press@yale.edu
(U.S. office) or sales@yaleup.co.uk (U.K. office).

Set in MT Baskerville & MT Bulmer type by IDS Infotech Ltd.,
Chandigarh, India.
Printed in the United States of America.

Library of Congress Control Number: 2021935874
ISBN 978-0-300-24612-4 (hardcover : alk. paper)

A catalogue record for this book is available from the British Library.

This paper meets the requirements of
ANSI/NISO Z39.48-1992 (Permanence of Paper).

10 9 8 7 6 5 4 3 2 1

For Leo, once more

CONTENTS

Acknowledgments, ix
Conventions, xi

Introduction, 1

CHAPTER ONE
A Plundering People, 26

CHAPTER TWO
Renegades and Reprisals, 65

CHAPTER THREE
Risks and Rewards, 94

CHAPTER FOUR
Piracy and Empire, 134

CONTENTS

CHAPTER FIVE

Sailors and the Company-State, 163

CHAPTER SIX

Englishness Abroad, 205

CHAPTER SEVEN

Sailors and the State, 243

Epilogue, 275

Notes, 281

Bibliography, 311

Index, 333

ACKNOWLEDGMENTS

Writing this book has taken me a long time, and it would have taken longer and been less enjoyable without the support of colleagues, family, and friends near and far, especially my husband Leonidas Nguyen, as well as the generous support of Princeton University. However, as I complete the book in the throes of the 2020 pandemic, after an interval of several months with no childcare, I am particularly conscious of the gratitude I owe to a different set of people, without whom the book would have been wholly impossible. I began research for it soon after the birth of my first child, in 2011. Now that the book is complete, my third and youngest child has turned four. My children, Delilah, Edward, and Chloe have been a source of tremendous joy for me, but they have in no way helped with my writing. Rather, during these long years, a small army of talented teachers and nannies made it possible for me to be a mother and a scholar at the same time. I am particularly grateful to the teaching staff at UNOW in Princeton, New Jersey, an early childhood center that has stayed true to its feminist and child-centered roots over fifty years. Day in and day out, their hard work has made school a delightful place for my young children, allowing me to go to work with a light heart. In August 2020, despite the dangers of working with groups of young children during the pandemic, UNOW reopened and teachers returned to work. Without their courage and dedication, my youngest child would still be home and this book would be even later than it already is. To the UNOW teachers and to all childcare workers whose essential but often unacknowledged labor makes parents' creative work possible, I extend my deepest thanks.

CONVENTIONS

Dates are given as they appear in the sources, but with the year beginning on January 1. Spelling, capitalization, and punctuation have been modernized for clarity.

ENGLISHMEN AT SEA

INTRODUCTION

In July 1609, a ship bound for Virginia was overtaken by a hurricane. Within minutes the sky turned black, and the screaming wind drowned out the shrieks of the passengers; even the sailors grew pale when they saw that the *Sea Venture* was taking in water at a fearful rate. With candles, the seamen searched the ship, but they could not find the leak. All the men on board were set to the frantic task of pumping and bailing out the ship, and so they labored "with tired bodies and wasted spirits three days and four nights, destitute of outward comfort and desperate of any deliverance." God seemed to have turned his face from the failing ship. On the fourth morning, however, as the exhausted people prepared to commit themselves "to the mercy of the sea," they saw land. By night, the *Sea Venture* was wrecked on a reef, and they were all on shore on Bermuda. To their immense relief the reputed "Devil's Islands" proved to be a welcoming refuge. The English people stayed there for almost ten months, admiring the strange flora and fauna, eating turtles, and quarreling among themselves, while the master carpenter, Richard Frobisher, built the *Deliverance*, and the commander supervised the construction of the *Patience*. In due course, the two small vessels were complete, and they set sail for Virginia. Almost immediately the *Deliverance* hit a reef and nearly came to grief but was saved by the "quick spirit" of the coxswain, Robert Walsingham, in the ship's boat; he towed the pinnace to safety. On May 23, the *Deliverance* and the *Patience* came at last to Jamestown, where after all their travails they received a poor welcome from the starving colonists.[1]

This dramatic story is a well-known episode in the history of early America. For the *Sea Venture*'s sailors, however, it was just another ordeal in working lives that spanned the globe. The seamen who stepped unsteadily onto the shore of Bermuda had landed in other unfamiliar places before, and would do so again: Italy, Morocco, the Azores, the Cape Verde Islands, the Cape of Good Hope, Java, even China—these and more would be visited by members of the *Sea Venture*'s company, sometimes in the guise of merchant seamen, and sometimes as privateers, corsairs, or outright pirates. Placing the experiences of these mobile mariners at the center of the *Sea Venture*'s story reframes it from being one of westward settlement to one of global labor, connecting the Mediterranean, the Atlantic, and the Indian Ocean, the Old World and the New, the East and the West. The lives of the quick-witted coxswain and the ingenious carpenter wrecked on Bermuda illustrate the vexed roles sailors played in the projection of English influence abroad, and the conflicts that arose when merchant companies sought to shape and control overseas expansion, a corporate vision of empire that clashed with the freewheeling traditions of English seafarers. All over, sailors were essential to English enterprise, yet they made troublesome imperial subjects.

Like many of his contemporaries, Robert Walsingham served as a privateer during Elizabeth's reign.[2] He had already lost one hand by 1604 when, after the end of the Anglo-Spanish War, he joined a merchant vessel bound for Genoa, but soon relapsed into predatory ways when he was impressed—with the ship and his crewmates—into Medici service. Flying the Tuscan flag and prowling the eastern Mediterranean, he and others killed hundreds of Ottoman subjects, causing considerable diplomatic difficulties for the English Levant Company.[3] Unable to return to England, the ship's master, Robert Thornton, became a Catholic renegade, but Walsingham seems to have avoided punishment and later set sail on the doomed *Sea Venture*. After his return from Virginia, Walsingham served on the *Daisy* bound on a smuggling voyage to the West Indies, but he never got there: when his ship was captured off the Guinea coast by an English pirate fleet, he opted to join his captors.[4] He rose through the pirate ranks, crisscrossing the Atlantic world from Senegal to Newfoundland, eventually becoming captain of his own ship based in the English pirate enclave of Mamora on the Atlantic coast of war-torn Morocco. When Mamora was captured by Spanish forces in 1614, Walsingham moved first to Algiers, then Tunis, leading mostly Muslim crews, but quickly grew weary of this service and sailed to Ireland, where in 1618 he threw himself on the king's mercy.[5] His knowledge of North African corsair ports proved useful; pardoned, the ex-pirate served more or less loyally in the navy for the rest of his long career.[6]

Meanwhile, after his return from Virginia, Richard Frobisher entered the service of the East India Company and sailed to the Red Sea, Java, the Molucca Islands, and Japan. The skillful carpenter was a pillar of loyalty for his captain on a voyage plagued with mutiny and desertion. Frobisher even acted as a cultural ambassador for the East India Company, performing English music for Japanese dignitaries at Hirado.[7] After returning to London, lucky to have survived his dangerous travels, Frobisher made two more voyages to the Indian Ocean. On the last, then forty years old, he agreed to stay in the East Indies for seven years on the condition that he be permitted to bring his wife, children, and maidservant. Unfortunately, while sailing from Banten to Japan they were all shipwrecked off the coast of China; later they were captured by the Portuguese. Frobisher met his death in captivity in Malacca, apparently a faithful servant of the East India Company to the end.[8] If Walsingham's picaresque career exemplifies the continued vitality of the Elizabethan predatory seafaring tradition and the value the state placed on its warlike subjects, Frobisher inhabited a more corporate, disciplined form of empire founded on trade.

Like the elite travelers who roam through Alison Games's *Web of Empire*, seafarers were men with global horizons, cosmopolitans who moved fluidly across institutional, legal, and even national boundaries. Unlike Games's diplomats, merchants, governors, and clergymen, however, sailors were skilled laboring men. Sometimes their interests coincided with those of their merchant employers or of the Crown—but often they did not. Indeed, though their knowledge and labor were essential to the Virginia

Company, the sailors of the *Sea Venture* were largely indifferent to its aims and interests. They were troublesome in Bermuda, where they often challenged the authority of the governor, and they were troublesome at Jamestown as well. As the colonists went hungry, the sailors would sneak out at night in their longboats to Algonquian villages, where they bartered copper for furs, undercutting the struggling colony's effort to control trade. William Strachey complained that even when trading with the planters, the sailors insisted on making the same kinds of profits they made in the East Indies, four to one.[9] Sailors ignored the Virginia Company leaders' claim to speak for the common good; they disobeyed the instructions of their distant employers; and they had their own ideas about how to engage with local people, ideas shaped by their wide-ranging experience of maritime travel and trade.

This was a transformative moment for England in the world. Though the kingdom possessed no territorial empire to speak of beyond the British Isles, and the Crown generally lacked the ability to project power far overseas, English ships and sailors were going where they had never gone before. In the late sixteenth century, religious warfare in Europe and growing appetites for foreign luxuries spurred English shipping to new heights. The disruption of Antwerp forced English merchants to look farther afield to sell English cloth and buy foreign wares. Increasingly open war with Spain drew hundreds of ships and thousands of men to sea in privateering ventures, where Englishmen were schooled in navigation and gunnery as they hunted the vastly larger merchant fleets of Spain and Portugal. Other English ships entered the Mediterranean in pursuit of trade and plunder, eyeing its busy markets and rich, slow merchant vessels. When the rebellious Dutch states aggressively promoted East Indian ventures to make up for lost access to Lisbon's spices, the English were not far behind. In the Americas, militant Protestants and hopeful investors challenged Spanish preeminence. In Newfoundland, English seamen harvested abundant cod; in cold northern waters, they slaughtered whales and walruses. At Elizabeth's accession, English ships were largely confined to European waters; by the early seventeenth century they were all over the globe.

In contrast to other European seaborne empires, in which the state played a more central role, English maritime expansion remained largely a matter of private enterprise, more the uncoordinated product of a multitude of actors and their short-term interests than any coherent imperial plan. Both under Elizabeth and under James I, the Crown remained resolutely focused on European politics. Profits from the sea were welcome, but the periphery remained stubbornly peripheral—and even if the English state was interested in projecting national power beyond Europe, its creaky finances were a serious check. As a result, English expansion was semiprivate: individuals and corporations laid claim to goods, trade routes, and distant territories, basing their claims on letters of reprisal, commissions, charters, and letters patent as well as physical possession and occupation.

For the Crown, this indirect rule had its advantages; it attracted vigorous investment and produced new streams of customs revenues at little cost. Private expansion also presented problems, however: sometimes, the state's ostensible representatives in distant places pursued their own interests, oblivious to official policy. During the later war years of Elizabeth's reign, this was justly a source of scandal. Private naval ventures backed by men at the highest levels of the government veered greedily into piracy, weakly restrained by an admiralty that was itself run for profit and vulnerable to political pressure, leading Kenneth Andrews to question whether the Elizabethan state was indeed much more than the "mere conglomeration" of the interests of powerful families.[10] Later, as English investors shifted their attention to commerce and colonies, they produced an empire that was less likely to actively undermine the stated policy of the Crown but was still fundamentally a conglomeration of private interests. Inevitably, authority did not simply originate within the metropolitan state and radiate out to the periphery; it was also constructed within the corporations themselves and in the territorial colonies.[11]

Making money, making sovereignty: imperial corporations could do both, Philip Stern has argued, because they were political bodies from the outset, not just extensions of the state.[12] Indeed, the larger body politic of England was composed of myriad smaller ones. Guilds, incorporated towns, universities, and other corporations recognized royal rule, but they were also forms of "commonwealth" that, to varying degrees, ruled subjects and nurtured traditions of active political citizenship.[13] English people's lives were structured by plural forms of jurisdiction, overlapping layers of sovereignty, intersecting models of political participation. In

England, corporate claims to sovereignty hemmed one another in and were kept in check by the monarchy, but abroad they flourished luxuriantly. In India, Stern argues, the East India Company did not accidentally become a territorial state in the eighteenth century: it was state-like from its inception.[14] These diverse sites of authority were essential partners for the central state but also posed a challenge. Rather than commanding colonial elites, the state had to negotiate with them. By the time the British state attempted to discipline its unruly empire, subordinating the periphery to the core had become an intractable problem. The distinctive form English expansion took in its freewheeling, experimental early years left an enduring imprint.

If profit-driven trading companies and colonial corporations were forms of commonwealth, we might well ask what was common in them, and whose wealth counted. After all, the idea of "commonwealth" rested on the assumption that there was such a thing as the public good. But who were members of the commonwealth, and who were outsiders, of whom less account need be taken? In practice, the public good was less of a calculation—the greatest good for the greatest number, for example—than the claim that only the interests of certain people mattered, the people who *belonged*. Were those who labored abroad citizens or servants? How much allegiance did they owe to their merchant masters—and what were they owed in return? Belonging was, of course, already a fraught question in England: as landowners strove to squeeze more income out of their holdings and a growing population strained traditional social structures, the division between those who were deemed worthy of aid and those who were excluded took on greater salience. Since poor relief was administered by individual parishes, such belonging was necessarily local: one belonged—or did not—in a particular place, not in the commonwealth as a whole.[15] Vagrants were the outsiders within. Belonging looked different in the empire, however. In the early settlements, where labor was scarce rather than abundant, the boundaries of belonging had more to do with controlling labor than with poor relief.

New territories opened the way to the aggressive reshaping of social relations: private rulers and colonial elites fashioned societies that were advantageous to themselves, expecting much of their laboring subjects and granting little. The logic of indentured servitude, that characteristic form of early colonial labor, was that servants were indeed meant to become sharers in colonial commonwealths: to become full members of society, they were simply obliged to pay the debt they had incurred. They were, in theory, not so different from trade apprentices, who after the payment of a premium and years of unpaid service could hope to attain civic "freedom" and to set up their own households as citizens. But in practice many indentured servants found that the colonies offered them oppression, not inclusion. In Virginia during the years of the tobacco boom, for example, laboring English people were subjected to new degrees of naked exploitation. When making money was everything, and the ordinary constraints of custom and neighborhood did not apply, rapacious leading men fleeced the Virginia Company and brutalized their servants, whom they bought and sold in defiance of paternalist tradition. Severe mortality meant that many servants did not survive their terms of service, and those who did often found that land was much less accessible than they might have supposed. In Virginia, the best tracts of land were likely to have been claimed—even if they were not actually worked—by large planters, and in tiny Barbados the situation was even worse: servants who survived their tropical ordeals found that the little land available was priced far beyond their reach.[16]

Early English imperial investors were not motivated by profit alone, but among their various goals making money was generally central. To be sure, colonial promoters argued that the transportation of poor laborers served the public good by providing a means for England to rid itself of superfluous inhabitants. With population on the rise and poverty increasing, these writers argued that the colonies served as an outlet for excess humors whose corruption threatened the health of the body politic. It was "no new thing, but most profitable for our state, to rid our multitudes of such as lie at home, pestering the land with pestilence and penury, and infecting one another with vice and villainy, worse than the plague itself," one explained.[17] The transportation of convicts and political and religious undesirables similarly promised to turn worthless people to good use. Such patriotic explanations may have resonated with metropolitan audiences, but it is doubtful how important they were to the planters themselves. For them, indentured servitude and convict transportation functioned largely as a means of obtaining the labor they needed at advantageous rates, an alternative to African and Indian slavery.[18] When the supply of British servants and convicts failed to meet colonial demand, the planters' response was not to retract their activities but to turn to the mass exploitation of enslaved West Africans.[19]

Without the accretion of customary rights and traditional practices that governed English economic life, the field was open for merchants and wealthy planters to fashion governments and legal codes to serve their interests. Indentured servitude bore some similarities to coercive labor practices in England: pauper apprentices also served without pay, for example, and masterless men and women could be forced to enter service at set wages.[20] Domestic policy developed in the context of widespread unemployment, however, not of labor shortage. Just as young people could be forced to enter service, so householders could be forced to take them in. The central goal was to make the poor belong somewhere, to shore up a precarious social order.[21] In the developing plantation economies of Virginia and Barbados, servants' claim to belonging was far more tenuous. On land, laboring people lost ground.

The sea, however, was where the bulk of early English expansion took place. Elizabethan and Jacobean maritime enterprise did not create a territorial empire: it produced little more than a few straggling settlers, a handful of wary merchants here and there. Even when they were planted, colonies were slow to take root. Of far more import, in the short run, was the web of shipping routes that gave England access to Levantine silk and cotton, Mediterranean currants and wines, Brazilian sugar, West Indian hides, the rich fisheries off Newfoundland, the furs and wax of Muscovy, and the spices of the East Indies. In Kenneth Andrews's classic survey of early English maritime enterprise, *Trade, Plunder, and Settlement,* trade and plunder came first for a reason. Territorial settlements—especially those that endured, like Jamestown and Plymouth, not the fever-ridden failures on Madagascar or in South America—loom large in our narrative of early English empire, but in the early seventeenth century, places that produced no or few territorial possessions were often just as important, if not more so.

Pushing back against an older tendency to see the seeds of empire in Elizabethan sea exploits, modern scholarship has remained ambivalent about the relationship between maritime expansion and empire in the sixteenth and early seventeenth centuries. Andrews revealed the chasm between Elizabethan imperial rhetoric and reality, destroying "the illusion ... that some grand mercantile and imperial strategy was at work" in the haphazard and often disastrous ventures of the day. N. A. M. Rodger writes that with little room for cargo or passengers, heavily armed and handy English ships were "not, in this period, at all suitable for founding or sustaining a colonial empire overseas." Small wonder, then, that by 1625, as John Appleby concludes, "England had become an oceanic seafaring nation capable of rivaling Spain or Portugal, but it had yet to establish an overseas colony able to reproduce itself."[22]

For early modern Englishmen, of course, territorial control was usually not the object. By and large, early English imperial actors wanted wealth, and while acquiring land was one means of attaining prosperity, it was hardly the only one.[23] Sir Walter Raleigh thought "whosoever commands the sea commands the trade; whosoever commands the trade of the world commands the riches of the world, and consequently the world itself." He would have readily embraced Elizabeth Mancke's argument that "control of the world's oceans was a fundamental part of European empire building."[24] In Raleigh's lifetime, of course, controlling the oceans was impossible: Britannia did not yet rule the waves, nor did anyone else. For the most part, English imperialists sought not to command the sea but to enjoy it, but even this was a challenge. The sea was a conduit, not a barrier, but it could only be crossed with ships and sailors: maritime capacity was measured in tonnage of shipping, in thousands of mariners. These had to be armed if English ships were to pass through contested maritime space with sufficient strength to deter attackers and capture weaker vessels. Common routes and coastlines were heavily trafficked, shared—peacefully or not—by ships of many nations. Like highways, they attracted bandits: pirates and privateers did not cruise at random but lurked in the places where they expected to find prey. The sea was not an empty, frictionless space but one in which worlds collided; borders abruptly came into being then melted away as ships met and parted. If most early English settlements—fortified encampments of young men who hoped for plunder or trade—looked rather like stationary ships, ships were like mobile colonies.[25]

Before they settled foreign lands, then, the English settled the sea. They did not command it, but they were far more potent than their hapless early attempts at settlement suggest. Like the land empire that came later, however, the early English sea empire was a jumble of private projects, a tangle of conflicting interests. There too, participants disputed the allocation of the risks and rewards of overseas enterprise. The idea that merchant companies' interests were national interests was critiqued in printed tracts and also on shipboard, in word and deed. Merchant capitalism entailed the renegotiation of social relationships, all the more so because sailors were both "the tools of empire" and its rebellious subjects.[26] Asserting jurisdictional claims over overseas subjects was an early way that European rulers and their representatives claimed sovereignty in distant lands and seas, as Lauren Benton has argued, but that jurisdiction was contested when sailors mutinied, became pirates, or entered foreign service. Imperial conflict took place not just between rival fleets but also within English ships and around sailors' bodies as merchants and investors tried to mobilize sailors' labor and claim their allegiance, while seamen set their own courses for survival and gain.[27] Control over people, not space, was the key to seaborne empire.

The troubled, tightening relationships between mariners, merchants, and the state in this first phase of empire followed a path different from that of labor relations in the early colonies on land. Seamen found that their central role in overseas expansion carried certain advantages. Mercantilists theorized about seamen as human capital, but sailors had ideas about how best to spend their lives and labors and were often able to put those ideas into effect.[28] Their skills and mobility, the dangers and endemic violence of the seas, the weakness of the state, and the decentralized nature of the English empire all combined to give seafaring laborers more bargaining power than their fellows on land, a stronger claim to belonging.

Medieval maritime custom endowed English sailors with the belief that their interests ought to be central to maritime enterprise. Early modern ships were temperamental things, complicated pieces of technology that required expert handling, strenuous labor, and favorable winds to move from place to place. The men who provided that expertise and strength were also—as critical observers noted—temperamental and stubborn, "like to a stiff necked horse, which taking the bridle betwixt his teeth, forceth his rider to what him list, mauger his will."[29] Global navigation was novel for Englishmen, but the men who worked English vessels had a tradition of their own, one that made them less malleable than the servants shipped to Virginia. Though they usually negotiated their wages and terms of service individually with their shipmasters and had no guild to protect them, sailors regarded themselves as practitioners of a skilled craft, a collective body in their own right, with customary rights that they were eager to protect and, if possible, to extend.[30]

The long Anglo-Spanish War that prompted the earliest phase of large-scale English maritime expansion encouraged English sailors to expect their full share of power and profits. In this largely predatory period, with or without official papers, in ventures large and small, English seamen sailed in search of plunder, targeting Spanish and Portuguese ships and settlements as well as a host of others. The war attracted thousands of men to the sea, drawn by the hope of wealth, the promise of masculine honor, and private fighting ships that welcomed novices. Ordinary seamen assumed the right to make war, ventured their lives, received shares of plunder, and took part in important decisions. While investors and commanders hoped, of course, to maximize their share of plunder and glory, they were hampered by a splintered command structure and competing interests at all levels. Rather than pitting officers against men, shipboard disputes were typically factional, with rival officers martialing their own groups of supporters, doling out patronage, and appealing to personal loyalty.

The fact that English seamen were trained in plunder gave a particular stamp to English maritime culture, one that left sailors unlikely to retreat mutely into wage-earning obedience after the end of the war when far-flung merchant ventures increasingly replaced Elizabethan commerce raiding. For Peter Linebaugh and Marcus Rediker, who use the wreck of the *Sea Venture* to illustrate essential themes in their history of English Atlantic capitalism, the unruly sailors and settlers on Bermuda were wage earners cast off the land by enclosure, humble people who yearned for a world without property, rulers, or violence.[31] This may have been true for the settlers, but the common rights the seamen most valued were the rights to plunder and trade. This did not make them any easier to handle. Nothing could have been further from their experience than the notion that they ought to sacrifice their own interests to those of the merchant companies.

Moreover, English sailors' scarce skills as oceanic mariners with experience in gunnery and close fighting enhanced their value to a throng of actual and potential employers. In the violent maritime world of the early seventeenth century, shipowners and merchants needed fighting sailors to defend goods and passengers, and states both at home and abroad appreciated English sailors' naval capabilities. Unlike their fellows on land, maritime laborers were extraordinarily mobile. Facing unfavorable conditions on shipboard, they could desert to find work elsewhere, even across borders or legal barriers: some became renegades, others pirates. Unlike the Virginian servants whose only real alternative was to join the Indians, English seafaring men were in demand wherever fighting seamen were needed: not only in rival European fleets but also in North Africa and the Ottoman Empire.[32] The Stuarts could order their subjects home but lacked the power to enforce their commands. When imperial corporations wanted men to man their ships, they had to compete with one another, the Royal Navy, and foreign recruiters.

Further negotiations took place on shipboard, for merchant ships were responsible for their own defense, which meant that merchant crews were regularly called upon to take up arms against pirates, privateers, and other hostile vessels. Would the sailors fight, and if so, on what terms? Guns were useless without men to fire them. When East India Company captains rallied their men with rousing patriotic speeches to fight against the Portuguese or the Dutch, sailors were quick to negotiate rights to participate in monopoly trade. From their perspectives, the risks they took in the service of English enterprise entitled them to shares of its proceeds. Their demands challenged the assumptions that undergirded the trading companies: the assumptions that sailors were owed wages rather than a share in lucrative trading opportunities, that they were servants and not citizens of these state-like entities. Corporate, codified, and exclusive "company-states" made appeals to a "nation" broadly based on martial comradeship, shared language, and a shared homeland, but they had to pay for the loyalty they claimed.

The structural conditions of English maritime enterprise in the late sixteenth and early seventeenth centuries enhanced the bargaining power of

English sailors. In addition to transporting cargo, they were fighting men, handy with swords, pikes, and muskets as well as larger guns, and they sailed in fighting ships. This is a critical difference between the volatile maritime world described here and the more familiar one of the eighteenth-century Atlantic, in which merchant ships were less responsible for their own defense, and merchant interests and a powerful fiscal-military state appear to have gained the upper hand over unruly seamen.[33] Like Rediker's beleaguered merchant seamen, however, Elizabethan and early Stuart sailors worked together to defend their interests. Knowledge about distant places, markets, and legal regimes circulated widely in seafaring communities, and sailors were quick to mutiny in the face of unacceptable risks: it is no accident that the word "strike" derives from seamen's collective refusal to work. Others turned to outright piracy, a form of collective maritime enterprise that substituted the interests of seamen for those of the state and its merchant company partners. The professional and social ties that bound the English seafaring community were a potent counterpart to the formal structures of the merchant companies.

As in the English settlements on land, then, private expansion at sea entailed the reworking of the social fabric and the renegotiation of labor relations. As on land, the results of those renegotiations shaped the long-term trajectory of the empire, but in a different direction. Mobile, knowledgeable, skilled, and valuable both to merchants and to the state, sailors enjoyed more leverage than imperial laborers on land, and they used it effectively to defend their interests. Unlike the supply of immigrants to Barbados, the supply of seamen did not dry up, even as the English population ceased to grow in the middle of the seventeenth century.[34] Slavery took root in English possessions in the West Indies and on the American mainland, but seafaring remained a viable career for free Englishmen even as new technologies and commercial structures reshaped the old rough egalitarianism of late medieval shipping.

This is not to say that the sea was a paradise for laboring men: the work was hard and dangerous, and merchants did their best to keep the fruits of maritime enterprise for themselves, while the turn from plunder to commerce eroded seamen's sense of themselves as men of martial honor. Sailors did, however, win some victories. They negotiated the right to take part in monopoly trade, though in a small way. Despite common assumptions about the tyranny of the lash, in an age in which disciplinary violence was widespread on land, shipboard discipline remained comparatively mild. The sea offered opportunities for upward mobility unavailable on land, and while wages were not high, they exceeded those offered to laboring men in most of England. Fiercely defended customs surrounding the provision of food insulated seamen from the harsh impact of rising prices. A multitude of individual negotiations and confrontations in the late sixteenth and early seventeenth centuries produced a robust English seafaring culture. By the time the protectionist Navigation Acts were passed in the mid-seventeenth century, England had already acquired a seafaring community capable of sustaining an empire that stretched across the globe.

By word and by act, sailors asserted the importance of their interests in private ventures as large as imperial corporations, and as small as lone ships. More broadly, however, they identified—and were identified by others—as members not of corporate commonwealths but of the "English nation." The nation was a key organizing principle for the sailors and merchants who participated in overseas enterprise, so one of the aims of this book is to show why nationhood was important to them and what it meant. Categorizing people by nation was a widespread practice in the early modern world, but it is not well understood, in part because early modern nationhood is usually measured (and found wanting) against modern nationalism, and in part because of its variable meanings and uses in the early modern period. While some scholars have made bold claims for the emergence of modern nationhood in early modern England, others break down the concept into its component parts, avoiding the word in favor of "patriotism" or "ethnicity," or emphasizing narrowly juridical uses of the term.[35] It was precisely the fluidity and ambiguity of the "nation" that made it so useful for early modern actors, however.[36]

At sea, the idea of the English nation had less to do with preserving the integrity and unique qualities of the English church and state than with managing and containing the risks of maritime enterprise. Protestantism, the common law, and the ancient constitution took pride of place in texts presenting England as a special nation enjoying special privileges that it had to safeguard against perils within and without, but the constitution had little traction abroad, and even religion was less salient: in the Mediterranean, English merchants and seamen had to be discreet about their faith, and in the Indian Ocean, English actors often nurtured commercial bonds with Muslims and "pagans," while the Dutch, their religious allies, became dangerous and hostile rivals. Rather than referring to a core set of religious and legal values, the idea that English merchants and seamen were part of the English *nation* suggested that they were members of a single, coherent national community, sharing common interests and bound together in a web of mutual obligation. This was not self-evidently true: trading companies aimed at enriching their investors, not their workforce, while one of the most distinctive characteristics of seamen was precisely their ability to move across boundaries, to become renegades.[37] In the late sixteenth and early seventeenth centuries, however, persistent and lethal maritime violence and the difficulties of managing cross-cultural trade despite intense European rivalries made nationhood the glue that bound global English maritime enterprise together.

Calling on the English nation was a way in which English people made claims on one another, claims for loyalty, care, and protection. Commanders called on sailors to defend the honor of the English nation when they needed seamen to fight to defend English merchants' interests, but when sailors were expected to risk being maimed or killed, it was hard to dismiss them as mere laborers who were due no more than their bare wages: as Linda Colley has argued for a later period, plebeian people emphasized their commitment to the nation to advance their own interests.[38] While the Crown asserted its right to the service of its seafaring subjects, sailors presented themselves as loyal subjects to mobilize the protection of a distant sovereign. Sailors also called on the idea of English nationhood in dealing with one another: in distant settings the help of the Crown was often less accessible than mutual aid between English seamen. In this period, the growth of London and other major ports that attracted sailors from smaller coastal villages helped to produce a national English seafaring culture. Unlike subjecthood, which tended to weaken with sailors' distance from the center, this Englishness grew stronger in faraway places, where familiar speech and homely tunes took on a comforting resonance, and regional differences receded in comparison to the yawning gulf between Englishmen and a variety of foreign others.[39] Countrymen were not always friends, but they were almost always potential allies.

Nationhood was also important to English people abroad because foreign interlocutors found it useful to treat them as a national collective in which individuals could be held responsible for one another's actions. This was a common approach in the early modern world, for it allowed people from different jurisdictions to obtain redress—or at least revenge—for wrongs committed against them when the real wrongdoers were out of reach. Foreigners were often in need of such redress, since Elizabethan oversight of privateering was lax and English piracy remained notorious even after the country's ostensible transition to peaceful commerce. Ottoman, Mughal, and Javan authorities had no qualms about holding English merchants to account for the misdeeds of Englishmen over whom they enjoyed little control. As we have seen, Robert Walsingham attacked Ottoman shipping in an English ship pressed into Medici service. Though the ship flew a Tuscan flag, its victims recognized their assailants as English, to the chagrin of the Levant Company merchants who were held responsible. The boundaries of the nation were not always drawn from within.

English merchants did not enjoy being held responsible for English pirates, but they willingly presented the community of English seafarers abroad as a particular *sort* of people to foreign observers. In Mediterranean port-to-port shipping, English sailors' reputed readiness for battle attracted Catholic, Muslim, and Jewish passengers hoping to be preserved from corsair attacks: what Levant Company merchants termed "the honor of the English nation" was a valuable asset. And when English merchants ventured into new lands, they presented themselves to foreign eyes as a particular kind of people: a courteous, respectable, trustworthy nation, one worthy of trading privileges. Since sailors usually constituted the majority of the English population in distant lands, merchants enlisted them in this project: sailors were to differentiate themselves from their European rivals, behaving with decorum. The carpenter Richard Frobisher literally performed Englishness when he obligingly played music for a Japanese audience. In a period of first contacts, nationhood helped explain who the English were and what might be expected of them. It provided a means to assign blame for bad behavior, facilitated the development of trust, and mitigated the risks of cross-cultural trade.

The structures of maritime empire encouraged English sailors to think of themselves in national terms, but it is not always easy to know what Englishness meant to them. Some seamen slipped readily into foreign service; many others were more firmly rooted. Robert Walsingham abandoned his country to attack Christian shipping in Tunisian and Algerian ships, as we have seen, only to return home a few years later at real personal risk, hoping for a pardon. These winding and diverse trajectories contribute to the debate about the malleability or fixity of early modern identities.[40] They remind us that there was no single way of being in the globalizing early modern world even among members of a single occupational group. Some sailors exhibited a protean ability to remake or disguise themselves; others were less amenable to dissimulation. Some may have wished to reinvent themselves but were trapped within identities imposed from the outside. Their stories show that early modern identities could be more sticky than fluid, that self-fashioning could come at a personal cost, and that coercion and violence could fashion people against their wills.

Despite its global sweep, this book strives to present sailors as individuals, not faceless masses. This presents a challenge, for few sailors are as well documented as Walsingham and Frobisher, and in the archival record even these two appear mostly in fleeting glimpses. The task of teasing meaning out of these biographical fragments is made feasible, if not light, by the sheer volume of information available. Many sailors—more than ten thousand in all—appear in the legal records, travel writing, and state papers that form the archival basis of this book, and in a number of cases they can be traced across different archives.

Legal records supply an essential body of source material: the examinations of thousands of seafaring men provide essential insight into dangers and conflicts at sea, the complications of cross-cultural shipping, labor negotiations, piracy, and more. In foreign courts, such as the Inquisition, testimony was often extracted during frightening interrogations. For the most part, however, the process of providing evidence was more routine: this book makes extensive use of sailors' and merchants' examinations for the High Court of Admiralty.

The admiralty court was intended to provide reasonably speedy justice to merchants and mariners, and it sat, conveniently, in Southwark. The court handled a wide variety of business. Civil suits encompassed a broad range of sea disputes, such as liability for spoilage, traffic accidents on the Thames, wage disputes, and so on. Piracy dominated its criminal business, and in war years, prize cases flooded the court. The court offered litigants some benefits they could not expect to find in competing common-law courts, such as a relatively rapid process and a legal structure intelligible to foreign merchants: it was a civil law court that operated on the basis of equity and the law of the sea, though according to Henrician legislation criminal offenses were tried with common-law procedure, *oyer et terminer.*[41]

While the High Court of Admiralty offered an international community of seamen and merchants swift and convenient justice tailored to their needs, its other main function was to generate income for the Lord High Admiral by means of a wide variety of fees. This income came most notably in the form of a tenth of all lawful prizes. As one might imagine, the judge who was appointed to adjudicate maritime cases was obliged to consider the interests of his noble master. From 1584 to 1618 the Lord High Admiral was Charles Howard of Effingham, Earl of Nottingham; Howard was succeeded by James's favorite, George Villiers, Duke of Buckingham. The judge for much of this period was the careerist Sir Julius Caesar, a man more interested in the promotion of his interests than in ideas. Despite these inauspicious circumstances, the High Court of Admiralty was an important site for the development of international law, since it offered a venue for the resolution of international disputes. The lawyer who represented the Spanish ambassador at the admiralty court, for example, was none other than the celebrated jurist Alberico Gentili.

As an archive for maritime legal history, the early records of the High Court of Admiralty leave much to be desired. Until 1729, the law dealing with sailors' legal rights and duties was unwritten, resting instead on a "custom of the sea" that bore only a familial resemblance to medieval written codes and that necessarily evolved with England's rapid maritime expansion.[42] As one sea captain wryly put it, it was hard to know what was "lawful or unlawful" because "at their going to sea they are forbidden many things which at their being at sea they do notwithstanding."[43] Wage agreements between sailors and shipmasters were made orally, and disputes were generally resolved out of court. Even when a suit was begun, many and perhaps most cases never reached a verdict, and when sentences were given, they were recorded in a form that was "summary in the extreme," with no evidence of legal reasoning.[44]

Still, dozens of volumes of examinations of hundreds of merchants and thousands of seafarers are the most accessible class of documents within the archive and have undergirded much scholarship.[45] Examinations were taken routinely: written documents, rather than oral evidence, formed the basis of the judges' decisions. First, the plaintiff or plaintiffs took out a warrant against another party or property, such as a ship or its cargo. After the warrant was executed by the court's marshal or his deputy, the plaintiff presented a libel laying out his complaints. At this point the defendant and witnesses were questioned about the contents of the libel and made sworn statements, which were carefully recorded. Sometimes witnesses were also asked to answer interrogatories, a written form of cross-examination. Most of the witnesses were English, but Scottish, Irish, French, Dutch, Portuguese, Spanish, Italian, and Greek sailors and merchants also gave evidence, sometimes with the help of translators who worked regularly for the court. In addition, English witnesses often provided accounts of their experiences at the hands of foreign authorities as part of the process of establishing official grievances, or in the relitigation of disputes initially handled elsewhere.

These examinations offer a remarkable view of seamen's experiences from England's ports and rivers to distant coasts. This is not to say that they are uniformly believable. By early modern standards, sailors were not desirable witnesses: they were too poor, too ungentlemanly, too interested to be deemed impartial. To compensate for these faults, those who did give evidence tended to be drawn disproportionately from the middle and upper ranks of ships' companies: shipmasters, their mates, boatswains, gunners, quartermasters, and other more experienced sailors were examined frequently, while young boys, for example, rarely appeared. It is noteworthy in itself that important mercantile business *could* depend on sailors' words, even those of the more experienced and reputable sort. Despite their manifest imperfections, sailors were often as close as the admiralty judge could come to neutral witnesses. The High Court of Admiralty saw with sailors' eyes.

In this book, the factual credibility of individual depositions is less important than the dynamics they reveal. Large sums of money could and did depend on admiralty verdicts, and sailors had their interests to consider. Accused pirates presented themselves in the best possible light or, if they had agreed with their victims to give evidence in exchange for leniency, sought to satisfy their new patrons. Sailors who deposed in civil suits were usually not in direct legal jeopardy, and when they were, the greatest punishment that could be inflicted on them was usually some sort of loss of wages; still, they generally wished to justify their behavior or, if the case dealt with injuries they had experienced, to gain redress. Sometimes they were directly interested in the suit: in prize cases, or when sailors laid claim to wages or disputed charges that their negligence had led to losses. At other times, they might have wished to support a popular shipmaster or to undercut a disliked commander in a suit between a shipmaster and his merchants. Sailors may have been coached: although we know little about their involvement, civil lawyers were presumably employed to compose libels and interrogatories; they presumably also advised witnesses on how to answer. Even without coaching, of course, sailors had their own blind spots. The stories they told had heroes and villains; often, we must imagine that they omitted information that did not fit. Understanding how sailors framed their evidence offers insights into the disputed distribution of risk and profit at sea, and into how they represented themselves as deserving, important, innocent members of the English nation.

A wide variety of travel writing—voyage narratives, ships' logs, diaries, reports, and pamphlets by English and foreign authors—offers more sustained views of English experiences of cultural contact, and the external and internal difficulties of long-distance voyages. These texts survive in large numbers, in part because so many were printed in the voluminous compilations of Richard Hakluyt and Samuel Purchas. While much valuable work has been done by literary critics on Hakluyt and Purchas as editors, these collections have yet to receive the attention they deserve from historians.[46] They contain many narratives whose manuscript sources have been lost; some are sensational, but others are not. Purchas's compilation includes many accounts of early East India Company voyages, for example. While travel accounts are often thought to contain as much fiction as careful observation, East India Company ship journals were written for anxious investors, not for a breathless popular audience, and revealed what Richmond Barbour has termed "a disciplined commitment to the actual." These journals constituted proprietary knowledge and were kept in the East India Company's private archive, but Purchas obtained permission to publish edited—often sadly shortened—versions; in several cases the originals are no longer extant.[47]

Other useful sources are found in the archives of states and corporations: correspondence, council minutes, memoranda, petitions, and so forth. English state papers provide insight into the state's efforts to track, control, and deploy English mariners, as well as English sailors' attempts to access state aid, while the rich and detailed correspondence and minutes of the East India Company offer a view of that state-like corporation's management of its own sailor "subjects." In addition, the accessible *Calendar of State Papers Relating to English Affairs in the Archives of Venice* supplies a valuable foreign perspective on the activities of English seamen. In keeping with its focus on English nationhood, my book relies primarily on English sources, but the depositions of foreign seafaring men, French, Dutch, and Portuguese travel accounts, and Venetian diplomatic correspondence provide instructive counterpoints.

This book begins with the rapid expansion of English shipping in the reign of Elizabeth, and it traces English maritime expansion and the fortunes of the English seafarers through the difficult transition from warfare to commercial trade and corporate empire in the reign of James, ending with the challenges of renewed warfare and foreign piracy in the 1620s. It shows that a distinctive warlike and predatory English seafaring culture developed in the late sixteenth century, that this generation of seamen challenged the decentralized corporate vision of imperial Englishness that succeeded state-sponsored plunder, and that a younger generation of sailors, trained in commerce, faced their own problems in a persistently violent maritime world—problems that would only be solved by the development of a much more powerful state.

The first chapter, "A Plundering People," argues that insofar as fighting Elizabethan seamen shared a collective identity, violent plunder was central to it. Surviving records provide little evidence of militant Protestant or anti-Spanish attitudes; instead, the men who flocked to the sea to man private warships were largely attracted by the prospect of material gain and martial masculinity. To live by the sword was honorable in a way that living by one's labor was not. Few Elizabethan seamen—either common privateersmen or their commanders—seem to have had any notion of subordinating their own interests to an overarching national purpose. Instead, investors and seamen took on risk in hopes of private profits, with little regard for broader naval strategy. Common seamen were shareholders in these voyages: like other participants, they had interests to protect and expected to take part in important decisions. Though shipboard conflict was common, especially on voyages in which seamen faced grave risks, commanders rarely pitted themselves against common men. Instead, officers quarreled among themselves, fighting over spoils and prestige, and appealing to common seamen for support, and whole ships' companies faced off against one another in disputes over prizes. As a form of maritime empire, then, for all its rapacious violence, lawlessness, and widespread corruption, Elizabethan privateering offered seamen material and social rewards and a loose and broadly inclusive structure.

England's predatory seafaring culture attracted sailors but posed a problem for merchants who sought to promote a different kind of maritime empire. The second chapter, "Renegades and Reprisals," explores the conflict between these two models in the early seventeenth century. After James's accession, some discontented seamen drifted to the Mediterranean, where they entered the service of both Muslim and Catholic patrons of the religious privateering war known as the *corso;* others were already there, plundering local shipping despite Elizabethan prohibitions. Independent English ships also sailed along the coast of North Africa carrying goods and passengers between coastal cities, stirring up unrest when their men purchased stolen goods or kidnapped their own passengers. English sailors often found it convenient to treat their countrymen as a loose affinity regardless of whether they were loyal subjects or corsairs, but English maritime abuses created diplomatic difficulties for the Levant Company. Along with its outraged trading partners in Venice and the Ottoman Empire, the

Levant Company strove to sever the links between England and its renegade seamen, tightening the diffuse English nation into something more
orderly and bounded.

The third chapter, "Risks and Rewards," explores how sailors and merchants struggled over the allocation of profits and danger in commercial and
colonial enterprise in the Mediterranean, the Atlantic, and the Arctic Ocean.
Conflict over maritime risks and rewards was not new, but as English ships
ranged farther away and undertook increasingly lengthy voyages in violent
seas, the stakes rose. Where markets opened up, sailors attempted to extend
traditional trading rights in the face of new corporate monopolies. Armed
English ships were popular with merchants and travelers in the violent
Mediterranean, but when corsairs attacked and sailors were expected to fight
back, daunting risks—including death, injury, and enslavement—tempted
seamen to cut deals with their assailants. When colonial governors made
sweeping claims to authority over English subjects, they were frequently
irked by seamen's defense of their customary rights and perquisites. The social relations of merchant capitalism were negotiated in stubborn resistance,
in open disobedience, and in court.

While some sailors chafed under company rule, others took to the seas.
Chapter 4, "Piracy and Empire," shows that for a brief but significant period hundreds, even thousands, of English sailors in formidable and semi-
coordinated fleets ranged the Atlantic, preying on European shipping of
all kinds, facing down royal ships, and basing themselves sometimes at
Mamora in war-torn Morocco and sometimes in Ireland, on the peripheries of state control. Keeping their distance from the perilous and unre-
warding West Indies, English seamen moved fluidly in and out of piracy,
developing practices that reduced their legal and physical risks, and
Mamora remained linked to seafaring communities in London by a dense
social network. Jacobean Atlantic piracy may be considered an alternative,
illegal form of private imperial expansion, one that retained a strongly national quality exemplified by the lethal rivalry between English and Dutch
pirates but that was more lucrative and less dangerous for seamen than
legal commercial and colonial projects.

The fifth chapter, "Sailors and the Company-State," explores labor and
allegiance in the early East India Company, an imperial corporation
whose dual roles as a private merchant corporation and a semi-sovereign

entity raised questions about the relation between the public good and private gain. These questions were deeply significant for Company sailors, who faced punishing mortality and were expected to risk their lives in battle against numerically superior European rivals. Company governors initially hoped to bar sailors from the profits of trade, and commanders typically sailed with sweeping martial law powers, but in practice the difficult conditions of East India voyages forced commanding officers to cast their voyages as a national venture, tolerating some private trade by the seamen and embracing a more consensual approach to discipline.

The sixth chapter, "Englishness Abroad," shows that sailors engaged with a wide variety of non-European peoples and reflects on English identity and cultural encounter from a maritime perspective. The demands of cross-cultural trade played a central role in the construction of English identity in the early seventeenth century as merchant companies hoping to establish commercial relations in distant lands tried to convince local rulers and populations that the English were more desirable trading partners than their European rivals: lacking Dutch firepower, they presented themselves as a formidable but courteous and trustworthy nation, and needed sailors to play the part. For English sailors, then, what mattered was not what they thought about foreign people but what foreign people thought about them, though this new "courteous" Englishness was at odds with their traditionally warlike seafaring culture. Even more painfully, when English sailors were captured by rival empires, they were sometimes publicly exhibited in humiliating triumphs designed to illustrate English national weakness.

The last chapter, "Sailors and the State," argues that English sailors gained leverage vis-à-vis their employers because the state valued sailors as essential resources for defense and commerce. Pirates were lured home with generous pardons, and criminals with valuable navigational knowledge escaped unscathed. In wage disputes, admiralty judges recognized that the law might need to bend toward sailors' interests to make sailing an attractive profession. While the state broadly favored sailors, however, its fiscal weakness prevented it from being able to protect them abroad or pay their wages on time. In the later 1620s, when England had developed a large and vulnerable merchant fleet, the combined impact of slaving pirates, enemy privateers, and heavy impressment into disastrously underfunded naval expeditions gave English seamen reason to complain that while their labors sustained English commerce and security, the state failed to uphold its own obligations; they voiced their grievances in petitions, mutinies, and riots. The state's light hand had spurred the rapid expansion of English shipping, but as peaceful commerce replaced the commerce raiding of earlier days, a more expansive state role would be required.

Examining England's early empire through the lens of maritime labor helps to explain the kingdom's singular path to oceanic dominance. It provides new evidence of the scale and complexity of global English entanglements beyond well-known colonial outposts. It reveals the importance and practical usefulness of the early modern idea of the nation, and the complex relationship between the nation and early imperial corporations. Most importantly, perhaps, this approach centers the remarkable experiences of early English mariners, flawed and forgotten men who played a central role in their nation's rise to global prominence, but whose small victories and devastating defeats were very much their own.

CHAPTER ONE

A PLUNDERING PEOPLE

Christmas in 1591 must have been joyful for the newlywed William Cradell. The young gunner's mate had recently returned from a lucrative cruise in the *Little John*, a warship belonging to the investor John Watts. His shares alone had come to £42, at least three years' pay for a few months' work, testimony to Cradell's labors and luck but also to his participation in maritime enterprise that placed gain first: above the priorities of the Crown, English solidarity, and responsibility toward his fellow venturers. The single-minded pursuit of plunder did not pay off for everyone, but for this seaman, its rewards had been substantial.

Watts's fleet had been at Plymouth in April, ready to sail for the West Indies, when its plans were threatened by a major royal expedition. The expedition's commander, Lord Thomas Howard, planned to sail to the Azores to lie in wait for Spain's silver-laden fleet. Watts's captains were commanded to go along with him, but they protested "that they were servants to their owners"—their investors—and insisted on a written agreement limiting their obligations. Reluctantly they sailed with Howard, but after a few weeks, the sailors allegedly rebelled. "They would not hinder their voyage any longer," reported William Lane, the captain of the *Centaur*, unless Lane could promise them "the Queen's pay."[1] He could not, and so they steered away, leaving Howard in the lurch. By the time the English fleet met its Spanish counterpart in late August in the Battle of Flores, Howard's fever-ridden seamen were heavily outnumbered, and the silver passed on safely to Spain.[2]

Watts's men fared better. In early July, they captured several prizes off Cuba, ships carrying hides, cochineal, and silver. But it was not enough to capture prizes; one also had to keep as much plunder as possible for one-self. Cradell's ship, a modest vessel of about 140 tons, carried around seventy men, and the other three ships were similarly crowded with eager fighters, some four hundred in all.[3] Watts's ships were consorts: their crews shared their plunder on an equitable basis no matter which ship had taken what, encouraging them to cooperate closely. They could and did do their best, however, to exclude outsiders, in particular the *Swallow*, which had also been in the West Indies, where it had allegedly worked with Watts's fleet for a time. Once the sea battles were won and the ships returned home, the legal battles began, as Watts's men denied in court that the *Swallow* deserved any share of their gains.[4]

Nor were Cradell and his comrades averse to cheating their owners and the seamen of Watts's other ships by embezzling the spoils. According to one seaman, when the goods aboard one prize ship were being invento-ried, the sailors hid three chests of cochineal, later bringing the bags of ex-pensive dyestuff onto the deck, "where the company cut the bags and some got their pockets full and others their hats full of cochineal." The rest was smuggled into a carpenter's house in Dartmouth, and the sailors all had their share of the proceeds—some £3 apiece. Cradell was accused of embezzling other spoils as well: with others, he secretly shared a bag of Spanish money at sea, and another fifty-pound bag of cochineal mysteri-ously disappeared from the gunroom where he and two others worked.[5]

In pursuit of gain, men like William Cradell sailed across the Atlantic to attack the enemy. They also ignored the aims of the Crown, main-tained fierce legal battles against their compatriots, and cheated their in-vestors. Their private ambitions prevented English sea power from being used effectively for state purposes, but for individuals the results were worth it. In February 1592, when Cradell appeared before the High

Court of Admiralty, he was only twenty-four but already comparatively wealthy, the veteran of three voyages with letters of reprisal, including two to the West Indies in Watts's ships. He was also a married man: in December, he had wed Clemence Bridges, a sixteen-year-old Stepney girl. They were both very young, but with Cradell's bright prospects, they could afford not to wait.[6]

Unfortunately for the young couple, fortune proved fickle. Cradell suffered an injury that was slow to heal; they had no children; and Clemence went mad and died young despite her husband's vain attempts to seek a cure.[7] In addition to his domestic griefs, Cradell was buffeted by changes of state. Once the war with Spain came to an end, it proved far more difficult for him to find a profitable niche. He lost his savings and nearly his life in a disastrous attempt to set up a colony on the Oyapock River in 1604. He rose in the ranks, becoming a shipmaster, but his ship was cast away along with one hundred pounds he had borrowed. Around 1614, his second wife, Benedict, persuaded their neighbors to petition the shipmasters' fraternity at Trinity House in Deptford to support a charitable collection for their family. The following year, Cradell managed to be appointed as master of the East India Company's ship *Expedition*—but was demoted for want of navigational skill. With the help of Benedict, a midwife, Cradell survived into his late fifties, but his life probably never again seemed quite so golden as it had in 1591.[8] Like thousands of others, he had been drawn to oceanic seafaring by the prospect of plunder, a participant in a freewheeling private war in which seamen's interests were central. This would rarely be true in the Jacobean years of commercial and colonial expansion.

English sailors at the outset of Elizabeth's reign were not known for their navigational expertise or daring. English ships sailed regularly to familiar destinations, to be sure: to Bordeaux and other French ports, to the Low Countries, to Iceland for fish, and even to Spain and Portugal. More exotic destinations had also been attempted in recent years: the ships that sailed vainly in search of the northeast passage established a trade route between England and Muscovy, and a number of ships ventured to Guinea.[9] For the most part, however, ships stayed close to home, and their numbers were few. English shipping had expanded in the sixty years before 1520, but that energy waned thereafter: ships as moderately large as two hundred tons, "fairly numerous" in 1520, were rare by 1560, when concerned officials were only able to locate six in all and a paltry fifty thousand tons combined of merchant shipping in English hands. "A meagre coastal traffic, a fishery of moderate scale, a trickle of carrying traffic with the Low Countries, Spain, Portugal, France, and the Baltic" made up English maritime enterprise. Much of English trade was necessarily carried in foreign ships, controlled by foreign merchants.[10]

Early Elizabethan seamen were few, and they were a conservative lot, abiding for the most part by maritime custom dating back to the medieval Rolls of Oléron. No very clear distinction was made between labor and capital: the same men might own a ship, load it with merchandise, and perform manual work on shipboard. They were bound by a "far closer community of interest" than later ships' companies, and their close relationships, both financial and social, defined the tenor of shipboard life. The shipmaster—not yet expert in mathematical navigation—was only the first among equals, and while he possessed the right to inflict punishment, he was limited in turn by the rights of the crew. They could decide not to sail if they thought the weather was dangerous, and they possessed the right to arbitrate between the master and individual seamen in cases of serious disagreements. Even along well-traveled coastal routes sailing was risky, and customary modes of resolving conflict helped to contain those risks.[11]

In the following decades, especially after 1585, English shipping was transformed. Building on a tradition of marauding and trade, merchants, West Country gentry, and seamen rapidly expanded their horizons.[12] Between 1577 and 1580, after he and his kinsman John Hawkins had struggled to wrest profits from the Spanish New World, Francis Drake sailed around the globe, plundering undefended Pacific shipping on the way, returning with enough treasure to buy forgiveness and a knighthood from the queen. His feat proved difficult to repeat, but the promise of gain won by force of arms reverberated among ambitious young men. After the definitive breach between Elizabeth and Philip II in 1585, England became a stronghold of seaborne predators. Thousands of young men learned to sail the ocean in private warships where little experience was necessary: since privateers were not paid wages and close fighting remained as important as cannon fire, backers tended to welcome as many fighting men as their ships could reasonably hold, and often more. Predatory voyages in the Atlantic and the Caribbean as well as more distant seas offered ample opportunity for seamen to practice the art of oceanic navigation, honing skills that had been rare among Englishmen.[13] By Elizabeth's death, few ocean-going Englishmen could remember a world without war and plunder. In the eyes of their victims, they had become a nation of pirates.

If war was the violent nursery of English seafaring, we may well wonder what sort of seafaring culture formed under its auspices. The impact was clear on English shipbuilding: for decades, shipyards continued to turn out fast, heavily armed, handy ships well suited to battle, but with little space for cargo and uncompetitive with Dutch merchant ships.[14] The war with Spain also left its mark on English mariners. A new seafaring culture emerged, a hybrid of older maritime traditions and driving rapacity. The sea offered the prospect of gold and glory—and nothing was quite so glorious as gold—to young men who were willing to venture their own lives, and take those of others. These ventures could be fraught, however. Predatory enterprises required close cooperation, but participants' interests sometimes collided. The most ambitious ventures, those that aimed at the Pacific Coast of South America, were also fearsomely dangerous, exposing seamen to navigational and logistical challenges for which they were poorly prepared, while those who ventured their money, lives, and reputations were naturally anxious to maximize their shares of potential rewards. If English identity was forged in this war, its content remained diffuse. Seamen did as they pleased, seeking to survive, to enjoy themselves, and to profit. Trading companies would later take a strong interest in defining Englishness and policing its boundaries, but in this early period, there was no such unified leadership, no one to say that the English were a particular kind of people who behaved in a particular manner.

Swordsmen at Sea

As Elizabethan ships sailed toward distant destinations, Englishmen saw much that was new to them, marvels of nature that inspired delight and curiosity. Some animals seemed uncannily human, like the long-tailed monkeys in Sierra Leone who muttered together on a rock "as if they were in turn conspiring or determining dubious matters." In 1582 one such monkey was bestowed on Captain Edward Fenton by the legate of a local ruler, pleasing him "inordinately" until he realized it was not housebroken, according to Richard Madox, a disaffected chaplain whose official and private diaries provide one of the most vivid early voyage accounts. When a mariner stretching his legs on an island found "a great company of seals . . . sleeping, with their bellies toasting against the sun," he fetched reinforcements to attack the giants. Their "sentinel" gave the alarm, however, and the seals galumphed to the sea, mowing down the seamen in their path. Once safe, "they did, as it were, scorn us, defy us, and danced before us," until the bruised, angry sailors put them to flight with musket fire.[15] Even birds amazed English observers with their nests artfully woven out of grass, hanging above streams in Sierra Leone, or crowding rocky islands in the South Atlantic. Sir Richard Hawkins marveled: "In all the days of my life, I have not seen greater art and curiosity in creatures void of reason, than in the placing and making of their nests; all the hill being so full of them, that the greatest mathematician of the world could not devise how to place one more than there was upon the hill, leaving only one pathway for a fowl to pass betwixt."[16]

Whenever possible, sailors ate what they found, for the most cherished discoveries were those that refreshed their weary bodies. Oranges were "very sweet and delicious." A gunner who sailed with John Hawkins on his last slaving expedition thought that "sugar is not more delicate in taste" than ripe plantains, and that waterfowl eggs were "very good meat," crabs too were "very good meat," and avocados were "an excellent good fruit."[17] Coconut meat was "as good as almonds blanched," and potatoes were "the most delicatest roots that may be eaten, and do far exceed our parsnips and carrots."[18] In their enthusiasm, English seamen even enjoyed prickly pears, which they considered to be "very pleasant in taste," and sometimes devoured poisonous fruits, enduring vomits and purges as a result.[19] They were unsqueamish eaters of animals as well. Off the Cape Verde island of Boa Vista, the men of the *Edward Bonaventure* spied a huge she-turtle "engendering with her mate" and hauled the unwieldy reptile on board, where the reverend John Walker rode cross-legged on its back as it scraped its way along the deck, searching for freedom. In vain: it tasted like veal. A manatee's flesh was "white and marvelous savoury and interlarded."[20] Gull chicks were "one of the delicatest foods that I have eaten in all my life," Sir Richard Hawkins claimed. Even the conspiratorial monkeys did not escape. When Walter Hooker killed one in Sierra Leone, the Englishmen ate it—starting with the liver—even though they had plenty of alternatives.[21]

Hunting strange animals was great fun for all the voyagers, gentle and common alike. Laboring men in England were barred from hunting deer, but the wilder game of Africa and the Americas was open to all, and the seamen took to it with relish. They hunted buffalo with "great pleasure" in Sierra Leone, a chaplain recorded in 1582, and "one Russel" caught a sawfish that had been injured by a crocodile. Two seafaring men from the *Galleon Leicester* had the good fortune to see an elephant; they shot at it, though with no success, and told the others how the giant pushed over trees with his armored shoulder.[22] The Englishmen enjoyed slaughtering penguins, "a great recreation to my company," wrote Sir Richard Hawkins, "and worth the sight, for in determining to catch them, necessarily was required a good store of people, every one with a cudgel in his hand, to compass them round about." The birds nested in burrows, so whenever one escaped from the encircled herd, the pursuing sailor was likely to break through the ground and fall "up to the armpits in the earth." This, Hawkins chuckled, "was the sport." Indeed, the English were not too dignified to laugh at their failures—or at least at one another's mishaps. On one shooting expedition in Sierra Leone, some men hunting a peacock chased the fowl into some bushes—and right onto a bees' nest. Stung unmercifully, they beat a hasty retreat, while their captain, Luke Ward, "seeing this battle betwixt us and them held his hat about his ears . . . laughing at the skirmish."[23]

English sailors took more savage delight in assaulting dangerous beasts. When men from Fenton's expedition glimpsed "a great crocodile" in a river at Sierra Leone, for example, they immediately sought to catch the monster. When it eluded their nets, they set themselves in battle array: "some with calivers, some with fishgigs, some with spears and other with swords and targets, purposing to fight it out with him." The crocodile put up a stiff resistance, but after several hours it was killed and brought in triumph to the *Galleon Leicester*, where the carcass was flayed, and the men, giddy with victory, began at last to feel tired. Like so much else, the crocodile purportedly tasted like veal, but eating it was not the point. "Certain men of this country did not think that we durst attempt the killing of this beast," the chaplain Walker boasted, "for he feedeth on land and used to eat the Negroes whom he met withal nigh the shore."[24]

Killing an alligator was one of the highlights in Job Hortop's account of his travails. Hortop sailed on John Hawkins's last, ill-fated slaving expedition to the Spanish New World, a voyage in which the slavers were denied access to colonial markets and then defeated by a Spanish fleet; he was one of the men who tried his luck in Mexico rather than starve on the way home. The young gunner was stripped naked by Indians, questioned by Spanish authorities, imprisoned, shipped back to Spain, punished for attempting to escape, and imprisoned again. He spent twelve years rowing in the galleys before he was finally liberated by English sailors and returned home. Throughout, the fishing of the alligator remained bright in his memory: "Seven of us," he recalled, "went in the pinnace up into the river, carrying with us a dog, unto whom with rope yarn we bound a great hook of steel." The poor dog was thrown overboard, and "the alagarta came and presently swallowed" him up. The men rowed as hard as they could while the alligator plunged and frothed the water. When it finally succumbed, the sailors leapt on shore and dragged out their prize, all twenty-three feet of it, as Hortop remembered. They "flayed him, dried his skin, and stuffed it with straw, meaning to have brought it home, had not the ship been cast away." While Hawkins bargained with Spanish merchants over the price of captive Africans, the alligator was the sailors' own trophy.[25]

Killing sharks was a favorite sport. On Fenton's voyage in 1582, the clergyman Walker recorded that they had "great pastime this day with taking of so great sharks that three men could scarce draw them into the boat." When they took two more sharks that night, they threw them overboard, "for the other plenty we had of fish." Writing toward the end of his life about his 1593 voyage, Sir Richard Hawkins recalled that his men fished for sharks "to recreate themselves, and in revenge of the injuries received by them; for they live long, and suffer much after they be taken, before they die." The sailors devised ingenious torments for their victims: they tied logs and barrels to their tails to prevent them from diving, or blinded them and threw them back overboard. Once, they threw one into the sea "with his belly slit, and his bowels hanging out," a prey to his fellows. Sailors hated sharks because the sinister predators "deprived them of swimming, and fed on their flesh being dead."[26]

Indeed, by the time ships reached shark-filled waters, their crew numbers were already usually diminished. The lucky ones perished when the ships were close to shore, like young William Burges, who died in 1582 of a burning fever and was buried in Sierra Leone with an epitaph that its proud author, Richard Madox, recorded in his diary:

> Thy soul to heaven whence it fled
> Thy body to earth which first it bred
> Though far from country little WILL
> Yet in thy country BURGESS still.[27]

Men who threw their dead comrades into the sea must have wondered whether their bodies, too, might be torn by sharp teeth. The men in Fenton's fleet were all young—"not ten were thirty years of age"—and many would never grow old. Madox himself was probably buried in Brazil in February 1583, but there was no one to write witty verses for him. His friend and fellow chaplain who had ridden on a turtle in happier days had died of dysentery a few weeks before, his body heaved overboard while a single cannon shot echoed across the water.[28]

From monkeys to crocodiles, Elizabethans seemingly ate anything that moved. Several decades later, when a merchant named Richard Jobson journeyed up the Gambia River in West Africa, this had changed. When a local notable sent Jobson and his fellows a gift of elephant's meat, Jobson recorded, "our dainty stomachs looked asquash at such gross flesh," and the Englishmen passed on the game to their less sensitive "black neighbours, who eat it very merrily." Similar delicacy allegedly prevented the Jacobean traders from purchasing human beings. When an African merchant showed Jobson "certain young black women, who were standing by themselves, and had white strings cross their bodies, which he told me were slaves, brought for me to buy," Jobson famously answered: "We were a people, who did not deal in any such commodities, neither did we buy or sell one another, or any that had our own shapes." When the merchant "seemed to marvel much at it," and pointed out that other white men on the coast "earnestly desired them, especially such young women," Jobson stressed that those white slavers—presumably

Portuguese—"were another kind of people different from us."[29] In Jobson's narrative, the English were a particular *kind* of people, one that did not eat gross flesh or buy slaves. Like the African trader, the men of Hawkins's early slaving expeditions would have marveled at this notion. They did not succeed in carving out a lasting role in the slave trade, but it was not for want of trying.

Slaving was not a foregone conclusion. The first English ships to sail to West Africa were merchant vessels: nine voyages composed of twenty ships were undertaken in search of gold, pepper, and ivory between 1553 and 1565.[30] Despite the peaceful trade links so recently developed between Englishmen and West African traders, the participants in John Hawkins's three slaving voyages in the 1560s seem to have had few qualms about their murderous attacks on African villages even though they understood their victims to be "civil." Thus, on the earliest voyage the first targets were people on the Cape Verde Islands, described as being "more civil than any other, because of their daily traffic with the Frenchmen . . . of nature very gentle and loving," who had recently rescued some French castaways. Hawkins's men did not care about the upright character of their intended victims, but other Englishmen did: the slaving raid was foiled by men from a trading ship who "gave them there to understand of our coming, and our pretence, wherefore they did avoid the snares we had laid for them."[31] Undeterred, the slavers passed on to the mainland, where again they attacked precisely those they considered to be most civil and industrious. The region was war-torn, as Mane invaders from the interior and their local recruits, the Sumbas, conquered coastal Zape towns, acquiring fearsome reputations for brutality. Hawkins's companion John Sparke understood the place to be inhabited by two groups, the Sapies (Zapes), who had traditionally been hardworking, rich in gold, and peaceful, and their attackers the Samboses (he conflated the Sumbas and the Manes), who preferred to "live most by the spoil of their enemies, both in taking their victual, and eating them also." According to their own account, the English also preyed upon the Zapes, capturing people and burning villages.[32]

On Hawkins's third voyage, Job Hortop later recalled, Hawkins and his men helped three Mane or Sumba commanders capture a town. For their services, the English slavers were allowed to take five hundred captives, but most of the townspeople were murdered: "The three kings drove seven thousand Negros into the sea at low water, at the point of the land, where they were all drowned in the ooze, for that they could not take their canoes to save themselves," Hortop wrote. The battle lines were drawn not between civil and savage but between prey and predators: English and African attackers murdered and enslaved peaceful villagers. It is conceivable that the Englishmen were troubled by this monstrous act: in Hawkins's own account, he recounted that the captured town had held eight thousand inhabitants, of whom only two hundred and fifty were enslaved by the English and six hundred by the local victors, despite the fact that the English had hoped for more—but he seems to have remained silent on the fate of the rest.[33] Still, had Hawkins been able to find a reliable market for his captives, there is every reason to think that English slaving would have continued to expand.

One English sailor who lived for months in the interior of Africa in the late sixteenth century seems to have perceived little moral distance between himself and his companions, a mercenary cult whose customs were horrifying not only by English standards but also—and much more to the point—by the standards of the African people on whom they preyed. Cannibalism, witchcraft, and the deliberate destruction of the productive landscape made the Imbangala raiders in Angola a living nightmare for their victims, and useful allies for Portuguese slavers.[34] If anything, however, the description of the Imbangala by a sailor named Andrew Battell is surprisingly positive. The devil was clearly a potent ally, and Battell admired their martial discipline and boasted of his own high standing among them.

Battell had left England on a plundering voyage bound for the Río de la Plata in 1589. He and several others were taken prisoner by Indians while searching for food in Brazil, and he became a captive of the Portuguese, who sent him, as an expendable person, to work in Angola. About twenty years later, he made his way back to England, where he was ultimately interviewed by Samuel Purchas.[35] In Angola, Battell ended up trading for slaves along the coast. The second time his ship came to the Bay of Benguela, where the slave port would later be founded, he and the other slavers saw a great company of men on shore: the Jaga, or Imbangala, who sold them "good cheap" slaves. The Portuguese and the

Imbangala joined together to wage a devastating attack on the Benguelas. Battell seems to have taken his allies' cannibalism in his stride, though he thought it "strange" that they ate "man's flesh, having all the cattle of that country." While the Imbangala were making spoil of the country, Battell and his companions traded with them for five months "and gained greatly by them," sailing back and forth between Benguela and Luanda.[36]

When the Portuguese later found that the Jaga soldiers had departed to the interior, they followed them and became entangled in the wars of a different chief, who would only allow them to depart, Battell recounted, if they promised to return and left "a white man with him in pawn." As Battell explained, the "Portuguese and Mulattos . . . consented together that it were fitter to leave me, because I was an Englishman, than any of themselves." They did not return, and fearing for his life, the sailor "ran away, purposing to go to the camp of the Jagas." With the Imbangala, at least Battell was safe, and he had plenty to eat and drink.[37]

Battell fought side by side with his predatory hosts. His account of their movements switches revealingly between the first person and the third: "They took the spoil all the way as they went," but "we arose and entered into the province of Tondo . . . we passed over mighty high mountains." "Having spent sixteen months among these cannibals, they marched to the westward again" to the realm of the Lord Shillambansa, where "we burned his chief town . . . we found great store of wild peacocks . . . we marched to the westward." The sailor recalled with some pride: "I was so highly esteemed with the Great Jaga, because I killed many Negroes with my musket, that I had any thing that I desired of him." Battell called this leader "a man of great courage," believed in his supernatural powers, and was impressed by his strict discipline and rhetorical prowess: "He is always making of sacrifices to the devil, and doth know many times what shall happen to him. . . . He hath strait laws to his soldiers: for those that are faint-hearted and turn their backs to the enemy are presently condemned and killed for cowards, and their bodies eaten. He useth every night to make a warlike oration upon an high scaffold, which doth encourage his people." The Imbangala general was splendidly arrayed with expensive shells entwined in his long hair, a chain of other shells "for the worth of twenty shillings a shell" about his neck, and "a palm cloth about his middle, as fine as silk."[38] There is strikingly little judgment in Battell's descriptions even of routine infanticide and human sacrifice, prompting an aghast Purchas to add disapproving marginal notes: "Butcherly rites," "Cruel funerals."[39] If Battell felt any moral discomfort, it did not prevent him from joining the group and enjoying its strength and wealth. He seems not to have been so different from the rank and file of Imbangala soldiers: thirsty for palm wine, determined to survive, ready to kill.

To be sure, some Englishmen did have misgivings about the predatory nature of English maritime enterprise in the later sixteenth century. In Edward Fenton's expedition in 1582–1583, for example, merchants and soldiers struggled for control: though the voyage was ostensibly set to sail around the Cape of Good Hope toward the East Indies on a trading venture, it soon became clear that Fenton hoped instead to pass through the Strait of Magellan and plunder the Pacific Coast, as Drake had done and as Thomas Cavendish was then doing. In Sierra Leone, those peaceably inclined—the merchants as well as the chaplain, Richard Madox—were optimistic about the prospect of establishing friendly trade relations, while the fighting men remained suspicious of the local people. Madox thought that Portuguese stories of cannibalism and witchcraft were tall tales designed, as he put it, "to scare us and frighten us away from all trade." He noted with scorn that the soldiers aboard seemed to swallow all they were told, exclaiming how much the situation reminded them of war-torn Ireland. Soldiers make terrible explorers, Madox decided, because "they can never enter into dealings with others without suspicion. Suspicion, however, breeds hatred and hatred open war, and thus those they ought to attract and attach to themselves by human kindness and clemency, they frighten off by impudence and malice."[40] Restrained, perhaps, by his opinionated chaplain, Fenton left the local people in peace, though his diplomatic gestures were half-hearted.

The next two fleets to visit Sierra Leone were more purely predatory, with predictable results. According to the accounts in Hakluyt, when the ships under the command of Thomas Cavendish anchored there in August 1586, at first the Englishmen "played and danced all the forenoon among the Negroes," but the mood quickly turned sour, and a larger armed contingent of Englishmen disembarked, "drave them from their town, and sacked their houses, and burnt their dwellings." Similarly, they destroyed Africans' houses on a nearby island, one of Cavendish's companions recorded, "because of their bad dealing with us."[41] A few months later, a fleet set out by the Earl of Cumberland followed Cavendish's example: a merchant on board recalled that when a Portuguese trader told them "there was Negroes inhabiting not far off and that in giving unto the king a butizia of wine and some linen cloth he would suffer us to water and wood at our pleasures," the commanders thought it "not good to give more than others which were here before us" and refused.[42] Like Cavendish's men, they sacked and burned a town, looting all the rice they could find. Both 1586 fleets were bound for Brazil and the Strait of Magellan, with the plan of attacking Spanish shipping and towns on the Pacific coast. Though there was little of value to be had for them in Sierra Leone, the commanders seemed unwilling to perform even modest friendly gestures or to exercise the forbearance that would prevent "vexation" from spiraling into violence. Theft was their raison d'être, after all, whether their victims were enemies or, as in this case, complete strangers.

Religion seems to have done less to sharpen the hazy boundaries of maritime English identity in this period than previous scholars believed. Kenneth Andrews, the foremost historian of Elizabethan privateering, cast its culture in familiar terms: Protestant, doggedly anti-Spanish, bombastic, and hopeful of gain. While poverty and rapacity fueled privateering, he contended, "material forces and motives do not . . . seem fully to explain this great wave of maritime aggression." Celebratory broadsides and poems "unmistakably reveal widespread anti-Spanish, Protestant and nationalistic sentiments." These had been particularly strong in English ports before the war, he suggested, "where the stories of seamen and merchants who had suffered at the hands of the Inquisition in Spain lost nothing in the telling."[43] More recently, it has become clear that Protestantism was less broadly popular in the late sixteenth century than previously believed. The new faith, so dependent on scripture reading and sermon hearing, was often not easily accessible.[44] It is not altogether surprising, then, that deeply felt anti-Spanish hostility and Protestant zeal can be hard to find in voyage narratives and admiralty examinations. While pamphleteers trumpeted their hostility to Spain, for most privateers and their backers the central purpose of privateering was to make money. Injuring Spain was a distant second, and in many cases privateers seem not to have cared whom they injured, so long as they filled their purses.

The ambiguous religious identities of early Elizabethan seamen can be traced in the experiences and narratives of those who were left on the coast of New Spain in 1568, after the defeat of John Hawkins's last slave-trading expedition. Some were killed by Chichimeca Indians, while the survivors made their way on foot to the nearest town, where they were held and questioned. In Job Hortop's account, the religious differences between the Englishmen and the Spanish Catholics were barely visible: when "some of their clergy asked us if we were Christians," he recalled, "we said, we praised God, we were as good Christians as they." When the priests "willed us to bless ourselves, and say our prayers in the Latin tongue, that they might understand us, many of our company did so, whereupon they returned to the vice-king, and told him that we were good Christians." The Englishmen complied with the command to recite Catholic prayers, but they did rebel some time later, when they were commanded "to card wool among the Indian slaves, which drudgery we disdained, and concluded to beat our masters, and so we did."[45] Following their revolt against this feminized and racialized work, some of the seamen were sent to Spain, but most were permitted to assimilate into Mexican society as servants, mine overseers, muleteers, and artisans, seemingly melting into a loosely governed and highly diverse population in which heterodoxy was common.[46]

In 1571, however, the Inquisition was established in Mexico, and soon thereafter the sailors were rounded up as suspected Lutherans. Detailed records of their interrogations reveal their varied religious upbringings: depending on their age, these "Lutherans" had received their initial religious education under Henry VIII, Edward VI, Mary, or Elizabeth. Richard Williams of Bristol, who had left England with John Hawkins as a boy of thirteen or fourteen, told his interrogators that his parents had conformed to Catholic practice until Mary's death, when he was about five years old, and to Protestant practice thereafter. He was able to tell his interrogators quite clearly why reverencing images was forbidden in England: one ought not to pray to sticks that can neither see nor hear. Bread and wine are consumed in memory of Jesus's sacrifice, and one must confess one's sins only to God, not to priests, who are only men and cannot absolve sins. Williams knew these arguments well and was accused of mocking the Mass and holy images, though he insisted that he had immediately conformed to Holy Mother Church when he arrived in Mexico and learned the truth. He admitted that aboard ship religious worship had been "Lutheran," with English prayers and mandatory services centering on readings from English books. In essence, he explained, he had always believed what he was told to believe.

For Williams, real sustenance seems to have come from friendship rather than faith. After months of seemingly endless imprisonment, he climbed up to the high barred window of his cell with the laces from his shoes and stockings and tried to hang himself, only to be thwarted when the makeshift rope broke and he fell to the ground. Williams resisted when a cellmate took the tight noose from his neck, and he was carried to the bed, where he lay weeping. When the Inquisitor rebuked him, he replied lamely that he had wanted to hang himself because he didn't know why he was there or why his companions were there. His cellmates explained that Williams had stopped eating and seemed very sad ever since a boy named William Low had been removed from the cell a few days before.[47]

In the case of some captive seamen, of course, their sufferings for the reformed religion and endless Inquisitorial interrogations about doctrine prompted them to conceive of themselves in strongly Protestant terms. Miles Philips, also a boy on Hawkins's last slaving voyage, presented himself as an ardent Protestant patriot when he eventually returned home. Most of the captured seamen were ultimately sentenced to galley slavery, and a few were burnt. Philips was spared a harsh punishment on account of his youth, yet after several years of surveillance, when the surviving Englishmen (including Richard Williams) were marrying and settling down, he revolted:

> For mine own part I could never thoroughly settle myself to marry in that country, although many fair offers were made unto me of such as were of great ability and wealth, but I could have no liking to live in that place, where I must everywhere see and know such horrible idolatry committed, and durst not once for my life speak against it: and therefore I had always a longing and desire to this my native country: and, to return and serve again in the mines where I might have gathered great riches and wealth, I very well saw that at one time or another I should fall again into the danger of that devilish Inquisition, and so be stripped of all, with loss of life also.[48]

The motives that drove Philips to return to England were tangled: love of country and hatred of idolatry mixed, it seems, with an aversion to the "Negro" and mestiza women the other Englishmen married, and certainly with the fear that his life in Mexico would never be secure while the Inquisition held sway.[49] Job Hortop—an older man whose initial religious formation may well have been Catholic—was less doctrinally committed. Reflecting later on his ordeal, he concluded his account with a secular meditation on fortune's wheel rather than the spiritual narrative so strongly suggested by his given name.

> Extremities cannot always last,
> Each thing doth bow and bend:
> In time both joy and woe doth waste,
> And all things have an end.[50]

For some English seamen, Protestant zeal may have been a consequence rather than a cause of maritime aggression. In the early voyages of the 1570s and 1580s, shipboard chaplains suspected some seamen were not Protestant at all, while others counterfeited zeal to justify plunder. Francis Fletcher, the chaplain of Drake's voyage around the world, recorded that when he and some others destroyed a crucifix with "an evil faced picture of Christ" that the Portuguese had set up on a headland of the island of Santiago, the act occasioned "great dislike as well to some of our own company being so much addicted to that opinion as to the Portugals themselves."[51] Well supplied with preachers and Bibles, Fenton's 1582 expedition had a staunchly Protestant air, but this may have been deceptive. The chaplain, John Walker, was initially impressed by the devotion of the crew, writing enthusiastically to the Earl of Leicester: "No doubt but God will bless us, for our people are wonderfully reformed both in rule of life and religion towards God. . . . Every Sunday I preach and after dinner we have conference in the scriptures wherewith the mariners who never heard sermon in their lives are marvelously delighted."[52] But not all spiritual teachings were equally delightful: around the same time, Richard Madox, the other chaplain, recorded that the men had been eager to seize a Flemish hulk, but he and Walker had dissuaded them with some difficulty. The next day, Madox and Walker preached against piracy, and Madox noted that "those . . . which at the shore did counterfeit most holiness were now furthest from reason affirming we could not do God better service than to spoil the Spaniard both of life and goods, but indeed under colour of religion all their shot is at the men's money." Madox found a teachable moment the following day when the carpenter's boy was to be ducked for stealing a shirt; he preached that "because we carried felonious hearts, therefore God sent us felons among ourselves." Some resented this instruction. When Madox proposed that the boys who waited at meals ought to learn and recite biblical proverbs, the navigator, Thomas Hood, "would not in any case that his boy should learn any such thing." Conferring together privately in Sierra Leone, Walker and Madox lamented "how much reproach we should bring on ourselves, what shameful disgrace upon the church of God," if the voyage turned altogether to piracy.[53]

Like the abandoned sailors from Hawkins's 1568 voyage, Elizabethan seamen continued to adapt as best they could when they found themselves in Catholic territory. The youth Anthony Knivet, who sailed with Cavendish in 1591 and soon found himself in captivity in Brazil, quickly realized that he could afford neither pride nor principles. When his small band of English stragglers was attacked by Portuguese forces, he saved his life by clinging desperately to his captors, offering to tell them everything he knew if they let him live. He would remain in Brazil for most of the next decade, working for his Portuguese master in the sugar *engenhos*, serving on inland military expeditions, trading for Indian slaves on his master's behalf, and living with Tupi-speaking tribes for months on end—once when he ran away, thinking he had killed a hated overseer, and once after he and some Portuguese soldiers got profoundly and hopelessly lost. In Knivet's narrative, Brazil was a claustrophobic wilderness, full of serpents, with Indian communities scraping a living, selling "their wives and children" for knives and hatchets, hemmed in by the extractive violence of the Portuguese on one side and by murderous enemy tribes on the other.[54] With a gift for languages, Knivet survived, convincing Portuguese captors that he was Catholic and Indians captors that he was French.[55] His life was not a happy one, however; his courage was often the recklessness of despair. The only glimpses of comfort that emerge from his story are his accounts of his friends, other young men struggling to survive in a hostile and indifferent world: Christopher, a Japanese boy on the Cavendish voyage whom Knivet loved so much that "we had nothing betwixt us unknown together," the runaway Indian slave Quarisiacupa, who shared his fugitive travels through a perilous desert ("Never man found truer friendship of any than I did of him"), "my dear friend Henry Barrawell," the one other English survivor, and "my dear friend Domingos Gomes," a mulatto slave who belonged to Knivet's master.[56] Friendship was something the young Englishman could not do without, and although he was sometimes disappointed, it is easy to see why. Friends saved Knivet's life, and he saved theirs, not in heroic battle, but by looking after one another when starvation, sickness, and exhaustion left them incapable of fending for themselves. Affective openness was a life-saving advantage.

Evidence of visceral hatred for Catholics is sparse, too, in the records of everyday privateering. When capturing Spanish and Portuguese ships, English privateers appear to have used no more violence than necessary, and while prisoners were stripped, robbed, and usually abandoned on shore to shift for themselves, they were not the objects of English loathing. When two English ships captured a Havanan ship in 1600, for example, the violence was largely symbolic. According to Portuguese witnesses, the Englishmen spotted the Spanish ship during the night, having glimpsed a cookfire the mariners had made on deck. When the *Diamond* caught up with *La Señora del Rosario* around noon, one of the Englishmen waved at the Spaniards "with a naked sword from the poop" crying, "Amaine amaine" (the command to strike their sails) while another from the more distant *Centaur* waved a cloak. The *Diamond*'s men shouted in Spanish, "Do you see this great ship which is not far off? She will sink you if you yield not," and they gestured that the Spaniards' throats would be cut. The Spanish captain responded as derisively as his broken English allowed, and after the two ships shot at each other intermittently for two hours, the *Centaur* came up, the *Rosario* yielded, and the victors fell to rifling the ship. They were rude but not cruel, according to a captured friar. No throats were cut, no one was killed, and for a fee the English surgeon attended a wounded man from the *Rosario*.[57]

The most violent encounters were not with Spanish ships but with well-armed Dutch merchantmen engaged in Iberian trade. A bloody battle took place in 1602, for example, when the *Affection* of London accosted the *Hope* of Emden not far from Lisbon, where the *Hope* was bound with brazilwood and sugar. The *Hope*'s thirty-five mostly Dutch sailors fought hard in defense of their goods and wages, and only yielded after five were slain and fourteen or fifteen wounded. Then the English surgeon shared his salves with the Dutch surgeon, and, as one Dutchman ironically reported, the English treated the Dutch "in kind manner and did them not any hurt more than take from them all that they had."[58] English privateers were not always so kind. When the *Content* of Plymouth took a French ship in 1594, for example, the Englishmen were determined to force their captives to admit that their goods belonged to supporters of the Catholic League, not to loyal subjects of Elizabeth's ally Henri IV. Some of the prisoners' fingers were "utterly spoiled" by being hammered into holes, but the Frenchmen stood firm, to the irritation of the privateers. When one French captive was "weeping" by the side of the ship, a frustrated Englishman knocked him overboard with a pike.[59]

When neutral or allied captives refused to cooperate, English privateers often tortured them with ropes. After two English ships captured the *Brown Fish* on its way back to Amsterdam from Madeira, the privateers "took the carpenter and hanged him up by the neck a foot from the ground until he was speechless, and that his eyes began to turn out of his head, and others they wrested about the head until the blood issued out, and also they tied a rope about the shipper's neck and threatened to hang him up, and then three or four of them came to [another sailor] and set naked swords to his breast saying they would thrust him through, and another showed him a cord and told him he should be used as the carpenter was if he would not declare that the goods were Spaniards' goods." Understandably, the company of the *Brown Fish* complied.[60] When choosing their victims, English privateers were pragmatic, targeting those who were most likely to speak and who had valuable knowledge. Carpenters were often tortured, perhaps because they were suspected of building hiding places for valuables.[61] Boys, too, were frequent targets. When Captain Jacob Wheddon in Sir Walter Raleigh's *Roebuck* took the *Fox* of Bergen in 1591, he was so eager to find out whether treasure was hidden in the cargo of salt that "two carpenters and three boys were cruelly dealt withal and wrested about the head with ropes, and otherwise tormented to confess what money was in the ship."[62] John Crosse, the prize captain of the *St. Jacob* of Delft, sailed the ship to North Africa and there "caused the boy of the said ship to be hanged up by the arms and so to be whipped to cause him confess where the money in the ship was hid." The boy did not know, but when Crosse "threatened to sell him to the Jews in Barbary," the carpenter came forward to tell the child the secret.[63] No one seems to have cared whether the Dutch seamen were Protestant or Catholic. Inflicting pain was a means to an end; plunder was the point.

Private War

The mobilization that transformed Elizabethan seafaring was no single national undertaking, controlled and directed by the state. Instead, a host of private ventures were launched for private gain, beginning well before the official breakdown of political relations between Elizabeth and Philip II in 1585. Drake's early raids on Spanish shipping, including the circumnavigation of the world, took place in the 1570s, when many English merchants were still trading with Spain and both the English and the Spanish Crowns still hoped to preserve peace.[64] Drake justified his attacks as reprisals for the losses he and his kin had suffered in John Hawkins's third slave-trading voyage. These were private ventures and losses, though Elizabeth herself was one of the investors.

Even the Elizabethan navy was a conglomeration of private interests in which private objectives could trump those of the Crown in blatant ways. With their rare oceanic experience, the sea captains of the Hawkins family were essential allies for the queen, but they never forgot their personal ambitions in the service of their country. The experts who managed Elizabeth's navy often had shady pasts, and even shady presents.[65] In most naval offensives, the Crown was only one of many investors who expected profits and influence over objectives and strategy. In 1589, for example, when Drake and Sir John Norris sailed to Spain with a large fleet financed partially by the queen and partially by private investors, their core mission was to destroy the remnants of the 1588 Armada. That would not be profitable, however, so Drake left the warships largely undisturbed. Instead he attempted to spark a Portuguese uprising in favor of the pretender Dom António, and when that failed Drake headed for the Azores in hopes of finding the silver fleet. When he limped home with the remnants of a fleet devastated by sickness, he had nothing to show his outraged sovereign.[66]

Since full-blown naval expeditions remained sporadic, the private war-ships that hunted Iberian ships and goods and raided Iberian settlements remained at the heart of the Elizabethan sea war: at least one hundred ships sailed on privateering voyages every year of the war, and often many more. They brought in prize goods constituting some 10 to 15 per-cent of the total value of English imports, amply making up for the loss of Iberian trade.[67] Remarkably, the vast majority of these predatory ven-tures continued to be justified on private grounds. Letters patent that au-thorized their bearers to capture and seize enemy ships were available only to men with influence at court. Most privateering voyages sailed with letters of reprisal, which were intended to be used in peacetime when a merchant suffered losses at the hands of a foreigner and was un-able to obtain justice through normal channels.[68] Thus if an English mer-chant lost goods to a French pirate and found no redress in French courts, he could obtain letters of reprisal to the amount of his loss and seize equivalent French goods at sea. After Spain seized English ships and goods in Iberian ports in 1585, many aggrieved English merchants ap-plied for letters of reprisal along these lines, but the practice quickly be-came a legal fiction. The requirement that privateers present proof of their losses was abandoned, and the High Court of Admiralty made no attempt to limit the value of Spanish goods seized. "Her Majesty shall not need to espy the faults of those that will venture their own to do her service," as Sir George Carey put it.[69] In almost two decades of warfare, the English government did not devise a legally coherent mode of autho-rizing privateers.

The private nature of the war shaped seamen's experience of it: condi-tions in the navy were abysmal, but for the most part, when not serving as impressed naval sailors, seamen were one of the many interest groups who collectively produced English maritime aggression.[70] Indeed, each privateering venture was itself a coalition of interested parties great and small. The queen conferred legitimacy and claimed roughly 5 percent of the value of prize goods, the Lord Admiral granted letters of reprisal and expected his tenth, and the remainder was divided in thirds between the owners of the ship, the victualers who financed supplies, and the ship's company. From the queen down to the ship's boy, all stakeholders had a financial interest in the outcome of a voyage.[71]

A wide range of investors fueled the privateering boom. Some fool-hardy gentlemen invested thousands in grandiose ventures. The London magnate John Watts owned several large ships and regularly sent them to prowl the West Indies, with profitable results.[72] While the great expeditions that made and broke their promoters' fortunes were likely to be financed by a few wealthy individuals, the modest ships that sailed out of Bristol and other smaller ports attracted much small fry. The expense of victualing the *Consolation* of Bristol was shared by some larger investors, like "one Mr Gall a weighter for the Custom House," who put in £40, and a number of smaller ones: a surgeon paid about £12, a gunner named Miles Burley paid about £11, "one Wainwright of Bristol or his wife who keepeth a victualling house . . . adventured a rundlet of acqua-vita of sixteen gallons," and a landlady near Tower Dock held a £3 stake made over to her by a ship carpenter.[73] Commanding officers were often also small investors. Some made their fortunes, like the seaman Michael Geere, who went to sea on reprisals every year after the war began when he was nineteen, often serving in Watts's ships. He became a master in 1589 and a captain in 1591. Scrappy fighting and sharp business practices built up his savings, and after 1592 he sailed several times as captain and part owner of the *Michael and John*.[74]

Even if they did not invest money, privateering sailors were shareholders who expected their shares of the proceeds. Sometimes they explained that they had adventured *themselves*. A gunner who "ventured not anything in the said ship but only his life" expected four shares, for example, and another who "adventured his person . . . was to have six shares."[75] Shares were allocated according to rank and custom, with the highest-ranking officers receiving three or four times as much as ordinary men. Usually the captain and master both received seven or eight shares, the lieutenant six or seven, the master's mates six, the gunner four to six, the boatswain four or five, the quartermasters three to five, the corporal four, the steward four, a little less for the petty officers' mates, perhaps two or three shares for an ordinary sailor, and one for a boy. Some of the poorest sailors on board shared their shares with backers who had paid for their clothes and supplies. One "young man little or nothing worth" received £11 but had to pay part of it to his brother, who had "set him to sea." A carpenter might receive four or five shares but often chose, like

Robert Harwin, "rather to have wages, than to hazard his voyage upon taking of prizes."[76]

The ship's company also enjoyed the customary right to pillage the prize ship of any goods that did not belong to its cargo. While Trinity House tried to establish rules governing the distribution of pillage in 1594, proclaiming that the captain received the defeated captain's chest, the master the defeated master's chest, and so on, in the heat of the moment, as the victorious sailors broke open sailors' and passengers' chests, all seem to have pocketed as much as they could.[77] When the *Galleon Shute* took a rich prize in 1594, for example, John Golding came away with "two old cloaks, a ring, an image of stone and glass," Richard Taylor had six pieces of eight "and nothing else save a pair of old stockings of silk," and Edward Maynard had "eighteen shillings in Spanish money, a crucifix of silver of four shillings value, [and] three quarters of a yard of crimson damask." Others were not so lucky. Anthony Man had "nothing but a few clothes," and Josiah Moore "was not on board while the pillaging was [happening], neither had anything out of the prize more than two old cloaks, which were given him by Harry Brewer and James Denton two of his company."[78]

Everyone involved in privateering ventures had interests to defend. English participants cooperated together in pursuit of common ends but also struggled to enhance their shares of the gains. The money designated for critical supplies sometimes found its way into private pockets: the greatest noble privateering promoters were thoroughly fleeced by their servants. The seamen—who often suffered shortages as a result—could be just as individualistic. On Cavendish's last voyage when a landing party was readied to plunder the town of Santos in Brazil, Anthony Knivet remembered, "there were so many that would have gone, that we began to fight and cast one another overboard into the sea." Whenever these privateers did find food or treasure, they hid it away and kept it for themselves. In the event of a rich prize, everyone aboard ship had an incentive to embezzle or dissimulate as much as possible of the spoils before they were taxed and shared with authorities and investors on land—and with one another. Once a prize was safely brought home, the vice admirals and customs officers were at least as interested in lining their own pockets as in guarding the interests of the Lord Admiral and the Crown. Privateering worked by aligning the common interests of the queen, investors, and fighting men, but self-interest permeated the system from top to bottom.[79]

The Nation

Elizabethan privateers may not have been drawn to the sea by religious or patriotic fervor, but the experience of maritime warfare did foster the development of collective identities. No sea battle could be won without close cooperation, as sailors worked in the rigging, hastily repaired damage, and manned the unwieldy guns. If victory was to be achieved, it had to be achieved together, so commanders did what they could to strengthen mutual bonds. When the *Golden Dragon* prepared to join the *Dainty* in the attack against an enormous Portuguese carrack in August 1592 off Flores, "Christopher Newport the captain said, 'masters, now the time is come that either we must end our days, or take the said carrack' and wished all the company to stand to their charge like men and if any displeasure were amongst any of them, to forget and forgive one another, which everyone seemed willing unto." Robert Keyball "took a can of wine and drank to John Locke and John Locke drank to him again and so throughout the ship every one drunk to the other" in secular communion.[80]

Battle-forged collective identities tended to take on a national form: the content of Englishness was uncertain, but the fact of English nationality was not. Local and regional identities receded when sailors migrated from coastal villages and small seaports to London, where they settled in untidy suburbs along the Thames.[81] Moreover, unlike most laboring men, sailors regularly fought with foreigners, and in the aggressive posturing that proceeded these fights, nationality loomed large. When the *Centaur* met with the *Esperance* and the *Princesse* of Le Havre in the West Indies in 1594, for example, the Frenchmen allegedly waved at the Englishmen with drawn swords, crying, "Amaine English dogs." Similarly, when the *Refusal* accosted the *Double Des* near Tenerife, hearing that the *Double Des* was Scottish, "the English thereupon called them Scottish dogs" and shot at them.[82]

The queen's honor was taken to legitimize English aggression: when privateers accosted foreign vessels, they commonly commanded them to "amaine for the queen of England" or "strike for the queen of England," threatening righteous wrath if the foreigners resisted putting themselves at the mercy of their assailants. Asked in 1594 why he had captured a Hamburg ship, Thomas Atkins claimed to have been angered in part by "hearing vile speeches uttered against Her Majesty as 'skite upon the queen of England.' " When Captain Matthew Bredgate of the *Truelove* commanded the men aboard the *Black Eagle* of Middelburg "to strike their topsail for the queen of England," the Flemings allegedly first told him to do it himself and then performed a perfunctory gesture, saying: "This is for the queen of England. What wilt thou have more?" Bredgate angrily gave the order to fire, and the *Black Eagle* resisted fiercely until its master's head was blown off.[83]

Even some of the most indiscriminately rapacious English adventurers cast themselves—to foreigners, to domestic audiences, perhaps even to themselves—as Elizabeth's loyal champions. The author of a pamphlet defending the gentleman Captain Edward Glenham and his men seized every opportunity to present them as defenders of the queen and the Protestant faith, despite the fact that Glenham had pawned captive Dutch Protestants into slavery at Algiers in exchange for supplies. The hapless shipper of the *Hare* of Enkhuisen complained that Glenham had given four young Dutch mariners to the "king" of Algiers, and that two of them—including the shipper's own son—"were shorn and clothed in Turkish apparel . . . and kept by the king to be allured to become Turks." Glenham had done this, the shipper alleged, to extort money from him. Selling Christians to Muslims was surely wrong, but in the pamphlet Glenham and his companions were presented in a pious and patriotic light, gallantly defending "the name of our most gracious sovereign lady" against rude Frenchmen.[84]

Violent encounters in which English seamen robbed foreign sailors underlined national boundaries, hindering the development of professional solidarity. Privateers routinely rifled captive sailors' chests and seized the clothes off their backs. Dutch and French seamen who had suffered at their hands trooped to the High Court of Admiralty to enumerate their losses in litanies of resentment. Limping from a wound to his thigh, a French pilot complained that Englishmen had taken his ship and stolen "the mariners' apparel and necessaries and left them nothing not so much as a knife to cut their meat or a can to drink with and besides did beat and misuse them very badly." Peter Arents of the *White Greyhound* lost everything, down to his "six linen night caps," to the men of the *Lioness* in 1601. A common sailor on the *Blue Sheres* had hidden his modest savings by letting them down on a rope in a hole in his cabin, but his wily captors found the coins and took them, along with his small stock of trade goods: "grapes to the value of thirty shillings sterling, and three canary birds worth nine shillings, and one jar of oil, and a pound of green ginger worth two shillings sixpence, more he had in musk to the value of three shillings which were all taken away by the Englishmen that came on board."[85]

Personal injuries fed political animosity. When a Flemish flyboat was manned with Englishmen and sent to London in 1591, it was captured again on the way there by French Catholic Leaguers, to the delight of the pillaged Flemish seamen, who "with vile and unseemly words professed that they were for the king of Spain and not for the queen of England, and with billets and such other things as they could get up they helped the Frenchmen to stow [the English prize crew] saying they should be all hanged up." They hoped, they allegedly said, "to overrun the land of England with Frenchmen and Flemings ere long." The English seamen remembered this injury when, some months after, they ran into the Flemings on their own ground in Wapping. One of them recognized the "villains" and seized the Flemish cook, exclaiming that "he had him now in England and he would use him well enough." The cook drew his knife; his fellows took his part; and the Englishman "called out for the constable and charged the people to assist them in the queen's name." "Skite on the queen of England and all her well willers," the angry cook shouted, before being hauled to Newgate.[86] National divisions took on heated emotional significance.

Some Englishmen did serve abroad, however—and not just Catholics. Some sailors drifted onto foreign ships by happenstance, signing on to foreign vessels when they were stranded in European ports. Others—particularly gunners—seem to have been actively recruited. A later case suggests how underground recruiters operated: when an English gunner was obliged to explain his presence on the *Esperance* of Dieppe, he recounted being "hired in London by Monsieur le Grove of Dieppe, by the means of Jeffrey Ilford a gunner dwelling at the sign of the Gun in

Limehouse." Ilford had paid him £4 in advance for two months' wages on behalf of the Frenchman, and the gunner received another forty shillings once he reached Dieppe.[87] Some Elizabethan sea commanders worried about the consequences of these movements. After one particularly disastrous sea battle, Sir Richard Hawkins speculated that his gunner had been corrupted by foreign service and was "more friend to the Spaniards then to us; for that he had served some years in the Tercera" and also "had a brother that served the king in the Peru, and that he thought he was in the armado; and how he would not for all the world he should be slain."[88]

Sailors' personal ties across battle lines could indeed complicate naval engagements. For example, some renegades retained a certain fellow feeling for their former colleagues even as they attacked English shipping. John Allyn, a Muscovy Company pilot who was implicated in a theft, fled England in 1599 and then entered Spanish service, hunting the very ships he used to sail.[89] One of these, the Muscovy-bound *Speedwell*, was chased by Allyn's Dunkirk privateer after losing its consort in a fog. Realizing that they could not escape, the English master John Monie drank to his men and willed them do their duty. They reportedly did their best to defend ship and goods even though Monie soon received a mortal wound, but were no match for the Dunkirkers' aggressive attack. After roughly seven hours (the sailor who kept the hourglass was killed) the master's mate, John Hare, saw that they had the advantage of the wind and called up the men to turn the ship around, but the ropes had been cut by enemy fire, and "they durst not go about to put any new for that the small shot came so thick about their ears, that they could not stand on the deck." The surviving sailors took refuge under the deck to figure out what to do. Some suggested blowing up the ship to slay their enemies, but they eventually agreed to surrender. Young Roger Donne ran up on deck and cried, "Masters, if you will use us like men, we yield."[90]

When the Dunkirkers entered the *Speedwell*, it turned out that several of them were Englishmen, including John Allyn, who demanded to see the shipmaster. The youth Donne hastily called to Hare: "Master you must come to John Allyn else he sayeth he will heave us all overboard." When the Dunkirkers asked Hare why he meant to fight so long, saying that John Monie would not have done so, Hare answered grandly: "Mr Allyn, will it not behove a man to fight for his liberty and to save all that he had?" "Mr Hare, content yourself, you shall not lose a penny," Allyn allegedly replied. They knew each other—Jonas Stephens of the *Speedwell* had once been a servant to Allyn's brother—and now that the battle was over, their relations became almost collegial. Not entirely, of course: the Dunkirkers took the ship's broadcloth, and they also exercised their customary right of pillage. Still, rather than leaving the shivering Englishmen with only the shirts on their backs, they gave them the remnants of the *Speedwell*'s cargo.[91]

Allyn also decided, remarkably, to give the English prisoners the *Speedwell* itself as a gift. His first thought was to give half of the *Speedwell* to John Hare and half to his brother's old servant. But Hare, "thinking his company would grudge thereat, did entreat the said Allen that one half of the ship might be bestowed upon the company." Together, Allyn and the Dunkirk captain wrote up a peculiar deed, giving one quarter of the *Speedwell* to Hare, one quarter to Stephens, and the rest, divided equally between them, to the remaining members of the company, allegedly threatening that if they refused to accept the ship, it would be burnt.[92] To assuage Hare's legal concerns, an English fisherman was fetched from a nearby Danish ship to serve as a witness. Then nothing was left but the final ritual of possession: Allyn told all the men of the *Speedwell* who could walk (the carpenter was gravely wounded) to come out of the ship into the man-of-war and then to ceremonially reenter the *Speedwell* as its owners. If this were not enough to establish their ownership of the vessel, the Dunkirk captain told the Englishmen, "if they did send him word thereof to Dunkirk, he would send them the king of Spain's broad seal to justify his deed." When the *Speedwell* limped into port at Archangel, the English sailors' unorthodox claims were met with suspicion, despite their wounds and the silent testimony of the dead. In their examinations they were at pains to show that they had not yielded voluntarily for gain. For merchants, English sailors' social networks were a cause of concern.[93]

In this unsettled period, fears that sailors would not fight hard enough to save ship and goods were aggravated when crews were mixed: national divisions weakened a ship's defenses. Portuguese sailors on a Spanish ship complained that English privateers were able to take it because of the treachery of its Flemish gunners, for example. When the *Rose Lion* attacked, the Flemings "shot at random over and wide that scarce any shot did harm the Englishmen." After the ship was captured, the Flemings "cursed and banned the Spaniards and Portugals and threatened to be revenged on them for misusing them in the voyage." When the English captain commanded one of the Flemings, a surgeon, "to dress some of the Spaniards that were hurt in the fight," he "denied to do it, and called them dogs, and said that if Captain West would give him leave he would help to cut all their throats."[94] English sailors could prove similarly unreliable on foreign vessels. In 1599 Christopher Cornelison of Middelburg unwisely hired Thomas Flood at Lisbon, where Flood was posing as a Scot. When the *St. Mary* was captured by English ships on its way to Venice, Cornelison insisted that the ship and goods were owned by men from Zeeland, and therefore not good prize, but Flood contradicted him. After Flood deposed that the goods did indeed belong to Spanish subjects, the Dutch carpenter hotly accused him of lying. Incensed, Flood slashed him in the face with a knife.[95] As a result of these dynamics Englishmen were rarely found on foreign merchant ships in this period, and English vessels contained no more than a sprinkling of foreign seamen.

Even allies found mixed crews hard to manage. Sailing in winter 1591–1592 with a Dutch captain, an English master, a mixed crew, and commissions and letters of marque from the English Lord Admiral, Holland, and the king of France, the *Tiger* of London was riven by conflict. According to the steward's mate, the ship sailed with twenty Dutchmen and eighty Englishmen on board, having left Plymouth early because the master, William Ivy, and the main owner, William Holliday, wanted to avoid taking on sixty more Dutchmen who were on their way. The Dutch captain "greatly disliked thereof," and with good reason: "Captain Barnstraw was not regarded by the Englishmen but greatly reviled and set at nought all the voyage, and called coppernose, and that he was fitter to drink ale than be a captain." A gunner from Hamburg agreed, claiming that Ivy had sole command of the Englishmen, and "the captain had no more government over them than any other mean person of the ship, but was threatened to be cast overboard many times if he sought to rule there."[96]

Barnstraw's insistence on following prize rules particularly irked the Englishmen. When the *Tiger* took two ships with spices and other valuables, the Englishmen were eager to open up their cargo at sea.

Barnstraw charged Ivy with violating the terms of his commission, but Ivy exclaimed: "Shite on their commissions, we have nothing to do therewith, we know what commission our owner Mr Holliday hath given us."[97] Part of the problem was that the prizes were from Holland and Bremen though they had most recently sailed out of Lisbon—good prize for the English, but perhaps not for the Dutch. Later on, when they took a wine ship, Barnstraw scrupulously forbade "the poor men that had taken great pains in the taking of her to draw out so much as a bottle of wine to comfort themselves withal, but sent the whole lading for England."[98] At Dartmouth, where the English privateers were anxious to go on land, Barnstraw "spake against the company for carrying the goods on shore before they were perused by the officers," but in vain: "Thomas Bowden master's mate and the quartermasters threatened to cast him overboard and one struck at him with a dagger."[99] When possible, sensible shipmasters sailed with more homogenous crews.

Shipboard Politics

Purely English ships could also be riven by internal strife, however. Elizabethan seamen's ambitions remained largely personal, and their aims sometimes collided. Single-mindedly focused on their own honor, some commanders put their men in unnecessary danger, for example. Famously, near the Azores Sir Richard Grenville deliberately sailed the *Revenge* into the middle of a large and threatening Spanish fleet, even as other English ships stayed well out of range. According to Jan Huyghen van Linschoten, who spoke with survivors after the fight, the shipmaster gave orders to escape, but Grenville "threatened both him, and all the rest that were in the ship, that if any man laid hand upon [the great sail], he would cause him to be hanged, and so by that occasion they were compelled to fight." After at least twelve hours and a hundred casualties, the *Revenge* had sunk two ships but could no longer resist. According to Sir Walter Raleigh, the mortally wounded Grenville "commanded the master gunner . . . to split and sink the ship," but the survivors refused and negotiated an honorable surrender. Grenville's fearlessness was renowned, but Linschoten reported that "his own people hated him for his fierceness, and spake very hardly of him." Probably many of them would have agreed that Grenville, who allegedly chewed and swallowed wine glasses in company, was "a man very unquiet in his mind."[100]

Few commanders were prone to such suicidal excesses, but the most ambitious of them were perfectly willing to sacrifice seamen's lives for their own gain and prestige. Thomas Cavendish casually abandoned some sick men to die of cold and starvation in the Strait of Magellan, for example, and left others—including Anthony Knivet—to the tender mercies of the Portuguese. And in general, commanders were apt to seek to monopolize the proceeds of maritime enterprise. For ordinary seamen, negotiating the politics of predatory enterprises was fraught with difficulties. It was hard for them to challenge officers who embezzled supplies, or to withstand merchants who pressured them to sell their shares at below market rates. Nonetheless, no sailing ship could operate without the active cooperation of the company, and seamen could make their voices heard.[101] Their efforts were all the more successful because richer and more powerful participants were often divided: at sea, it was easy to disregard the desires and interests of those investors who remained at home, and officers rarely acted as a single bloc.

Shipboard relations in the sixteenth century tended to be more familiar than would later be the case: captains addressed their men courteously as "masters" or "my masters," for example.[102] When commanders with pretensions to gentility looked around their ships, however, they tended to see servants and rivals rather than comrades in arms. Ships setting out on ambitious voyages needed to carry more than one potential commander, for safety's sake, but like their queen, commanders often held their heirs apparent in mortal dislike. Some only accepted lieutenants under duress, like Martin Frobisher, who being told that he had to bring Edward Fenton and others with him in 1577, "utterly refused the same, and swore no small oaths, that he would be alone, or otherwise he would not go in the voyage."[103] At sea, discord often followed. Francis Drake notoriously launched a lethal campaign against his lieutenant, Thomas Doughty, accusing him of mutiny and sorcery, and engineering his quasi-judicial murder. Fenton, the general of a fleet by 1582, hated his lieutenant, William Hawkins, and maintained cool relations with his captains. Thomas Cavendish blamed the failure of his last voyage on John Davis, a leading captain in his fleet, penning an impassioned denunciation before dying on the homeward voyage, allegedly of a broken heart. Few could stomach threats to their personal prestige and future gains.

Elizabethan sailors' ability to negotiate with their commanders was enhanced by the factional nature of shipboard politics: rival officers needed to cultivate groups of supporters, so divisions at the top offered opportunities for those below. Seeing that Drake disliked Doughty, for example, the trumpeter John Brewer and the ship carpenter Edward Bright reportedly took issue with the lieutenant's leadership. When Doughty joined in giving Brewer a ritual spanking upon his return to his ship, laying "his hand upon his buttock," the trumpeter "began to swear wounds and blood to the company to let him loose," refusing to be struck by a gentleman who "was not the general's friend." Drake demoted Doughty, and as the voyage wore on made it clear that Doughty's friends were his enemies. As a result, Doughty and other gentlemen were allegedly badly treated "by a sort of bad and envious people, as sailors and such like," including the ship's master, who refused to eat with them. When Drake later put Doughty on trial, Bright allegedly provided damning testimony against the lieutenant, claiming that he had long plotted against Drake. After Doughty was executed, the chaplain Francis Fletcher asserted, Drake rewarded Bright by making him captain of the *Marigold*, an astonishing promotion for a carpenter.[104]

It was hard for subordinate officers to uphold their authority when they were undercut by their superiors. When Edward Fenton sailed as lieutenant to Martin Frobisher in 1577, for example, "the boatswain, and others of the *Aid*'s mariners" refused to obey him. Fenton complained, but the general turned a deaf ear, leaving Fenton to rage that "he had offered him great disgrace."[105] A subordinate officer could try to bolster his position by slavishly proclaiming his loyalty to the general, but this also carried risks. Thomas Skevington, captain of the barque *Elizabeth* in Fenton's 1582 fleet, attached himself ardently to the general. When he appealed to Fenton for help with his insubordinate shipmaster, Ralph Crane, Skevington cannily repeated Crane's disrespectful words about the general. Predictably, Fenton took the matter seriously, calling a council "to examine certain words tending to mutiny and derogation of Her Majesty's authority (unworthily laid upon me) as also against certain principal officers in my ship." Crane was briefly punished in the bilboes, and order was apparently restored; but the sailors were disgusted with their captain and told him so: "So long as he went fizzling to the general with tales to pick him a thank, so long they should never be in quiet." "Privy talebearers were called fizzelers," Richard Madox recorded with relish, because "he which fizzleth doth stink worse than a plain farter and doth also lead many into suspicion." By tattling to the general, Skevington lost his men's esteem.[106]

Cultivating seamen's loyalty was easiest for those who had rewards to dispense. When Drake appealed to his men to support Doughty's execution, he allegedly told them that if the voyage went forward "the worst in this fleet shall become a gentleman," but that they could not continue with Doughty alive: "Therefore my masters they that think this man worthy to die let them with me hold up their hands, and they that think him not worthy to die hold down their hands."[107] Fenton allegedly bought loyalty by doling out extra supplies at the expense of the voyage's investors, handing out liveries of popinjay green to build up support for his secret plan to conquer St. Helena and make himself king of that island: "While he hoped to be able to rule without sailors and a captain, he hated them all worse than a dog or a snake, but after he realised he could become nothing without these people, he now embraces them alone."[108] So long as Fenton was able to make big promises, it was hard for his rivals to attract followers. Luke Ward, a captain in the fleet, told his chaplain he would desert "if his company would go with him," crying "that he had received discourtesies at the General's hands."[109]

The sailors' obedience to Fenton depended on their confidence that he was acting in their best interests. This had become clear even before the ships left England. When a favorable wind arrived while the pilots and the lieutenant, Hawkins, were still on shore, Fenton had commanded the ships to set sail without them, but "answer was made that in as much as each man went upon his venture, they would not run headlong into an unknown coast without those pilots that were appointed by the council." The sailors explicitly linked their disobedience to the fact that they sailed for shares: "The general commanding to weigh the anchors, the mariners utterly refused, saying that they ventured for the thirds and would not therefore go without the pilots." Later that day, when Fenton and the other high officers discussed what to do, "every impudent boy leaned over [their] shoulders."[110]

As the voyage progressed, the sailors continued to view themselves as essential stakeholders. They had hoped to cross the Strait of Magellan into the Pacific, but once the fleet reached the Río de la Plata, most of their supplies were exhausted, and they heard troubling news that a Spanish fleet was bound for the strait to repel them. In his advice to Fenton, Richard Madox, the chaplain, emphasized that whatever was decided, the sailors had to be persuaded to go along. He warned Fenton that there was already "great gratching" among the ship's company: the men were complaining that they would "starve in the end and that they [would] return home beggars." When the fleet turned around and headed north, leaving the dangers and promises of the strait behind, the other chaplain, John Walker, recorded that "our men greatly murmured fearing for the voyage." To maintain order, their captain had to promise that they would return south after obtaining more supplies. Still, one of the small ships left the fleet, continuing south on its own. The other ships limped north, thirsty and hungry. For a while, Fenton entertained hopes of sailing all the way to Newfoundland to attack Spanish fishermen, but once it became clear that this was not realistic, they headed for England "by the consent of the whole company."[111]

By the time the fleet arrived in Ireland, the men's dreams of wealth in tatters, Fenton's authority was in shreds. When he commanded his men not to depart without leave, a quartermaster, Edward Robinson, replied that he would come and go as he pleased "and cared not a fart for the best in the ship." The next day, two men refused direct orders, and when Fenton hit Robinson with his cudgel, the quartermaster struck back. Fenton could hardly complain to higher authorities about his men's insubordination: he himself had disregarded his instructions and lost the investors' money. His hated lieutenant, William Hawkins, was only too glad to provide damning details.[112]

Other attempts to cross the Strait of Magellan were abandoned when sailors persuaded or forced their commanders to turn back in the face of catastrophic mortality and adverse winds. Battling fierce gales and currents in the strait in early February 1590, having lost many men, the *Delight* of Bristol faced mutiny: the captain, Matthew Hawlse, stockpiled weapons and food in his cabin, while some of the sailors believed they would be starved to preserve the lives of a favored few. Hoping to save themselves, they exploited division in the upper ranks: they petitioned the ship's master, reminding him of the slights he had suffered from Hawlse and the master's mate, and pleaded to "return back into England, rather than die here among wild and savage people." Two days later, the ship turned back.[113] Similar resistance foiled Cavendish's plans the following year. As men died of cold and want in the strait, unable to pass through it, Cavendish purportedly determined to sail to the Cape of Good Hope instead. The captain of the *Desire*, John Davis of Sandridge, reportedly implored Cavendish to "consider the great extremity of his estate, the slenderness of his provisions, with the weakness of his men": the fleet was in no condition to sail so far. It was not until "a petition delivered in writing by the chief of the whole company," however, that Cavendish resolved to sail to Brazil for supplies.[114] He was never able to return south. When "most boldly they all affirmed that they had sworn that they would never go again to the straits, neither by no means would they," Cavendish was so enraged that he tried to strangle the spokesman, shocking the rest of the men into silence for a time. They remained obdurate, however, and when Cavendish ordered them to sail to St. Helena, "they all plainly made answer they would not," steering Penelope-like for England whenever he slept. Their implacable resolution seems to have put an end to their furious and despairing commander, who wrote before expiring that his "spirit was clean spent" by grief and "the continual trouble I endured amongst such hell hounds."[115]

Pacific-bound voyages were fearsomely dangerous and accordingly rare. Davis's ship, the *Desire*, returned to Ireland with only sixteen men and boys alive out of seventy-six.[116] Most privateering voyages were much safer, consisting of short cruises in familiar waters, mostly off the coast of Spain, and since the interests of ships' crews were fairly well aligned, their internal politics were far more harmonious. Still, sailors demanded full political participation: they had financial stakes in the voyages and expected a say in shipboard decisions, particularly about consortship.

Consortship—agreements between two or more ships to aid each another and share their gains—was a regular practice in the late sixteenth century. Ships consorted for the purposes of both defense and offense, for periods that could be as long as a voyage or as short as a few hours. For predatory ships, the question of whether or not to consort was a gamble, because consortship diminished not only the risk of returning home empty-handed but also the hope of having a rich prize to oneself. As in William Cradell's case, disputes over prizes often hinged on the validity of particular consortships, especially on the question of sailors' consent.[117] If captains did not consult their men and obtain their agreement, consortships could be invalidated. In a richly documented case between the *Diamond* and the *Prudence* of Weymouth in 1600, for example, the men of the two ships disagreed vehemently about whether the ships had been consorted but agreed that consent was required.

The two ships had left Weymouth together in the early spring of 1600 and came together again off the Azores, where the *Prudence* had tried and failed to take a village, losing its boat and eight men, and its captain had drowned. Some sort of agreement was evidently reached between Captain William Jolliffe of the *Diamond* and George Browne, the master of the *Prudence*, but it was not put into writing—indeed, Browne could barely write.[118] Instead, two men were exchanged to seal the agreement: Ansell Rise, quartermaster of the *Diamond*, and Richard Philmore, midshipman of the *Prudence*. On May 22nd or the morning of the 23rd, the ships lost sight of each other while the *Prudence* was chasing a Portuguese ship. When the luckless *Diamond* arrived home at Weymouth, news arrived that the *Prudence* had come to Dartmouth with the prize. The men and investors of the *Diamond* claimed their share, but those of the *Prudence* denied them, with typical early modern thoroughness, on all possible grounds: Browne had not had the authority to consort; the company had not consented; the consortship had expired; and so on. Because of these wide-ranging arguments, it is difficult to isolate the legal weight of consent; in the examinations of men from both sides, however, it featured prominently. According to some witnesses for the *Diamond*, when the master of the *Prudence* had proposed the consortship, he did so "saying he had talked with his company and they had given consent to consort."[119] Philmore admitted that this story was true, and that Browne had indeed sought his company's consent beforehand, saying: "Masters, you see the *Diamond* is in our company and she saileth better than we do, and there is no contract betwixt us. If we should give chase to any prize, and the *Diamond* fetch her up before us, we shall have no part with them, therefore advise what you will do, whether we shall consort, or leave their company." The men allegedly answered: "We had rather consort with one of our town than with any other." Later, when Browne formally "asked them if they would consort with the *Diamond* or no," they said "they were content to consort," so long as "the men which they had lost should be taken in as if they were on board." When Browne called, "Dick, fit your clothes and come on board," Philmore answered he was ready and only waited to make sure that he would still receive his shares as a man of the *Prudence* before he changed ships.[120]

Others from the *Prudence* told a very different story. The boatswain first denied ever having heard about it: "If there were any pretended consortship made, the same was made secretly and closely for [he] and the rest of the company and mariners of the *Prudence* never heard thereof till after their arrival in England." Later, he acknowledged having heard Browne's proposal but insisted that he "and the rest of the *Prudence*'s company told him they would allow of no such matter."[121] The quartermaster, John Lockyer, insisted that as soon as Browne returned to the *Prudence* after his negotiations with Jolliffe, angry mariners went to his cabin "and told him they heard, he had made a consortship with the *Diamond,* and if he had, they answered, they would not stand unto it." When the master "asked who spake . . . they answered, one and all." Abashed, Browne replied that "he had done nothing but that they might brake out of when they would."[122]

Browne's flexibility was typical. Though some gentlemen raged at any check on their authority, professional privateering commanders often found it useful to acknowledge the limits of their sway. They were as eager to invalidate unprofitable consortships as their men, after all, and sailors' willfulness could be used to mask their own disobedience to higher powers. When the *Prudence* of Barnstaple brought an illegal prize to England in 1592 and the *Prudence*'s anxious owners told them to release it, for example, the officers protested they were willing to obey but seemed powerless to resist the mutinous seamen. The captain soon showed his true colors, however, when he and others broke into the warehouse where the prize's sails were kept and sailed the ship away to Safi in Morocco, having first given "vile and intemperate speeches" against the owner, "saying he had compounded with the Flemings for £1500 to defeat and cozen him and his company of their said part of the said goods."[123]

Facing rival ships and domestic authorities, common Elizabethan privateers and their officers often saw the advantages of making common cause. In both maritime attacks and legal suits, they banded together to reap profits from the sea.

The maritime plunder and raiding of the later Elizabethan period attracted young men to the sea and encouraged them to regard themselves as Englishmen, members of a nation at odds with foreign enemies and victims. This private warfare did little, however, to clarify what being English meant, beyond allegiance to the queen: quarreling with one another and attacking neutral and friendly shipping, the privateers did more or less as they pleased. While the fortune of the seas was inconstant, for sailors this loose structure had clear advantages. It mostly aligned their interests with those of their masters, and few effective restraints were placed on their behavior. Even the dangers of battle were mitigated by the fact that English warships generally attacked merchant ships that had smaller crews and fewer guns.

When Elizabeth died, the privateering war died with her. James had little taste for anti-Spanish bombast and lost no time in drawing the conflict to a close: a proclamation of 23 June 1603 recalled all letters of reprisal, and peace with Spain was finalized in August 1604. For some merchants, the privateering years paved the way to commercial success: the wealth and knowledge accumulated in predatory voyages provided a foundation for long-distance trade.[124] Some sea captains, too, turned smoothly to trade and settlement. Christopher Newport, whose capture of a rich carrack was one of the greatest victories of the war, returned to the West Indies in search of trade after 1604. He took on a leading role as a maritime commander in the early voyages of the Virginia Company, then commanded ships in three East India Company fleets before succumbing to fever in Banten in 1617, a wealthy man. For ordinary ex-privateers, however, the path forward was less clear. Their skilled labor was still in demand: England's battle-hardened sailors were an asset that could usefully be repurposed, their martial skills deployed to protect merchants' goods. It was one thing to fight for gain, however, and another to die for other men's property.

CHAPTER TWO

RENEGADES AND REPRISALS

In September 1602, as the sailor John Norway made his final preparations for a voyage on the *Margaret and John,* the ship's young captain, Thomas Tomkins, scrawled a note for Sir Robert Cecil about his ardent desire to serve his "prince and country" against the Spanish threat. The secretary of state was probably not impressed: the youth, a former follower of the Earl of Essex, had been under a cloud since the late rebellion. Still, even a cynical observer could not have predicted quite how much trouble Tomkins and his men would make. Rather than remaining in the Atlantic according to royal command, the *Margaret and John* sailed to the eastern Mediterranean. There, Tomkins and his crew captured a ship carrying valuable leather and oil belonging to François Savary de Brèves, the French ambassador at Istanbul. They sold the goods in Patras despite the French captain's pleas that France was an English ally; then in April 1603 off Cyprus they took an even richer prize, the Venetian ship *Balbiana,* laden with rich textiles. Norway had his share of the plunder, including costly materials that few of his status would ever have even seen up close. A few months later, when his ship was at Tunis, Norway used these goods as security for a long-standing debt he owed to William Chester, the carpenter of the *Alcedo* of London: lacking ready money, the pirate gave Chester twenty-three yards of cloth of gold as collateral, saying he would redeem the cloth when he returned home.[1] By this time, however, James was king and the political climate had altered: newly arrived in London, a Venetian ambassador complained pointedly about the *Balbiana*. When Norway came to Chester's house to redeem his cloth of gold, Chester was afraid to give Norway the goods; these were soon seized, and Norway fled. Tomkins himself was obliged to spend several years in exile, explaining apologetically to the Privy Council that he had planned to seize only the goods of "Jews and Armenians" on the ship but had been "crossed by a secret commission given underhand from the owner of [his] ship unto the master, one of his mates, and the gunner," whose "faction [was] so strong amongst the mariners" that he could not withstand them. As for Norway, the sailor lost little time in returning to the Mediterranean waters that had proven so rewarding: he joined the company of John Ward, a notoriously successful renegade. Tunis would be Norway's new home.[2]

For a generation of seamen who had known nothing but war, the end of privateering came as a shock, leaving some men at dangerously loose ends. Days after the initial proclamation against reprisals, the mayor of Plymouth complained about the "intolerable outrages" committed by "a great number of sailors, mariners and other masterless men, that heretofore have been at sea in men-of-war, and being now restrained from that course do still remain here and pester our town." Daily, he lamented, they stole boats and went to sea to "rob both English and French," which he feared would "be the means that our goods shall be stayed and confiscate in other places abroad."[3] Honest merchants might be held responsible for the ravages of unemployed predatory sailors.

Even during the war English commercial shipping had expanded along multiple fronts. The destruction of the northern trade emporium at Antwerp prompted merchants to look further afield for markets for their wares. English fishermen had long spent their summers catching and drying cod in Newfoundland, and they gained ground there in the 1580s and 1590s as their Portuguese and Basque rivals were pressed into Spanish royal service. In the 1590s, Dutch merchants who had lost access to spices at Lisbon financed ambitious ventures to the Indian Ocean, and the first English fleets followed close behind. And since 1573, English ships had sailed into the Mediterranean in increasingly large numbers, bound especially for Livorno, Venice, and the Greek islands.[4]

Englishmen arriving in the Mediterranean found a relative vacuum of power. The Ottoman Empire suffered a devastating defeat at Lepanto in 1571, and Spain was too exhausted by decades of warfare in the Low Countries and elsewhere to make hay of the allied victory. Venice, another ostensible victor although it had suffered from Ottoman advances, found its naval superiority to be both a blessing and a curse. The Serene Republic proved unable to meet the combined challenges of defending its maritime possessions and integrating them commercially, leaving its discontented Greek subjects amenable to English overtures. Meanwhile, Elizabeth pursued diplomatic and commercial relations with the Ottoman Empire, whose extensive military commitments fed demand for English tin and lead.[5] Eager to control the trade in Levantine luxuries, English merchants in the Turkey Company and the Venice Company obtained royal monopolies in 1580 and 1583, respectively. To Venetian chagrin, the separation of the two companies proved impractical, as Turkey Company factors (commercial agents) purchased currants and sweet wines in the Ionian islands on their way to Ottoman ports, circumventing Venetian customs regulations, and the two companies were merged into the single Levant Company in 1592. The Levant Company was a regulated company, not a joint-stock company: merchants paid a premium for the right to participate in lucrative eastern Mediterranean trade, but they traded for themselves. Politically, however, the Levant Company played a unified role, representing the English state in Venice and the Ottoman Empire and lobbying the English government to support its interests. The English ambassador in Istanbul and the consuls in other ports were employees of the Levant Company as well as representatives of the Crown, and until 1619 the Levant Company not only paid these diplomats but also selected them.[6]

The Levant Company spoke for England, but its semi-sovereign control faltered when it came to the motley community of English seamen. Predatory Englishmen were notorious among the pirates and corsairs who thrived in the poorly policed waters of the early seventeenth-century

Mediterranean. This disorder ultimately helped strong national fleets—including the English—to establish a dominant role in Mediterranean trade by weeding out their local rivals. English pirates and renegades have accordingly often been viewed as the unofficial agents of a policy of national expansion.[7] The Mediterranean was not a battleground between disciplined representatives of their national commercial interests, however, but a chaotic space in which a wide variety of traders, sailors, and pirates did as they pleased.[8] English corsairs were generally indifferent to the fortunes of their merchant compatriots and sometimes injured them, because national reprisals were a useful way for the victims of English violence to obtain satisfaction. The legal structures that later fostered the growth of European shipping in Ottoman service were still being developed.[9] A rogue English sailor could cause endless trouble for his countrymen, and there were plenty of rogues to be had.

At some times, ordinary English merchant sailors paid the price for English crimes, at others, the Levant Company was left holding the bag, a national corporation at odds with an unruly nation. These reprisals were intended not only to compensate victims and avenge abuses: like diplomatic complaints, they also sought to pressure the English Crown to strengthen its control over its predatory subjects. Progress was slow, for the state's reach was limited overseas, but Ottoman and Venetian efforts did tighten the loose affinity of English seafaring men abroad into something more bounded and more orderly.[10] In the meantime, bearing the brunt of local anger about their countrymen's abuses, English merchant seamen learned a painful lesson about national collective responsibility.

Revenge and Redress

Indiscriminate raiding by Elizabethan privateers left English sailors with a bad reputation in the Mediterranean. In theory, no private English men-of-war were to enter the inland sea, but the repetition of royal proclamations to this effect in the queen's last years attests to their ineffectiveness. As good prizes dwindled, rogue privateers cruised Mediterranean waters, prowling for Venetian ships. One victim remembered: "They came on board us, and thrashed us all for not taking in sail fast enough. About thirty of them swarmed on board, using great violence and foul language to us. They took all our artillery; sent us all below and fastened down the hatches. They then proceeded to help themselves to everything, including thirty casks of wine. We were all in terror of death, for they bullied us, and went so far as to put the noose round our necks every day." Venetian officials who pushed back were targeted by vengeful English sailors. Maffio Michiel, the governor of Zante, earned their rancor by hanging English pirates when he could, which was not often. When the pirates took a vessel carrying "some doves that [Michiel's] womenfolk were sending home for their particular delight," the Englishmen spitefully threw them into the sea.[11]

For Levant Company factors, this lawlessness was a problem. One wrote to the leading Levant Company merchant Richard Staper in February 1603: "If you may not continue your trade with more security, but evermore to rest in fear to have your goods troubled for the abuses committed by pirates and rebels, it were better for the company to have no trade here at all. [E]very day we fear to hear of their bad dealing; therefore it doth behove your worship and the rest of the company who trade into these parts to procure some good redress from Her Majesty for these matters." Redress was not to be had: Cecil himself dabbled in Mediterranean plunder, and orders to stamp out piracy were used as excuses to outfit *even more* predatory warships.[12]

In any case, it was hopeless to bar private warships from the Mediterranean when Elizabethan merchantmen carried letters of reprisal. For captains like Hugh Whitbrook of the *Thomas,* trade and plunder went hand in hand. On one voyage, Whitbrook sailed to Civitavecchia and Livorno with herrings and then seized a Spanish ship laden with "cinnamon, cloves, carpets, quilts of silk and cotton" and other valuable goods. On another, he sailed to Guinea with iron, sold it peacefully, and then captured a Portuguese prize, trading its cargo of iron to African merchants for ivory and hides. Then Whitbrook sailed to Livorno, where he sold his African wares before sailing farther to capture a Barcelona ship, selling *its* cargo to "Turks, Greeks, and Jews" at Patras.[13] Similarly, on the way to Italy the *Alcedo* of London took a Portuguese ship from São Tomé; the prize and most of its goods were sent to England, but fifty-six African captives were taken on to Venice, where they were sold for about £200.[14] For merchant seamen, pillage and plunder made a welcome addition to monthly wages.

When the pilot Thomas Pipe was killed in the Mediterranean by a Spanish javelin, in addition to his seaman's effects (a silver whistle, clothing, a featherbed, a rapier and a dagger, a compass, and a tinderbox) and goods he had purchased (currants, oil, sponges, linen cloth, and nutmeg), he owned half a hundredweight of dates, some fishing lines, and "a Negro" seized from a prize.[15]

At the beginning of James's reign, some English merchant sailors continued to plunder, as a Venetian shipmaster lamented in 1604. Relations had been cordial when the *Moresini* first met an English ship: the English ship's master identified himself as Abraham Lawse (he had made a peaceful merchant voyage to Venice and Zante the year before), the ships saluted, and the seamen ate and drank together. Later, all the Englishmen but Lawse went back onto their ship, taking two English members of the *Moresini*'s company with them. When the *Moresini*'s master, Marco, later went to fetch his two crewmen, he was taken to a cabin while a number of Englishmen boarded the Venetian ship again. It seems that the English members of the *Moresini*'s crew had told their countrymen what was worth stealing. "When night came," Marco recounted, "I saw the boat come back from our ships full of things, which they had taken after breaking open all the boxes and trunks, though their chief officer made us understand that if any of us saw anything belonging to himself he was to point it out, and it would be restored." Then the Englishmen began to fight among themselves because, Marco continued, "some wanted to carry off the ship, others to give her back to us." By the time Lawse succeeded in pacifying them, the *Moresini* had been thoroughly plundered. Faced with such rapacity, Venetians could well suspect "that there is not a sailor of that nation but is a pirate."[16]

Aggrieved foreigners sometimes struck back at English merchant ships, disbelieving their protestations of innocence. These national reprisals threatened the goods of English merchants and upended the lives of their seamen.[17] In 1603, for example, the *Salamander* of London was carrying goods for an English merchant in Zante when it was unexpectedly attacked by a large French man-of-war at Milos. "So soon as the Frenchmen had gotten the wind, they set up a bloody flag in the foretop, and sounding with drum and trumpet in the poop, they ran presently on board the *Salamander* and filled the ship with men," the shipmaster, William Browne, recalled.

The French warship had been fitted out specifically for reprisals against English shipping by Savary de Brèves after his loss to the *Margaret and John*. After several hours of battle, Browne, "having two of his mariners killed and seven hurt[,] . . . was enforced to yield himself and the ship . . . upon condition to have their lives and liberty."[18]

The ordeal of Browne and his men had just begun. The defeated Englishmen were rowing to land when "they were called back and asked if any of them would go to Marseille, they should have four crowns a month and a passport to carry them for England." Five accepted the offer, but when they arrived at Marseille, they were accused of being pirates. As one of the Englishmen, John Weddell, later reported, the hapless sailors "were committed to prison the next day after their coming to Marseilles, and kept prisoners about six months, and then they were condemned by the judge there to the galleys, viz., two for their whole lifetimes and [he] and two others for the space of ten years, and the *Salamander* was adjudged for prize." Their appeals were rejected, and they spent twenty months in the galleys. "Then upon letters from the French king [Weddell] and three others were released, paying ten crowns a man for their ransom to the captain of the galley . . . for the captain of the galley affirmed that if the king sent as many letters as his galley could carry he would not release them without money."[19] Servitude also awaited some of the seamen who had remained at Milos. Browne made his way safely to Istanbul, where he complained to Ottoman authorities and the English ambassador, but one of the crew, John Cotterell, petitioned King James five years later, lamenting that he had lost both his estate and his freedom, having been "put into the galleys of Scio [Chios], where he still remaineth in slavery and bondage, to the great danger not only of his life, but also of his soul, by the cruel enforcement of the Turks in their blasphemous religion, and having set his ransom at £40 the which he is utterly unable to pay." He begged that the bearer, Mary Pierce, be permitted to collect charity on his behalf.[20]

After the first few years of the seventeenth century, incidents like this became rarer as the distinction between English merchantmen and pirate ships became more clearly established. Diplomatic pressure played a key role: Venetian ambassadors were regularly sent to London from 1603 on, in large part to deal with maritime grievances, including disagreements over how English merchant ships should behave when challenged by

Venetian galleys: galley commanders claimed the right to exact submission and search for contraband in the Adriatic, but the English were loath to submit. While disputes persisted, James's orders that English ships should show the galleys due courtesy helped calm the tempers of prideful commanders on English and Venetian ships alike.[21]

Seamen in Foreign Service

English merchant sailors slowly reformed, but the presence of English corsairs in the Mediterranean continued to cause trouble for their law-abiding compatriots. Many old privateers were attracted by the corso, finding ready patrons among both Catholic and Muslim rulers. Aristocratic renegades sought positions of command and influence—Sir Robert Dudley designed ships for the Grand Duke of Tuscany, Sir Anthony Sherley commanded fleets for Philip III, and Sir Francis Verney became a corsair captain at Algiers, for example—but humbler berths abroad were occupied by hundreds of English sailors who ended up in foreign service by design, coercion, or the luck of the sea.

Maritime war had endowed England with warlike ships and many fighting seamen. For these battle-hardened mariners, employment was easy to find. English sailors fanned out across Europe, meeting with open arms: even the governor of Zante hired English ships. The Spanish ambassador complained that "many English ships, under colour of merchandise, go into Holland, where they become men-of-war . . . and so go with commission of reprisal from Count Maurice to the coasts of Spain," and that the States General even sent their own ships "all manned with English" to prey on Spanish shipping.[22] Indeed, the Dutch ambassador reportedly explained that "for matter of hostility and reprisals . . . the States had found more aptness in our seamen to serve their turn and more obedience to their captains, than in their own men." Englishmen also served in Catholic ships, including in the Spanish Navy, where gunners were paid especially high wages. James recalled his roving subjects, but they do not seem to have listened.[23]

Warlike English sailors also made their way to the Mediterranean, the richest hunting ground for predatory ships, where the needs of bustling cities ensured that merchant ships put to sea despite the long-running maritime conflict between Catholic and Islamic states. While the corso derived its legitimacy from religious conflict, some patrons of corsairs were broad-minded to a fault: English sailors were welcomed on both sides and sometimes actively recruited. They were especially prominent in Livorno and Tunis, two port cities on the rise.

Grand Duke Ferdinand I de' Medici was eager to acquire English sailors for his fleet. Aspiring to make Florence more formidable at sea, he built up trade and naval power with the construction of Livorno. Originally "semi-deserted malaria-ridden swamps," Livorno was endowed with a Renaissance city plan, excellent fortifications and port facilities, a cosmopolitan merchant population attracted by tax exemptions and religious freedoms, and its own order of corsairs, the Knights of St. Stephen.[24] For fighting men and sailing ships capable of taking Ottoman prizes, Ferdinand looked in part to England—and indeed, after James's accession, predatory English seamen flocked into Tuscan service, where they took part in attacks that destabilized Mediterranean trade, tarnished nascent efforts to promote English commercial respectability, and endangered their countrymen.

One of the foremost of these was Richard Gyfford, a well-connected young gentleman whose talent for getting into trouble was matched only by his ability to wriggle out of it, leaving his countrymen to deal with the consequences. Gyfford had been imprisoned in Livorno in 1601 after having arrived in command of an illegally captured Ragusan argosy. Letters from Elizabeth helped Gyfford to obtain a pardon and his sequestered goods, and the adventurer left Livorno on good terms with the grand duke.[25] Two years later, on a cruise supposedly bound for the Pacific, Gyfford heard that James had banned privateering; leaving his ship the *Lioness* at Majorca, he offered his services to Ferdinand. The *Lioness* was then captured by Spanish ships, and its men were committed to the galleys, "where [the] most part of them perish[ed] with hunger and stripes." The loss of his ship weakened Gyfford's position, and the grand duke was at first reluctant to employ him, but he ultimately suggested that Gyfford burn the galleys at Algiers, "alluring" him with the false assurance that James would not object.[26] England and Algiers were on good terms at the time, so Gyfford could sail there unmolested: he was valuable to Ferdinand precisely because he was English.

After setting barrels of wildfire ready to explode in the galleys, Gyfford absconded in the night in company with another English ship that happened to be there, abandoning nine of its hapless men on shore. The two English captains then sailed to Bugia, where, allegedly flying English flags, they invited a number of unsuspecting Muslim merchants to come on board, then carried them to Livorno to be held for ransom.[27] In Algiers, meanwhile, the lit matches had been discovered and extinguished. The luckless English sailors were put to death "to appease the fury of the people," while two English merchants were kept alive as hostages for the Bugia captives. Gyfford had sacrificed English relations with Algiers for personal gain, with lasting consequences: several years later, the Levant Company consul in Pisa was still laboring for the release of the captives from Bugia "that thereby twenty English mariners kept in miserable captivity in Argier may be released who daily solicit us with pitiful letters to that purpose."[28] Fearing reprisals for these sneak attacks, the Levant merchants sought to mollify the Ottoman sultan and prevented Gyfford's friends at court from protecting him. Unable to return home, the adventurer pressed Grand Duke Ferdinand for payment but was imprisoned instead; the next few years found him writing letters to his contacts in England, promising to do the king great but unspecified services if he could obtain release.[29]

Despite his disappointment with Gyfford, Ferdinand continued to recruit Englishmen in England, the Mediterranean, and the Atlantic.[30] In 1604 and 1605, in addition to buying some English ships, the grand duke pressed others and their crews into his service, again with repercussions for Levant Company trade. The *Merchant Royal*, a powerful merchantman with about fifty men that anchored at Livorno early in 1605, was just to his taste. With a Ragusan captain and roughly eighty Italians and Greeks supplementing the English crew, the ship was impressed into Tuscan service and "was sent forth in warlike manner against the Turks." Toward the end of the ten-month cruise, as the ship passed between Rhodes and Cyprus, it came across a huge Ottoman galleon "manned with six or seven hundred persons on board her, both men women and children." After a lengthy fight, "it so pleased God" that the *Merchant Royal* took the galleon, killing about four hundred Ottoman subjects in the assault. The crew took the survivors as captives and set the badly damaged galleon on fire.[31]

Despite its Tuscan commission and extra soldiers, the *Merchant Royal* was clearly an English ship with an English crew. The merchants of the Levant Company were "in great alarm" at the news of the sinking of the galleon, for it had carried goods belonging to powerful members of the Ottoman court; they urged the arrest of the *Merchant Royal*'s owners and complained about the grand duke. The attack may indeed have sparked reprisals: when an English ship was burned at Istanbul in January 1606, Sir Henry Wotton, the English ambassador at Venice, had no doubt that it had been done "on the Grand Signior's orders," possibly at the instigation of the Venetian *bailo*, who had reportedly told the sultan that the English were responsible for all maritime disorders. Hoping to avoid further troubles, Wotton wrote to the sultan to protest that the *Merchant Royal* had sailed under Tuscan command.[32]

The trouble they had caused left the *Merchant*'s English sailors in a tricky situation. Robert Thornton, the master, brought the *Merchant* and its spoils back to Livorno but lingered nervously outside the harbor, so Ferdinand wrote to Wotton asking him to tell Thornton that he might as well enter Tuscan service, since he would be safe nowhere else. Reluctantly, Wotton agreed, and the shipmaster finally brought the *Merchant* to his new home, where he converted to Catholicism and raised his children as Tuscan subjects. Few of the crew stayed with him. The quartermaster, Francis Magner—actually an Irishman—reported that after a brief imprisonment he and the English sailors were offered "wages and other good allowance and kind usage," but they refused and were expelled from the ship. With their wages for the first cruise, he "and seven more of his company travelled away from Leghorn by land fearing to be impressed again in such service." Most of the rest trickled back to England after the *Merchant Royal* sank soon thereafter.[33]

In England, the *Merchant*'s mariners were called into question for the deaths of hundreds of Ottoman subjects, the sinking of the Ottoman galleon, and the loss of two English ships. In their defense, they claimed that they had been coerced not only by Ferdinand but also by their English superiors. Magner protested that Ferdinand's officers had seized the ship "contrary to the wills and liking of all the company . . . for they would have forsaken the ship and returned for England when they perceived the ship should serve as a man-of-war." They had only agreed to serve when

Thornton and the ship owners' representative told them that they would not be paid "unless they would consent to stay in the ship." The argument that "they should have no wages for the time past if they would not continue in the ship" was a strong one, and it helped that "they knew that the *Roebuck* and the *Darling* were employed by the said Duke in warlike manner the summer before, and were well used and the mariners had their wages well paid, and were suffered to depart home with their ship when the service was ended."[34]

Having entered Tuscan service under duress, the *Merchant*'s sailors claimed, they had done their best to avoid sparking reprisals against English subjects. At Scanderoon (Iskenderun), they asserted, where the grand duke's officers had been eager to take "twelve vessels belonging to the Turks," the English sailors had refused to attack because there were four English ships there as well, and English merchants on shore. The master's mate claimed that he "and the other Englishmen being in the *Merchant Royal* feared that the English ships . . . would have been seized on and hardly dealt with" if they captured the Ottoman vessels. They also claimed to have interfered when, a few days later, Ferdinand's officers complained to other Catholic corsairs about their recalcitrance. The other warships made straight for Iskenderun, but so did the *Merchant Royal* "to defend the said English and Turkish ships . . . and would not suffer them to do any damage." As for the bloody capture of the galleon, they asserted implausibly that the Ottoman ship had forced the fight on them.[35]

For the Levant Company, Ferdinand's use of English ships and mariners was a major embarrassment. According to Wotton, by 1607 the grand duke's "fleet abroad [was] great and for the increase of one year very enorme but the success thereof principally founded upon English pirates." He warned James that Ferdinand's employment of Englishmen "did ruin the public commercement, endangering the fortunes and peradventure the lives of Your Majesty's people in the Levant: for the Turk was not likely to be satisfied with the banner of the Grand Duke or of the order of St. Stephens upon the top of a flagstaff."[36] He may have overblown the danger: it is not clear that English privileges were ever in serious danger of being revoked, but familiar as they were with national reprisals, English merchants feared Ottoman wrath.[37] Wotton did his best to convince the Venetian cabinet that the English corsairs at Livorno were mere outlaws for whom James was not responsible. The grand duke, he complained, "receives, shelters and caresses the worst of the English, men who are publicly proclaimed pirates by the king." In London, while the Levant Company agitated against Florentine use of English ships and sailors, the admiralty attempted to tighten its surveillance of English mariners, though it was hampered by solidarity among seamen. Admiralty officials inquired after the names and addresses of the *Merchant*'s company, but while Magner provided a list of names, he was studiously vague about the men's whereabouts: they had come "some to London, some to Bristol and to other places, but where they or any of them are now remaining he knoweth not more than some poor men of his company that dwells here in and about London."[38]

While the Levant Company tried to clarify the legal boundaries of the English nation, seafarers found their informal national affinity useful. After settling at Livorno, Robert Thornton helped to recruit other English sailors, perhaps including the five men of the *Thomas* who "left the ship at Leghorn and served the Duke" in 1607 or 1608.[39] Compatriots could also aid sailors languishing in Tuscan captivity after being captured by the Knights of St. Stephen. Since the late sixteenth century, English merchant ships had been intermittently liable to Tuscan attacks because they carried Muslim passengers and their goods. One victim was William Davies, a surgeon who had left England in 1597 on the *Francis* of Saltash, which was "bound to Scio within the Arches of Archipelago, and freighted with Turkish goods by Turks, and some Turks aboard with us" when the ship was "most fiercely set upon by six of the Duke of Florence his galleys, who being in continual war with the Turks, took us as a Turkish prize." Hard labor and humiliation awaited the captives: "We were all shaven both head and beard, and every man had given him a red coat, and a red cap, telling of us that the Duke had made us all slaves, to our great woe and grief." After three years "chained in a cart like a horse," working on building projects in Livorno, Davies and the strongest of his fellows were sent to the galleys, "where our former diet lessened, but blows increased, to the loss of many of our lives. We were shaven head and beard every eight or tenth day, being always naked, but only a pair of linen breeches and chained continually. . . . The misery of the galleys doth surpass any man's judgement or imagination, neither would any man think that such torture, or torment were used in the world, but only they that feel it." To survive this ordeal, Davies depended on his national network, receiving "much comfort and relief from English merchants that were Protestants, and also from many English masters and owners of ships." It was the renegade Thornton, however, who ultimately procured Davies's liberty so that he could serve as a surgeon on a Tuscan expedition to South America.[40] After visiting the Amazon and enduring a final run-in with the Inquisition, Davies was finally able to return home.

While some Englishmen served in Catholic men-of-war, others flocked to the corsair ports of North Africa, where renegades from Christian Europe joined native Berbers and Arabs, Ottomans from Anatolia and the Balkans, Moriscos, Jews, and sub-Saharan Africans: as in Livorno, the corso coexisted profitably with vibrant trade and remarkable ethnic and religious diversity.[41] Algiers and Tunis were formally subject to Istanbul, ruled in theory by a rotating cast of pashas. By the early seventeenth century, however, their local rulers had come to enjoy considerable autonomy, which was tolerated by the central Ottoman government: for the Sublime Porte, the corsairs were an essential reserve of maritime power.

English sailors were already familiar with the coast of the Maghreb: they had watered and sold prize goods there during the Spanish war, co-operating with Muslims against the shared Catholic enemy. For some, continued raiding out of North African ports may have been an extension of the previous struggle. The Cornish gentleman Ambrose Sayer sailed out of England as a privateer shortly before Elizabeth's death but was captured and spent four years imprisoned in Florence, then three more as a prisoner of the Inquisition in Rome. Sent out with the Spanish fleet as a galley slave, he "and divers others Flemings and English" mutinied and sailed to Algiers, and from there he set out with "about two hundred men English, Scottish, and Turks," he said, "to revenge the wrongs that he had sustained and to take Spaniards, Italians, and all papists that he could meet with." Captured and tried for piracy in England, Sayer may have exaggerated his anti-popish fervor, but it is easy to believe that his ordeal left him with hard feelings.[42]

Other English renegades were simply looking for gain. Chief among these was John Ward, a man of obscure origins and a stratospheric rise to notoriety.[43] According to Andrew Barker, a shipmaster who was taken prisoner by some of Ward's men and published an account of the pirate, the beginning of James's reign found Ward on a small naval ship, the *Lion's Whelp*, reminiscing with fellow malcontents about the old days "when we might do what we list, and the law would bear us out . . . when the whole sea was our empire, where we rob at will, and the whole sea but our garden where we walked for sport." When his listeners urged him not to pain them with talk of "that golden world," Ward protested that a remedy lay at hand, "if true resolution were not bankrupt in England, if we had not women's hearts to bearded faces, nay, and we were not all cowards." Spurred on by his assurances, the sailors seized a barque in the night and went to sea. Posing as harmless merchant sailors, they took a small French ship by surprise, recruited more men near Plymouth, and set sail to the south. On the coast of Spain, they captured a larger Flemish flyboat and made for Algiers. In addition to putting eloquent speeches in his mouth, Barker exaggerated Ward's early stature. In fact, these pirates' first leader was probably Edward Fall, a privateering captain who had been imprisoned in 1602 for piracy in the Mediterranean; Ward seems to have taken charge only after Fall's capture. Barker was right, however, that dissatisfaction and nostalgia for the lax Elizabethan days prompted some seamen to turn pirate, and that they could readily do so by stealing small vessels in English harbors.[44]

Ward's arrival at Algiers was poorly timed, since the city was still smarting from Gyfford's surprise attack. Ward and his now considerable crew quickly decamped and presented themselves at Tunis instead, where they sought the patronage of the dey. Uthman Dey had reduced the role of the pasha to a largely formal one, initiating a period of quasi-monarchical deylical rule.[45] Like Ferdinand I de' Medici, he was intent on increasing his city-state's wealth and maritime power, supporting both the corso and trade. It is hard to know what Ward thought of the Anatolian commander or what Uthman made of the uncouth Englishman, who was said to be "very short with little hair, and that quite white, bald in front; swarthy face and beard. Speaks little, and almost always swearing. Drunk from morn till night. Most prodigal and plucky. Sleeps a great deal, and often on board when in port. A fool and an idiot out of his trade."[46] According to Savary de Brèves, who visited Tunis in 1606, when Ward was asked why he took French vessels, since the French were friends of the Muslims, he answered in garbled Italian—the original Lingua Franca—that "people of his sort did not care for such alliances, that he could not refuse what his good fortune offered him." He would sell his own father if he found him at sea, he claimed. De Brèves thought Ward and Uthman Dey were birds of a feather: men of lowly origins, greedy, and ambitious; both needed money to keep their unruly followers happy.[47] Indeed, Uthman was as quick as Ward to see that they had interests in common, and he both permitted the English to install themselves in Tunis and invested in their voyages.

Ward attracted scores of English seamen drawn to Tunis by ambition or misfortune. Many had attacked Spanish shipping under Dutch flags after James's accession. Jeffrey Wiseman married and settled in Southwark when the Spanish war ended, for example, but after a few years his money seems to have run out, and he got employment on the *Blessing*. With a Dutch commission, the *Blessing* took a Spanish prize, but it was recaptured the next day with many privateers on board. The remainder of the *Blessing*'s crew sailed in disarray to Salé on the Moroccan Atlantic coast, and when Ward appeared there shortly on the *Gift*, all the *Blessing*'s men— including the future pirate "admiral" Richard Bishop of Yarmouth— elected to join him, since their own ship was rotten and leaky. Walter Hancock, Thomas Mitton, and Richard Parker also came to Ward by way of Dutch privateering. As Mitton later recounted, he sailed on a Dutch ship out of Bristol bound for Guinea, but it was "blown up with powder in a fight that they had with a Spanish man-of-war on the coast of Spain." Fortunately for the thirty-four survivors, they were rescued by the Dutch pirate Captain Simon Danseker, who took them to Tunis. William Longcastle, his brother, and Samuel Cade arrived on the *Greyhound*, a Dutch ship allegedly destined for a voyage to the West Indies that stopped in Tunis—not exactly on the way—for repairs.[48]

The recruits' previous experiences had prepared them well, since many, like John Norway, had previously raided Venetian shipping and sold plundered goods in the Maghreb. Prior to entering Dutch service, the Longcastle brothers had sailed on a Plymouth privateer that captured a Venetian ship in 1602 or 1603.[49] Richard Atkins and Francis Martin sailed with the piratical Cornish privateer Captain Hugh Tolkerne, who lost his ship off Mamora and pawned Atkins, Martin, and his own brother to

Saletan merchants in exchange for a vessel. When Ward later came to Salé, he convinced another English captain, John Muckell, to redeem Atkins and Martin, "being his countrymen."[50] According to reports, Muckell himself had been sailing with a Dutch commission but illegally took an Emden prize and sold it in North Africa; when he went on board an English merchantman to write a letter, most of his crew, including his lieutenant, Anthony Johnson, ran away with his ship and joined Ward.[51] John Lilburn was one of the company of the *George* of Southampton; they had taken an illegal prize called the *Wagon* and sold its cargo at Tunis.[52] These men were old hands at Mediterranean piracy.

For several years, the English corsairs' valuable skills and great success at sea won them toleration for unruly conduct, and Uthman Dey accorded them considerable independence on the condition that they sell him and other officials their plunder at cut-rate prices.[53] De Brèves reported: "The great profit that the English bring to the country, their profuse liberality and the excessive debauches in which they spend their money . . . makes the janissaries cherish and support them above all other nations. Such that no one else is noticed there but them; they carry their swords at their sides and run drunken through the city. . . . They sleep with the wives of the Moors and when discovered, buy their way out of being burned. . . . In short, every kind of dissolution and uninhibited licentiousness is allowed them, even that which is not tolerated among the Turks themselves."[54] Another French observer, Captain Foucques, claimed that the English corsairs—especially the captains John Ward, Richard Bishop, Sampson Denball, Anthony Johnson, and Toby Glanfield—transformed the fortunes of Tunis, making Uthman a wealthy man, and powerful at sea: "These Englishmen have taught the Turks to arm and set vessels out to sea, to take and enslave all Christian nations, and by the riches they have stolen and taken in the last three years they have so far enriched this Carosman and his associates, that . . . they now put six well-armed galleys to sea, and twelve great ships of which the least are of 300 tons . . . and with this force they will destroy Christendom, if measures are not taken, and France will suffer the most."[55] Ward's glory days culminated in the 1607 capture of the fabulously rich Venetian argosy *Reniera e Soderina*, whose unwarlike sailors allegedly hid below and forced their captain to surrender.[56]

In England, though they were a cause of scandal, the renegade corsairs in Tunis were seen as less of an urgent problem than those in Livorno. Indeed, they could even be seen as assets. Writing in March 1607, Wotton claimed that Venice would not openly attack English trade in the Levant for fear of provoking a privateering war: "So timorous a state cannot but apprehend these effects seeing that one only Captain Ward . . . hath kept them in such awe . . . and done upon them almost what he hath liked." The Venetians had their revenge, however, by frustrating Ward's hopes of reconciliation with his sovereign. Ward quietly opened up negotiations for a pardon for himself and his men, offering to return some plunder to Venetian merchants if they would support his bid, and Wotton urged the doge to accept: "If your Serenity could see a way by which he could, in part, give satisfaction to the gentlemen and citizens who are owners of the booty he has plundered, I do not think the return to the king's favour would be so difficult a matter, and that would be a public benefit." The Venetians were not impressed, and Ward remained outlawed, his bribes wasted. For aggrieved foreign merchants, national reprisals were one way to discourage English maritime abuses; diplomatic insistence on permanently severing the bonds between rogue Englishmen and their country was another.[57]

As Ward's discreet overtures suggest, the Tunis renegades were less cut off from home than one might think. Treating the English "nation" as a loose and fluid affinity continued to appeal to many seafarers. Letters could easily be carried by the English ships that regularly called at Tunis and other North African ports, allowing for contact and exchange between pirates, merchant sailors, and minor English traders. These contacts are well documented because in 1607 and 1608 three English ships returned from the Mediterranean carrying goods that bore a marked resemblance to those captured aboard the *Reniera e Soderina*. The Venetian ambassador took their masters and merchants to court, and the resulting depositions make it clear that personal and economic ties between the corsairs and "honest" Englishmen persisted despite the official condemnation of Ward and his crew.

The mariners and merchants of the *Seraphim* and *Husband* of London and the *Unicorn* of Bristol were all careful to avoid direct trade with the pirates, but this posed no serious barrier, since in Tunis all prize goods were first purchased by local intermediaries who resold them at marked-up prices, a practice that simultaneously enriched the intermediaries and shielded European buyers from legal action.[58] Accordingly, Richard Bromfield, the master of the *Seraphim*, condemned Ward and his company in public, "blam[ing] them for living in so barbarous and heathenish a country to the scandal of his nation insomuch as they could never after abide [him] so long as he was there." Bromfield's mate, John Durson, said "there were divers great brawls and fallings out" between them and "Ward used Bromfield hardly in speeches and gave him many opprobrious words and called him puritan knave and puritan rogue and divers other ill words."[59] Englishmen testifying on behalf of John and Jacob Pountis, the master and merchant of the *Husband*, said that they could not have dealt with Ward or any other pirates, because if any Christian were to buy any goods from Ward "he should lose his head or be galley slave as long as he lived." John Pountis "gave express commandment to his mariners not to have any dealings with any of Ward's company."[60] Others admitted to casual conversations with the corsairs, however. Durson said "he hath spoken to some of them aboard and as he hath met with them in the streets and that one of them gave [him] an old bed of cotton wool."[61] The master's mate of the *Husband* too "had speech with some of Ward's company as he hath met with them in the town about ordinary matters which he remembreth not," and a carpenter conceded that "as they met with Captain Ward's men they saluted them as being their countrymen."[62]

Despite his alleged aversion to Ward, Bromfield was happy to purchase cotton from Uthman Dey. He and other seamen claimed that there was nothing unusual about such dealings. The gunner of the *Seraphim* deposed that Tunis was a port of great trade, that many English ships transported Turkish, Moorish, and Jewish merchants from there to the Levant and back, and that those merchants brought Levantine commodities like cotton, rice, and indigo to Tunis. The greatest Tunisian merchant of all, the Englishmen agreed, was Uthman Dey. "It is usual in those parts," the gunner said, "that the greatest men are the greatest merchants, as the Signores of Venice, Genoa, and Ragusa and sundry other places are, and their greatest state is maintained by trade." Bromfield explained he had often seen Uthman sitting on a stool in the street and administering justice to the people; indeed, Bromfield himself had craved justice from him. "Carosman is a great merchant as most of the chiefest men of the towns within the Straits are," he said. "The greater that men are in those countries, the greater merchants they be."[63]

Elaborate ritual surrounded the transactions. When Bromfield bought thirty bags of cotton wool from Uthman, the bags were openly weighed at the common beam by Uthman's servant Morato Jennesa and an elderly "Turk" who was the sworn weigher for the city, in the presence of the officials of the customhouse. A gunner then marked the bags as lawfully purchased goods and sent them on board the *Seraphim*. Similar procedures legitimized the purchase of cotton yarn, indigo, cinnamon, and drugs by the master and merchant of the ship the *Husband*. Thomas Morse, the carpenter, said that the *Husband* had originally sailed to Cartagena in Spain but, finding little demand there, put over to Algiers, where it sold its corn and took in passengers for Tunis. Morse and the French consul were present when Uthman viewed the cargo of cloth in his tent near the castle of La Goulette. The *Husband*'s cloth and gunpowder were then carried up to Tunis and exchanged for cotton wool and yarn that was weighed at the common beam. The consul wrote out a certificate in Italian and sealed it, the pasha's secretary wrote out a second certificate in Turkish, and the pasha "took out a seal from his bosom" and sealed it. The English purchasers had, as the jurist Gentili put it in his analysis of the case, done their business with "the highest Tunisian officer, who had, moreover, the administration of the main fiscus."[64] The Venetian ambassador was unimpressed by these explanations, and he must have found the *Husband*'s chance arrival at Tunis with a cargo of gunpowder suspicious, to say the least. His appeals to James's sense of justice met with some success: in January 1609, in response to Venetian pressure and the Levant Company's request, James forbade English merchants to "buy, barter, exchange, or receive directly or indirectly any goods taken at the seas, upon any pretext whatsoever."[65]

In fact, the merchant sailors and the corsairs had been on far more familiar terms than the former initially admitted. Thomas Mitton, a corsair who was captured and pressured to give evidence against the English merchants by the Venetian ambassador, said that Bromfield and his men "were aboard the *Soderina* and did converse and make merry with . . . Ward and the company of the *Soderina* and did buy and had given some trifles of the said Ward and other of his company." Walter Hancock, another corsair in similar circumstances, reported that "the *Unicorn*'s company had familiarity and speech oftentimes with Captain Ward and his company as Englishmen usually do meeting in foreign parts."[66] The Pountis brothers were "often in the company of the said Captain Ward in his own house in Tunis, being invited for dinner and supper in regard they were his countrymen." Moreover, it eventually became clear that John Pountis carried quite a lot of money for Ward and other corsairs, to "be delivered here in England to their wives."[67]

Pountis also gave passage to George Dix, John Thomas, and Humphrey Dallamore, former corsairs who transferred themselves to smaller ships near Cartagena to avoid a public homecoming. Nine or ten more embarked on the *Unicorn*, paying high prices for their passage.[68] Nearly all managed to avoid the snares of justice, and Ward's forces were replenished when three sailors from the *Husband* joined his company. Similarly, when Henry Pepwell sailed to Tunis with orders to "persuade Ward and his confederates to forsake their wicked course of life," he not only failed but even lost his *own* crew: "What with gifts and further hope of spoils, Ward so won my sailors that they became pirates with him, whereby I was compelled to part with my pinnace at a under rate unto the Turks."[69] Political pressure could prevent corsair commanders from safely returning home, but ordinary renegades were far harder to track.

Vulnerable Passengers

Cross-cultural commercial relations were also jeopardized when English merchant sailors abused their Ottoman passengers. They had ample opportunity to do so, for English ships and sailors quickly became popular for the transport of goods and passengers from port to port. Carrying "the goods of Argier . . . to Constantinople, the commodities of Constantinople to Scanderoon, and the wares of Damascus to Sio," the adventurer Thomas Sherley related, English merchant made good profits, and "in all these transmigrations from one Turkey port to another they transport many passengers, Jews and Turks."[70] Richard Bromfield, master of the *Seraphim*, claimed he had served "near three years together . . . in carrying Turks, Jews, and Moors being merchants of Tunis and their goods from Tunis to Alexandria and back again to Tunis, and that one hundred and fifty of those merchants at the least have been transported at one time in the *John and Francis* with their goods." Anthony Bullock, the *Husband*'s master's mate, said that he had done the same in the *Mary Anne* of London, and that "the *Darling,* the *Angel,* the *Isaac,* and sundry other ships of London have been employed by the Turks and Moors of Tunis."[71] Though Venetian, Ragusan, and especially French ships dominated Ottoman trade in European ships in the eighteenth century, English ships may well have been preferred earlier.[72]

The reasons were clear: English ships were strong for their size, and their crews were skilled in combat. Thomas Sherley boasted: "Our ships are the gallantest and best fitted for the war of any; our mariners are most apt for such enterprises, as men daily trained and experienced in fight, by reason of the long war that hath been between England and Spain."[73] English merchant ships were designed for battle as well as trade, and cheap domestic iron made it possible for English merchantmen to go heavily armed. These "defensible ships" were expensive to man, and they could not compete with Dutch shipping on most trade routes—especially since English seamen were accustomed to more and better food—but lower insurance costs and greater security made them attractive to merchants and passengers of all creeds in the hazardous Mediterranean.[74] Some English seamen robbed and even enslaved Muslim passengers, however, prompting reprisals against English merchants, who then sued the original miscreants for damages. These cases reveal the precariousness of cross-cultural shipping: crowded together in cramped quarters, seamen and their passengers lived in fear, especially when rumors of English-Muslim violence elsewhere raised the risk of retaliation.

The first major such betrayal of passengers took place in the aftermath of Gyfford's attack on Algiers. Just before the attack, a trader named William Mellin and his associates had bought the *Hopewell* at Algiers from the corsair Ambrose Sayer. Under the command of the part-owner Richard Lux, it sailed to Alexandria, where, according to a youth, "there came news thither both of Her late Majesty's death and peace made with Spain, and that Captain Gyfford had fired the galleys at Argier. By means whereof the English grew in contempt with the Turks and Moors insomuch that the said master and company were misused and beaten in the streets and threatened to be made slaves when they had them at Tunis and Argier."[75] The master's mate of the *Trial,* also at anchor at Alexandria at the time, remembered worrying about possible reprisals: "He and his company durst not deny the Turks anything that they desired and would have, and suffered them to take out of their ship powder and wine at their pleasure, and if they should have been denied, they would have beaten [him] and company like dogs, for as he sayeth there came a Turk on board and would have had wine, and [his] mate denied him, and for that cause he was fetched by force ashore and beaten on the soles of his feet with a pizzle of a bull, and he gave five pieces of gold to the Moors, and so had but ten blows, otherwise he thinketh they would have killed him."[76] In these tense times, the nervous Muslim and Jewish passengers "would not lade any goods into the *Hopewell* at Alexandria until they had the command of the gunner's room, and all the weapons of the ship were in their hands," except for a dozen pikes or so that lay about the poop. Their fears were fanned by the fact that the *Darling* and the *Roebuck* had been impressed by the Grand Duke of Tuscany to attack Ottoman shipping: the passengers worried that the *Hopewell's* men would not fight against their compatriots to defend foreigners and their goods, and might have heard rumors that some of the *Hopewell's* own company had previously been "shipped . . . at Leghorn and had served in men-of-war and taken Turks." For their protection, the travelers brought along on board "a company of janissaries . . . without agreeing for their passage, or bringing any victuals on board for their diet." The Englishmen were nervous as well, having heard that "one Mahomet . . . who came as passenger in the said ship from Argier" had "wished them to be wary and to look well to themselves," warning them "that the Turks meant to confiscate ship and goods."[77]

These mutual suspicions proved fatal. After leaving Alexandria, the *Hopewell* stopped at the island of Kastellorizo. When about a hundred of the passengers went ashore to refresh themselves, the Englishmen attacked those who remained on board. "The Turks leapt out of the ship and swam ashore, and some of the Turks leapt into the boat and put her off from the ship so as no more of the said Turks could get in the said boat, but were forced to leap into the sea and as many as could swim got ashore and the rest were drowned."[78] The *Hopewell* promptly sailed away to Civitavecchia, where the owners sold the passengers' goods as their own. Their crime did not go unnoticed: in England, the *Hopewell*'s master, Richard Lux, and its other owners were eventually indicted for piracy on the evidence of Levant Company factors resident in Algiers. One of them, Devereux Morgan, complained that the pasha of Algiers seized *their* goods because "of an insurrection of the people who had their husbands, children, and friends in the *Hopewell* and went with open mouths to the king to cry out against the English nation." Morgan had been obliged to pay a heavy fine to escape with his life. In England, meanwhile, Lux bought his freedom with a judicious bribe.[79]

The Gyfford attack and the *Hopewell* episode dampened English merchant shipping at Algiers, but by 1610, English sailors there were once again in a position to betray their passengers. Hundreds of Moriscos who had been banished from Spain during the wave of expulsions between 1609 and 1614 were bound for Tetouan from Algiers, so the English consul, Richard Allen, arranged with the pasha for three ships to carry them: the *Blessing*, the *Transporter*, and the *Seaflower*. The *Seaflower* was let to the merchant William Garrett by its master, James Motham, while the *Transporter* and the *Blessing* both belonged to Allen himself.[80]

Allen's continued presence in Algiers was supposed to guarantee the passengers' safety, so Algerian authorities were alarmed when, after the departure of the three ships, he was nowhere to be found. Ominously, he had left with the ships. The pasha immediately sent a frigate to warn the passengers of their peril. As Robert Tendering, boatswain of the *Seaflower*, remembered, "Thereupon the said passengers began to be all in an uproar and were greatly discontented." The frigate also brought letters from the hapless English merchants left in Algiers, asking Allen to return and to bring the passengers back safely, but the ships did not turn back. Instead, Allen spoke with leading passengers, calming their fears.[81]

The following evening, however, trouble began to brew. Tendering said that "about six of the clock that night, as the said Motham and his company were going up to prayers on the steerage, sundry of the Turks stood looking at them and viewed them, and as it seemed numbered how many they were, and after prayers, they came to the master and merchant and required to have their weapons delivered them." Motham promised them that if they would wait until morning, a satisfactory compromise would be arranged: "Two Englishmen and two Turks should be appointed to have the keeping of them so as they would swear they would do the master and his company no wrong, as they the said master and company would swear the like oath to them." Nonetheless, that evening, the *Seaflower*'s mariners claimed, the passengers tried to seize the ship. William Ivery, the cook, reported that they "secretly got two spits out of the cook-room and a half pike and three or four swords betwixt the decks" and that "missing the spits" he had told the master, who, "fearing they would rise upon him and his company that night watched himself until about midnight and then going to rest prayed his mate to watch diligently lest the said Turks should offer them violence. And about an hour after the master was gone into his cabin, [he] being in his cabin asleep, awaked with a great noise which he heard in the ship and coming out found the master and most of his men and the Turks together by the ears, the master's mate having his deadly wound given him in the belly with a knife and another sore hurt."[82] Tendering said that some of the passengers had tried to wrest the helm from the helmsman, who cried out for help. When the master's mate and another man came over to help him, the passengers mortally wounded the mate. The noise drew the rest of the ship's company from their cabins, and "after about three hours' fight" the seventeen sailors "stowed the said Turks and Moors being an hundred and upwards, and freed themselves from their fury and violence."[83] Embroiled in the fight, they had called to John Reekes, master of the *Blessing*, for aid, but he simply sailed away.

On board the *Blessing*, the consul's brother Thomas Allen had a very different view of the incident. "Between one and two of the clock," he said, "Motham, Garrett and company did set upon the passengers . . . and killed divers of them and hurt some others and at the length stowed them under the hatches." Hearing the "hurly-burly" on the *Seaflower*, Reekes had come to the consul's cabin "and asked him if he were ready, and told him that if he were ready, they were all ready to join in the said spoil." To his amazement, "Richard Allen protested upon his soul he neither had nor would have any finger in the matter, but would be the first which should lose his life in the defense of the passengers aboard the *Blessing*." Reekes was incredulous, explaining that "Motham and Garrett had made him acquainted with the plot before their departure from Algiers and had made him believe that he the said Richard Allen was also acquainted with the said intention." Reekes allegedly confessed that he would have attacked his own passengers if Allen had not prevented him, "and was very joyful and gave God thanks that he did not." While the *Blessing* apparently sailed to Tetouan as planned, the *Seaflower* and the *Transporter* (on which the passengers had also been locked up) sailed to Alicante in Spain. Tendering and Ivery claimed that Motham only agreed to sail to Spain under pressure from Garrett and other crew members who feared they would be enslaved in Morocco. Thomas Allen's account, however, suggests that he, Garrett, and Anthony Townes, master of the *Transporter,* had planned all along to sell their passengers into slavery.[84] For the luckless Morisco refugees, the forced return to hostile Spain must have been a double tragedy.

These episodes demonstrate the precariousness of trust between English sailors and Muslim passengers: once it seemed likely that relations would break down, it was safer to strike first. Such glaring abuses of passengers did not happen often, however. National reprisals were a reasonably effective form of deterrence: not only did they satisfy popular demands for justice, they also helped to prevent future attacks, because Englishmen who robbed and enslaved Muslims were sued by the English merchants who shouldered the blame for their compatriots' misdeeds. As powerful English merchant companies increasingly forged durable commercial relations in foreign ports, it became more difficult for rogue Englishmen to plunder abroad and bring their gains safely home: trade links inhibited English piracy. Any resulting cross-cultural trust owed as much to measured violence as it did to cultural understanding, however.[85] English seamen and Muslim passengers who spent weeks together in uncomfortably close quarters may have come to appreciate their shared humanity across national, ethnic, and religious lines, but sensible people would hesitate to venture their fortunes on such fragile foundations.

Renegades and Englishness

Mutual understanding was also elusive among Ward's corsairs: coalitions of Englishmen and "Turks" were riven by distrust and failure at sea. After the stunning capture of the *Soderina,* their fortunes were less brilliant: converted into an unwieldy warship, the *Soderina* sank in 1608 with almost all on board, mostly Muslims, leaving a handful of survivors to be picked up by a French ship. When Ward—who had chosen a more seaworthy vessel—returned to Tunis, he "was nearly torn in pieces by the janissaries, who heard what had happened from five Turks who were saved on some planks of the *Soderina*."[86] Another corsair ship was "forced" by Uthman Dey to sail to Chios to rescue shipwrecked janissaries; it was taken by a Venetian galleass, and the captured pirates, including "divers Englishmen," were hanged.[87] In August 1609, it was said that several of Ward's ships had been burned in the harbor by Frenchmen, and a number of English corsairs deserted him, discontented with their shares of plunder.[88] Already, Ward had made overtures to the Grand Duke of Tuscany, hoping for a safe haven in Livorno, but negotiations fell through.[89]

In 1610, after failing to procure English and Tuscan pardons, John Ward finally converted to Islam, "to the great indignation of the whole [English] nation," but few of his men followed his example: most drifted to the independent English pirate ships based in Mamora on the Atlantic coast of Morocco, or discreetly returned home.[90] Despite their years of cooperation, relations between English and Muslim corsairs seem to have remained tense. Some forged lasting ties, like Thomas Mitton, who had formerly been enslaved and stayed in the house of his old master Murat when he was in Tunis. But violence and betrayal were common. In March 1609, one powerful Tunis warship was apparently taken to Malta by "forty English, six French, one Ragusan and four Turks" who had run away with the ship when the bulk of the company, all Muslims, were ashore. The following May, a Venetian diplomat reported that a corsair ship "manned promiscuously in Barbary" had come into the Aegean Sea, where "the crew quarrelled, and the English slew all the Turks."[91] As in Livorno, then, many English sailors were willing to enter foreign service on a temporary basis, but few chose to convert and settle permanently, especially since they had less to gain than commanders like Thornton and Ward. Their reluctance suggests that rather than seeing conversion to Islam as an enticing path to a prosperous and powerful new identity, as Nabil Matar has suggested, most English sailors preferred to live and work with their compatriots, and feared subordinating themselves to foreigners they did not trust.[92]

The handful of English corsairs who remained in Tunis (there were almost none in Algiers) were increasingly integrated as converts to Islam.

For these, return to England was difficult to contemplate. Captured at Salé and carried toward England in 1613, the renegade and possible convert Toby Glanfield was overcome by horror. He lamented "that his sins were so great that they should not be forgiven him" and seemed "sick and weak-headed, and in desperation, and sometimes like a man lunatic." One day he told the sailors "that within a day or two or three he would make some of his friends sorrow or mourn for him," and indeed soon after, while his attendant slept, he cut the netting over the gallery, stripped off his gown and slippers, and threw himself into the sea.[93]

Other Englishmen served on North African corsair ships as slaves. When Sampson Denball, alias Captain Sampson, alias Ali Reis, captured a ship from Southampton, his corsairs were described as "being for the most part Turks" but included the English carpenter Robert Morecock, who called sadly to the apprehensive merchant sailors: "O countrymen you are undone, for you have fallen into the hands of Turks that will take all that ever you have from you even to the hats off your heads and shoes off your feet, and I for my part am a poor slave amongst them that have lost all that ever I have and live in captivity." Englishmen—both renegades and slaves—now supplied maritime expertise and labor to local elites, rather than operating independently. "At first these Englishmen were the masters, but now it is the Turks," the French captain Foucques noted wryly.[94]

From his conversion until his death in 1622, Ward maintained an ambiguous relationship with his erstwhile countrymen.[95] He was complicit in the slaving economy that increasingly snared English sailors. In November 1610, for example, an English merchant arriving at Zante reported that his ship had encountered six corsair vessels from Tunis, commanded as he thought by Ward. When the English master refused to yield, Ward "declared that if he fired a single shot they would all be made slaves." Ward's residual Englishness did, however, remain meaningful to him and others. In 1614 or 1615, for example, the Scottish traveler William Lithgow found him a welcoming host. Lithgow wrote that Ward had turned Turk because of "his denied acceptance in England," and that despite living in "a fair palace, beautified with rich marble and alabaster stones," attended by "some sixteen circumcised English runagates, whose lives and countenances were alike, even as desperate as disdainful," he seemed to be quite happy to entertain a fellow Briton. A "placable" old man, Ward invited Lithgow to eat with him several times and gave him a safe-conduct for Algiers. When Lithgow returned to Tunis some time later, Ward played the role of a knowledgeable local, telling Lithgow how to tip his dragoman and even sending his servant to take Lithgow to admire the chicks being hatched in large ovens—a standard tourist attraction. In 1620, when the sailors of the *Elizabeth Anne Judith* were brought to the bagnio of Tunis as slaves, one of them reported that "Captain Ward became pledge for them and so procured their liberty to walk up and down the town"; a few were later allowed to return home. As a renegade, Ward scandalized his country but as a cultural broker he remained a friendly face and a useful contact in a foreign city.[96]

The entangled fortunes of honest and piratical English merchants and seafarers in the Mediterranean reveal the tension between different models of English nationhood. Treating English people abroad as a moral collective, national reprisals offered compensation and revenge to the victims of rogue English attacks. Angered by what they correctly perceived to be a corrupt and porous system in which outlaws were pardoned and stolen goods were laundered, Venetian and Ottoman officials pressured English authorities to plug the holes that allowed James to condemn piracy while his subjects profited from it. Aggrieved by the ease with which warlike English seamen moved across boundaries, plundering under foreign flags then returning home with their gains, the Venetians and Ottomans aimed to define the English nation more distinctly. When Ward and Thornton were denied pardons and permission to return home, it was because Venetian and Ottoman actors and the Levant Company pressured the Crown to repudiate those it could not govern. For them, a more bounded English nation promised to reform this swarm of unscrupulous adventurers into a morally and legally responsible collective, making the sea safer for commerce and travel. For English seamen themselves, however, this jurisdictional view of their nationality was at odds with their own customary freedom to seek their fortunes wherever they chose and to appeal to their countrymen for help—even when they were outlaws and renegades.

CHAPTER THREE

RISKS AND REWARDS

In 1602, six English merchant ships sailing toward Elbing in Poland were chased by two Dunkirk men-of-war. The ships were supposed to aid one another against enemies, so when the *Prospect* lagged behind, William Malem, the master of the flagship, stayed to help. Unfortunately, the small crew of Malem's ship, the *Michael and Barnard,* could not simultaneously sail and prepare for battle, and soon the Dunkirkers attacked, crippling the topsail. "By those shots the master's son lost his life, Robert Sexton was shot in the right leg, one Roger Dellam had a piece of both his buttocks shot away, and others were hurt with splinters," a survivor reported. Unable to flee, Malem signaled with his cap for the merchantmen to come to his aid. When a Dunkirker came up and asked whether he would yield, however, he answered he would not "so long as he was alive." He proved to be a man of his word.[1]

No help was forthcoming from the Eastland ships, even from the escaping *Prospect,* though its gunner reportedly asked the master to stay and fight. The *Michael and Barnard* withstood one attempt at boarding, repelling the assailants with pikes and the guns called murderers, but then, the

Michael's gunner reported, a broadside killed two men, wounded himself and another, and shot off the helmsman's leg. The Dunkirkers came alongside the English ship and killed Malem with small shot. The two men left on deck fought "until the boatswain was shot in the shoulder, and then none being left to resist, the Dunkirkers entered and took the ship." A passenger claimed that the company had been so determined to avoid capture that they had planned to blow up the ship as the Dunkirkers entered. However, "seeing no help like to come, and fearing they should all die if fire were given to the powder, [the passenger] thereupon put away the powder and suffered not fire to be given unto it." When the Englishmen finally surrendered, only four of them were "sound without hurt." All but the trumpeter, "who hid himself," had fought "as stoutly as any man alive might do."[2]

Entering the blood-splattered prize, the victorious Dunkirk captain was allegedly struck by the contrast between its crew's resolution and the rest of the English fleet, goading the wounded seamen: "What cowards were the rest of your fleet to run away and never offer to help you. If they had cast about and aided you, we had been gone and left you." By the time the Dunkirkers left the plundered ship, taking a passenger for ransom with them, the fleet was long gone, and the survivors were left "adrift in the sea some ten days . . . not having any surgeon or linen rags to wipe their wounds" before the waves drove them to Norway.[3] At least some of the wounded men lived through the ordeal: the gunner, Robert Atkinson, and the quartermasters, Robert Sexton and Lewis Roberts, gave evidence in a suit against the English shipmasters who had abandoned their admiral, though Sexton had lost his leg, and probably his livelihood.

This slaughter and the litigation that followed illustrate the contested distribution of risks and rewards in maritime trade. The ships in the fleet were to stay together if attacked—sharing risk between them—but only the *Michael and Barnard* proved true, at the expense of Malem's life and the lives of several of his men. When the ships' actions were called into question, the carpenter of the *Phoenix* explained that helping the *Michael and Barnard* would have been too dangerous: "The wind was contrary and the ships so laden that some of them could not put out their lower tier of ordinance, and besides they were so slenderly manned, that the men which they had were few enough to handle their sails, so as they could not set themselves for fighting without endangering their ships."[4] Liability for the lost goods could be determined in court, but there was no redress for the dead men. For them, fighting was part of the job.

Although seaborne commerce could be very profitable, it was dangerous, and for seamen, the dangers—of battle, sickness, and misadventure— struck at their bodies as well as their purses. In the early years of the seventeenth century, as English merchants increasingly invested in far-flung trading ventures, the uncertainty of the sea and the difficulties of long-distance trade forced both investors and seamen to grapple with the possibility of catastrophic loss. In some respects, this was a technical problem, as recent work on the commoditization of risk has shown.[5] But it was also a political problem: how were the dangers of maritime trade to be divided between the ships of a consorted fleet, or, for each individual ship, between the shipowners, the merchants who owned the goods, and the seamen who transported them? In the long term, the British state would help secure English trade from enemy attacks, but in this early period even the Channel was not free of hostile men-of-war, and merchants depended on sailors for their defense—not always to their satisfaction. Danger was part and parcel of a sailor's profession, yet there was no consensus about how much seamen ought to sacrifice for merchants' profits.

The problem of how to allocate the risks and rewards of maritime trade was not new, but it was growing. Legal custom rested on the assumption that sailors would not work diligently or fight bravely unless they were forced to share their employers' losses. In the late sixteenth and early seventeenth centuries, as English ships ranged farther away and undertook increasingly lengthy voyages in violent seas, there was both more to gain and more to lose. Sailors had traditionally carried trade goods with them, but their right to do so was challenged by new merchant companies whose charters endowed them with monopoly trading rights and sweeping powers over English subjects abroad. Merchants depended on sailors to defend their goods both in battle and in foreign courts, but for some seamen the costs of doing so were too high. Nor did the law provide clear guidance on what was expected: it was based on custom, but custom could change. As maritime enterprise pushed past the boundaries of settled practice, those involved struggled to maximize their shares of the rewards, while minimizing their shares of the risks. These conflicts often pitted seamen against investors, but as in the case of the Eastland fleet, they did not always play out simply along class lines. Some sailors were also small traders; others were not. Sailors, shipmasters, shipowners, the merchants who chartered ships, and passengers all had their own interests.

This was a formative period in which the social relations of merchant capitalism were negotiated in tense shipboard conversations, quiet resistance, open conflict, battle, and the courts. With their diversified investments, early modern merchants were often more ready to accept danger as they chased shifting profits. Seamen had to be more cautious. They stolidly defended their customary perquisites and adopted diverse tactics to avoid excessive danger: surrendering to the enemy, accepting bribes for favorable testimony in prize courts, refusing to sail to dangerous destinations, deserting, and mutinying. English sailors were famed for their willingness to fight, but Malem's suicidal valor was exceptional—and in James's peaceful reign, fewer seamen were trained in warfare.

Colonial ventures to the Americas were similarly fraught with conflicts of interest. The sailors who transported the earliest English settlers to the New World privileged their own well-being over investors' plans. Though settlers frequently faced famine, sailors stubbornly defended their rights to customary rations. When enticing new opportunities for trade arose, they demanded their share—and when denied, often took it anyway. Colonial governors who asserted authority over English people abroad were irked to find their claims disregarded by these supposed subjects. The complaints about sailors' misbehavior that permeate reports about early settlements should be taken with a grain of salt, for these were failures, by and large, and scapegoats had to be found. Still, they leave little doubt that English seamen, for whom the Atlantic was a familiar working environment, were largely unmoved by the imperial visions of their superiors.

Compensation and Custom

Men who went to sea exposed themselves to grave dangers. Ships could be wrecked by storms, or founder on rocks or treacherous sands. Accidents were common: sailors might fall from the rigging or be struck by heavy objects; they might be swept overboard and drowned. Diseases both familiar and strange lurked in unwholesome holds and busy ports. Sailors could be maimed, killed, or enslaved when pirates or other enemies attacked. Seamen ventured their lives when merchants ventured their goods—and like merchants, they were obliged to set their potential losses against their potential gains. What, then, did seafaring life offer to merchant seamen? Their pay was respectable but not high: during the first two decades of the seventeenth century common sailors could expect seventeen or eighteen shillings in money a month, plus their food and drink, which was worth about as much again.[6] Because sailors were so mobile and London dominated long-distance shipping, sailors' wages had to be competitive with those of London laborers, who earned more than their provincial peers.[7] Of course, like laborers, sailors could expect to spend a certain amount of time out of work, which could quickly erase any accumulated savings.[8] Victuals of a type and quantity firmly fixed by custom were a valuable benefit in times of scarcity and high prices, and seamen resisted efforts to alter their diets, which were rich in animal foods. Writing in the 1630s, a colonial governor wished "we did more conform ourselves, if not to the Spanish and Italian nations, who live most upon rice meal, oatmeal, biscake, figs, olives, oil, and the like; yet at the least to our neighbours the Dutch, who content themselves with a far less proportion of flesh and fish than we do." He hopefully suggested a simple and economical diet of maize.[9]

A good chance of promotion was another attraction of going to sea. One proposal to set up an English herring fishery suggested that beginners be paid sixteen shillings a month, while skilled mariners would expect twenty shillings.[10] There were many specialized officers on board ship, and with English shipping expanding despite high mortality, ambitious sailors could hope to step into dead men's shoes. On a ship with a crew of twenty men, for example, one would expect to find a master, a boatswain, a gunner, a carpenter, and a steward, all with their mates, as well as two or so quartermasters. Sailors describing a Mediterranean voyage in 1608 reported that the quartermaster was to be paid twenty-four shillings a month and the carpenter twenty-eight shillings. The gunner had agreed to accept a lump sum, which turned out to be a mistake because the voyage dragged on, but two years later the same man expected twenty-seven shillings a month.[11] Higher-ranking officers could earn more. Becoming a master's mate increasingly required mathematical learning—not a possibility for everyone, though surprisingly many seamen knew something of navigation—and becoming a master was more difficult still, since capital and connections were required. It seems likely, however, that only the unluckiest or least capable sailors failed to attain some kind of office by their mid-thirties, if not much earlier. Older men who served as ordinary sailors may have been partially disabled or otherwise unsatisfactory, like Edward Dole, who at forty was hired for a mere seventeen shillings a month for a Mediterranean voyage and "gave not [his] attendance in the said ship for the performance of [his] duties therein as [he] ought to do."[12] For an industrious and clever young man of poor family, the sea was one of few occupations by which he might hope to obtain significant preferment—a gamble, to be sure, but perhaps a gamble worth taking.[13]

A shrewd sailor might also enhance his earnings through small-scale trade, as Richard Blakemore has shown.[14] English ships spent lengthy periods in foreign ports, where sailors often went ashore: with their firsthand knowledge of foreign markets, they were well placed to know what commodities to buy and sell, and their right to trade was supported by custom. On Mediterranean-bound ships, sailors claimed, "merchants . . . never denied anyone of their ship's company to lade some small matter in their ships freight free, or any other of ability to lade 1/2 or a whole ton paying reasonable freight for the same."[15] Edward Dole clubbed together with a quartermaster to buy a sack of currants at Venice, and the gunner Thomas Gaylord sold linen cloth at Majorca and bought olive oil with the proceeds.[16] Not every sailor had the resources or skills to trade, but many did, on credit if they lacked ready money. John Foster, who sold some saffron at Elsinore then died of the plague at Elbing in 1602, left behind a bag of tobacco and sixty-two pairs of coarse worsted stockings purchased with funds borrowed from the shipmaster and other seamen. The quartermaster of the *Cynthia*, Thomas Edmunds, earned only twenty shillings a month, but he brought barrels of tin and pewter, cloth, shoes and stockings, and a few pistols on board with him. He bartered the stockings and kerseys for currants at Zante but then fell mortally ill at Iskenderun and sold his remaining goods to the purser, leaving £70 for his heirs after his shipboard debts were paid.[17] Sailors' personal and professional acquaintances on other vessels helped extend their reach. When the *Dorothy* was at Hispaniola in 1604 for illicit trade, three of the crew sent barrels of tobacco back to their wives on a homeward-bound privateer. Alexander Cox, the master's mate of the *Gift of God,* sold rabbit skins at Alexandria, then entrusted the proceeds to Roger Cross, the surgeon, who was bound for Cairo, to buy cloves and pepper on his account.[18]

Sailors' personal involvement in trade blurred the line between wage earners and traders: like merchants, sailors risked loss if their stock of goods was captured or cast away. Apprenticed to a master's mate, Richard Norwood quadrupled a small sum of money borrowed from a cousin in just two voyages, inspiring him with "a very earnest desire of gain," but he lost his enthusiasm for the seafaring life when he considered "the continual toil and many dangers whereunto that course of life was liable, and though a man might make some profit by an adventure, yet if once in many voyages he fell into the hands of pirates or should suffer shipwreck, all was lost."[19] Even without personal trade, however, the line between venturers and wage earners was indistinct, for custom obliged sailors to shoulder some of the risks of the sea. Freight was the mother of wages, as the saying went: if a ship sank and the shipowners received no freight, the sailors received no pay for the work they had done since freight had last been earned. This was a bitter pill for the survivors of misfortune. When a ship laden with silk sank in a tempest off Cadiz with forty-seven men, the common sailor Thomas Baker did his best in the following days to save what he could from the wreck, but he "had not the value of two pence of all the goods and furniture of the said ship that were saved, or anything else but only allowance of victuals for the time that he remained there to save of the ship's provision, neither hath he received any wages for all that voyage." Since one case of waterlogged silk had indeed been recovered, Baker thought he should have received *something.* Questioned about his worth, he reported bitterly that "his labour is his living, and he is little worth for that he lost all he had in the said ship the *Dragon.*" The law favored shipowners and merchants, reducing their exposure to risk by forcing wage earners to share their losses, on the pretext that otherwise they would not labor to preserve ship and goods in tempests or fight when attacked. In general, sailors seem to have taken this legal regime for granted, but Baker seemingly lost his taste for merchant shipping: by the next time he appeared in admiralty court records, he had joined a pirate crew.[20]

When ships were wrecked, sailors who struggled to shore were desperate to save what they could in hopes of being paid their wages or earning a salvor's share of the saved goods, but this often put them at odds with local people.[21] When the *Carnation* of Ipswich broke up on the coast of Yorkshire in late November in 1613, the master's mate alone survived the wreck, clinging for hours to a piece of wreckage until he was able to get to land "almost starved to death with the violence of the cold." There he "found a great number of people with hatchets, hewing and cutting the hull of the ship and whatsoever they could lay hands on." He begged them to desist but was obliged to go to a nearby mill to warm himself and dry his clothes. By the time he returned the next day, hundreds of people had flocked to despoil the wreck. The mate hired men to help him save part of the rigging, but even this was carried off "in the dead of night," leaving the survivor with nothing for his pains in the voyage. Some opportunists did not even wait for a ship to be wrecked. When the barque *Thomas* was lying at anchor off Audierne after being damaged in a storm in 1579, Breton villagers attacked it. The shipmaster and his men did their best to guard the cargo of wine, but "the country people . . . came down with force and violence, striking and misusing the company of the said ship" and stealing the wine. Losing one's wages for a single short voyage was a relatively minor mishap, but as merchant ships ventured farther afield and spent months and years away, sailors risked losing large sums.[22]

Merchants also transferred risk to sailors by holding them responsible for damage. When goods were spoiled by seawater, for example, sailors could be penalized. To avoid having their wages docked, they told harrowing tales of violent storms, arguing that they had done their utmost to safeguard ships and goods. The quartermaster of the *Rose Lion* described vividly in 1600 how the ship's perishable cargo of prunes, raisins, and paper had been damaged. Because of "a marvelous great and tempestuous storm," he recounted, the sailors had had to pump and bail out the ship for thirty-six hours without rest: "And therein they laboured with all their force for safeguard of their lives, and did submit themselves to death for they made no account but that the ship would have foundered under them and if they had not laboured continually during the storm he verily thinketh they had all perished, and if it had not pleased God to mitigate the rage of the tempest in time they had given over labour for they were so overwearied with the continual labour that they could not have held out much longer." In twelve years at sea, the thirty-year-old claimed, he had never been as close to drowning. Others told similar tales to explain why goods had been cast overboard, like John Skutt, who explained that during a fierce storm the *Falcon* of Poole "was able to bear no sail but piteously lay driving in the sea and the master and company yielded themselves wholly to God's mercy never thinking to have escaped that brunt," though they pumped diligently and, of necessity, threw some goods into the sea. Sailors had strong reasons to tell compelling stories, but the risk of foundering was very real: perhaps 4 percent of ships wrecked or burned every year.[23]

New Opportunities, New Dangers

The dangers and profits of increasingly expansive maritime commerce heightened the tensions and conflicts of interest that both seamen and merchants accepted as an unavoidable aspect of merchant shipping. Companies of merchants trading in new, distant markets often sought and received exclusive monopoly rights from the Crown, but their attempts to bar their sailors from trade ran counter to long-standing tradition. When merchant seamen risked their lives to take prizes, sailors and investors quarreled over the distribution of the gains. The alluring profits of forbidden trade in foreign empires enticed investors but put seamen in mortal peril. In the Mediterranean, long itinerant voyages strained the conventions that governed English maritime life. In a rapidly changing world, law lagged behind as merchants, shipowners, and sailors struggled over the allocation of profit and risk. Seamen stubbornly defended their interests, but they had to act warily to avoid catastrophic losses. The stakes were high.

Armed with royal charters, merchants attacked sailors' private trade in promising new markets: exclusive rights to desirable imports underlay the logic of early modern merchant companies. When trading companies imposed restrictions on sailors' trade, however, sailors pushed back, often successfully. The early experience of the Muscovy Company illustrates a pattern that was often repeated. In 1553, the Company commanded its shipmasters not to "privately bargain, buy, sell, exchange, barter, or distribute any goods, wares, merchandize, or things whatsoever (necessary tackles and victuals for the ship only excepted) to or for your own lucre, gain or profit," and to prevent the mariners from trading privately as well. This was evidently difficult to enforce. In 1556, pursers were enjoined to report any goods being laden that did not bear the mark of the Company and, in the words of the Company directive, to "spy and search as secretly as you may, to learn or know what bargaining, buying and selling there is with the master and the mariners of the ship and the Russes." The next year, the Company commanded its agents, as it put it, "not to suffer any of our nation to send any wares to their wives or friends in any of our ships; but to take their money there to be paid here by the Company and not otherwise." Despite these restrictions, sailors continued to trade, and Company merchants seem to have come to accept it. They wrote to their agents in 1560, for example, that they had learned that fox skins were "vendible" commodities in England, not because the official factors had sent any, but because "there were mariners that brought many." Rather than forbidding future private trade by sailors, they instructed their agents to keep it within bounds and to have sailors' goods registered in pursers' books, "to the intent we may know what they be."[24]

The Muscovy Company and English seamen also disagreed about who had the rights to valuable English maritime expertise, particularly in whaling ventures. Expert whalers were mobile, and the Company itself readily employed foreign talent: for a 1611 voyage, the owners "provided themselves of certain Biscayners expert men for the killing of the whale." Hiring foreign experts was an essential means of mastering new forms of maritime enterprise, and skilled seamen tended to assume that they could sell their services to the highest bidder.[25] When English seamen sought to enter the service of the Muscovy Company's competitors, however, the Company strenuously objected, hoping to impede foreign access to Bear Island in the Svalbard archipelago, home to a rapidly dwindling population of walruses, and a useful base for whaling. In 1612, to the dismay of the merchants trading with Russia, "by means of English pilots there were two outlandish ships brought into that country," one piloted by Allen Sallowes, "who had served the said fellowship in those parts twenty years before and had fled his country for debt," and one by "Nicholas

Woodcock an Englishman." Sallowes was a persistent thorn in the side of the Muscovy Company. The following year, in 1613, he was whaling again as pilot of the *Jacques* of Bordeaux, along with the English gunner Thomas Fisher. The Muscovy Company fleet that challenged the *Jacques* seized both men and brought them back to England.[26] Sometimes, the Muscovy merchants were able to reincorporate renegade pilots into their own ranks. After being discovered on a Dutch ship, Nicholas Woodcock "for that offense was afterwards worthily punished here in England," and then was hired to work for the Muscovy Company; he helped it oppose Dutch interlopers.[27] Similarly, when Muscovy Company seamen found numerous Englishmen and Scots on two Dunkirk whalers in 1613, including the pilot Cuthbert Appleyard, they forcibly took them on their own ships; Appleyard sailed with the English fleet the following year.[28]

In other novel situations, there was similar jostling as investors and mariners angled for what they could get. When merchant ships took prizes and private warships dabbled in trade, questions of the division of the spoils and sailors' compensation raised lively debate on shipboard and in court. In 1597, for example, three formidable English merchantmen on a Mediterranean voyage took several prizes, including a Flemish ship carrying three hundred Spanish soldiers bound for Oran. Were the shipowners obliged to pay the sailors wages for the whole voyage? If so, were the sailors were also entitled to shares? According to Thomas Rowe, the master of the *Report,* he had asked the sailors to accept lower wages after a prize had been taken, but "the mariners answered they would not abate any part of their wages, and willed [him] and the other masters to cast off the prize, sink her, burn her, or give her to the enemy, or else do with her what they would for they would have their whole wages." They believed that they were entitled to both shares and wages, and precedent was on their side: in his experience, the *Mermaid*'s master, Thomas Best, admitted, "After deduction of all charges the mariners have had their shares and their wages"—but on those voyages, he claimed, the sailors had been paid lump sums, as was usual for short voyages, not monthly wages. In this case, their taking of prizes had delayed their voyage considerably. Best proposed that the sailors were due wages for the trading part of the voyage, from November 1596 to the end of April 1597, but not thereafter, because the ships had become privateers. The admiralty court generally favored sailors in wage disputes, however, and this was likely a profitable voyage for the seamen. Depositions dealing with the estate of the *Mermaid*'s pilot, Thomas Pipe, suggest that he would have been comparatively wealthy if he had lived.[29]

There were fewer gains and more losses in the Caribbean, where English merchants invested in trade and plunder. The 1494 Treaty of Tordesillas had granted Spain sovereignty over the territory west of a meridian about halfway between the Cape Verde Islands and the islands discovered by Columbus, and in theory the Spanish Crown maintained its exclusive claim to these territories. In practice, of course, it was primarily interested in the most profitable parts of the Caribbean and New Spain, and could not police the entire area. Since much of the Caribbean was neglected by Spanish colonial authorities, illicit trade tempted both Spanish colonists and European interlopers, but it was risky.

For English smugglers, the years of transition between the reigns of Elizabeth and James were particularly fraught. Possibly hoping to establish a "*de facto* basis" for trading rights in the Caribbean in the anticipated peace after the queen's death, some substantial London merchants invested in voyages with a major trading element around the end of Elizabeth's reign.[30] John Eldred and Richard Hall sent the *Mayflower* to the West Indies at the very end of 1602 on a mixed voyage of plunder and smuggling, for example. According to the charter party, its sailors agreed to work for shares of prizes and half wages, but this was a perilous undertaking for them, for while some Spanish subjects were eager for black-market European wares, all English presence in the Caribbean was illegal by Spanish law, and interlopers could be captured and punished by any convenient means, including subterfuge.

Dashing the merchants' hopes, some of the *Mayflower*'s pinnaces were captured and their men slain or imprisoned. For the Englishmen, this was sheer treachery. The survivors of such actions, when there were any, were quick to emphasize that they had been perfidiously attacked during peaceful trade. Arthur Chambers, the young master of the pinnace *Richard*, stated that in September 1603 on the northern coast of Hispaniola, Spaniards came on board with a flag of truce, and after drinking with the Englishmen, persuaded them "to go ashore with their boat to fetch certain hides aboard which they had bargained for." Three of the English sailors went ashore, leaving the pinnace's remaining four men with the Spaniards. Seizing the opportunity, the Spaniards struck: twelve ambushed the sailors on shore; in the cabin, two others attacked Chambers and the merchant Thomas Goddard. Goddard leapt overboard; after being repeatedly stabbed, Chambers broke away and jumped into the water as well. He was too badly wounded to swim, however, and was saved by "a Spaniard on shore being more pitiful than the rest," who brought him back on board. Meanwhile, as an English merchant later heard from Spanish witnesses, the remaining two sailors on the *Richard,* who had been working in the hold, were attacked by three Spaniards but "resisted and found them play" until the boat returned with reinforcements, who "presently slew them, one being a Scottishman called Robert and the other Thomas Applebee." Chambers was left lying on the shore for two days without water or help as two captive English sailors looked on from the trees to which they were tied. Finally they were carried to Santo Domingo, and after eleven months Chambers was brought to Seville, where he was ultimately released "by means made to the king." The others—except for Goddard, who escaped—remained in prison at Santo Domingo.[31]

Arthur Chambers escaped lightly in comparison to Ambrose Birch, the master of the pinnace *Mary,* who was on shore in Hispaniola inspecting hides under a flag of truce when he and his twelve men were attacked. Birch was "stripped naked and tied . . . to a tree in the wood there where he was stung with mosquitoes or flies of that country" so that "he fell mad with the pain thereof." The Spaniards then took the pinnace and killed all the sailors except for two who leaped into the sea. The Spaniards returned to Birch on shore "and there cut off his nose and his ears and afterwards his head and cast his body into the river and set his head upon a pole." So much was reported, at least, by "letters written by the said Spaniards to certain Flemings . . . and also by the report of those two that escaped that violence." After the loss of its two pinnaces, the *Mayflower* may have turned to plunder, consorting with the raider Captain Christopher Cleeve. By then, however, the queen had died, and James had recalled ships sailing on reprisals. The prize goods that were brought to England were immediately challenged by the Spanish ambassador; the *Mayflower* more prudently sailed to the Mediterranean with its illicit cargo.[32]

For the sailors, the voyage had been emphatically unsatisfactory. Many of them been captured or killed on the pinnaces, and in more than two years in the West Indies they had not taken enough prizes to compensate them for their half wages. They soon met other malcontents: sailing toward Livorno, they were chased and caught up by John Ward and his men; some of the *Mayflower*'s men went on board the corsair ship, where they drank with the pirates and exchanged information. Emboldened, perhaps, by this encounter, the *Mayflower*'s seamen rebelled at Livorno. Together, the master and thirty-six mariners wrote a letter to the merchants' agent, "underwritten with all their hands in a circle . . . demanding greater wages than was agreed upon by the charter party." They would not deliver the cargo, they said, until they were paid full wages for their time. By signing their names in a circle the men concealed who signed first.[33]

The factor reluctantly agreed, fearing that otherwise the sailors would run away with the ship to join Ward. The sailors were paid, but their victory was short-lived: when they went on land, the factor procured their arrest, and their money was seized. In August 1605, the English sailors were given a Spanish dollar each and banished from Livorno to make their way home as best they could, since Grand Duke Ferdinand I of Tuscany had impressed the *Mayflower* for a cruise against Ward. They did not give up, however, and in England pressed their case both at Trinity House and in the High Court of Admiralty. This time, the seamen were successful, receiving "for three months' time that Queen Elizabeth lived after their going to sea half wages, and for all the rest of the time whole wages contrary to their own agreement formerly made," according to Eldred and Hall's irritated representative. To make matters worse for the shipowners, the *Mayflower* sank in Ferdinand's service.[34]

After England and Spain made peace, and war gave way to commerce, English ships' popularity in Mediterranean shipping produced its own economic complications. These voyages were often lengthy, with uncertain itineraries, since shipmasters and merchants responded to local demand. A common model was for English ships to call first at Livorno or Venice, where they discharged their original cargo, and then to make a series of short trips between Christian and Islamic ports, transporting goods for local merchants as well as passengers, before taking in their lading for England. These complicated voyages bred conflict, not only between merchants and laboring seamen, but also between shipowners and the merchants who chartered their vessels. One could always lose a ship to ill fortune, but in the Mediterranean, the risk of shipwreck was joined by those of capture and impressment. The most dangerous itineraries and cargoes offered the highest profits, but when merchants chased these opportunities, shipowners fretted. Sailors were caught in between: their wages were paid by the owners, but only if the merchants paid their freight, and by custom sailors were paid only at the end of the voyage, no matter how long it took.

The troubles of the *Joshua* of London in 1606–1608 illustrate these tense dynamics. A modest ship, the *Joshua* had originally been chartered by Richard Staper of the Levant Company for a fifteen-month voyage to the Levant. Joshua Downing, a quarter owner who acted for the owners, hired a master for the voyage, one Silvanus Man, who had experience piloting Venetian ships. Rather than wholly trusting Man with the ship, however, Downing chose to go along as purser and master's mate—a decision that suggests that he and his partners were concerned about the shape the voyage might take. Man hired the rest of the crew, as was customary.

They sailed to Livorno, then to Sidon, where the *Joshua* took in "Turks and Jews and their goods" for Istanbul, "and great profit was made thereof as the speech went" for Richard Staper. The voyage was going well, but Downing and Man soon fell out over the ship's supplies: Downing wanted to husband them, while Man and Staper's agent, John Bruckhouse, were keen to gain the sympathy of the crew and the goodwill of guests by showing a liberal hand. In Istanbul, for example, much gunpowder was wasted in honorific salutes, to Downing's dismay: the powder was supplied by the owners, and any lack might endanger the ship in the case of a real battle. On the six-week voyage back to Sidon, Downing lost much of his remaining support among the crew because the ship ran out of drink. Downing had not bought wine in Istanbul, "because it was extreme dear there," but he had expected the *Joshua* to stop in Greece for supplies.[35] By that point, however, Bruckhouse had let the use of the ship to a Muslim merchant, who was unwilling to go to the Greek port "for fear of [Catholic] men-of-war on [the] coast." As a result, the crew had nothing but water to drink for two months at Sidon, "and six or seven of the company were sick there at a time, and one died."[36] As the purser, Downing was blamed. The mariners became insolent to him, and the master's mate, William Hubbard, whipped Downing's boy, "then took a live cat and drew her over his buttocks and so scratched him, and then bade him go tell his master again." Ominously, a visitor heard "an inkling amongst the company of the *Joshua* . . . that it were a good deed to cast the said Downing overboard."[37]

Fifteen months were almost up, but Staper's factor in Sidon, William Pate, was determined to continue to hire the ship out for the profitable Ottoman port-to-port trade. Initially Pate wanted to send the *Joshua* back to Istanbul, but then the ship was freighted instead "to carry a present to the Bashaw at Scanderoon from the Emir of Sidon." Appalled, "Joshua Downing stood against the carrying of Turks in the *Joshua* as much as in him lay, and was very desirous to have her laden for England." When he failed to change Pate's mind, "Downing went on board the *Joshua* and told the mariners that the owners would not pay them wages longer than the fifteen months for which they were hired, and therefore wished them to foresee how they should be paid if they served longer than the time appointed." In the struggle for the sailors' loyalty, however, Downing's close-fistedness had cost him dearly: "The mariners went ashore to William Pate . . . and the said Pate made them answer that if they would be quiet they should be paid before the owners were paid." This was highly irregular, and Downing read the charter party to the mariners to show them that they were in danger of losing their wages, but they seem to have been convinced by Pate's assurances. Short of mutiny, in any case, they had little choice.[38]

Ill, miserable, and fearing for his life, Joshua Downing returned safely home to England on another vessel. The ship that bore his name was less fortunate. Downing had probably objected to carrying Muslims and their goods because of the risk of attacks by Christian corsairs. Indeed, returning from Iskenderun to Sidon, the *Joshua* was assaulted and captured by Maltese corsairs. When its steward, Thomas Bourne, returned to London sometime in 1608, eight of the company were still in Malta.[39] The *Joshua* was ultimately recovered: Silvanus Man's wife testified in 1610 that her husband had brought the ship to Flushing after a year's enforced stay in Malta. But the surviving sailors seem to have had to wait through the legal wrangling in the High Court of Admiralty and Chancery to be paid their long-overdue wages, and they were probably not paid at all for the long months of captivity.[40]

The voyage of the Genoese shipping magnate Filippo Bernardi's *Susan Bonaventure* was similarly troubled by concerns about danger and an expired charter party. When the *Susan* arrived at Genoa in 1612 or 1613, perhaps after several months spent in itinerant trading, the owner's factor, Dominico Bernardi, informed the master, William Okes, that they were to proceed to Candia and the islands of the Aegean for grain, in direct violation of Ottoman policy. Nearly to a man, the English crew refused to go to the Aegean, "for that they said it was a dangerous place by reason of the Turks' galleys who if they should have taken them laden with corn would have made them all slaves."[41] In the Levant as in the West Indies, smuggling was profitable but dangerous. The men's refusal soured their relationship with the owner. The *Susan* stayed at Genoa for almost three months, at a heavy cost to Bernardi, before being sent to Seville, where it received orders to take in cargo and return to Genoa. This time, the men refused to depart "for that their charter party was expired," and they wanted assurance that they would be paid their wages.[42] Realizing that their strength lay in unity, the seaman George Penwarden bound sixteen of his crewmates "to go to law for their wages" at Seville. Unfortunately, they did not know how to proceed: "By the space of ten days after the arrival of the ship at Seville the company did go up and down exclaiming against the said owner and endeavoured to procure somebody to protect them for the recovery of their wages there."[43] No one was willing. The English merchants there were put off by the sailors' "ill behavior and mutinous carriage" and especially by rumors that some of the *Susan*'s men were thinking of running away with the ship to become pirates. John Walker, who kept a drinking house, where he sold English beer and Rhenish wine to English sailors, reported that Richard Londe and Thomas Spittie initially fell into talk with him about buying tobacco to sell to the corsairs at Villafranca, then told him that they and nine others planned to put the rest of the *Susan*'s company into the boat and send them ashore, and "go for the Islands to take Spanish shipping."[44]

In the end, the English consul appears to have brokered a compromise. Bernardi's factor consented to pay the sailors three months' wages and to "bind ship and goods to them for the payment of the rest and to clear them of the charter party." Most of the sailors then agreed to return to Genoa, although one took his wages and was discharged, and George Penwarden and his brother James seem to have remained obdurate. As for the mutinous plot, the consul told the sailors that "if the matter were further proceeded he must put all the company that were found guilty into the galleys," but he settled for removing the two "chief plotters," Richard Londe and George Cornish, from the ship. Reconciled, the master and the remaining men departed for Genoa, and with the exception of a battle with two "Turkish" warships, in which "divers of [the] company fought valiantly, but some others . . . hid themselves behind chests," the voyage seems to have proceeded uneventfully. The Seville agreement would not stand unchallenged, however: when the ship returned to London, Bernardi sued the sailors for his losses.[45]

Being paid only at the end of a lengthy voyage left sailors at a disadvantage, forced to wait for months for the money they had earned while contracts expired and disaster struck. The voyage of the *Dorothy* of London around 1611–1613 shows how perilous the wait could be. The *Dorothy* was a tramp ship: its master, Gideon Johnson, himself decided where to go, crisscrossing the sea in search of profit. From London, the ship first sailed to Ireland to take in pilchards, dealwood, hoops, and West Indian hides brought there by pirates. The pilchards and hides were sold at Venice, and the timber was brought to Zante. From Zante the *Dorothy* sailed to Vitala in Greece for corn, then back to Zante, where the corn was delivered, then back to Vitala, where it took in acorns. The *Dorothy* took in some passengers and goods at Zante and then more at Corfu, which it brought to Venice. After seventeen weeks in Venice, the ship took in steel and iron, which were carried to Palermo in Sicily, where some of the metal was sold and corn was bought in exchange. Then the *Dorothy* sailed to Alicante and Cartagena, where it stayed for two months before somehow taking in "550 Morisco passengers and their goods being banished out of Spain" and carrying them to Algiers at the extortionate rate of twenty-five shillings per person.[46] At Algiers Johnson bought one hundred and twenty butts of muscadel wine from the English corsair Ambrose Sayer, which he intended to bring to Alicante.

These Mediterranean meanderings took a toll on the *Dorothy*'s sailors, who had been hired for a much shorter voyage. Johnson had planned to pay his men upon their return to London, but when that return was indefinitely postponed, and the company saw him collect freight in port after port, they demanded their due. According to the two men who did eventually make it back to London, Johnson was slow to part with his money. William Cane, who was to get about twenty shillings a month for his wages as quartermaster, said he received fifty-eight shillings at Venice, nine shillings at Palmero, and eight pence when they touched at Venice the second time, all in a mixture of local currencies: a total of £3 7s. 8d. out of about £25 due for twenty-four or twenty-five months of labor.[47] Over time, the company dwindled. Out of twenty-four mariners, two left the ship while it was still on the English coast "and six more died in the said voyage, whereof the carpenter and gunner were two, whom the said Johnson displaced and set ashore at Venice before they died." Johnson "displaced" still more of his men at Cartagena, replacing them with "four Dutch men who came out of one of the king of Spain's ships of war."[48] The surviving Englishmen lost their patience at Algiers: "The mariners knowing the said Johnson had received great store of monies for freight demanded their wages of him and had him before Mr Allen, consul there, and the said Johnson denied to pay them any wages." The consul imprisoned Johnson briefly, to no avail.[49]

All but four of Johnson's frustrated English sailors deserted in Algiers to become corsairs. Johnson was left with Lancelot Fisher, William Cane, Hugh Burdwell, and Allen Montgomery, as well as the various "Flemings" he had hired before to make up his numbers. He supplemented them with more Dutch seamen "who had served the pirates" and seemed ready to return home. This strategy went badly awry when the Flemings and the gunner, a Scot, "joined together and rose up in arms" against the Englishmen.[50] Johnson, two sailors, and some passengers were put into the ship's boat and set adrift, while the pirates detained Cane, and Montgomery died of his wounds. On their return to England, the surviving mariners sued for their wages, arguing that they were due for the parts of the voyage for which freight had been paid, and that Johnson himself was responsible for the loss of the ship.

Talking together on shipboard and in taverns, sailors learned about their rights. They needed as much knowledge as they could get, because jurisdictions varied in their friendliness to seamen: it was important to know how much weight a master's threats carried. When the sailors of the *Elizabeth* of Leith demanded their wages at Alicante in 1609, their year of service having expired, their merchant, William Fursman, and the shipmaster and part owner, Thomas Gurlee, "would not suffer them, but enforced them to sail in the ship for Venice or else they would have put them into prison." Cowed, they served another eight months, then were captured and enslaved by corsairs under the command of the renegade Captain Sampson. Several years later, the seaman Godfrey Consell had managed to return home and was still trying to get Gurlee to pay his back wages.[51]

Sailors faced setbacks and uncertainty, but they did make gains. Over the course of the seventeenth century, in response to seamen's agitation, sailors on itinerant voyages in the Mediterranean came to be paid a large portion of their wages at sea. The Trinity House fraternity of Deptford certified in 1677, for example, that after discharging their cargo abroad, English shipmasters paid their sailors what was due to them, only reserving six months' worth of wages in hand until the return to England to discourage desertion.[52] In the second half of the seventeenth century, moreover, when shipmasters refused to pay a sufficient portion of their wages abroad, English sailors demonstrated their ingenuity—and irritated English merchants—by suing for their wages in places like Venice, where according to custom sailors were paid every month. In Livorno, for example, where shipmasters were particularly anxious not to have to pay sailors their full wages for fear of desertion, canny sailors appealed to Tuscan courts over the head of the English consul.[53] By going to law, appealing to consuls, and simply by voting with their feet, sailors were able to obtain much-desired changes in maritime custom.

As expanding commercial horizons opened up new opportunities for gain, sailors and investors moved quickly to defend their interests. Sometimes simply continuing old practices in quiet defiance of new orders was enough to induce merchants to tolerate sailors' trade. When seamen were convinced the law was on their side, they were loud in their opposition to infringements of their rights; when they were less sure, they sought safety in numbers and written petitions, dissimulating mutinous leadership. When informal negotiations failed, both sailors and merchants appealed to authorities and sought redress in a variety of courts, angling for legal advantages. Desertion was always a possibility, and merchant sailors' familiarity with English pirates lent strength to veiled threats to turn to piracy. Collectively, they asserted sailors' rights to safety and fair compensation in merchant shipping.

Resistance and Capitulation

How hard sailors ought to fight to defend ship and goods was an enduring point of tension between seamen and merchants, one that took on heightened importance in the early seventeenth century. English ships' guns and skillful, battle-tested sailors attracted Mediterranean merchants and travelers despite the expense: as a Venetian observer noted sourly, "Passengers do not think their lives safe except aboard an English vessel, although the fares are double."[54] While English merchants courted foreign business, to be killed, maimed, or enslaved were dreadful prospects for seamen, even those who prized their manly resolution.[55] When corsairs attacked merchant vessels, then, labor conflicts became entangled with commercial aspirations. The honor of the English nation—and the fortunes of the Levant Company—depended on the courage of the mariners under fire. Would they fight to defend their passengers, the reputation of English shipping, and cross-cultural trust?

Some English sailors did indeed defend their passengers, like those of a ship that fell in with four Catholic warships in the Aegean around the beginning of 1605. According to one report, when the corsairs wanted to seize the Muslim and Jewish passengers and the ship's gunpowder, a battle ensued, and the outnumbered English surrendered only "after considerable slaughter on both sides."[56] Others cut deals with their attackers, like the master of the *Triumph* in 1607. Sailing from Sidon toward Algiers or Tetouan, carrying mostly Englishmen's goods but also Muslim passengers, including the merchant Khūjā Hammett and his bales of English broadcloth, turbans, and dry goods, the *Triumph* was accosted by two Tuscan warships and a pinnace. An English renegade shouted from one of them "to the master, and told him, he had order from his captain to tell him, that he had no intent to wrong the ship or company or the English merchants' goods, but if he would yield without any compulsion, he would only take out the Turks and their goods, and pay the master his freight for them, and suffer him and company to proceed on their voyage." When the master, Thomas Gardner, denied having any "Turks" on board, the renegade scoffed "that his captain knew what Turks and goods of theirs were on board as well as they themselves, and therefore wished them to yield"—and that is what they did.[57] According to a Levant Company factor who had spoken with the men of the *Swan,* a nearby ship, "they yielded upon composition without making any fight at all . . . very basely to the great dishonour of our nation." He worried that, in his words, "our people will be troubled in Algiers about it." The *Swan* had not exactly covered itself with glory either: its master, Walter Whiting, had been warned by the English renegade not to interfere, and although Whiting protested that "it were a shame to his nation to suffer his consort to be fought withal, and not to take his part," he submitted quietly to the subsequent events.[58] Sailors who wished to preserve their lives, freedom, and goods and shipmasters who answered primarily to the shipowners had interests at stake that were very different from those of Levant Company merchants like Richard Staper, whose factor, William Pate, had arranged Hammett's passage.

It was doubtful, of course, whether the *Triumph,* a modest ship of 120 tons, could have prevailed against the Tuscan fleet, but the authorities thought it should at least have tried. Defending himself and his comrades, the *Triumph*'s quartermaster, John Browne, claimed that it was the passengers who lost heart, not the mariners. The Muslims, who had prepared themselves for battle, "cast down their muskets and put forth their matches, and told the master and merchant they would willingly lose their goods rather than endanger their lives in fight, so as they might by composition obtain liberty for their persons." Then, Browne recounted, Gardner sent three men "to treat . . . for the liberty of the said Turks . . . being in number about twenty-six men, women, and children." After a while, the corsair captain agreed to let the passengers go and to pay the Englishmen their freight in exchange for the peaceful surrender of the Muslims' goods. The passengers consented, and, after some discussion, so did the wary English sailors.[59] In this narrative, the English mariners had done their very best for their passengers, and the decision to surrender was mutual.

Browne may well have been telling the truth. Although seamen manned the ordnance, musket-wielding passengers took on the risks of combat too, and they surely participated in hurried shipboard consultations. The same cannot be said of merchants' goods, which English seamen sometimes surrendered to attackers in hopes of gentle treatment. When the master of the *Mary Anne* of London did so around 1605, the aggrieved merchants could only take him to court after the fact. The *Mary Anne,* a ship of about 180 tons, manned by thirty mariners and carrying seven passengers, was becalmed on the coast of North Africa when it was approached by three galleys and a galliot. The merchant ship was "pestered" with merchandize, and its guns were not readily accessible. While the master, Robert Rickman, allegedly prepared the ship for a fight, when the galleys fired several warning shots, he "called up his company and commanded the gunner and the rest not to shoot off a piece," angering a merchant on board who felt that the ship "had been able to have withstood a greater force . . . and to have defended themselves and the merchants' goods."[60]

When the merchants sued Rickman for not fighting, his men came to his defense, arguing that it was simply too dangerous for sailors to fire on North African galleys. A quartermaster explained that "Turks and Christian galleys are different for although a ship fight with any Christian galley and be afterwards taken, if they belong to friends they do not make prize of them . . . but if the Turks do meet with any merchants' ships and the said ships do resist them and shoot but one shot . . . if they afterwards take them they make prize of ship and goods and commit the men to the galleys for slaves." A young boatswain's mate similarly asserted: "If a ship once make one shot at the Turkish galleys, if she be overcome they lose both ship and goods, and the people are made slaves during life, which he knoweth to be true . . . he hath often traveled into those parts and knoweth and hath seen the evidence thereof." Indeed, Rickman himself had previously been a galley slave in Algiers for three years.[61]

Rickman's negotiations saved him and his men but not the merchants' goods. He sent seven men in a skiff to speak with the commander of the galleys, Muhammad Bey of Tunis, who sent back two of them to fetch their papers and the cape merchant (the supercargo). When the cape merchant refused to go, Rickman sent another merchant pretending to be him, "one Richard Sotherne who spake the French language and did also understand the Italian tongue." Muhammad Bey told Sotherne that the *Mary Anne* "had Venetians' goods on board," which he denied, saying untruly that the ship was bound for the Levant. The corsairs disbelieved him and "demanded a present." Sotherne wrote to Rickman and the other merchant, asking them to send ten kerseys, but the merchants thought the quantity too large and sent four instead. After some angry talk among the corsairs, the *Mary Anne* was then boarded and captured.[62]

According to an aggrieved merchant, Rickman allegedly urged the corsairs to treat the seamen well, telling Muhammad Bey explicitly that "if he used him the said Rickman and his company well, he might haply take more Englishmen, but if he used them not well it would make other Englishmen rather die than lose their goods." Indeed, the seamen were not harmed in any way: "The admiral of the said galleys . . . told the said Rickman that in regard he had declared him his ship's books and acquainted him truly with his lading as he had found it, that neither he nor any of his mariners should lose any goods that were appertaining unto them, and said moreover unto him that he would pay him his freight." The *Mary Anne* was towed to Tunis, where the merchants' goods were removed; those claimed by the mariners were left on board. The opportunistic mariners even "purloined" one merchant's tin as their own; they sold it back to him later.[63] As for the merchants, they were out of luck.

Merchants faced an aggravating principal-agent problem when corsairs and merchant sailors agreed to avoid fighting. When three warships commanded by the Dutch renegade Simon Danseker and manned by several hundred men attacked the *Consent,* a merchant ship, in 1609, for example, it surrendered without firing a shot, and Danseker treated its men generously, taking the cargo but giving them back the ship and the goods they claimed as their own. Following the advice of their master, Hugh Bullock, the sailors of the *Consent* promptly claimed not only their own goods and clothing but also forty-two bags of currants, two large looking glasses, and a box of comfits, marking the goods "which they fathered as aforesaid some with one mark and some with another." Moreover, "whiles they were in durance with Danseker some of Bullock's company broke open the great chest of looking glasses and secretly conveyed them into the mariners' chests, and after they were cleared of Danseker the said Bullock did divide those glasses being about fifteen with his own hands amongst the company."[64]

Submission carried its own dangers for merchants and mariners alike, however. To strike one's sails and submit to boarding was to put oneself at the mercy of one's attackers—either unconditionally or hoping that a negotiated agreement, if made, would be respected. "None that come into the hands of men-of-war escape out again without loss," one merchant wryly concluded.[65] Even when a warship was friendly, extortion was to be expected. When a Tuscan captain asked for a present from the shipmaster Walter Whiting, saying that "it was by custom of the sea to be given," Whiting denied the custom but gave him "a hogshead of wine and two or three hens and a pair of worsted hose."[66]

As Whiting knew, the encounter could have been much worse. A few years before, for example, the *Trial* had met with disaster when it submitted to Spanish warships. Bound on a merchant voyage, the *Trial* had stopped first at Livorno and then sailed east to Malta, where "by reason of the Inquisition they stayed not," Corfu, Zante, Ragusa, and Alexandria, selling herring, tin, and kerseys and lading flax, indigo, and other goods. On the way from Alexandria back to Ragusa, they met with five Spanish vessels. At first, when the Spaniards tried to search the *Trial,* they were kept away by the eighteen English sailors. Finally, the Spaniards agreed with Edward Collins, the merchant, that six Spaniards could board the *Trial* while six Englishmen went on board one of the Spanish ships. The wary sailors still objected, fearing "they should be pillaged if the Spaniards came on board." Naively, Collins said "he would warrant them their wages and goods." With this assurance, the sailors finally consented to let four Spaniards board.[67] Once the Spanish ships came close enough, however, some forty of them boarded the *Trial* and took the English sailors prisoner.

Once the *Trial* was captured, the victors turned to eliciting confessions, accusing the Englishmen of piracy—not a wholly implausible accusation, given the presence of rogue privateers in the region at that time.[68] The English captives were distributed among various ships, and the *Trial* was converted into a man-of-war. After about seven weeks in which all the Spanish warships cruised against Ottoman shipping, the *Trial,* fifty Muslim captives, and most of the Englishmen were sent to Messina. There the master, purser, and merchant "were put into prison in a dark dungeon and kept eight days, and then brought up into the common jail where they had no allowance but bread and water," according to the young master's mate. Within sixteen days, all three had died.[69] Torture seems to have contributed to their deaths. The gunner, Robert West, claimed "they took the purser, and gave him the strappado three times, and at the last (by hanging weights and a live goat to his heels to give him by strangling the more torment) they brake his arms so as they could not torture him any longer. Which they did to cause him [to] confess that he and company had taken a ship of Marseilles and spoiled her." The men did not see the tortures, since they were kept chained on the *Trial*, but "by such as came on board [they] heard how the merchant, master, and purser were used and died."[70]

At length, the sailors were distributed among different galleys, where they were kept chained and isolated from one another, so that they "were brought so feeble and weak that they could scarce shift a foot." After twenty-five days, West remembered, he, the carpenter, Thomas White, and the quartermaster, William Conway, were "brought ashore before the king's secretary . . . and told by him, that the master's mate of the *Trial* had confessed that they had robbed a Christian ship . . . and sold powder and ordnance to a man-of-war." They were told to confirm the confession, "or else they must be tortured and imprisoned as the rest were." The three frightened men "were contented to put their hands to a writing which the said secretary had made to that purpose," and four or five others also confessed.[71] They may also have been bribed: Humphrey Goddard, a young sailor, claimed that he was told "he should be tortured and have his bones broken and put to death. . . . And if he would confess as he was promised he should be set at liberty, and should have a hundred or fourscore ducats to put in his purse to carry him home." The *Trial* and its rich cargo were pronounced good prize on the basis of the men's confessions. Their interrogators were quick to recognize (as English privateers had recognized in the past) that few seamen would brave torment to preserve merchants' investments.[72]

Meanwhile, the surviving relatives of the *Trial's* men who died silently in prison struggled vainly for compensation. Led by the master's widow, Alice Lile, their widows petitioned the Privy Council twice in the following years, lamenting their deaths "by torture, imprisonment, famishment, and poisoning, and by enforcing of them to serve to take Turks." As for the survivors, the widows claimed, "all their hairs went off their heads and beards" because of their sufferings. They stressed that their husbands had surrendered not out of cowardice but because they were loyal subjects: "Because the said master and company of the said ship would not offend his Highness's proclamation . . . they did not resist the Spaniards." As martyrs for their country, the *Trial's* dead seamen deserved consideration, the petitioners implied, yet the widows had been unable to obtain their husbands' wages or any redress: the English merchants had told them that they were suing for recompense in Spain, but the law moved slowly.[73] As loyal Englishwomen, they looked to the Privy Council for aid, but none would come, at least directly: the Earl of Salisbury, the secretary of state, scrawled on one of the petitions that the lords of the Privy Council had "had long conference" about the matter with the Spanish ambassador a week before and planned to write to the king of Spain. In the meantime, "patience must be had." It seems to have been a point of principle for the merchants and the Privy Council that English money should not pay for a Spanish fault. The *Trial* arrived home, finally, by the end of May 1607; perhaps the widows received their husbands' wages then.[74]

As we have seen, Thomas Gardner, master of the *Triumph*, similarly made an agreement with his assailants and submitted, trusting them to respect it—and like Edward Collins he was swiftly undeceived. Shortly after Gardner allowed a handful of Tuscan corsairs to board his ship, at least twenty men spilled onto its decks, and more came the next morning, when the Englishmen were seized along with the Muslim passengers and were divided among the ships in the fleet. When Walter Whiting of the nearby *Swan* asked the Florentines what would happen to the *Triumph*, he was told that the ship would be carried to Livorno. There the passengers were held as captives, and so were the English sailors. They were kept close in different places, including the slave bagno, to prevent them from talking together, the quartermaster, John Browne, said, and eight of them were tortured to make them confess that the ship's whole cargo belonged to Muslims, even those goods the sailors claimed as their own. This pressure appears to have been effective, as almost all of the goods were pronounced good prize. Browne, aged twenty-seven, said he had ventured his savings from more than a decade of seafaring on the voyage and lost the indigo and silk he had purchased at Sidon, as well as the grosgrain and "Constantinople platters of earth gilded" another seaman had bought for him at Istanbul. False Turkish notes of lading were inserted into the Englishmen's goods, he complained. As the seamen of the *Trial* and the *Triumph* discovered, the falsifiability of ships' papers raised the importance of their testimony. Bills of lading and account books could be faked and altered; it is conceivable, as the Tuscans asserted, that the goods on the *Triumph* claimed by English merchants really belonged to Muslims. When documents were so unreliable, sailors' words—even words wrung by torture—provided valuable legal evidence.[75]

Sometimes the agents of Grand Duke Ferdinand I of Tuscany sought to persuade captured English sailors to confess to piracy so that he could claim the ships and men as well as their cargoes. After the outcry over the *Merchant Royal*, Ferdinand had ceased to impress English ships, but he still wanted more of these warlike vessels and was not particular about how he got them. The *Thomas and William*, attacked while bound from Alexandretta to Istanbul carrying "160 Turks and Jews among which a *qadi* and the rest men and merchants of good import," was surely no pirate ship. Under the command of Captain Bradshaw, the passengers and sailors had fought for four hours, "in which space were slain twenty Turks and no English but some hurt whereof three or four are since dead." At that point, an English merchant wrote from Livorno: "The Turks desired Captain Bradshaw to yield, which he effected." The passengers were now imprisoned, "and the English in chains with them for company except Captain Bradshaw and one or two more of his men. [U]nless our shipping may pass with better security our Turkish trade will go to ruin shortly," he glumly concluded. For the unfortunate English seamen who were charged with piracy, ruin had already arrived.[76] A sea captain who stopped in Livorno in November 1607 reported that the companies of the *Triumph* and the *Thomas and William* had been "made slaves, no earthly miseries exceeding theirs." To add insult to injury, Ferdinand had ordered "the colours of England with the several ships' ensigns to be hung up with the Turk's colours in the chief church at Pisa as a trophy of his victories."[77]

When the *Matthew* of Plymouth was similarly captured and treated like a pirate ship, its stricken owner, Walter Matthew, sent the secretary of state a desperate missive. He recounted how a great galleon had chased and fired at the *Matthew*. The dismayed master had asked his men if any of them recognized the galleon's flag, but none did, except for a Greek who recognized St. Stephen's cross because his father had worn a shirt with that emblem. He suggested that the galleon might be Florentine, but the others were by no means convinced. Meanwhile, the galleon attacked them with cannon and musket fire, killing four. Concluding that it must be a "Turkish pirate," the Englishmen fought back, resolving to die rather than surrender. Three hours later, when a shot killed their helmsman and the ship swung around so that they could see the grand duke's arms on the stern of the galleon, the relieved master yielded. The survivors' misery had just begun, however: "For the usage of our people, it is so bad and unchristianlike: that I cannot but shed tears when I see or think on them," Matthew lamented. With shaven heads, "fettered with chains and irons," and poorly fed, they were put to hard labor, sick, disheartened, and "like to perish." Matthew vehemently denied that his ship had been the aggressor, pointing out that it would have been madness for a ship with twenty-seven men and twelve or thirteen cannons to attack a giant galleon manned with six hundred men and fifty great guns. In fact, he argued, Ferdinand targeted English ships "because he will have our ships and men to be slaves for his galleys: for he findeth our shipping to be stronger and fitter for his purpose than other shipping are." Matthew beseeched Salisbury to consider his misery, "as also the miserable estate of the families of these poor men that are killed and those perished in his prison: and likewise those remaining yet in slavery . . . all undone and brought to beggary."[78] In addition to pitying the sailors' fate, the shipowner may have feared that the cruelty with which they were treated would elicit the incriminating evidence the Tuscans sought, allowing the *Matthew* to be condemned as a captured pirate ship.

Spurred by these pleas, James sent a special ambassador to Florence to remonstrate with Ferdinand. In May 1608 Stephen Lesieur met with a friendly welcome but scant success, as Tuscan officials blandly insisted that all procedures had been correctly followed. The prisoners, meanwhile, were lured with promises of freedom to sign a "supplication" admitting their guilt. "These poor men not understanding the Italian," a Levant Company merchant reported, the men of the *Thomas and William* "underwrote they knew not what and were delivered." However, the *Matthew*'s men, of whom some at least could read Italian, "would not underwrite the thing, so they are again shaved and used as slaves." They continued in prison until ten of them, perhaps all who remained alive, were quietly released about a month later, having paid a heavy price for their defense of English honor.[79]

Already obliged to answer for the depredations of English corsairs, Levant Company merchants had to hope that English merchant sailors would be strong in battle and resolute in captivity, protecting their goods and their nation's reputation. Fortunately for them, Ferdinand's death in early 1609 lessened the tensions between London and Florence, though Maltese corsairs continued to attack English ships. In addition, the Levant merchants increasingly turned to larger and more powerful ships, sending formidable merchantmen of four hundred tons to the eastern Mediterranean rather than smaller, cheaper vessels like the *Matthew* and the *Triumph*. These large ships still needed fighting crews, however, and when they lacked them the diplomatic fallout could be serious: when Stephen Mitchell gave up his Muslim passengers to Maltese galleys in 1651, for example, the dey of Tunis seized an English ship in reprisals, and war followed.[80] A decade later, when Edward Coxere became a Quaker, he found that shipmasters bound for the Mediterranean simply would not hire a pacifist, even though he was a skilled seaman expert in those routes. Legally, they had little choice. Even if their charter parties did not bind them to employ only fighting men, following the 1663 peace articles between England and Algiers, Tunis, and Tripoli, Charles II directed English consuls in North Africa to take bonds from English shipmasters for the security of their passengers and commanded the shipmasters to defend their passengers and their goods "to the utmost of their power, by fighting or otherwise," from all attackers. In the long run, only naval power and an elaborate Mediterranean pass system would remove the burden of protecting English commerce from merchant sailors.[81]

In the meantime, the North African corsairs' increasing turn to enslaving English seamen complicated the sailors' calculus. Fighting back aggressively might be worth it to obtain better terms: in 1614, when a corsair ship from Algiers attacked the small *Tiger* of Bristol, the Englishmen fought desperately until all but five of the crew were slain. Only then did they yield up the cargo, on the condition that they be left their ship and their freedom. By the 1620s, ships and men themselves were often the prime targets, and some who surrendered in hopes of favor learned the hard way that times had changed. The *Elizabeth Anne Judith* was manned by eighteen men and a boy in 1620 when it was on its way back to England from Zante with currants. When the ship was chased by three "Turkish" men-of-war about twenty leagues off Malta, the master, John Stephens, did his best to encourage his men: once he saw they could not outsail their pursuers, he "went to prayer" with his company, "and after prayers ended, he the said Stephens did persuade and exhort his company to fight and defend his ship against the Turks," saying that "he had rather sink or burn his ship and goods and lose his life than yield his ship and goods to be taken by the Turks." The company promised to fight and made the ship ready for battle, but when the master's mate, George Barefoot, went down to tell the gunner to fire, the men changed their minds. The warships were large and well armed, manned by hundreds of men, and so "perceiving the force of the Turks and the impossibility to defend themselves," the sailors extinguished the matches "and would not fight, some of them saying that they had known the misery of being slaves before, others saying that they had wives and children and taxing the master that he had friends or monies to redeem him, which made him so willing to fight." Stephens argued with them, but to no avail: they struck the sails and yielded without his consent. They were enslaved anyway, to their dismay. Bitter resistance seems to have become more common: in January 1622, for example, Elizabeth Young of Poplar applied for a license to beg, explaining that her late husband, Henry, had been master and part owner of the *Delight* of London when the ship was attacked the previous fall by three "Turkish" men-of-war. Resolving to die rather than surrender, the men had apparently drowned after their ship caught fire.[82]

Though the routine enslavement of English sailors helped to align the interests of investors and seamen, conflict over maritime losses and gains persisted: even seemingly providential escapes from slavers could degenerate into sordid struggles over profits and losses. Around 1620, for example, three captured English seamen—the master, mate, and boatswain of a Dover ship—rebelled against their eleven captors as they sailed toward Salé, and after a ferocious fight managed to wrest control of the ship. With one of their party badly wounded and the other two hurt and exhausted, the English seamen made an uneasy peace with the defeated corsairs and, with their help, sailed the crippled ship to a village near

Lisbon. The would-be slavers were then enslaved, and the English sea-men were granted their price as a reward. When the Englishmen re-turned home with the money, however, the owners of the Dover ship demanded a share of it; "neither would they give them wages, which yet demanded this money," actions that struck Samuel Purchas, who chroni-cled the episode, as an impiously grasping response to "the unspeakable grace and bounty of God."[83]

To fight or surrender, to remain silent, tell the truth, or lie—merchant sailors faced hard choices as they navigated perilous encounters in the Mediterranean, hoping to save their wages, their goods, their freedom and their lives. For those who remembered privateering, there must have been a bitter irony to the fact that English sailors' belligerence had be-come a selling point for merchants touting the safety of English shipping, part of the country's newfound respectability as a commercial nation. Yet as the years went on there were fewer who remembered. In the 1620s and '30s, a generation after Elizabeth's death, the corsairs of Algiers, Tunis, and Salé took hundreds of English ships and thousands of men. A nation of pirates had become prey.

Colonial Conflicts

Quarrels over losses and gains roiled the western Atlantic, too. In the earliest stages of imperial expansion, English colonies were private proj-ects, often managed by groups of investors who formed joint-stock com-panies and enjoyed royal charters. This arrangement had its strengths. It suited the Crown to allow private individuals to take on the costs of colo-nization, while investors could pool their resources, protected by monop-olies. Promotional literature blurred the lines between the common good and private profit, heralding the benefits that colonization would bring to the participants and to the commonwealth as a whole: growth of ship-ping and mariners, new products to replace current imports, increased royal dignity and revenues, and opportunity for the poor.[84] In practice, however, such gains were hard to realize, and early English colonies were rife with conflict.

Sailors in particular did not fit easily into colonial administration. They were essential, of course, to the establishment and survival of the colonies: they carried settlers and supplies, explored the coast, and transported colonial products back to England. Sailors were not often direct employees of the companies, however, and they certainly did not subordinate their own interests to company aims. They clashed with colonial governors, challenging the lofty authority that they assumed. When the *Sea Venture,* bound for Virginia with Jamestown's new prospective commander, Sir Thomas Gates, was wrecked on Bermuda in 1609, sailors made particularly troublesome subjects in the de facto colony. As Gates oversaw plans to sail to Jamestown, William Strachey recorded, "the major part of the common sort" began to murmur of staying in Bermuda, where there was plenty to eat and little danger. These "dangerous and secret discontents . . . began first in the seamen," who spread them to the landsmen. Later on, when one sailor, Robert Waters, murdered another, he was captured and sentenced to be hanged. Though he was bound and guarded, "his fellow sailors . . . in despite and disdain that justice should be showed upon a sailor, and that one of their crew should be an example to others . . . cut his bands, and conveyed him into the woods, where they fed him nightly."[85] Sailing to the New World represented a life-changing transition for prospective settlers, but it was no such thing for the sailors, who defended their rights and perquisites as they would on any other route. While seamen's infractions were hardly the greatest challenge facing the early colonies, they were a consistent cause of complaint.

These complaints began with the first colonial expeditions to the New World, when would-be planters traveled on privateering ships. The most common route to Virginia passed through the Caribbean, and strong ships provided necessary security. The Roanoke backers were not opposed to raiding Spanish shipping; indeed, they hoped to establish a privateering base in American waters. In practice, however, combining privateering with planting was not easy. The mariners' focus on taking prizes impeded John White's attempts to establish and relieve a settlement in present-day North Carolina. Commander of the 1587 Roanoke expedition and captain of the *Lion,* White left a scathing account of his difficulties with the ship's master, the Portuguese Protestant Simon Fernandes, and the other seamen. Sailing through the West Indies on the way to Roanoke, for example, Fernandes refused to stop where White thought they could take in useful supplies, preferring a route by which he apparently hoped they would encounter prizes. When White wanted to land at Boqueron Bay to take in fruit trees, "Simon denied it." Later, they anchored off Roanoke Island, where White intended to speak with the handful of Englishmen left there the previous year before proceeding to Chesapeake Bay to found a permanent settlement. When the pinnace set off for Roanoke with a number of settlers, however, "a gentleman by the means of Fernando . . . called to the sailors in the pinnace, charging them not to bring any of the planters back again, but leave them in the island . . . saying that the summer was far spent, wherefore he would land all the planters in no other place." Eager to attack Spanish ships sailing by the Azores, Fernandes canceled the plans to sail for the Chesapeake, and the sailors sided with him: "Unto this were all the sailors, both in the pinnace, and ship, persuaded by the master, wherefore it booted not the governor to contend with them."[86]

The following year, 1588, White—who had returned to England to seek urgently needed additional supplies—was frustrated in his attempt to reach Roanoke, where he had left his daughter and his infant grand-daughter, because nearly all shipping was stayed to counter the Armada. In April, two small ships were allowed to depart, and White traveled on the *Brave*, whose captain, he learned to his dismay, was more interested in plunder than in relieving the vulnerable settlement. They indiscriminately robbed a number of ships before being attacked by a stronger enemy, a warship from La Rochelle, and being given a deadly dose of their own medicine. After a battle that left twenty-three men dead from both sides and others badly wounded, the English surrendered and were pillaged. There was no question of continuing on: "By this occasion, God justly punishing our former thievery of our evil disposed mariners, we were of force constrained to break off our voyage." By the time a relief expedition finally reached Roanoke in 1590, the colonists had disappeared.[87]

Charles Leigh also struggled with his sailors in 1604 when he sought to establish a settlement on the Wiapoco (now Oyapock) River. Once he found what he took to be a suitable spot for settlement, his men "grew generally discontented" at the thought of the tremendous physical effort required to cut down the thick forest. They had been "suborned," he claimed, by the shipmaster and "his lewd consorts he brought with him." Leigh thought that "intending spoil and purchase in the West Indies [they had] from the beginning sought the overthrow of this voyage." He persuaded the men with some difficulty to consent to remain at Wiapoco for one year, but their acquiescence did not come cheap. "My loose commodities, as hatchets, beads, knives, looking-glasses, &c. are almost all gone; a great part in buying of victuals, but the most part to stop the mouths of my mutinous and monstrous sailors; to whom also I have promised two third parts of my iron," Leigh lamented.[88] The sailors clearly hoped that trade with local people would make their stay worthwhile.

Unmoved by Leigh's persuasions, the shipmaster, Martin Pring, promptly shipped himself on a Dutch ship trading nearby and went on to enjoy a long and prosperous career. Other sailors returned to England on Leigh's ship the *Phoenix*, seeking reinforcements and supplies. The men left behind at Wiapoco, including Leigh himself, were less fortunate: by the time the *Phoenix* returned, disease and malnutrition had killed many. Leigh himself died shortly after of the flux, and all the surviving members of the abortive colony forsook it, taking passage on the European ships that called at Wiapoco to trade. Meanwhile, on the *Olive Branch*, sent for the relief of the Wiapoco colony, hostility simmered between the prospective settlers and the sailors—men of "contrary natures" according to the colonist John Nicholl. After a difficult voyage the expedition ran short of food, and the settlers landed on the island of Saint Lucia, where they traded with Caribs and remained after the departure of the ship and its company, "seeing," one of them recorded, "it was in vain for all of us for to venture home in the ship with that small allowance." Tensions between the seamen and the landsmen were so high that they shot directly at one another with cannons in lieu of a civil salute.[89]

Mindful of the dangers and temptations of the West Indies, the North Virginia Company experimented with northern routes to present-day Maine but found its seamen refractory. George Waymouth sailed north of the Caribbean in his successful 1605 voyage of exploration, and Henry Challons was directed to follow the same course in the *Richard* the following year. Contrary to his instructions, the *Richard* sailed through the Caribbean anyway. While Challons was ill, the colonial entrepreneur Sir Ferdinando Gorges explained, "his company shaped their course for the Indies" and made landfall at Puerto Rico, where they spent "some time . . . hunting after such things as best pleased themselves" before being captured by Spanish ships.[90]

The *Trial* never sailed to America at all. A syndicate of London fishmongers and others obtained a passport for a voyage to Virginia in 1606, but they made a fatal error in hiring Arthur Chambers as master. Much to the dismay of the purser, rather than proceeding to Virginia the *Trial* loitered on the coasts of England and Ireland for months, as Chambers embezzled its stores and threw riotous parties, setting a bad example for the mariners, who "seeing his slender government invited likewise many of their mates and acquaintances" to drink healths at the investors' expense. Finally, after the charter had expired, the ship sailed to the coast of Spain for piracy rather than to North America, and the syndicate dissolved amid mutual recriminations. For the more respectable Virginia Company, Chambers's exploits were a public relations disaster.[91]

In the first years of the seventeenth century, when the North American coast was still relatively unfamiliar, sailors could also sell their knowledge of precarious English settlements to Spain. One was even actively recruited by a Spanish agent: Francis Magner, who sailed to Virginia in 1607 or 1608 and subsequently took a ship to Guinea. On the return voyage from Guinea, Magner fell out with his shipmaster and was summarily discharged at Naples. Traveling home overland, the aggrieved seaman met an Irish priest who convinced him to travel to Spain, where he provided the authorities with a detailed if highly exaggerated account of the settlement at Virginia and offered to serve as pilot for a Spanish expedition against it. Magner was an attractive target for Catholic recruiting because, though he lived with his wife near London, he was "an Irishman born." Talking with "Father Patrick," Magner must have complained about the master of the Guinea ship, for when the priest discovered that Magner was Irish, he revealed his identity and "persuaded him he should become a Catholic and that he should not adhere unto the English nation, who had not only wronged him . . . but the whole kingdom of Ireland [his] native country."[92] A shipboard dispute could prompt a shift in allegiance.

More commonly, sailors and planters quarreled over access to victuals. Even after privateering ceased to tempt America-bound sailors, English ships remained built for war, with meager cargo space. They were unable to carry the ample supplies planters needed to establish self-sufficient settlements: famine often undermined English colonial ambitions. As planters starved, the sailors guarded their customary rights to provisions—which, after all, they needed to sail safely home, and which formed a large part of their renumeration. In late 1608, John Smith complained: "For the sailors (I confess) they daily make good cheer, but our diet is a little meal and water, and not sufficient of that."[93] The ships' commanders tended to side with their men. In 1602, for example, when the colonial promoter Captain Gosnold wanted to establish a trading post in North Virginia, the *Concord's* captain, Bartholomew Gilbert, would allocate only six weeks' worth of food for the planters, rather than six months' worth, and so plans for settlement had to be abandoned. Even so, they had "not one cake of bread, nor any drink, but a little vinegar, left" by the time they reached Portsmouth: Gilbert's caution was fully justified.[94]

Shortages also created strife on the *Gift of God* while the ship made the homeward journey from the fledgling colony in North Virginia in 1607. It had become clear that the colony had too little food for its population, and so the *Gift* carried roughly thirty settlers homeward as well as the sailors, with enough food for only about six weeks. When they reached the height of the Azores, "there was a general mutiny in the ship among the company that they wanted victuals and should be starved if they had not supply." The captain, John Elliott, resisted demands that they stop at the Azores, telling them that the planters in Virginia depended on their haste, but "the company of the ship answered that their want being at sea was more desperate, and that they should perish if they were not relieved." Elliott gave way, and the master, John Havercomb, sold the cargo of masts and bought victuals. When they finally arrived in England, two investors, Sir Francis Popham and his mother, sued Havercomb for having sold the masts, but the sailor John Deoman affirmed that they "must of force have perished if they had not been relieved in the Islands"; as it was, several men had died of hunger.[95] In contrast, Elliott blamed the crisis on the sailors, who "underhand as he believeth consumed and spent more victuals than were necessary to be so spent in excess, and by reason thereof the rest were in want and a mutiny grew amongst them." If a man had died before reaching the Azores, he said, the fault lay in "his own beastliness in not clearing himself of lice and vermin." Unconvinced, the admiralty judge dismissed the Pophams' suit.[96]

Sailors sometimes used their food as trade goods. At Jamestown, the settlers remembered, seamen pilfered biscuit to "sell, give, or exchange with us, for money, sassafras, furs or love." If some recognized that "whilest the ships stayed, our allowance was somewhat bettered," William Strachey thought their rates were exorbitant, blaming the settlers' misery on "the mariners, who never yet in any voyage hither but have made a prey of our poor people in want; insomuch, as unless they might advance four or five for one . . . they would not spare them a dust of corn, nor a pint of beer, to give unto them the least comfort or relief . . . I myself have heard the master of a ship say . . . that unless he might have an East Indian increase, four to one, all charges cleared, he would not part with a can of beer."[97] Rather than sacrificing for the success of the colonial enterprise, as Strachey apparently thought they ought to, the seamen persisted in regarding Jamestown as a market like any other, a place to buy cheap and sell dear.

When sailors supplemented their wages by foraging or bartering with local people, this, too, put them at odds with merchant companies. In 1606, the royal council for Virginia directed the North and South Virginia Companies to trade together with one stock for five years, preserving their goods in common storehouses and appointing one person in each colony to take charge of all commerce.[98] Unity strengthened the settlers' ability to barter profitably with Algonquian people and keep prices for colonial products high. Many sailors disregarded these strictures. In June 1607, the council at Jamestown complained: "Our easiest and richest commodity being sassafras roots were gathered up by the sailors with loss and spoil of many of our tools and with drawing of our men from our labour to their uses against our knowledge to our prejudice." The council directed the Virginia Company in England to take action, "since they be all our waged men," but recognized that sailors had a customary right to trade on their own account and that compromise would be necessary. To avoid dumping sassafras on the English market, the Virginia Company probably bought up the two tons the sailors had gathered.[99] In 1610, when the settlers at Jamestown were in desperate want, William Strachey wrote much more harshly about the misdemeanors of the sailors. He reported caustically that the mariners secretly traded with the Indians, undercutting the planters' interests: "To do us more villainy and mischief, they would send of their longboats still by night and (well guarded) make out to the neighbor villages and towns and there (contrary to the articles of the fort, which now pronounce death for a trespass of that quality) truck with the Indians, giving for their trifles, otter skins, beavers, raccoon furs, bears' skins, etc., so large a quantity and measure of copper as, when the truckmaster for the colony in the daytime offered trade, the Indians would laugh and scorn the same, telling what bargains they met withal by night from our *mangot quintons* (so calling our great ships)."[100]

Some seamen who ranged up and down the coast of New England trading with Indians also sought opportunistic profits at the expense of those interested in colonization and developing the fur trade for the long term. In a whaling, fishing, and fur-trading expedition in 1614, for example, the shipmaster Thomas Hunt enticed more than twenty Patuxet and Nauset men on board, "under colour of trucking with them," and allegedly sold them as slaves for twenty pounds apiece at Malaga, where he had sailed with his cargo of cod, "like a wretched man . . . that cares not what mischief he doth for his profit." He left the captives' aggrieved tribes "ill affected towards the English," including the dismayed settlers of the Plymouth Colony. John Smith even suspected that impeding English settlement was Hunt's object: he hoped "to keep this abounding country still in obscurity, that only he and some few merchants more might enjoy wholly the benefit of the [fish and fur] trade."[101]

Interloping mariners continued to trouble colonial promoters in the region even after Sir Ferdinando Gorges and his associates formed the Council for New England, to which James granted sole rights in 1620. In 1622, at the council's behest, James issued a proclamation condemning the "sundry interlopers, irregular and disobedient persons" who allegedly cut down the council's timber, spoiled the harbors by casting out their ballast, and, worst of all, "not so content, by their promiscuous trading, as well mariners as masters with the savages, have overthrown the trade and commerce that before was had . . . as if they resolved to omit nothing that might be impious and intolerable, they did not forbear to barter away to the savages, swords, pikes, muskets, fowling pieces, match, powder, shot, and other warlike weapons, and teach them the use thereof." Selling arms to native people was dangerous, James proclaimed, to English settlers in the area, and he forbade English subjects not associated with the council to go to the coast or trade with the people.[102] Such proclamations were easy to make but difficult to enforce. Raiding and trading, the sailors in early colonial expeditions preferred time-tested ways of seeking gain from the lofty and often illusory goals of settlement—whose profits would not, in any case, accrue to them.

Chartered monopoly corporations were designed to make overseas expansion easier and more profitable, increasing the likelihood of success by preventing English people from competing with one another. Both in Atlantic projects and in commercial ventures in the Mediterranean, however, the "English nation" was fractured by clashing interests. The dangers were great, the gains tempting but uncertain and unevenly distributed. Settling in the New World under the authority of a merchant company was one way for Englishmen to seek their fortunes abroad, but for most early settlers the experience was a dismal one. Many must have longed for home, but escaping was not easy, even for sailors. Leaving letters complaining of "their hard and bad usage" in Bermuda, for example, in 1616 the mariner Richard Sanders and his companions borrowed a compass and set to sea in a tiny fishing boat, miraculously reaching Ireland before their supplies gave out.[103] Other disillusioned settlers were more ambitious. In 1609, after a number of Jamestown planters on the *Swallow* traded with the Patawomecks for corn, "the most seditious of them conspired together, persuaded some and enforced others, to this barbarous project. They stole away the ship, they made a league amongst themselves to be professed pirates, with dreams of mountains of gold, and happy robberies." The runaways failed, perhaps because they lacked the necessary skills.[104] They were not alone, however, in seeing piracy as an attractive alternative to corporate empire.

CHAPTER FOUR

PIRACY AND EMPIRE

Jonas Prophett sailed for Virginia in December 1606, on one of three ships under the command of the old privateering captain Christopher Newport. It was a long and anxious voyage, but one in which Prophett saw a great deal: the ships stopped at the Canaries for water, at Dominica for trade with indigenous people, and at Guadeloupe, Nevis, Mona, and the Virgin Islands, where the hungry company feasted on iguanas, turtles, and whatever else they could catch. In mid-May they finally settled on a site for Jamestown, and hard labor began for the ill-prepared settlers. When Newport sailed for England in June, Prophett was the only man described as a sailor to be left behind. In the following months, as the starving Englishmen struggled for subsistence, fishing and trading up the river with Algonquian people, Prophett's ability to handle a boat surely came in handy. He was one of the handful of men who accompanied John Smith in summer 1608 in his exploration, by boat, of Chesapeake Bay, parleying uneasily with a number of different Powhatan and Chikahominy communities. In late December 1608, when Smith led a more considerable expedition to the Powhatan headquarters Werowocomoco in hopes of purchasing or seizing a large supply of corn, Prophett served as master of the pinnace.[1]

Prophett was a useful man at Jamestown, but he soon lost enthusiasm for the colony. By early 1613, he was back in England, pressed into service on the *Anne Royal* as a boatswain's mate or coxswain as the fleet escorted Elizabeth Stuart to Flushing as the bride of the Elector Palatine. When the fleet returned to England, many sailors seem to have been discharged unpaid. One of these, young James Jackson, recounted that at Gravesend he happened to pass by the Red Cross alehouse when Prophett called him in to join twelve other poor seamen. If Jackson would accompany them to Ipswich, Prophett allegedly promised, he would help him find work. "Being very poor and having neither clothes nor money," the boy walked to Colchester with the men. There, Prophett hired a boat "to carry them to Ipswich because they said they were weary." Once the sailors were afloat, however, they turned pirate. Prophett explained frankly to the distressed boatman "that they were poor men, and wanted money, and that they would take some other ship at sea, and then he should have his boat again."[2]

First the ragged pirates took a Guernsey boat carrying cockles, eating enough to satisfy their hunger, and then they had the good luck to set upon the *Nightingale* of Middelburg. They told the frightened merchants not to be afraid, because they were Englishmen and would not hurt them; they "were poor men, and were in great want, and desired them to give them something." The ransom of the *Nightingale* was set at about £500, a substantial sum. No longer poor, the sailors divided the spoils and went their separate ways. One of them, young William Isgrave, went on a spending spree: he laid out a few pounds on clothing, presented his aunt with a new hat, paid his hostess, Rosamund Newport, his debts for lodging and food, paid Newport's husband his debts for tobacco, and sent some money to one Mary Sound. Unfortunately for Isgrave and the rest of the crew, their newfound wealth drew official attention, and most of the men were arrested.[3]

Imprisoned in the Marshalsea, Prophett staunchly denied everything, but his accomplices were less resolute. On their evidence and that of the *Nightingale*'s passengers, he was found guilty and sentenced to be hanged. While he languished in prison, his friend Joan Mitche, a sailor's wife, did what she could to obtain his pardon. Mindful of Prophett's colonial experience, she appealed to the Virginia Company to intervene on his behalf, suggesting that he could sail with Captain Adams on a projected voyage to Bermuda. Her efforts came to nothing, so one Saturday afternoon Mitche went to the Marshalsea to visit Prophett and tell him of her disappointment. Over "certain trotters, about a pennyworth of bread, and a double jug of beer," she ate and talked with the prisoner in the porter's lodge, telling him "she had been with Sir Thomas Smith and Captain Adams for his discharge, but she had little hope to get it."[4]

Mitche may have brought more than refreshments on her visit, though she denied giving Prophett any ropes: the sailor escaped from the Marshalsea two days later. According to Mitche, a little girl saw him at her door, dripping wet. Then, Mitche claimed, Prophett disappeared. In fact, he had gathered a small crew and took "a small barque of Lynn laden with grocery" in the Thames. This time, the pirate knew better than to stay in England. Instead, he would seek out a small, nondescript port on the Atlantic coast of Morocco, a pirate haven that had become famous among English sailors. This time, he sailed to Mamora.[5]

In his turn to piracy, Jonas Prophett had plenty of company. More English seamen sailed on pirate ships in James's reign, proportionally, than in the famous golden age of piracy a century later. Since 1608 or so, a fearsomely large community of English pirates had become active in the Atlantic, congregating on the western coast of war-torn Morocco and on the southwest coast of Ireland, where royal authority was weak. For the authorities, English Atlantic piracy became impossible to ignore in July 1611, when Sir Ferdinando Gorges sent the Earl of Salisbury a troubling report from Plymouth. Some London merchants had been taken by English pirates near the Isles of Scilly, not ragtag miscreants but a major force. The captured ships were the *Concord*, a large and powerful merchantman of 240 tons, and the *Philip Bonaventure* of Dover. Their opponents had been even more formidable: four ships, of which three were of 160 tons or more, well armed, and manned with "some 600 men all English." The four pirate ships captured the merchantmen with ease, and during the week that they kept them, three more pirate vessels came to join them, all between two hundred and three hundred tons. The merchants reported "that there is in all, of these kind of vermin to the number of 40 sail, and 2000 men, all English, their common *rendez-vous* is La Mamora in Barbary, where they have merchants of all sorts that trades with them, for all kinds of commodities, especially those of Leghorn."[6]

In an age of imperial projects, the Mamora pirates created a project of their own, one that put the interests of seamen first, as the merchant companies clearly failed to do. To be sure, they lacked the charters and commissions that merchants and courtiers obtained. From their perspective, however, the differences between their ventures and those approved by the Crown were probably less salient than the similarities: they too were a group of Englishmen seeking to make money abroad, working closely together and bound to England by a multitude of personal and cultural ties. A handful of foreigners sailed on their ships, but they collaborated above all with other Englishmen and even fought their national rivals for access to valuable markets. Unlike the angry, even nihilist Anglo-American pirates who marauded after the Peace of Utrecht a century later, they did not usually cooperate with foreign freebooters or seek to kill representatives of British authority. Indeed, they promoted the interests of English people, though they favored the close-knit community of English seafarers over the state or commercial interests: their mostly collegial relations with English merchant sailors raised some merchants' suspicions. And while the Mamora pirates were well aware that their gains were illegal, they hoped these would be legitimated after the fact. The captured merchants reported: "These men . . . threaten the world and gives it out, they expect to be called in very shortly by His Majesty's pardon for 40,000 pounds, of whom notwithstanding they speak very opprobriously, but withal they say if they be not they will take and spoil all they meet with."[7]

Defiant of royal authority and threatening commerce, the Mamora pirates nonetheless expected to negotiate a return to England in due course, as indeed most of them would. Their achievements were fleeting but impressive. During their brief glory days, the Mamora pirates far outnumbered the inhabitants of England's settlements in the New World, projected more power, and handled more trade. Their imperial project may have been unlawful, but unlike many others in the early seventeenth century, it was a success.

Routes to Mamora

The colonial investor Sir Ferdinando Gorges represented piracy as the product of desperation: "This peaceable times affords no means of employment, to the multitude of people that daily do increase, and many are enforced (by necessity) to seek some ways to sustain themselves." The solution, he argued, was "the planting of colonies in barbarous and uninhabited parts of the world." Few sailors would have agreed with Gorges's self-serving assessment, however. For sailors who knew how many dangers and how few gains awaited them in trading and colonial ventures, Atlantic piracy was an enticing alternative, not a desperate last resort. It attracted discontented settlers like James Gentleman, who was hired along with other fishermen around 1611 "to go to Virginia, and to be employed there in fishing." Sent to sea from Virginia in the *Discovery* in July 1612, the entire crew decided that they "would not come any more in Virginia, but would for England," and summarily abandoned the colony.[8]

While Gorges was surely right that piracy flourished in peacetime, unemployment does not adequately explain the rise of the Atlantic pirates. After all, five years separated the end of privateering from the gathering of English pirates at Mamora, and their numbers only continued to grow in the years after 1608. Many sailors worked at sea only briefly in their twenties before settling on land, and commercial English shipping was expanding vigorously in the early seventeenth century. The end of the war with Spain produced a surplus of seamen, but it cannot have lasted long. Rather, for the men of the first English pirate ships that congregated at Mamora in the years around 1608, piracy seems to have offered opportunity that was otherwise hard to find for seafaring men after the end of Elizabethan privateering. In their own narratives, ambition played a larger role than desperation. Thus John Jennings, a pirate captain who had marauded even during the queen's reign, explained his turn to crime in terms of his high aspirations when, captured and condemned to death, he recounted his life for posterity: "From my childhood," he recalled, "I was wholly addicted to martial courses, especially in the manly resolution of seafaring men." His bravery and experience gave him "the name of a skillful mariner," but he longed for a command of his own. Lacking the "means and friends" to become a captain "lawfully"—and indeed the

essential business skills, for he could neither read nor write—he had become a pirate.[9]

Many—probably most—of the early Jacobean Atlantic pirates had
served on privateers, then struggled to adjust to peacetime after the war,
often serving foreign masters for a period before finding that life too re-
strictive. Some of them were old Tunis corsairs, unhappy with the increasing subordination of English seamen to Muslim elites. The Atlantic
pirate captains Gilbert Roope, Thomas Hussey, and Richard Bishop all
sailed out of Tunis in the years after 1603, for example. According to
James Harris, who was a captive there when Bishop purchased his freedom and recruited him into piracy, Bishop depicted piracy as a path to
independence, wealth, and status, a way of retaining the gains of
Elizabethan privateering. Bishop allegedly declared: "It will be unsavory
for us now, to pick up our crumbs in a low ebb, to live in baseness, and
want means even to sustain nature, to walk under the check of some such
as have perked up their heads to authority in this time of quiet, whom we
durst have buffeted . . . in days of war."[10]

Bishop was seen "drinking and plundering" together with John Ward, but
he was far less prosperous than the other corsair captain and lost his independence when Muslim investors asserted their authority over the English
outlaws. In spring 1607, Bishop was "appointed" as captain of a ship owned
by Uthman Dey and Muhammad Bey of Tunis, with a crew of "forty
Turks . . . and eighteen or twenty Englishmen."[11] Attempting to regain a
measure of freedom, Bishop then bought a ship of his own, but he was
obliged to borrow money from local *armatori* to furnish it for the sea—and
both he and Harris were forced to remain in Tunis as security for the loan
when the ship set sail on a fruitless cruise. Seafaring men reported that he
was then "a very poor man" and "in poor estate." Fed up, Bishop and
Harris borrowed more money to outfit their ship and decamped for the
Atlantic with an English crew, leaving four unlucky hostages behind as security.[12] The pirates William Longcastle, William Taverner, and Samuel Cade
were also veterans of Ward's company; they were among the small group
of pirates who left Ward after the capture of the *Soderina*, paying an extortionate sum for passage back to England on the *Unicorn* of Bristol. They
shipped out again soon on the *Ulysses*, belonging to the merchant Richard
Hall, a major investor in West Indian smuggling. Longcastle went as

captain, though Hall can hardly have been ignorant of his past. Old habits were hard to shake: stopping for water at Safi on the western coast of Morocco, Longcastle, Taverner, and Cade plundered the *Susan* of Bristol.[13]

Other seamen sailed illegally with Dutch letters of marque in the Atlantic before turning pirate entirely. Pardoned for his earlier attacks on Dutch shipping, John Jennings sailed on a Dutch warship before joining the larger community of English pirates.[14] Thomas Sockwell, an old privateer, was the captain of the *Lion's Whelp* when Ward deserted from it to begin his Mediterranean ravages. Sockwell's naval career did not last much longer than Ward's: in 1606, he left Flushing as captain of a piratically inclined Dutch privateer with a mixed English and Dutch crew. He sailed to Safi to sell French plunder, then conspired with his Englishmen to capture a Flushing vessel at Mogador.[15] For English seamen who had flouted James's proclamations against serving in foreign war ships, the 1609 truce between the Dutch Republic and Spain may have precipitated a final move into outright piracy.

For these warlike seamen, the Atlantic coast of Morocco was a natural haunt. As privateers under English and Dutch flags, they had regularly anchored there for water and supplies and to sell illegal plunder. Safi, Mogador (now Essaouira), and Mamora (now Mehdya) were also well-known ports of call for English merchants who traded cloth and arms for sugar and—after Morocco's 1591 invasion of the Sudan—gold. Moreover, domestic Moroccan politics were propitious for pirates around 1608. In the late sixteenth century, Ahmad al-Mansur had been allied with Elizabeth against Philip II, who strove to retain and extend Spanish enclaves on the Moroccan coast. When al-Mansur died in 1603, Morocco fell into a ruinous civil war, disputed between three of his sons. As tightening local control made the Ottoman regencies of Tunis and Algiers less attractive to English corsairs, Moroccan unrest opened up opportunities for independent maritime raiders. Persistent local warfare seems not to have bothered the English pirates, whose cut-rate commodities and skill in gunnery made them generally welcome: a number of English mercenaries, including the pirate Captain Roger Isaac, served the contender Moulay Zidan (Zidan al-Nasir) for good wages in May 1608, for example.[16]

While the rival Saadi brothers focused on events inland, English and Dutch pirates congregated at Mamora, a reasonably safe roadstead on that choppy Atlantic coast. They do not seem to have established any base on land, unlike the Morisco corsairs who established themselves at Salé about twenty miles down the coast. They remained free from local control, however, coming and going as they pleased. In some ways, their lack of territorial control was an asset, providing cover for the English merchants who wished to buy plundered goods. Instead of buying directly from the pirates—which was strictly forbidden—the merchant Richard Grice explained in 1609 that he had purchased sugar and brazilwood from "Ben Washe, Juda Lavia, and Ben Josan three Jews merchants for the king of Barbary." The goods, he argued, were all taken out of warehouses on land, and there was no way of knowing whether they were recently brought in by the pirate Captain Franck. Similarly, Thomas Burton told the admiralty court that at Mamora he had sold guns to Moulay Sheikh of Fez (Mohammed esh Sheikh el Mamun) for ginger, sarsaparilla, and hides; it was not his fault if the Moroccan pretender had originally obtained these New World trade goods from Captain Jennings.[17]

While the pirates could launder their plunder through Moroccan intermediaries, they also traded with merchants on anchored vessels in the Mamora roadstead. One ambitious English trader set up a floating emporium, stocking a captured slave ship, the *Angola Man,* with "barley, beer, bread, beef, hats, bands, shoes, stockings, boots, doublets, breeches, shirts, aqua vitae and rosa solis, pistols, knives, cards, and other commodities" for both European pirates and "the Moors."[18] A Dutch shipmaster supplied herring, butter, bread, candles, and hats; an English resident of Seville sent a barque from Sanlucar "laden with tobacco and wine, to trade there with the said pirates"; and a Frenchman sold them "wines, munition, rapiers, daggers, pistols, and many other things."[19] Because this trade was forbidden by English law, by and large the Mamora pirates were supplied by foreigners and English expatriates, including some who had settled at Livorno under the protection of the grand duke. The renegade Robert Thornton traded with Mamora, for example, and so did William Mellin, who had fled to the pope for a pardon after sharing in the spoils from the *Hopewell*'s Muslim passengers. The more respectable of the Duppa brothers sent a flyboat from Livorno to take in sugar and spices captured by his pirate sibling.[20] Operating beyond the reach of English authorities, these traders contrived to supply the pirates with every commodity they might desire. Soon the pirates were even reported to be buying "a drug called opium" imported from Spain.[21]

The pirates' spoils were not divided as equally as would be the case in the later golden age of piracy; rather, they mimicked the ways in which privateers divided their plunder, with the lion's share going to the captain as the owner and victualler of the ship.[22] Still, for sailors, they were flush: without other investors and taxes to pay, ordinary pirates seem to have shared at least half the plunder rather than privateers' customary third. When the pirate Captain Harris took a French ship with £1,000 in plate, for example, Harris kept £300 for his share; his crew of roughly fifty-five men divided £500 between them; and the remaining £200 seems to have gone to Captain Bishop, Harris's senior partner.[23] For Edmund Morish, a merchant sailor from Munster whose ship anchored at Mamora on business, the pirate haven was practically a land of Cockaigne. Questioned about his dealings with the pirates, he confessed that he "had given him amongst the pirates forty ducats at times in regard he attended upon them, and did many base offices for them when they were drunk and disordered themselves." At seven shillings for a Barbary ducat, this amounted to £14, roughly a year's pay.[24]

Morish's account of free-flowing wine and gold at Mamora suggests that Jacobean piracy was more than a survival strategy for laborers "who were unable to make ends meet from their usual employment," more than a humdrum activity that "served to supplement irregular work and wages ashore." It is true, of course, that in their depositions captured pirates spoke not "in the bold language of protest but in the submissive speech of men desperate to save themselves from execution." At sea, however, they sounded rather different. Thomas Sockwell's quixotic claim to be king of the island of Lundy seems to have offended his fellows, but he was not the only one to proclaim himself free from royal authority.[25] When John Bracke, master of the *Golden Dragon*, met the pirate Peter Easton at Santa Cruz (now Agadir) and told him that he was forbidden to have anything to do with the pirates by royal proclamation, Easton allegedly replied: "We are all kings," swearing "by many prophane oaths that His Majesty's law should be of no force there." He then forced Bracke and his men to come on board his ship, where they "were made very drunk against their wills" before returning to the *Dragon*. Bracke's mate,

Isaac Spere, seems to have enjoyed the pirates' hospitality, for he soon became a pirate himself.[26]

Compared to other sorts of maritime labor, piracy had obvious appeal. In the "discourse on piracy" he wrote for King James I in 1618, the pardoned pirate captain Henry Mainwaring explained that sailors turned pirate because it was more attractive than the alternatives, "there being now no voyage to speak of but Newfoundland, which they hold too toilsome, that of Newcastle which many hold too base, and the East Indies which most hold dangerous and tedious, and for Your Highness' ships the entertainment is so small, and the pay so bad that they hold it a kind of slavery to serve in them."[27] If honest work was toilsome, base, dangerous, tedious, and slavish, what would-be pirates sought, it seems, was ease, honor, safety, adventure, and freedom. They would not necessarily succeed, but the rumors filtering back from Mamora must have been enticing.

As the rendezvous at Mamora became well-known among English seafarers, many found their way there. The merchant ships that visited Mamora to buy the pirates' plunder sometimes brought recruits, for example. The shipwreck survivor Thomas Baker left England in 1611 with Captain Henry Gifford, then left him at Naples and traveled to Livorno, where he signed on to a merchant ship bound for Mamora. There he joined the pirate Captain William Baugh and participated in a lucrative cruise.[28] Others came directly, like Jonas Prophett, who sold his stolen barque to a Spanish merchant and then served as shipmaster under the pirate Captain Wilkinson. Some seamen even mutinied against their officers to sail to Mamora. On an island in the West Indies in May 1613 fourteen men of the *Little John* of London were cutting wood when they decided to put their plan into action. They overpowered the master and put him on shore and then took the surgeon and a quartermaster along with them by force. The quartermaster, William Jackson, later reported that they sailed first to the Azores and then to Mamora, where he escaped. There were some thirty sail of men-of-war at Mamora when he was there, he said, all English, "unless some few Flemings were amongst them."[29]

The proximity of Mamora also tempted English sailors bound for the Mediterranean. In September 1612, John Keepus, the owner and master of the little *Tindealer* of Yarmouth hired seven sailors and sailed to Cadiz "to seek a freight," bringing his eleven-year-old son along. At Cadiz, the ship was freighted by a Bristol merchant, but when it was ready to depart, Keepus later recounted, two sailors came to his cabin "and said, they must have his ship, and he asked them what they would do with her, and they answered they would carry her to Mamora, and willed him make no disturbance for if he did, they would kill him and his child." When Keepus cried out for help, they "shut him into his cabin, and laid hold of his son insomuch that the boy cried out 'father they will kill me,'" and so he "prayed" them to free the child and "do their pleasure, which they did." Unfortunately for all of them, when they arrived at Mamora the English pirates were away, and the ship and its crew were captured by Salé corsairs. Keepus obtained his liberty after a few months, but his son, "enforced to turn Turk," did not.[30]

It was probably safer to join the pirate ships by traveling to Ireland, where the pirates typically spent part of the year. In Munster, English settlements were still being rebuilt after the devastation of the Nine Years' War. As John Appleby has shown, for the settlers in southwest Munster, where the economy centered on farming and a growing pilchard fishery, the pirates were welcome trading partners. Much of the settler community traded regularly with the pirates, exchanging meat, bread, and butter for plundered goods and money, and some pirates settled on the coast, where they maintained regular and profitable contacts with their erstwhile colleagues. Meanwhile, the officials entrusted with suppressing piracy were plied with a constant stream of gifts and bribes, and unless it happened upon a single pirate ship, the lone naval pinnace charged with patrolling the coast was generally outmanned and outgunned. Under these favorable conditions, both men and goods regularly moved between the shore and the ships. Some of the men who joined the pirates at Munster were seamen who sought them out; others were settlers "for whom the opportunities of migration remained unfulfilled," dissatisfied with life in the fledgling English plantation. In Ireland as in the New World, dreary realities clashed with colonists' hopes.[31]

Complicity and Coercion

As the pirate fleet grew, most new recruits did not travel to Mamora or Munster but were taken off other ships under intentionally murky circumstances. When Cuthbert Appleyard escaped from the pirate Captain

Heath in Ireland in 1612, he reported that most of Heath's company had been pressed into piracy:

> There were very few of the old crew of the pirates on board the said pinnace when she came into Ireland, but most of them were such as had been taken out of other ships in Newfoundland and elsewhere, for as he sayeth Matthew Pringsley taken in Newfoundland was master, Thomas Browne of London taken out of the *Daisy* was master's mate, Robert Walsingham taken out of the *Daisy* was a gentleman in the ship, Mr Legg a western man was a gentleman also in the ship, John Roope cousin to the captain was taken out of a ship in Newfoundland, George Coles taken in Newfoundland was quartermaster, and one Ambrose a trumpeter, Joseph a Londoner was gunner.

These forced pirates were often promoted to higher office. When the *Concord* was taken in 1611, for example, its mate, George Barker, became master of the vice admiral of the pirate fleet, while the common sailor Walter Bray became the *Concord*'s boatswain.[32]

In the many accounts of merchant seamen forced to become pirates, observers consistently emphasized their lack of consent. Thus when the *Gift of God* was taken by Captain Parker, Thomas Hunt lost not only his cargo of grain but also four men who were taken "against their wills, as namely Walter Prise, Philip Vaughan, Thomas Paxley, and Philip an Irishman." At Mamora, Hunt's carpenter, John Compton, was also impressed into piracy by Captain Stephenson, even though Hunt "made great means to the said Captain to have him the said Compton released . . . and the said Compton weeping on his knees desired to be discharged from the said Captain."[33] Thomas Perse reported that when his ship was captured by English pirates, they took away two men "who did intreat the pirates with weeping tears and wringing of their hands to suffer them to stay in [Perse's] ship, but the pirates by force took them and flung them into the boat and carried them away." Three men were taken off the *Marigold* by Captains Stephenson and Franck in 1611 "by force and violence," even though the men "desired them by all means and upon their knees with weeping tears" to let them go.[34] In 1613 the master of the *Vine* of London lost three men to Captain Jolliffe, who took them "against their wills." The pirate Captain John Ellis pressed "Thomas Sicklemore who was unwilling to go, but yet the pirates by force detained him and much abused him for offering to go from them," Sicklemore's former shipmaster reported. The *Mayflower* of Dover was taken in 1614 by English pirates who forced two youths "against their wills into the ship of war and carried them away although they made great lamentation and means to be spared."[35] Shipmasters consistently recounted that men were forced into piracy against their wills, and they often described the sailors kneeling and weeping, begging for their freedom.[36]

It seems implausible that pirate ships could operate effectively against the will of most of their men and officers. With a strong majority, after all, they could seize control of the ship.[37] Indeed, the ex-pirate Henry Mainwairing was adamant that the lamentations of "perforst-men" were carefully staged. The shows of force were theatrical, he claimed: "Having fetched up and commanded a ship, some of the merchants-men would come to me, or to some of my captains and officers, to tell me they were desirous to serve me, but they durst not seem willing, lest they should lose their wages . . . as also that if by any occasion they should come home to their country, or be taken by any other princes, it would be a benefit to them, and no hurt to me, to have them esteemed perforst-men." Accordingly, Mainwaring would give the merchant seamen a document attesting to their innocence and send men aboard their ships to take them away "by force." Then, on their return to England, "concealing their wealth, they offer themselves to the next officers or justices, complaining of the injury they have received in being so long detained by force."[38]

It does seem that seafaring men knew exactly how to behave if they wished to appear to have been forced to join a pirate crew. Henry Trall, master of the *Humphrey Bonaventure,* deposed in 1612 that his gunner, Henry Spring, was taken away "by force and violence" by the pirates of Easton's fleet. The following year, Trall himself was allegedly forced to become a pirate, despite begging with other sailors "upon their knees to remain in the ship."[39] A few months later at Mamora, a more cheerful Trall handed the merchant seaman John Jennings "a ducat to drink amongst his neighbours in Ratcliffe."[40] Sometimes, however, there was credible evidence of coercion. When trumpeter William Wright's ship was captured by the pirate Captain Stephenson and he heard that Stephenson needed a trumpeter, Wright allegedly hid his trumpet and asked his fellow sailors to deny that there was one on board. Nonetheless, rifling through the ship, the pirates found the trumpet, "by threats" discovered that it belonged to Wright, and compelled him to join them—though not before he wrote to his wife explaining his detention. After a lengthy voyage with the pirates, Wright arrived in Ireland and "escaped away . . . into the mountains where he lay eight days close fearing to be pursued," before boarding a barque bound for England. Corroborating his story, a Dutch sailor who was held by the pirates for a few weeks before being set ashore in Ireland reported that Stephenson forbade Wright to go ashore, and that the trumpeter "greatly lamented and for grief was sick and refused his meat."[41]

The only way to tell if someone had genuinely been forced, Mainwaring claimed, was to see whether he had received any shares or pillage: anyone who had was "absolutely as willing and as guilty as is the commander."[42] This was a strict measure and probably not one that would have been accepted by most seamen. There was nothing unusual in being forced into maritime service: naval impressment was a fact of life, and even foreign rulers sometimes impressed English sailors. No one would have suggested that a pressed seaman should refuse his wages, and few "perforst" pirates seem to have rejected their shares of plunder. The otherwise respectable Thomas Digby had every intention of keeping his, for example. Before being taken by the Dutch pirate Captain Pecke in 1612, Digby had been employed for six years by the North Virginia Company, most recently as the master of the *Rainbow* of Topsham. Carried to Mamora, Digby left the Dutch ship and "got entertainment with Captain Baugh to come for Ireland." Baugh had negotiated a pardon that would allow him to keep his plunder, and even on the way to Ireland to surrender he assiduously amassed more gains. Serving as a navigator in Baugh's fleet, Digby helped take three Dutch ships, three French ships, and one from Hamburg, laden with sugar, pepper, sweetmeats, linen, hollands, silk garters, copper, silks, damasks, and more. In Ireland, when a dispute arose about the division of the spoils, Digby blandly declared that he expected "his shares of such goods as he was at the taking of, according to His Majesty's gracious grant."[43]

When pirates captured their ships, then, merchant sailors wrung their hands, fell to their knees, wept, and pleaded to be set free—some sincerely, others not. The resulting uncertainty about the culpability of "perforst men" gave valuable cover to seamen who wished to join the pirates. What is most remarkable about this practice is that the shipmasters who lost their sailors to pirates rarely betrayed a hint of a doubt about their innocence. Instead, when giving evidence in court, they seem to have done their best to ensure that the sailors in question would be able to collect their wages and avoid hanging once they returned to England.

Shipmasters' unwillingness to incriminate their men was part of a larger pattern of friendship and familiarity between English merchant sailors and English pirates, a pattern that perturbed merchants who lost their goods. The shipmaster Thomas Hunt was even prosecuted in the High Court of Admiralty for his excessively friendly relations with pirates. With a crew of eleven and three passengers, Hunt's *Gift of God* was bound from Lisbon for the Spanish enclave Ceuta on the North African coast with grain in early 1610 when it was attacked by a large pirate ship under the command of John Parker. As Hunt and his men deposed, the *Gift* was completely outmatched, and after attempting to flee and making a token attempt at resistance, they surrendered. They were carried to Mamora, where the pirates sold the ship's grain to the "Moors" but left Hunt some lead, timber, pickaxes, and other things. They kept them, in all, for eleven weeks, during which time—the despoiled merchants alleged—the *Gift*'s men ate, drank, and made merry with the English pirates.[44]

Called into question for this unseemly conviviality, the sailors argued that there was nothing unusual or blameworthy in fraternizing with pirates after capture. As Hunt's mate, John Harman, explained: "All men that are taken by pirates when they are once in subjection and under their command do eat and drink with the pirates and do anything else that they will appoint them to please them in hope to free themselves from them neither doth it stand with reason that they should refuse so to do when they are in the nature of slaves to them and not at their own disposition." Two veteran shipmasters concurred. The elderly Thomas Milton deposed: "It is the custom amongst English pirates at sea that after they have taken English men or of any other nation although they do fight with them or resist them to the uttermost of their power, yet if they have once them under their subjection they will use them kindly and eat and drink together neither can the eating and making merry of together of the pirates and them that be taken be justly said to be a sign that they that are taken did yield willingly." Robert Rickman, who had faced a similar suit six years before and was now master of Trinity House, agreed that Hunt and his men had done nothing wrong.[45]

One could not expect eleven men to fend off well-armed pirates or to starve themselves out of principle. Still, the personal and professional ties between English merchant seamen and pirates raised suspicions in some quarters. In 1613 after the *Bennett* of Bristol was captured by Captain Lambard in the *Commongain*, the *Bennett*'s owner, William Jay, was so highly suspected of colluding with the pirates that he himself was arraigned for piracy. He may well have been innocent, but there was a marked difference between the pirates' warm familiarity with the seafaring men and the businesslike rapacity of their dealings with the passengers. As Jay deposed in court, he was preparing to fight and encouraging the passengers to do the same when the pirate captain "willed [him] and the rest to be of good cheer, they were all friends." Indeed, they knew each other well: Lambard had been apprenticed to the *Bennett*'s master, John Grace, before running away some time before. Jay affirmed that "he would rather die than lose his barque," but the pirate reassured him: "Come on board with quietness, and I will not diminish a hair of thy head." He would only, Lambard continued, take Jay's arms and powder, and would do so even "if [Jay] were his father, for that he needed it," offering iron in exchange. Lambard took a harder line, however, where the passengers were concerned, robbing them of their possessions.[46]

Some pirates felt more kinship with merchant seamen than others, of course. After the *Gift of God* finally left Mamora in 1610, Thomas Hunt was sailing toward La Rochelle in search of a new freight when the ship was attacked and captured once again, this time by Peter Easton. The merchant sailors seem to have asked Easton to let them go unharmed because they were his countrymen, but they only succeeded in angering him. Easton "ducked two of the company at the yard's arm, and otherwise used them with great cruelty for that they were loath to be spoiled of such things as they had," and told them, shockingly, "to tell the merchants on the Exchange that he would be a scourge to Englishmen saying he had no English blood in his belly, and therefore esteemed Englishmen no other than as Turks and Jews." Whereas Parker and his men had only taken the *Gift*'s cargo, respecting the seamen's own possessions, Easton robbed the mariners as well, "spoiling the company of all they had," even "their apparel from their backs," as well as ship's provisions that were important to their safety, such as "all their powder and shot, a mainsail, a piece of ordnance and some rigging."[47] English merchant sailors were more used to receiving this kind of treatment from Dutch pirates, who, they complained, sometimes tortured English captives or forced them onto their ships, where they were "made slaves and compelled to do the drudgery of the ships" without any pay or shares.[48] English pirates who showed no care for their compatriots violated an emerging convention. When Michael Duppa captured John Jennings's ship the *Margaret,* he left it in the sea with only three men on board, so that Jennings only got to land at Sanlucar "by God's mercy." Other English pirates seemingly disapproved of this behavior: when Jennings then sailed to Mamora on business, the pirate shipmaster John Prise of Ratcliffe passed the hat for him. "Pitying [his] misery being spoiled . . . of all that he had, [Prise] made a gathering amongst his company for some relief to buy [him] clothes, and got eight pieces of gold, whereof six were worth eight shillings apiece and the other two, two shillings apiece."[49]

Pragmatic cooperation with pirates shaded into criminality when English sailors helped the pirates commit their spoils. When James Gentleman and his crew raided the Westman Islands near Iceland, for example, he commandeered the aid of English fishermen. At first, when the pirate ships *Tiger* and *Amy* sailed into view, Richard Hall, the master of a Harwich fishing ship, took fright, thinking they were "Biscayners"— Basque fishing rivals. He sent his boat to shore with his crew's clothes for safekeeping but soon perceived his error. "Finding the pirates were Englishmen, and thinking they would not take their clothes from them," one of the fishermen went back to fetch them.[50] Gentleman then asked Hall to help the pirate ships into the harbor. Hall allegedly begged "for the passion of Christ" to be let off, arguing that "it were better for them to make spoil of half Spain, than that beggarly island, and that more trouble and mischief would come of it," but to no avail: Gentleman insisted that he would spoil the island, because "the year before his men were put on shore there and beaten and misused by the people." In the end, Hall gave in and towed the *Amy* up to two Danish ships in the harbor. The pirates, who were almost all English, but had a few Dutchmen in their ranks as well as a Welshman, an Irishman, "one Hammond a Turk," and "two Moors Simon and Francisco," took the Danish ships and ravaged the village for two weeks. According to a Danish witness, they "brake open the churches," stealing their ornaments and even their bells, broke open the king's storehouses, plundered people's houses, slaughtered oxen and sheep, "and ravished many women and virgins." Hall allegedly took a generous share: the Dane reported that the pirates loaded so much into his boat that the fishing master "willed them put no more, for that the boat was full and could carry no more."[51]

Henry Marsh, who had been master of the *Amy* before it was taken by the *Tiger*, was also accused of piracy despite claiming to have been coerced. The Danish shipmaster said that as far as he could tell, Marsh was not a prisoner of the pirates: instead, "they were very merry together drinking of healths and shooting of ordnance when they drank, and when they ransacked the warehouses and houses on land the said Marsh was present, and as busy as any of the rest." Cordial relations between the pirates and other English fishermen were sometimes strengthened by close personal ties. The master of the *Solomon* of Harwich, who arrived when the pirates were ransacking Vestmannaeyjar, was married to the pirate Thomas King's sister, for example. Naturally enough, "some of his men in their boat came ashore . . . and were drinking with the pirates in the storehouses, and very familiar with them."[52]

In exchange for being well treated by English pirates, English fishermen and merchant sailors helped the pirates maintain ties with their friends and families at home, serving as conduits of information and goods. When the fisherman Richard Hall returned to Harwich, he carried gifts for the pirates' relations: William Drakewood of Harwich sent a featherbed for his wife, and John Grant of Lee, boatswain's mate of the *Amy*, sent two pieces of Barbary gold and a Jacobus for his widowed mother. When Michael Rochester, master of the *Susan Constance*, met Captain Duppa near Mamora, Duppa gave him twenty ducats to bring home for his wife, and five more from the master's mate, Leonard Johnson, for Johnson's wife. Simon Tuching, master's mate of the *Margaret*, received "one ducat of Richard Brian of Limehouse . . . for a token for his wife" at Mamora, and nine more from John Adams of

Limehouse. Adams had been "a slave with the Moors and redeemed by the said Brian," and he sent the money, which he had borrowed from his new pirate colleagues, "to relieve his wife and children." The *Margaret's* master also carried home a ducat for the wife of Edmund Clifton, the pirate master of the *Ambition,* and ten ducats for John Prise's wife.[53] Pirates' wives considered these sums their due. When Anne Sayers received a note telling her that her husband, William (a pirate with Jonas Prophett), had sent her thirty pounds from Mamora, she went to collect it from "one Mr Fynne at Wapping" but was told that the money had been put in the Lord Admiral's hands. Backed up by her neighbors, and suspecting that Fynne still had the money, she boldly petitioned the Lord Admiral for a warrant.[54]

Their familiarity served the interests of English pirates and merchant seamen alike: fighting was a dangerous business; sailors hated to lose their clothes and trade goods; and the pirates wished to avoid angering witnesses who might give evidence against them later. Convinced that collusion was widespread, the author of one printed account even argued that upon taking ships, a pirate captain usually "demands forthwith for their bills of lading, whereby he knows what belongs to the merchant, and what to the mariners, when the merchant's venture is always taken for lawful prize, but the sailors' goods are most commonly restored, and this bill doth the pirate captain most carefully keep and lay up . . . for their own discharge."[55] This parody of prize law was a fiction, but it is true that even when shipmasters did give evidence against English pirates, they tended to be reluctant to name men who were not already in custody. When Anthony Wye, master of the *Susan* of Bristol, was asked for the names of the pirates who had plundered his ship, he said only that "there was one Longcastle and other called Cade the rest of their names [he] doth not remember but they were in all some sixty-seven persons." Given that Wye had spent a festive evening and morning with the officers of the *Ulysses* before they seized his ship and that he even remembered the precise size of the pirate crew, this forgetfulness seems remarkable. The fact that the pirates had left him a large amount of sugar to compensate for his lost freight surely contributed to it. Convicted pirates were just as loath to provide evidence about their absent colleagues. Telling his story while awaiting execution, Captain James Harris named only those four men who had been tried with him, explaining that as to the rest, "in hope they may live to do their king and country better service, I hope no indifferent man will condemn me for concealing their names." English authorities seeking to separate the sheep from the goats faced a wall of silence and willful ignorance.[56]

A Nation Abroad

In his classic history of early English piracy, C. M. Senior emphasized the rough patriotism and anti-Spanish fervor of these Atlantic pirates, writing that they "acted as though the Elizabethan war had never ended, concentrating their attacks against the Spaniards, and showing favour to British vessels which fell into their hands." They were very different, in his view, from the Mediterranean renegades "who renounced their country and their religion and who treated English vessels no differently from those of any other nation."[57] For Senior, these hardy Protestant seamen were the irregulars of English expansion, men who abided by the spirit of empire if not the law, and they were epitomized by the gentleman pirate Henry Mainwaring, who devoted himself in later life to the Royal Navy. In fact, however, there was substantial overlap between the Atlantic pirates and those who operated in the Mediterranean in the first years after the war. Explicit evidence of anti-Spanish feeling is difficult to find in the records, and there appear to have been no pirates who limited their depredations to Iberian ships: Dutch and French shipping suffered heavily at their hands, while some attacked English, Scottish, and Irish shipping as well. Mainwaring did indeed treat British and Irish merchants with ostentatious respect, but his crew was less enthusiastic. When Mainwaring took a Lübeck ship laden with goods belonging to Irishmen, for example, he dealt "royally" with the merchants' factor, to the dismay of some of his men, who were heard to "complain and grudge" that so much had been given away "before the goods were shared."[58]

In the early seventeenth century, however, English Atlantic piracy did have a strong national character. For a mixture of pragmatic and cultural reasons, the pirates tended to treat their countrymen well. They did, at times, compensate English merchants for their losses: when Easton's fleet captured the *Phoenix* off Senegal in 1612, for example, he gave Edward

Brimstead, the captain of the Guinea-bound merchantman, a captured Dutch vessel "with her furniture and eight hundred Guinea hides" worth more than £400 in exchange for beer, food, aqua vitae, gunpowder, ordnance, and other supplies.⁵⁹ Easton may have reconsidered his earlier aggression toward Englishmen because he was hoping for a pardon, as others loudly trumpeted their affection for Englishmen when they were ready to retire. When the English merchantman *Friendship* of London was at anchor at Mogador Island, and the pirate Captain Hughes arrived with three ships, Hughes sent word "they should not fear any wrong from him for that he never intended to do the least injury unto any of his countrymen," allegedly much to the irritation of his own shipmaster, who was Dutch. A little later, when Hughes feared that the Dutch pirate Captain Peter Pecke would take the *Friendship*, he made Pecke swear—in the presence of the *Friendship*'s cape merchant—"never thereafter [to] take any English ship or goods nor wrong any of the King of England his subjects," warmly "declaring his love and honest care of his countrymen's welfare." He even gave the *Friendship* some much-needed victuals. Not coincidentally, Hughes complained to the merchant "of a weariness of those courses, and professed much desire of His Majesty's pardon."⁶⁰

Hughes's devotion to his countrymen had a cynical side, but the hostility that grew up between the English and Dutch pirates was real, cemented by cycles of aggression and retaliation.⁶¹ In 1610, there had been "a great mutiny betwixt the Englishmen and the Flemings" at Mamora, and the English pirates had evicted the Dutch Captain John from his man-of-war and prize ship, selling "all the sugar and ginger" to a merchant from Marseille. Then in early 1611 or so, a serious battle took place, allegedly sparked by Dutch torture. According to an English gunner, the Dutch captains Stoute, Drinkwater, and Jacques had at one time captured the ship of the English pirate Captain Franck, "and spoiled him of all his wealth, and also burned his fingers' ends off, and tormented him otherwise by the privy members, and many others of his company in most cruel manner as it was reported." In retaliation, the captains Franck, Hussey, Plumley, Parker, and Baugh with their companies attacked the Dutch ships in a "most desperate" battle that lasted three days. Stoute was killed and his ships sunk; Jacques too was killed, but Drinkwater escaped. On the English side, Parker, Hussey, Plumley, "and many others of their company were slain."[62] In James's reign, only battles in the East Indies matched this scale of English naval violence.

As hostility became entrenched, English pirates frequently "rescued" English merchant ships from Dutch pirates, and weaker Dutch pirate ships came to avoid the English pirate fleets as much as possible, which made it hard for them to access the entrepôt at Mamora.[63] When the Pecke brothers from Rotterdam captured the *Hart* of Dover at Safi in December 1611, they treated the Englishmen roughly, torturing them "with burning matches between their fingers" to find out where the gold on board was hidden. The Dutch pirates took the gold, the *Hart*'s remaining trade goods, and a few captive seamen with them. Soon thereafter, they sailed to Mamora, "where finding many English ships [they] durst not go in," according to one of the English captives. After waiting vainly for the English ships to leave, for want of food the Pecke brothers were obliged to bring their ships into the roadstead. Their fears of English aggression were soon realized: the English captains Baugh, Mellington, and Brooke came on board, saw the captive Richard Beaumont, and listened to his story. Beaumont "desired them to free him from the said Flemings," and they did, attacking the Dutch ships in the night a few days later and setting all the Dutch pirates on shore. The English pirates kept the goods and money, while Beaumont soon found passage to Livorno and thence to England. Similarly, in late 1611 or early 1612, when Peter Pecke took a Spanish prize and sent it to Mamora, a number of English pirate ships were there along with John Luck, the aggrieved master of the *Love*—which Pecke had previously captured and plundered—and the Englishmen took "the said Spanish ships and goods from the Dutchmen . . . and shared the goods amongst them."[64]

While Senior suggests that the English Atlantic pirates were motivated in part by rough patriotism, it probably makes more sense to think about "patriotism" as an effect rather than a cause of piracy. By maintaining amicable relations with their law-abiding countrymen, the English pirates avoided unnecessary violence and obtained much-needed supplies, while also making it easier, safer, and more profitable for sailors to move in and out of piracy. When English pirates prevented Dutch pirates from attacking English shipping, "rescued" captured English ships, and excluded the Dutch from Mamora, they smoothed their own prospective reentry into law-abiding English society while also enriching themselves at their rivals' expense. Cooperation along national lines helped English pirates to survive and profit: even in this outlaw community, nationhood mattered.

Geographies of Piracy

In 1613, almost two years after being pressed into piracy, George Isaack of the *Concord* finally returned home and recounted his movements to the admiralty court, providing a striking picture of the Atlantic range of one pirate fleet. After the *Concord* was captured, Isaack said, he was put onto the *Swan*. Spending a few months on the coast of Spain, the *Swan* took a Hamburg ship laden with sugar from the Canary Islands. The pirates sold the sugar at Safi and then made the prize, the *Falcon*, into another man-of-war. Then, hearing that their leader, Peter Easton, was at Agadir with more ships, the *Swan* and the *Falcon* went to meet him. All the ships in the fleet sailed to Lanzarote, one of the Canaries, where they took a ship belonging to the magnate Filippo Bernardi. They also took a French ship bound for the West Indies and sailed to "Lacatatho road" in West Africa, where they captured a Flemish ship. They sailed briefly to "Riadora" to trim one of their ships, then to Cabo Blanco on the border between present-day Mauritania and Western Sahara, where they took some Portuguese or Spanish fishing boats and the Dutch *Jacob*, homeward bound from Guinea with hides and ivory. They kept the *Jacob* and made it into another man-of-war. They also captured the fort at Cabo Blanco but found nothing besides "bread and water and some ordnance." Then the ships in the fleet sailed to the mouth of the Senegal River, where they took two English ships, keeping the *Willing Mind* of Fowey. After these depredations on the coast of West Africa, the pirates sailed to the Cape Verde Islands to refresh and rest themselves, and to take in water. The unserviceable *Swan* and another ship were burned at Brava, and Isaack was transferred onto the *Jacob*.[65]

At this point, the fleet may still have had too many ships relative to men, but the pirates knew where to find recruits and victuals. They sailed across the Atlantic to Newfoundland, "where they took many ships, and spoiled them of their victuals and some ordnance," also pressing about one hundred fishermen into service. Easton and his fleet stayed for a while at Harbour Grace, where they built a fort for their security and compelled the carpenters of the fishing ships to repair and trim their vessels. Easton took on airs, going around with a "guard and a noise of trumpets and his set of viols." The fleet also took and kept two Basque ships, the *Lion Doré* and one other. Isaack moved from the *Jacob* back to his old ship, the *Concord*.[66]

In Newfoundland, the pirate fleet began to lose some of its coherence. Captain Harvey took a Washford ship and sailed for England with other pirates who were anxious to return home, while another pirate ship was captured by the Newfoundland fishermen. After further depredations, the remaining fleet sailed for Flores in the Azores; there another pirate ship split off and sailed for Ireland to find out whether James would grant Easton and the rest a pardon. The bulk of the fleet continued on to the coast of Spain, then to Fedala (Mohammedia) and Mamora in Morocco. At Mamora, the ships found "two Moors men-of-war" with a captured Brazilman and sank them, "the Moors swimming ashore." Finally, the fleet sailed into the Mediterranean, taking a Hamburg ship with almonds and soap, the *Thomasine* of London with currants, and an Amsterdam vessel with muscadel wine. With these last prizes, the fleet continued on to Villefranche, "where the said Easton had protection from the Duke of Savoy to dispose of his goods." Easton settled permanently in Savoy, but most of the other pirates did not, including George Isaack, who finally obtained leave to return home.[67]

English pirate ships regularly cruised along the West African coast, intercepting English and Dutch merchant ships, Portuguese fishing vessels, and the occasional slave ship from Angola. On the coast of Spain they plundered ships carrying wine and sugar from the Canary Islands and Madeira, Brazilmen returning with sugar and dyewood, and Spanish ships with West Indian hides. Further north, Ireland was conveniently located close to the major shipping routes along the western European coast. Newfoundland—a rich seasonal source of victuals and men—was just across the Atlantic. Remarkably, the only parts of the Atlantic maritime world the English pirate ships seem to have avoided were those now most associated with piracy: the West Indies and the coasts of Central and South America, the world "beyond the line."

The Mamora pirates' aversion to the West Indies stands in dramatic contrast to the picture of early Stuart piracy that Atlantic historians have provided in recent years. Tracing the trajectories of the first enslaved Africans to arrive at the English plantations, Linda Heywood and John Thornton have shown that these captives were taken by English and Dutch pirates from Portuguese and Spanish slave ships, and Mark Hanna argues that early seventeenth-century English piracy was closely tied to colonization in the West Indies and Virginia as well as Ireland. There were indeed some piratical English voyages in the Caribbean during this period, but they were mostly instigated by the colonial investor Robert Rich, second Earl of Warwick. These pirate slave traders are rightly remembered for their introduction of slavery to Virginia and Bermuda, but theirs was not the popular piracy of common seamen.[68] For most pirates, the West Indies were distinctly unattractive. A rare visitor, Captain Tibault Saxbridge sailed there on the *Phoenix,* but he and his men found food hard to come by, and after their boat was "betrayed and eight of their men slain by the Spaniards," the starving survivors fled to Newfoundland.[69] Capture by Spanish authorities was likely to result in immediate execution. A pirate ship that set out from Bermuda soon encountered disaster, according to Richard Norwood, who surveyed the island for the Somers Isles Company: "Afterwards roving at sea, they were driven to great extremity and at last, as I have heard, taken by the Spaniards who hanged up divers of them, and what became of the rest I know not for I could scarce ever hear of any of them that returned either to the Summer Islands or into England." With both Virginia and Bermuda chronically ill-supplied in the early years, pirates there were far from reliable sources of provisions, and colonial governors sometimes seized their plunder and arrested them.[70]

Rather than fleeing *to* the West Indies, sailors were more likely to do the reverse, like the wood-cutting mutineers of the *Little John* who sailed to Mamora. Such seamen were by and large uninterested in the slave trade, which was dangerous and cumbersome for slave ship sailors. Indeed, even in the small community of English sailors who cut wood and traded with indigenous people in the Caribbean, seamen seem to have been unaware of or indifferent to the colonies' appetite for slave labor. In one notable case, even after taking on stranded Africans, they kept their distance from Virginia and Bermuda. In 1614 at St. Vincent, the *John* of Sandwich took on a group of Angolans who had been on the island for seven years after their slave ship had been wrecked there, suffering—according to one of them, a baptized Christian—"under the tyranny of the savage people [the Caribs] who did kill many of them and knocked the children of the Negro women on the head so soon as they are born" to keep their numbers in check. The sailors' motives in taking these shipwrecked Angolans on board may not have been pure, but rather than carrying their passengers to the English colonies or the slave markets of the Mediterranean, they sailed to England, where the Spanish ambassador promptly claimed the hapless Angolans as Spanish property.[71]

The Jacobean Atlantic pirates' sensible avoidance of the West Indies probably accounts for the fact that they have been almost entirely forgotten. A recent survey of early modern piracy passes over them in silence, suggesting that the number of English pirates dwindled after 1604, although "they would later return to prominence among the late-seventeenth-century buccaneers." Hanna's account of English piracy and empire ignores them as well, except for briefly discussing the pirates' trade with colonists at Munster, drawing them into an account of "piratical colonization"; he assumes that the Munster pirates were a community separate from what he terms the "African marauders" of Mamora.[72] Yet trade off the Irish coast was only a part of the Atlantic pirates' activities: plunder was better vented in Mamora, close to the commercial Mediterranean, than in the tiny fishing and farming communities in Munster.[73] English pirates needed access to markets, but they did not need for those markets to be English.

The Mamora pirates' Atlantic was not one of westward settlement, slave plantations, or Protestant expansion. Instead, it was an ocean of trade and plunder, centered on the western coasts of Europe and Africa, and tied to Jewish and Muslim traders in Morocco and to the cosmopolitan trading world of the Mediterranean. There was no need for the pirates to expose themselves to the hazards of the West Indies when Iberian ships carrying colonial goods sailed faithfully to Seville and Lisbon. Piracy, for these seamen, was not an aid to the imperial projects of Rich and his partners but a means of enjoying independence and fortune before discreetly returning home. Building on knowledge, practices, and skills gained in previous years, the pirates created an imperial project of their own, one that reflected their priorities and existed almost entirely at sea.

Coda: Serving the "Turks"

For all its great numbers, this pirate community was short-lived: its depredations were intolerable, and Mamora was indefensible. In 1614, both
the Dutch Republic and Spain sent naval expeditions to dislodge the pirates and seize the town. When the English envoy John Harrison warned
his "dear compatriots" of the Dutch plans, urging them to flee and save
their lives, most of the English pirates seem to have complied.[74] Disaster
awaited the fifteen pirate ships that remained hemmed in by Dutch warships when a more powerful Spanish fleet arrived in force soon afterward.
According to a Spanish report, these pirates refused to surrender, killed
some of the men sent to treat with them, and were forced on shore,
where "the Moors did by and by set upon the said pirates and robbed
and spoiled them most cruelly."[75] The pirate experiment was over.

The loss of Mamora to Spanish forces stripped the surviving English
pirates of their independence, and many sought pardons in England,
resuming work in merchant shipping and naval service or settling on
land. Others prolonged their predatory careers by serving the Dukes
of Tuscany and Savoy or making their way to Algiers, Tunis, and Salé.[76]
These found that their relations with their countrymen took a sour turn.
By interest and by inclination, the Mamora pirates had treated English
merchant seamen relatively gently, but now that they answered to local ar-
matori and sailed with mostly foreign fighters, that changed. Some of the
free Englishmen on North African ships hoped to preserve friendly relations with captured English sailors, but others thought that trying to preserve such relations was futile. When the *Susan Constance* was attacked in
1615 by six Algiers ships, five of which were commanded by Captains
Walsingham, Haggerston, Clerck, Kelly, and Brown, the *Susan*'s sailors
were defeated and stripped of their clothes. In a sympathetic gesture,
Captain Haggerston "made a motion to his company to make a gathering
for them to buy them some clothes to cover their bodies," but he met with
a mixed response. One of the corsairs, a gunner's mate named Nicholas
Thompson who "was generally reported to be a voluntary man among
the said pirates," grumbled: "Shall we give money to them that will hang
us when we come home?" About a month later, when Thompson had returned to England, one of the *Susan*'s sailors was indeed only too eager to

hang him, telling the court with bitter precision that Thompson was "a short man with a little black beard," resident in Ratcliffe, and that he was infected with the French pox.[77]

English merchant sailors had good reason to fear the pirates who entered service in North Africa. There the refugees from Mamora joined old renegades, helping the corsairs set out sailing ships and making them even more formidable adversaries. Thus the *Dolphin*, a powerful ship manned by thirty-six men and two boys, was attacked by a fleet of five "Turks men-of-war" in 1617—not galleys, like those that assailed Rickman eight years before, but sailing ships. After preparing for battle, one of the *Dolphin*'s company recounted, "we went to prayer, and so to dinner, where our master gave us such noble encouragement, that our hearts ever thirsted to prove the success." The men defied the attackers with swords, trumpets, and ordnance, and a fierce battle began. Twice they were boarded but repelled the assailants with muskets and the breech-loading swivel guns called murderers, "choosing rather to die, than to yield, as it is still the nature and condition of all Englishmen." Again the pirates boarded, and this time the *Dolphin* was saved only by catching fire: thinking the ship would sink, the corsairs left. The company had lost "six men and a boy . . . killed outright," and another nine were wounded. The battle had proved the "magnanimity and worthy resolution of this our English nation," according to the author of a boastful printed account. Some of the "English nation" had fought on the other side, however: three of the "Turk" ships had been commanded by Captains Walsingham, Kelly, and Sampson.[78]

As with Ward's pirates before them, these English corsairs did not always stay long in North Africa. In 1618, for example, Robert Walsingham sailed to Ireland and submitted to the king. After he surrendered, he claimed to have commanded "Turk" warships under duress. When he first arrived at Algiers, he related, "the Turks kept him there by the space of six months and then sent him out to sea again and enforced him to carry Turks in his ship." He returned to Algiers with the *Susan Constance* and a Flemish prize, then sailed to Tunis, where again "the Turks took his ship from him and he stayed on shore by the space of a twelve months" before being sent out on a cruise. He put into Algiers for water, and while the men went to take in provisions, a fugitive named Mustafa helped him take in water and set sail for Ireland, Walsingham said. Others told simi-lar tales of coercion. Whether these men were more reluctant to attack their compatriots or more embittered by their subordination to foreign masters is hard to say.[79]

Some old Mamora pirates built more permanent lives in North Africa. Arthur Drake of Plymouth, a pirate since 1604, worked with Captain Gilbert Roope in 1608. After the loss of Mamora, he seems to have moved just down the coast to Salé: in 1625, Drake reportedly served as a pilot helping slavers navigate the waters of the West Country, his former home, where they preyed on English fishermen. Perhaps he had old scores to settle; perhaps he simply sought out advancement where he could find it. He left no record either way.[80] At least one old pirate who remained in Morocco took a more peaceful path. Samuel Cade had been a corsair with Ward, a piratical smuggling captain, and a partner with Captain Collins at Mamora. After the loss of Mamora, Cade ended up "in the court of a certain prince of Barbary called Sidi Ali, where never a Christian lived before." Having "obtain[ed] the love of the prince and people," by 1621 he had become a broker between Ali and a London merchant, spinning his personal ties into wealth and respectability. Petitioning the Privy Council in 1623 about a commercial dispute, Cade styled himself a gentleman, with no mention of his former life.[81]

CHAPTER FIVE

SAILORS AND THE COMPANY-STATE

When the East India Company fleet set sail from the Downs in April 1611, its men must have contemplated the voyage ahead with mixed emotions. For the *Clove*'s master carpenter, Richard Frobisher, it was his first to the Indian Ocean and his greatest office yet; heavy responsibility lay on his shoulders. In contrast, the *Hector*'s gunner's mate, Christopher Evans, was returning to waters where he had a long history. Some years earlier, Evans had been taken prisoner while smuggling on behalf of London merchants in the West Indies. According to hostile rumor, "he and one Muffett, being in the *Mayflower* . . . had betrayed their pinnace to the Spaniards there, and all the men instantly was put to the sword, all but them two." Evans and Muffett had been put in the galleys in the Philippines, "where they remained a long time" before Evans somehow returned to England. In reality, Evans was more likely a survivor of one of the surprise attacks on the *Mayflower*'s pinnaces than a deliberate traitor, but his behavior in the East India fleet did raise serious doubts about his loyalty to English mercantile interests.[1] As the *Clove* continued its journey, he would become a thorn in the side of the commander of the fleet, Captain John Saris.

Evans first came to Saris's attention in January 1612, when the fleet was frustrated by contrary winds and currents on the eastern coast of Africa, causing water to run low and tempers to rise. Several of the *Hector*'s men were rebuked for "great gaming at dice, five and six shillings a throw not only to the evil example of others, but to the beggaring of themselves." When the two ringleaders were set in the bilboes, they "accused Evans, gunner's mate, to be the enticer of them." Saris spoke sternly to all the gamblers, and they promised to reform. By March, desertion was in the air: many sailors on the *Hector* were unhappy with their rations and, the captain recorded, had "vowed to run away at the first port we should anchor at." Questioned by Saris, they asserted their innocence and promised "to be hereafter more honest."[2] In the Red Sea in April, however, twenty-one men did run away with the longboat, presumably intending to enter Ottoman service. They were speedily captured, and their two leaders, one of whom was Evans, were put in the bilboes on Saris's own ship, the *Clove*.[3] This crisis strained Saris's authority, especially after the *Hector*'s master, Thomas Fuller, made it clear that his sympathies lay with the mutineers, but the commander resolved the situation by transferring Fuller to a different fleet and keeping Evans on the *Clove*, away from his erstwhile accomplices.

When the *Clove* left the other English ships at Banten in January 1613 to sail for Japan, Evans was still on board. He enjoyed the port city of Hirado, "making a common practice of going ashore and lying out of the ship without leave, and in most lewd fashion spending his time in base bawdy places, denying to come aboard." Punished again with the bilboes, he swore to be avenged, and Saris even feared that "he might blow up the ship." At this point, the officers and the chief merchant told Saris what they knew of Evans's past. His history gave Saris pause, but two days later, after he had apologized, Evans was released.[4] He did another brief stint in the bilboes the following month for staying on shore overnight without leave, "but after prayer released, promising amendment; yet before we had dined [Evans] went ashore again without leave," Saris reported; the gunner's mate then fraternized against orders with Spanish and Portuguese sailors from Nagasaki, earning more punishment. In early August he and a carpenter were suspected of corresponding with the Portuguese in order to run away. After a search, they were found on shore with "their whores"; Evans baldly explained that "he was a man, and would have a woman if he could get her." By September, his unruly behavior had spread: many of the ship's company were sleeping on shore and getting drunk with Japanese women, quarreling with one another and even dueling.[5]

On October 2, 1613, Evans and six other men fled for good with the ship's skiff. Furious, the cape merchant Richard Cocks asked for Japanese help to capture the runaways, "either alive or dead." A few days later, the skiff was recovered, but the fugitives had taken refuge in sanctuary "in the papist churches" in Nagasaki, and to get the governor to help extract them, Cocks had to offer a present and promise that he would forgive the deserters.[6] Even this limited victory was to be denied him. Conflicting stories filtered back from Nagasaki—the fugitives had sailed for Macao, they were being hidden in Nagasaki by the friars, by local people, they had sailed for Manila—but the runaway Englishmen never returned. Nothing further is known of Evans. In England, his father petitioned to be accorded the deserter's wages but was denied, although the East India Company did grant him forty shillings out of charity.[7]

What are we to make of Christopher Evans? Traveling the globe from the West Indies to the East, he crossed national boundaries with ease, aided by his possession of skills that would have made him as welcome in an Ottoman port as in the Philippines. We might even call him cosmopolitan, judging from his willingness to serve the Ottoman Empire, his taste for low Japanese society, his fluency in Spanish, and his final flight to Portuguese service. In any case, Evans and his disaffected companions posed a challenge to governance on East India Company ships. Accustomed to thinking of ships as places of rigid hierarchy, we might be surprised by Saris's willingness to forgive miscreants over and over after mild punishments: he never seems to have flogged any of his men, despite the fact that he had a commission of martial law in hand. Yet the Company's Court of Governors considered Saris a harsh disciplinarian, one who carried "a strict hand" over his "unruly company."[8] His plight is a useful illustration of the practical limitations of maritime corporate sovereignty.

As Philip Stern has argued, from the beginning the East India Company was a body politic that claimed jurisdiction over English trade and English subjects in the Indian Ocean. It behaved like a state and had a "coherent, if composite, set of political ideas about the duties of subjects and rulers." For the later seventeenth-century and eighteenth-century Company, the relation between the corporation and its subjects was to be a mutually beneficial but top-down system in which the Company provided safety and good governance, while its subjects reciprocated with loyalty, service, and taxes. This vision of corporate rule was easier to describe than to institute, however. Stern readily acknowledges that in its territorial possessions the Company struggled to make its polyglot, multiethnic subjects embrace its views. They were rarely as loyal and obedient as might have been wished, and the Company balanced different castes and groups against one another to avoid challenges to its authority.[9]

Corporate sovereignty presented other challenges in the earliest years of the Company, when the vast majority of its "subjects" were English seamen. How could it elicit their allegiance? By the end of the seventeenth century, the Company hoped to "cultivate safe, populous, thriving, productive, and even virtuous colonies and colonists," expecting "its subjects in turn to return the favor through loyalty, duty, and service."[10] In its early years, however, circumstances made this an unlikely model of corporate rule. Sailors were not blank slates; they came to the Company with expectations developed on English privateers, merchantmen, and pirate ships as well as in foreign service. They had their own ideas about what loyalty they owed, and to whom. Moreover, the daunting conditions Company factors and seamen faced in the early years of the seventeenth century kept safety well out of reach, and their position in Asia was tenuous. Lacking much coercive power, their safety on land and ability to trade depended on the tolerance and interest of local rulers. They were beset by European rivals, the Dutch Vereenigde Oostindische Compagnie (VOC) in Java and the Molucca and Banda Islands, and the Portuguese Estado da Índia in India. Long periods at sea and in hot climates exposed merchants and seamen alike to debilitating and often fatal diseases. Finally, the very structure of the Company meant that its interests and those of its seamen were, at times, fundamentally at odds. Some of the benefits the sailors most prized eroded Company profits, while others undermined its authority.

Under these difficult circumstances, Company spokesmen and sea commanders often found it useful to present the East India Company as a distinctively national enterprise, one with a claim to the lives and loyalties of English seafaring men. How these claims were made depended very much on the nature of the audience. In tracts defending the Company against mercantilist critics, Company defenders tended to describe English seamen coldly as national resources whose lives could and should be ex-pended for national gain. At sea, however, the need to maintain morale and English solidarity led commanders to adopt a warmer language of care and comradeship. Enjoining sailors to fight foreign rivals, they spoke in stirringly national terms, praising English valor. As the Company's ri-valry with the VOC intensified, Company governors also found emotional appeals to English nationhood useful as they deployed sailors' stories of pain and humiliation at Dutch hands in their campaigns for political support. Appealing to the nation was a two-way street, however: when Company spokesmen hailed the seamen as brave Englishmen and patri-otic martyrs, the sailors made claims of their own. In these negotiations, sailors won less than they would have liked but more than the Company would have preferred, a balance that soon took on customary force.

Perils and Profits

English voyages to the Indian Ocean faced fearsome practical and politi-cal challenges. The first expedition in 1591 was very nearly a total disaster. By the time its three ships reached the southern tip of Africa, scurvy had made such heavy inroads that the *Merchant Royal* was sent home loaded with sick men. Another ship became separated from the *Edward Bonaventure* soon afterward, and was never seen again. The surviving *Edward* lost so many men to accidents, illness, and violence that by the time the Englishmen arrived, sick and weary, at Penang, they were left with "but thirty-three men and one boy, of which not past twenty-two were sound for labour and help, and of them not past a third part sailors." They cap-tured a few Portuguese ships, and by December 1592 the men insisted on returning to England, but this was not easily accomplished. Having crossed into the Atlantic, they were becalmed around the equator for weeks, their supplies running very low, and finally sailed for Trinidad. Captain James Lancaster and eighteen others were left on the island of Mona when the remainder sailed away and surrendered to Spanish authorities. A second English voyage to the East Indies, sponsored by Sir Robert Dudley in 1596, was an unmitigated failure. According to an intercepted Spanish letter, the fleet took three Portuguese ships but was nearly wiped out by sickness by the time any of the Englishmen reached the Caribbean on the way home, where four survivors took a boat and went ashore with as much treasure as they could, only to fall prey to Spanish adventurers.[11]

Meanwhile, Dutch merchants were operating on a vastly larger scale: by 1602, no fewer than sixty-five Dutch ships had sailed to Asia. Economic and political circumstances both spurred Dutch investment in East India voyages. In 1591, a powerful international syndicate won the Portuguese spice contract to the detriment of Dutch merchants, whose participation in the wholesale distribution of spices had already been hampered by the Dutch revolt and the decline of Antwerp. With hostilities continuing between the rebellious Dutch provinces and the king of Spain and Portugal, Dutch merchants had no qualms about attacking the Portuguese in the East—and neither did their governors. From the beginning, Dutch expeditions to the Indian Ocean were "state-backed and heavily armed," furnished with free guns and gunpowder by the States of Holland and Zeeland, and benefiting from customs exemptions.[12]

In July 1599, envious English merchants petitioned Elizabeth for a monopoly on Asian trade via the Cape of Good Hope, reminding her in October that the Dutch were already preparing a new voyage. Still, it was not until the very end of 1600 that she granted a royal charter to the East India Company. In February 1601 the Company's first fleet set sail, under Sir James Lancaster's command and piloted by John Davis of Sandridge. While the voyage suffered from high mortality, it was a commercial and diplomatic success. The ships in the fleet sailed first to the Cape, where scurvy obliged them to put their sick men on shore and purchase cattle and sheep from Khoekhoe herdsmen. They stopped again at Madagascar to buy "lemons and oranges, which were precious for our diseased men, to purge their bodies of the scurvy," but lost many men to "the flux." Having briefly anchored at the Nicobar Islands to ready their ships, they sighted Sumatra on June 2, 1602, and arrived at Aceh shortly thereafter. Lancaster was received courteously by the sultan, and also by the regent of Banten in western Java, and loaded his ships with pepper. Enough men remained alive to sail the ships home, and having left eight factors to establish a trading post at Banten, the fleet sailed for England. The *Dragon* nearly perished after a storm broke off its rudder, yet with the help of "the best swimmers and divers" from the *Hector*, a replacement was hung in place. In September 1603, the two ships finally arrived home, where the others had already arrived safely.[13]

The East India Company merchants were pleased to see their ships come home but less enthused to find them laden largely with pepper rather than rarer and costlier spices like cloves, nutmeg, and mace. Clove trees grew only on the Molucca Islands, while nutmeg trees—which produced both nutmeg and mace—were rarer still, found only on the Bandas, ten tiny volcanic islands south of Ceram.[14] In the years that followed, the Molucca and Banda Islands would be sites of bitter European rivalry and, for the English, bitter defeat. The Dutch had a head start in the Moluccas and by 1599 had even arrived at the Banda Islands, where they aided local elites against the Portuguese, demanding sole rights to Bandanese spices in exchange. Heavily capitalized and enjoying state support, they were prepared to make the necessary investments in warships, soldiers, and fortifications to enforce their monopoly. The VOC pursued long-term imperial interests, and its governors—if not its smaller shareholders—were willing to pay the price.[15] In contrast, in the early seventeenth century, each English East India Company voyage was responsible to its own investors: the factors from different voyages did not necessarily even cooperate with one another.

Over the next few years, Englishmen played a marginal, opportunistic role in the conflicts between the Dutch, the Portuguese, and Moluccan rulers. Hovering on the sidelines, they took in cargoes where they could and in the short run were able to make good profits. In the long run, however, their trade would depend on the tolerance of the Dutch as well as the will and ability of Asian traders to circumvent or defy the VOC. In the Banda Islands, the English aligned themselves with Bandanese resistance to Dutch imperialism, but to no avail. John Jourdain, the leader of the English merchants at Banten, was killed by a sharpshooter in an English naval defeat at the hands of the VOC in 1619, and Nathaniel Courthope, who had ceremonially taken possession of Pulo Way and Pulo Run on behalf of James I in 1616, met his own Dutch bullet the next year. Mass murder and enslavement in Batavia awaited the defeated Bandanese.

The East India Company also cherished hopes of establishing profitable factories at Mocha and Surat, but where the VOC did not bar its way, other challenges loomed. Ottoman officials humiliated English merchants and sailors at Mocha, denying their requests for trading rights. The Portuguese, who had a permanent base at Goa, were hostile to English efforts at Surat, attacking English ships and warning the city not to welcome the newcomers. English attacks on Surat shipping and victories against Portuguese fleets from Goa helped the East India Company to gain a foothold, but the very sporadic presence of English ships at Surat limited their efficacy. For enduring protection and support, the English appealed to the Mughal emperor Jahangir, but the Mughals had every reason to play the Portuguese off against the English. From his august height, moreover, Jahangir was disinclined to treat with the East India Company, and even the arrival of the formal embassy of the aristocratic Sir Thomas Roe in 1615 did little to persuade him to take the English more seriously. Bearing rich gifts and enjoying a stipend grudgingly paid by the Company, Roe did his very best to embody the dignity of his distant sovereign.[16] On the whole, however, his embassy made limited gains, and the London merchants remained reluctant to invest in either diplomacy or warfare without immediate returns.

Meanwhile, the ravages of disease devastated English ships and factories, prompting scrambles for remedies and explanations, and forcing commanders to come to terms with weak, demoralized crews and serious shortages of skilled labor. In 1615, even Sir Dudley Digges, a champion of the East India Company, conceded that of the first 3,323 men sent to the East Indies, more than two thousand had died abroad.[17] This immense loss of life was ammunition for the Company's critics and a grim reality for its servants. Death hung over the English ships.

Scurvy, the first disease to attack the English ships, was countered reasonably effectively after a dramatic natural experiment demonstrated the efficacy of citrus. On the first East India Company voyage, in 1601, by the time the fleet was close to the Cape of Good Hope, three ships "were so weak of men that they could hardly handle the sails." With the sailors ill, the merchants had to take "their turns at the helm, and [go] into the top to take in the topsails, as the common mariners did." Luckily Lancaster had "certain bottles of the juice of lemons, which he gave to each one, as long as it would last, three spoonfuls every morning." The men on his ship were noticeably healthier than those on the other ships, and so when the fleet reached Madagascar, the officers eagerly bought up local citrus. On later voyages, the men and officers on board East India Company ships gathered and purchased lemons and limes whenever they could. On the third voyage, for example, when the men were beginning "to be weak and very many to be touched with the scurvy," the Company ships stopped at Sierra Leone, where they purchased limes and hens; the merchant Anthony Marlowe reported: "With the limes our men made them lime water, with which (it pleased God) and the shore, they recovered which were infected with the scurvy."[18] When another fleet stopped at St. Helena on the return journey in 1617, the Englishmen picked all the lemons they could, both ripe and green, "which we divided amongst our ships' companies to each man twenty lemons," the commander Walter Peyton recorded. Ships' officers spent significant sums on other sorts of fresh victuals as well, enriching and diversifying sailors' diets. On outward voyages at least, scurvy ceased to be an existential threat. In 1615, for example, John Oxwicke wrote buoyantly from Surat of God's "great goodness ... in keeping us from sickness and with so little loss of men, for betwixt England and this road we had not above six men which died, being men of no note but foremast men."[19]

The Company enjoyed less success in countering tropical fluxes and fevers. After months at sea, the leafy cities of Banten and Aceh must have been delightful to the sailors with their busy markets and compounds among coconut palms, bamboo groves, and banana trees, but these cities depended for their drinking water on the same rivers in which residents washed and relieved themselves.[20] For the *Expedition*, which set sail from Gravesend in late January 1614 with seventy-six men, dysentery became a scourge, easily surpassing other causes of death. The rhythm of mortality was slow at first: the first to die, only a few weeks into the voyage, may have suffered from a disease contracted on shore, then months passed with no deaths until Abraham Brackleman drowned at Socotra in August. At Surat, in November, another man died, then another in February 1615, as the ship sailed toward Calicut.[21] In late March, ominously, a midshipman succumbed to the bloody flux, but the pace of mortality remained slow: another month passed before the next death, again of the flux.[22] The ship arrived at Banten in May, then sailed farther to the spice islands. By June, the men were all falling ill; they were bled on the sixth, with great success according to the captain, Walter Peyton. On June 9 and 23, two men died of the bloody flux, then two more in early July.[23] On Sumatra, on July 20, the master of the ship, Thomas Bonner, died of "a calenture or burning fever," which along with the flux claimed two more men in August.[24] Peyton wrote with dismay of the fearsome contagious diseases that afflicted people in Pariaman, noting that "in these parts as in many other heathenish countries, the people are very ignorant in curing their maladies and diseases, they dying like incurable lepers, God grant we make true use of our knowledge they want." Whether by skill or luck, the pace of death eased in late summer 1615; it was October before a sailor died, of "the flux and burning fever together."[25] Another died later that month, and Peyton longed for a westerly wind: "God in mercy grant, we may get clear out to sea from this unhealthy place, for our ship's company fall down more and more every day ... God comfort them." By November one-third of his men were sick with the bloody flux; four died that month. With so many men suffering from dysentery, the ship must have been miserably foul. As the men sailed away from the islands, however, they began to recover: on November 27, Peyton recorded: "Most of my company in health God be praised."[26] A sailor died and was buried ashore at the Cape of Good Hope; he was the last to fall victim to the dreaded bloody flux. The next death was from "a corrosive consumption," while in January 1617 another sailor perished, of "a fever, proceeding of a cold taken in his stomach." In February, not far from St. Helena, another died of a "cold fever"; he was the twenty-third and last to die before the *Expedition*'s safe arrival in the Downs at the end of May.[27]

Sometimes the toll of disease doomed whole ships. When John Jourdain sailed in the *Darling* to Banten from the Moluccas in August 1613, he was startled to see the *Trade's Increase*, the Company's pride and joy, aground near the shore and to receive no reply to the *Darling*'s salute. After a while, he saw a proa coming toward him with a few Englishmen, "all of them like ghosts or men frighted." Inquiring anxiously for the commanding officers, he found he "could not name any man of note but was dead, to the number of 140 persons; and the rest which were remaining, as well a-land and aboard the *Trade*, were all sick." Helpless without its crew, the lovely *Trade* was wrecked on its maiden voyage. When the master's widow, Mary Thornton, petitioned the Company for "relief for the loss of her husband, son, and two servants, who all died in the voyage," the merchants "conceived it too dangerous a precedent."[28] Indeed, they were familiar with such disasters. The *Susan* and the *Hector* had left Java in March 1605, with forty-seven men on the *Susan* and sixty-three on the *Hector*, "many Englishmen sick." The ships' crews had already suffered greatly at Banten, where their masters had died as well as many others, so that the factors "were constrained . . . to hire as many as we could get of Gujarats and Chinois to help bring home our ships, to our exceeding great cost and charges." Nine months later, the *Dragon* came upon the *Hector* "driving up and down the sea about four leagues off the Cape Bona Esperanza" with ten Englishmen and four Chinese sailors on board, the only survivors. The *Susan* had been swallowed up by the ocean.[29] Similarly, in 1610, like a ghost ship, the massive *Union* drifted to the coast of France with only four living men on board, who "through feebleness . . . were scarce able to speak." Two of them, including one "Indian," died over the following days. According to Dudley Digges, the ship and its rich cargo could have been saved but for the selfishness of the sailors: after disease and misfortune killed most of the crew, fourteen of the ablest survivors had forsaken the ship once it reached European waters, leaving it to be pillaged by opportunistic Bretons.[30]

Unable to avoid the flux, the ships' officers often blamed its victims for their illnesses. When men died on Madagascar, the officers supposed that "the flux . . . came with the waters which we drunk," and also that men caught it "by going open, and cold in the stomach, which our men would often do when they were hot." Sometimes, men were thought to fall ill through "the feeding of the plantains and lemons, which they did devour immoderately."[31] Drunkenness and lust were favorite scapegoats. John Saris lamented that men died quickly "by surfeit and most filthily abusing of their bodies, which no courses mild or strict can prevent," and Peyton thought Aceh a place "somewhat contagious for the flux, especially for those who overstuff themselves with hot and fiery drink." Even in firmly Islamic port cities in Southeast Asia, alcohol was deeply embedded in festive culture, and arak was a potent temptation for Englishmen raised on beer. Peyton thought it contributed to many deaths "in East India, although all imputed unto the dangerousness of the voyage. How unruly the common sort of men are abroad cannot be imagined at home, for a great part of them never think themselves merry nor in health, longer than their brains are crowing with insatiable drinking, wherefore no marvel they die so fast." Venereal disease were also a concern. At Banten, John Scott died in December 1612 with "his guts eaten with the pox in the space of eight or ten days," Saris wrote, and many others were also infected.[32]

Commanders' eagerness to blame seamen for their own deaths may have reflected the East India Company's worries about its image. Sailors were essential to English security and prosperity, and with its catastrophic death rates, the Company was accused of weakening the commonwealth. In addition to exporting bullion, the pamphleteer Robert Kayll charged, the Company wasted seafaring men and timber, scarce resources that ought to be managed sustainably for the common good. Like its sailors, its ships often perished in faraway waters: "They die not the ordinary death of ships, who commonly have some rest, and after long service die full of years, and at home, much of their timber serving again to the same use, besides their iron-work, and the rest otherwise serviceable, and not in this bloody and unseasonable fashion. . . . For the rest that live, they come home so crazed and broken, so maimed and unmanned, that whereas they went out strong, they return most feeble: and whereas they were carried forth with Christians, they are brought home with heathen."[33]

Defenders of the East India Company could not deny that high mortality had afflicted the early East India voyages. To justify these deaths, Digges cast mariners—again, like timber—as a resource that had to be used lest it spoil through neglect: "The providence that bids us go and plant, commands us too to use our well-grown timber ere it rot, as that would soonest that is fittest for great shipping." Without employment in the East Indies, he argued, mariners were liable to go bad, ending on the gallows: "Nay mariners themselves admitting them to be so scarce, were better die in the East-Indies, than here at home at Tybourne, or at Wapping, for want of means to live; or else be forced to turn sea-robbers." Sailors, like all men, were destined for death; better that they should find it while working for "the public good," Digges argued, than lying safe at home. Writing a few years later, Thomas Mun echoed Digges's arguments. Rather than being scarce, he suggested, sailors were plentiful, even overabundant. Mariners' lives were only precious, he held, insofar as they served "the public good": "Take them from their laudable and accustomed employments, for want of voyages to sea; we see what desperate courses they do then attempt, by joining, even with Turks and infidels, to rob and spoil all Christian nations; so that we may conclude, we must not only breed up mariners, but also seek by trade, to give them maintenance." Moreover, the East India Company had taken steps toward sustainability: "To recompense the loss of those that die, do not the East India Company with great providence, yearly ship out at least 400 landmen in their fleets, which in one voyage prove good mariners to serve the kingdom and commonwealth, unto which many of them were a burden before they obtained this employment?" For these destitute novices, Mun continued, the Company was a savior: "When all the other doors of charity are shut, the East India gates stand wide open to receive the needy and the poor, giving them good entertainment with two months wages before hand to make their needful provisions for the voyage." If they died, the kingdom would be rid of unprofitable subjects; if they lived, the commonwealth would gain skilled seamen. Either way, Mun implied, England would be better off.[34]

Shipboard Communities

The profound challenges English ships faced in the Indian Ocean shaped sailors' relations with one another and their commanders. While commanding officers answered directly to Company governors and held commissions of martial law, they often found that their authority was more nuanced than their commissions suggested. Force was insufficient to maintain social unity: consensus building, attention to equity, and concessions for sailors' health and morale were also required. Discipline upheld collective values as well as the chain of command, and punishments for insubordination were sometimes remitted in shows of magnanimity or in response to crews' objections. Metropolitan spokesmen like Digges and Mun might write coolly about how most profitably to spend sailors' lives, but successful voyages depended on the creation and maintenance of tight-knit shipboard communities grounded in a traditional language of care and mutuality.

On tedious, dangerous East India voyages, mariners and merchants formed a community whether they wanted to or not. All depended on one another's skills and diligence for their survival. In life-and-death struggles against the elements, normal social hierarchies were all but erased: hardly anyone was exempt from the back-breaking work of pumping when ships had serious leaks.[35] Most of the time, however, venerable ideas about the social hierarchy offered clear guidance for how Company men ought to behave. All were to labor diligently and uncomplainingly in the positions in which God had placed them. Humble sailors were to respect and obey their superiors, and to treat one another with loving friendship. Commanders were to take paternal care of their inferiors while correcting their errors as occasion should require. Mutual respect and shared dedication to their masters would enable merchants and captains to treat one another with forbearance, forgiving slights and refraining from giving offense. In practice, however, unity was an ideal that remained constantly at risk. Voyages were long, labor was irksome, and tempers and provisions often grew short. Sailors were quarrelsome and unruly, while their betters were, if anything, even touchier, even though the Company avoided hiring gentlemen, who were the touchiest of all.[36]

Like the wooden ships that carried them, shipboard communities required incessant vigilance, or problems could grow to irreparable proportions. Gambling—a potent source of excitement but also of strife—was prohibited. Prayers were to be read daily, and while no one took Communion very often, William Keeling encouraged general reconciliation on Easter in 1615 by offering a feast of cheese to all communicants, as well as extra meal, currants, and beer for all.[37] Part of the job of a commander was to unite the Company's quarreling servants "in love one unto another," as Sir Henry Middleton did on Madagascar in 1610. Consensus was the preferred style of decision-making, and in times of danger commanders consulted with lower officers and experienced men, hoping to hear a full range of views.[38] When William Keeling consulted with the masters in his fleet and their mates about a proposed itinerary, he asked the youngest and most junior officers to speak first, to encourage frankness. When the *Hector* developed several leaks, the merchants asked not only the master but also his mates, the carpenter, the boatswain, and the quartermasters "whether they thought the ship suffi-cient to put to sea." Commanders who ignored advice could expect to be blamed for any subsequent mishaps, like those who "determined to follow their voyage for Cambaya, sore against the minds of the company," and promptly lost two anchors because of their "head-strongness."[39] The dan-gers of the sea called for unity.

Victualing and health were particularly potent issues for shipboard communities. Apart from private stores, all the men on East India Company ships were dependent on the same supplies of food and drink, and equity was important. In theory, victuals were distributed according to maritime custom, which was calorically sufficient though nutritionally unbalanced; spoilage and shortages were common, however, serious dearth was always a possibility, and many sailors were regularly hungry. The idea that status entitled certain individuals to more generous por-tions rubbed these sailors the wrong way. Writing from what he thought was his deathbed, and explaining his reasoning in choosing his successor, Captain Nicholas Downton ruled out Abraham Lawse in part because he suspected "the small store of wine yet left which hath been hitherto re-served for the relief and comfort of all by equal portions, at time of most need . . . should be wasted by few in a riot to the ruin of all" under Lawse's watch. On a later voyage, he cautioned the Company that it caused "much grief and dislike in the common people" when factors were allowed to consume more than their share from the common store, and advised that factors should bring "private provisions" if they needed extra supplies. In general, Downton worried that his cost-conscious em-ployers did not properly value the sailors' lives, and he chided the Company for providing inadequate stores: "God forbid that the ship's goods (with the lives of men which are rated at least value) should perish in the sea for want of supply." Although he thought them "very scandal-ous and troublesome," the captain was grieved by the sufferings of his "poor out-tired and long unrefreshed people." He realized that com-manders ought not only to care about their men but also be seen to care. His scrupulously equitable rationing was designed to preserve the sea-men's health and to reassure them that they mattered to him.[40]

Sailors, too, appealed to the ethos of care in times of need, collectively voicing their misery and exhibiting their pain to obtain more victuals or to induce commanders to seek "refreshing" on land, often successfully. On the Company's second voyage, Sir Henry Middleton had been instructed to sail for Madagascar and not to stop at the Cape of Good Hope. When the fleet sailed within sight of the Cape, however, Middleton reported, "our sick men cried out most lamentably, for at that present there were sick of the scurvy at the least eighty men in our ship, not one able to help the other." They "made a petition to the general, most humbly entreating him for God's sake to save their lives, and to put in for Saldania [Table Bay], otherways they were but dead men." After reading the petition, Middleton looked out of the cabin, where "a swarm of lame and weak diseased cripples" had assembled themselves, and "beholding this lamentable sight extended his compassion towards them, and granted their requests."[41]

A nearly identical series of events took place on the following voyage, for the directors of the East India Company continued—mistakenly—to believe that Madagascar was safer than the Cape, and they had given the commander William Keeling orders to proceed there directly. Better informed, the sailors were anxious to put in at the Cape in December 1607, and they followed the same script as their fellows on the preceding voyage. When Keeling directed the shipmasters to steer away from the shore, the company of the *Dragon* "did all with one accord come to our general and intreated him, as he did respect the lives of so many poor men which had been eight months and upwards without fresh victuals, that he would be pleased to put into Saldania," according to two factors on board. Bringing the weakest members of the crew with them, they appealed to Keeling three times. Meanwhile, the men on the *Hector* also "assembled themselves in the waist," and when the *Dragon* sailed close by and Keeling asked "what weak and sick men we had aboard," they exhibited their misery. Keeling gave way to the general will, to the relief of one merchant, who feared that otherwise "most of our men would fall down on a sudden being of themselves already weak and disappointed of their hopes." The factor Anthony Marlowe agreed that disappointment might have been fatal, for the "discontentment which they would take, would so much cast them down, hardly to be recovered, as might endanger the utter overthrow of the voyage." Since despair was seen as one of scurvy's more dangerous symptoms, maintaining stricken sailors' morale could be critical to their survival. In both cases, Middleton and Keeling may well have wished to stop at the Cape, but it was difficult for them to disobey their direct instructions. The sailors gave them the cover they needed to alter course.[42]

The flux posed more of a challenge to social unity, for it was a filthy disease and prompted as much disgust as pity. Humphrey Middleton was ill on the *Clove* in early 1612 when the surgeon complained about him to the captain, John Saris, alleging that Middleton was malingering. The suspicious surgeon secretly gave the sick man a purge, after which Middleton refused all treatment, "lying in his dung to the annoying of the company swearing most horribly he would not shift himself." Middleton's rank on shipboard had never been high: according to the purser, who had hired him at Deptford, he had been "begging door to door" there and was notable for nothing but blasphemy, being "the greatest curser and swearer that ever he heard." Saris usually favored the sick, supporting them in their quarrels with the surgeon and ordering that they be fortified with spiced wine twice a day, but he treated Middleton harshly. The boatswain was sent to rouse him to work, making the sick man "fearfully swear that if God would not let him live to be revenged on him he hoped the devil would." Outraged, Saris had Middleton "banged at the mast" and admonished him "to take a better course and not through sullenness and beastly behavior to spoil himself and the rest of us." Middleton's filth was offensive to man; his blasphemy was offensive to God. The next day, the surgeon again complained about Middleton "continuing his beastly manner dunging as he lay (notwithstanding at his feet was a convenient stool) cursing and swearing in such fearful manner as those which lay by him very weak yet kept themselves clean desired he might not be amongst them." Saris had the sick man left in the head, "where he might use his beastly manner without annoying his fellows." He died two days later without any comment on Saris's part beyond a terse record of the value of his clothes.[43]

As Middleton's case suggests, shipboard punishment often targeted men whose actions offended the community at large: discipline reinforced collective values. Thus captains took theft from other sailors seriously. William Jones, an elderly gunner's mate who "confessed he had narrowly escaped the gallows three several times" was punished for stealing shirts from other sailors, for example. Evan Lake received fifty lashes—a severe beating— "for stealing things out of Will Hoar's chest" on the *Dragon*. Keeling noted that the lashes were inflicted by five men who had purchased the stolen goods, perhaps to give them satisfaction or as a warning. None of them seems to have balked at whipping the thief.[44] Sailors were also punished for stealing food from common stores, with more serious punishments for thefts of luxuries. Evan Lake—an habitual offender—received thirty lashes for stealing a piece of fresh beef in 1615, while Edward Coldicutt was ducked for stealing a cheese. On the *Thomas*, two seamen were whipped at the mast for pumping out wine in the hold in 1613.[45]

For outcasts who were simultaneously ostracized by their peers and punished by their superiors, life on board could be unbearable. The *Hector*'s gunner's mate, George King, was driven to suicide in 1607, for example. King had been suspected of "committing filthiness with a bitch," a sort of "inhuman vileness" that threatened to call down "fearful judgments" on the fleet. King denied the charge and was acquitted: the evidence was "very ominous . . . yet not sufficient to induce the consciences of the said jury to allot him death."[46] But he was not forgiven. Whipped and transferred to the *Dragon*, King remained deeply unpopular. When he was accused of stealing shirts some months later, he tried to escape in the ship's pinnace onto the shore at Sierra Leone. Someone saw him, and the sailors pursued him in the longboat. Though King "cast himself into the sea," he was hauled up and bound. The following day, when King persisted in denying the theft, the captain ordered him to be tortured, and the sailor "confessed the stealing of the shirts, and one platter, and that he had hid them ashore." A search revealed nothing, however. In any case, innocent or guilty, King could stand no more. On his way back to the bilboes, he "desired that he might go to the beak head to ease himself," and under the pretense of relieving himself, "not having the fear of God before his eyes, did cast himself away and was never seen after."[47]

The fact that ships were so terribly vulnerable to providential punishment could lead to harsh remedies when grave sins were suspected; there is little evidence that illicit sex on board was tolerated. As the *Ascension* made its tedious way up the coast of East Africa, frustrated by contrary currents, a ship's boy named William Acton revealed that he had been sodomized by the coxswain, Nicholas White, and that Nicholas Cober had abused him to a lesser degree. A trial was swiftly held, and a jury of seamen found all three to be guilty of sodomy. Acton was not punished because of his youth, but the steward was whipped and White was hanged. Robert Coverte, the ship's steward, later marveled, "It was a wonder . . . that our ship had not sunk in the ocean" because of the sinful acts.[48]

Juries of seamen also convicted sailors of serious offenses against authority. A few months after White's execution, the *Ascension* was reunited with its pinnace, the *Good Hope,* at Aden. When the general Alexander Sharpeigh asked to see the pinnace's master, its seamen "told him very merrily that he was dead," for "they had slain him." At first the pinnace's crew kept a united front, asserting that they were all equally guilty and that they had killed John Lufkin because he refused to seek refreshing on land, for "it was better for one to die than all." Under closer questioning, however, it appeared that the men who took control of the pinnace after the murder had also coveted Lufkin's private store of aqua vitae. The *Ascension*'s officers were flummoxed at first: they could hardly execute the entire crew, and Philip de Grove thought it wiser "to wink" at the murder. In the end, however, three principal actors were tried by a jury of seamen, and the older two were hanged. If the mutineers of the *Good Hope* had counted on the support of the *Ascension*'s sailors, they miscalculated.[49]

Lesser crimes against authority were far more common and did not require jury trials. George Evans was forced to stand "at the capstan with a basket of shot about his neck for misordering himself toward Tucker one of the boatswain's mates" on the *Hector* in 1607, for example. Being ducked at the yardarm was another common punishment for insubordination: on the *Clove* in 1611, when the quartermaster was accused of inciting young sailors to disobey their superiors, he was ducked; so was Peter Martin for beating the boatswain. John Rickton of the *Expedition* was "ducked at the yardarm for resisting the boatswain with blows, he being commanded to work, refused obstinately."[50] Owen Bodman of the *Peppercorn* was punished "at the capstan for being ungovernable" and transferred to the *Dragon* in January 1616; later in the voyage, he was put in the bilboes "for misdemeanor to the boatswain etc in his drunkenness." A few years later, Bodman was hanged off Sumatra for burning a prize ship.[51] Threats of punishment were more common than the real thing, in part because malefactors were not necessarily easy to identify. At Surat, Keeling wrote, "we missed 7000 small shot and 400 lbs lead stolen and sold for toddy, whereupon I published in each ship that whosoever in such sort made away one more bullet should suffer 40 stripes with a whip upon the bare back," but he does not seem to have followed through.[52]

When punishments clashed with sailors' understanding of justice, they sometimes obstructed the punishment of their peers, so that a commander's desire to prove his authority had to cede to the greater need to build community on shipboard. Executions and whippings were theaters of power, but the script altered when ships' companies collectively entreated commanders for mercy, commanders gracefully gave way, and demonstrations of authority were replaced by celebrations of mutuality. On the first East India Company voyage, for example, a seaman named Thoroughgood "was arraigned and found guilty of mutiny and contempt, and therefore was condemned to be hanged, but by great entreaty he was forgiven."[53] The ritual did not always work quite so smoothly. When a carpenter's mate was to be punished in 1607, awkward timing led to an embarrassingly ambiguous outcome. In addition to fighting with John Ashenhurst, Goodman Lantro had struck "Thomas the captain's man to the ground with his fist." Since his servant was the victim, the captain recused himself, referring the matter to the shipmaster and the cape merchant, who decided that Lantro ought to be punished with heavy shot hung around his neck. When, however, the punishment was supposed to be inflicted, "the boatswain with thirty or forty of the company came up upon the deck, and with one voice said murmuringly, that they did labour and should be punished every boy abusing them, and growing very discontented." They were offended that a carpenter should be punished for striking a mere youth with no standing on board save his relationship with the captain. Meanwhile, the captain mistakenly thought that the punishment was being carried out and sent up his servant—Lantro's erstwhile victim—to order his release. Onlookers were left to wonder whether Lantro had been saved by the captain's generosity or the sailors' disobedience.[54]

When sailors refused to inflict punishment, they left commanders with a serious problem. Appealing to a higher authority was a popular solution. On the *Peppercorn* in 1617, when Richard Monke and others "abused" the boatswain, the captain consulted with his council and "adjudged the said Monke, being the original, to receive condign punishment at the capstan . . . and forthwith commanded the quartermasters to execute their duties therein." Unfortunately for Captain Harris, "all of them, William Currant excepted, disobediently refused," even when Harris read them his commission and "charged them by virtue thereof to obey his command." Not daring to press the issue further, he referred the matter to a larger council that decided the offenders would move to the *Globe* in exchange for other men. Once the ships returned home, the General Court of the East India Company pardoned the sailors in question and paid them their wages. When absolutely necessary, commanders could inflict punishment themselves, though doing so was undignified and bad for morale. When John Roan drunkenly murdered a Dutchman in Japan in 1621, the delicate political relationship between the English and Dutch merchants necessitated a harsh punishment, and he was condemned to death by an English jury. Roan himself made an exemplary end, "wishing all the ship's company to take example by him, and to beware of women and wine," and receiving the sacrament. When the time came, however, "Captain Robert Adams was forced to put the rope about his neck with his own hands, for none of the ship's company would do it, if he should hang them, and so told him to his face." Unlike the VOC, the English East India Company had no soldiers to suppress the sailors, so all punishment depended at the very least on the passive consent of the ship's crew.[55]

Gains and Losses

Unity was never more important than when ships went into battle, prompting commanders to frame conflict in stirringly national terms. Close to Surat at the end of November 1612, two English ships, the *Dragon* and the *Hosiander*, were menaced by a much larger Portuguese fleet. According to the surgeon, Ralph Standish, the fleet's commander, Thomas Best, came on board the *Hosiander* and made a rousing speech: "Although their forces were more than ours, yet they were both base and cowardly, and that there was a saying not so common as true: Who so cowardly as a Portingale?" As Standish recalled, "[Best] did therefore persuade every man to be of good courage, and show ourselves true Englishmen, famoused all over the world for true valour; and that God, in whom we trusted, would be our help. . . . [He urged us] to trust in God, and not to fear death, although for death we were ordained; and in a better action we could not die than on the behalf of so worthy a country as we have, the commonwealth of our land, the estate of our masters. For death, sayeth he, is the passage to Heaven." Mere professional obligation was not enough to motivate men to fight against great odds, and Best did not suppose that the sailors were likely to be enthusiastic about defending the company-state. They were enjoined to fight for their honor as Englishmen, for their commonwealth, for national glory, and for God, as well as for "the estate of our masters." These were brave words, but Best did not merely ask for sacrifice: he offered reciprocity.

> In this manner having encouraged our men, [he] further told them that, if it should please God that any of our men in fight were dismembered or lamed, he faithfully promised, upon his credit and reputation, in the hearing of all the company, that he would be a means unto the Worshipful [Company], whom we serve, in their behalves for reasonable maintenance to keep them as long as it should please God they live, and himself to be the petitioner upon his knees until his request were granted; but that we should not need fear, for that we served a religious and worthy company of masters that would never see a man go to decay or want by any harm sustained in their service.

If the seamen were to spend their blood fighting the Company's battles, they had to believe that the Company would, in turn, care for them. After the speech, Best drank a cup of wine to the master and the crew, "desired God to give us his blessing," and returned to his ship, while the *Hosiander*'s company went to prayer together. Fighting aggressively, Best's fleet was able to repel the Portuguese with few casualties.[56]

Best's sailors also knew how to appeal to unity for their own ends. About two weeks after the battle with the Portuguese, four men ran to the Portuguese enemy at Muzafarabad (Jafrabad) when sent ashore in the longboat to fetch water. Their leader, William Perfeit, had already been demoted and transferred to the *Dragon* for "swimming ashore of the Sabbath day and drinking drunk with whores." At Best's request, the local governor soon captured the runaways and returned them to the ship. The following day, Best called all the men of the *Dragon* and the *Hosiander* together to ask them whether or not they were willing to seek further battle with the Portuguese. The men proclaimed themselves ready to fight but also appealed to Best on behalf of the four prisoners languishing in the bilboes. At first, Best was adamant that he meant to hang Perfeit for his base treachery in abandoning his countrymen and his wife and child at home. Yet when the men persisted in entreating for the prisoners' liberty, Standish wrote: "The General told them that, if they had asked his right hand, he could not deny them it, for that they had proved themselves so faithful and stout to resist the enemy. The prisoners, having their irons taken off, gave thanks to both companies for their kindness towards them; and also unto the General upon their knees, promising to became new men and to endeavour themselves in their places to give content unto our General. So this being done, the cooper was called to fill some beer; and having drunk, we of the *Hosiander* repaired aboard our own ship."[57] By insisting that he had yielded to the seamen out of gratitude for their courage in battle, Best framed the pardon as a unifying moment, and the repentant runaways played their part to perfection. As they prepared to meet the Portuguese threat, this celebration of amity heartened the sailors and officers alike.

The men of Best's fleet got promises of maintenance and the pardon of the four runaways, but that was not all. When the *Dragon* returned to England in 1614, "the country was filled with spices" sold by the ship's men. When outraged Company governors demanded an explanation, Best explained that at Surat he had needed to encourage the crew for a battle with the Portuguese and had promised them "that they should have favour in laying out their means upon commodities."[58] If seamen were to be asked to lay down their lives for English trade, it seems, they needed to have a stake in it: both for Best and the sailors, appealing to national unity was an effective way of making claims on one another. Much of the time, Company merchants were wary of these appeals and the burdensome moral obligations they entailed; it was neater to frame sailors as simple wage workers. The violent clashes, however, between Company ships and their Portuguese and Dutch rivals and the magnitude of both the profits and the dangers of Asian trade made it impossible for the Company to suppress the sailors' claims to share in the benefits of trade.

Allowing sailors to trade ran counter to the economic logic of the East India Company. It was hostile to private trade by English subjects in Asia, either among its servants or by interlopers: such trade injured the Company's ability to control the supply of spices in England and lowered their prices. The "decrees and laws" set for the first voyage thus stated that all trade would be conducted on the basis of a single stock, and that "no private traffic, barter, exchange, or merchandising shall be used practiced or admitted by any particular governor, captain, merchant, agent, factor, master, mariner, officer or other person whatsoever employed in the said voyage," on pain of forfeiture of the goods in question and wages. The merchants did agree, however, that "for the better advancement of his salary" every sailor should "have two months' wages in adventure as his stock." By the second voyage, a small chest's worth of private trade in "China dishes or light trifles"—not spices or silk—was deemed permissible.[59] These small concessions were presumably designed to allow the Company to economize on wages, which still ran roughly 40 or 45 percent higher than usual for English seamen, around twenty-four shillings a month, reflecting the huge dangers of East India voyages.[60]

Company sailors were always more eager to trade for themselves than the merchants liked: since they had to risk their lives, they felt they might as well risk their money too. Those who lacked money or goods to trade abroad were sometimes visibly disaffected, like the master's mate John Mucknell, who spoke gloomily about a leak in his ship "to the discouraging of the sailors," because he "had nothing to lay out at Banten but was to return home as poor as he came forth his wages excepted." Some sailors even raised money by gambling on their own survival. In 1614 Rafe Hesam and William Warrey offered the Company "to resign all their right to wages and goods due to them on the purser's books should they die on the voyage" in exchange for an additional £5 upfront. Others, they said, were willing to give them those terms. The Company disapproved of private trade, but it knew that this was a good deal and offered to extend it to other mariners as well, so long as they were bachelors.[61]

Private trade by sailors was a persistent if minor headache for the East India Company. When the *Dragon* returned home in 1609, all the mariners on board were said to have pepper, and the ship was "pestered" with their belongings.[62] The coxswain reportedly had a chest containing 113 pounds of silk, while the gunner smuggled four hundredweight of pepper on shore. Hoping to avoid further problems, the Company governors strove to prevent mariners from landing goods without their knowledge, and they specified the maximum permissible dimensions of seamen's chests, allowing sailors to "bring home ... only such goods as the Company do not deal in."[63] Despite their efforts, smuggling continued, for once the East India ships reached home, they were met by willing purchasers in small boats. In the East Indies, moreover, the fact that so many different English buyers were looking for spices drove up prices.[64]

As corporate custom developed, East India Company sailors strove to make every favorable decision a binding precedent. William Keeling recorded that when he read the Company's commission to the men of the *Dragon* in March 1615, he encountered "much murmuring among my company who generally affirm they will not fight in whatsoever case to save the Company's goods before they have covenanted with me in that case how the hazard of their lives and limbs shall be rewarded." The men claimed a traditional right to some private trade, based on common practice in other long-distance routes, "producing the custom of merchants trading the Straits, who never denied anyone of their ship's company to lade some small matter in their ships freight free, or any other of ability to lade 1/2 or a whole ton paying reasonable freight for the same." Best's generosity was held up as a model to be followed: the seamen stressed "among themselves how worthily Captain Best dealt with them the last voyage in offering and permitting their private trade, to the reasonable advancement of their means and benefit of their long and hazardous voyage." The fact that Portuguese and Dutch sailors also enjoyed trading rights on East India voyages was another argument in their favor.[65]

Mitigating the damage from private trade was easier than banning it. On John Saris's *Clove*, sailors frequently bought pepper and even stole it from one another. Instead of preventing his men from purchasing spices in the first place, Saris's plan was to buy it up before reaching England. That, at least, was his advice to Gabriel Towerson: "And if you find that any of your company shall buy any quantity of pepper or other prohibited commodity it is necessary that you take it from them, giving them content as the price goes, for thereby you shall prevent stealing homewards and free the Company of jealousy in that point." Similarly, when Best's ships, the *Dragon* and the *Hosiander*, reached England, the purser was directed to buy all the mariners' pepper for the Company's use, and merchants were sent down to meet the ships with £300 to purchase the sailors' goods.[66] Some other commanders took a harder line. In the

Atlantic on the way back to England, Peyton confiscated 1,743 pounds of pepper from the surgeon Edward Wilson, noting that Wilson would have to go to the Company for satisfaction, and Keeling seized six parcels of gum benzoin—an ingredient in incense—from one John Smith, "to be by the honorable Company at their pleasures restored or disposed." Wilson and Smith probably got something for their goods from the Company, if not as much as they were hoping for. In October 1617, another surgeon, John Neve, was "discontented with the Company's offer to buy his indigo brought from Surat, although it was forfeited as a commodity absolutely forbidden."[67]

Sailors' trade came to occupy its own particular niche in the web of trade with Asia, intertwined with official Company commerce. Few European commodities were vendible in large quantities in Asia, but sailors found some of the smaller markets that did exist, trading sword blades, knives, and looking glasses for local goods.[68] These "toys" made useful presents when Company representatives hoped to curry favor with local officials. When the governor of Surat, Muqarrab Khan, visited the *Trade's Increase* in November 1611, he "busied himself in buying of knives, glasses, or any other toys he found amongst my company," Sir Henry Middleton wrote. As the governor toured the ship, Middleton continued, the captain "went with him and showed him the ship aloft and below: anything he liked belonging to the ship he carried away with him *gratis*, besides many toys of my companies, which he liked, I bought and gave him." Similarly, in 1617, the cape merchant Richard Cocks bought a parrot, a parakeet, and a monkey from English sailors to give to Japanese dignitaries.[69] In August 1615, acting for the joint stock on the advice of the merchant Thomas Dodsworth, Keeling bought all his men's sword blades for about three dollars apiece and traded some of them at Socotra for aloes. The officers may have regretted their decision at Surat, where they tried to sell the remaining blades. Peyton wrote in his journal that "straight blades [were] out of request, the markets being cloyed with the thousand blades, which were bought up of our fleet's companies."[70] The following year, the sailors were allowed to sell their own blades at Surat, leading the factors there to lament their undignified bargaining: "The commodity (by their shameful carrying them up and down the markets, home to men's houses, and bartering for high rated commodities at lower prices than they cost first penny in England) is extremely disgraced and disesteemed; whereby we have not sold a blade since their arrival, nor are likely in many years to come to the wonted price." Even worse, the sailors expected the factors to buy up any remaining goods. As the East India Company's factors in Surat, Thomas Kerridge and Thomas Rastell, wrote, "They think themselves highly wronged that we do not buy for your account their unvendible commodities that other men refuse."[71]

The volume of sailors' private trade did not approach that of merchants and commanders, but it probably made up a substantial portion of their earnings. The Dutch-born East India Company factor Peter Floris was surprised by how openly all Company employees—merchants, officers, and seamen alike—traded on their own accounts. The seamen of his ship, the *Globe*, even had an agent of their own: John Downes "like a factor lay on land," selling the seamen's goods and undercutting the Company's market. English sailors who were taken prisoner in the East Indies by Dutch ships often claimed to have lost valuable goods. A quartermaster on the *Swan*, taken by the VOC in 1617, listed mace, oil of nutmeg, oil of mace, looking glasses, and chinaware among his lost possessions, as well as maritime equipment, such as a cross staff and an astrolabe. His goods cost him £63, he said, and would have been worth about £250 in England. John Tucker, a gunner on the *Expedition*, gave a long list of the calicos, pintadoes, chintzes, chinaware, and other things he lost to the Dutch, coming to a total of £247 5s. 5d. Even poor men may have been able to borrow on the expectations of a long East India voyage, or to act for family or friends.[72]

Though Kerridge and Rastell emphasized the harm done by private trade, they professed themselves unable to counter it: "Private trade is too common to be reformed by us. There is not any seaman in your fleet that hath means but brings it, though the bad sales this year (we think) will be the forciblest restraint. To seize on their goods here were to hazard your ships and goods," they cautioned. In 1617, the Court of Governors considered whether to make a new effort to "debar the sailors and mariners wholly from all adventures . . . in regard they do so much abuse themselves under the colour [of limited permissible trade], by wronging the company in embezzling and purloining their goods." But the merchants ultimately agreed that "if the mariners be not encouraged by suffering them to bring somewhat for themselves, they will have no courage to defend the ship or goods for the merchants," and that it was "most safe to give way for so much as hath been formerly granted." If they wanted their sailors to fight, the East India merchants could not strip them of what had quickly become a customary right.[73]

Plunder was a similar subject of controversy. Even on ostensibly peaceful merchant voyages, sailors remained alert to the possibilities of pillage and resentful of efforts to restrain their traditional perquisites. In 1612, after being balked of trade in the Red Sea and at Surat, Sir Henry Middleton, the commander of the Company's sixth voyage, returned to the Red Sea to capture Gujarati ships and force them to barter their goods for English commodities. His belligerent arrival spoiled the delicate diplomacy of John Saris, the commander of the eighth voyage, who had been trying to obtain permission to trade at Mocha. After a heated discussion, Middleton and Saris eventually agreed to capture the Gujarati ships together, but Saris was determined to do as little damage as possible to the Company's reputation, and he gave instructions that "no man take the value of a penny out of [intercepted junks] or offer the least violence to their persons." This came as a severe disappointment, Saris recorded, to Middleton's men, who "did in their drunken meetings make a common course of cursing me and my voyage saying that if I had not come into the Red Sea they were promised the pillage of the junks." The following year, Thomas Best made himself more popular by condoning the pillage of several junks on the grounds that the sailors "had ventured their lives and showed themselves so full of courage" against the Portuguese.[74]

When Company ships captured other vessels, it was impossible for the factors to convince the sailors that they were due no part of prize goods. As Richard Cocks recorded in 1620, the *Elizabeth*'s men resolutely demanded what they saw as their rightful share: "These fellows ... demanded in mutinous sort the fifth part of the merchandise taken in the frigate, as also for other matters taken before, alleging Capt. Keeling did the like for prize goods taken before." Previous concessions took on customary force in the sailors' eyes, and perhaps in those of their commanders as well. Rather than rebuking his mutinous men, the *Elizabeth*'s captain went quietly on shore, leaving the merchants to cope. For officers who wanted to retain their men's affection, it was difficult to resist the pressure to share prize goods. When, on August 7, 1621, "the *Bull*'s company wholly mutinied, and thirty-six of them came to Firando [Hirado] and delivered a writing unto [Cocks], wherein they demanded their sixteenth part of prize goods," the merchants at first tried to punish the leaders, especially "one James Martin, a Scotsman . . . which stirred up the *Bull*'s men to mutiny." All the prisoners were set free a few days later, however, during the ceremonies celebrating a cooperative venture with the Dutch, and in October the sailors were paid their money, under the condition that "their wages should be answerable for it, if it were not allowed per the Honourable Company in England."[75]

The Company's exclusive claim to spoils was complicated by the fact that its own legal rights were unclear. When East India Company ships allied with Persian forces captured the strategic Portuguese fort of Ormuz in 1622, the hugely valuable spoils prompted political battles almost as intense as the military operation itself, setting the Company at odds not just with the Portuguese Crown but also with the Duke of Buckingham, who claimed his share as Lord Admiral. In the ensuing negotiations, all parties seem to have been more eager to maximize their share of the plunder than to establish a coherent vision of the relationship between the Company and the state. The East India merchants quarreled with their sailors over the spoils as well, but they seem to have known that they were on shaky legal footing. The Company first planned to dock the seamen's wages on the grounds that they had taken plunder and then, suspecting that the tactic might not hold water, they decided to claim instead that the sailors had damaged Company goods by stowing them poorly. Court minutes leave little doubt that these changing rationales were window dressing for the Company's real goal of reclaiming the gains.[76] As for the seamen who had actually done the fighting, they placed their faith, sensibly, in the maxim that possession was nine-tenths of the law.

The East India Company's political conflicts in England weakened its ability to cast private trade as selfish profit-seeking that injured common prospects. After all, the same accusation was leveled against the East India Company itself: by exporting silver and consuming ships and sailors, did the merchants weaken their country to fatten their purses? To the factor William Edwards's discomfort, this was a topic of debate on shipboard. In December 1614, he wrote to the Company about "a lewd fellow in the *Hector* . . . he is mutinous and scandalous and fit to work the destruction of a fleet." This man, the quartermaster, Henry Brighurst, had gathered other sailors together and told them "that if this trade were continued Sir Thomas Smith and his crew for their private benefit will overthrow the state of the commonwealth of England; which grew unto a public question among themselves *pro* and *contra*." Politically informed and determined to assert their rights, these sailors were not passive corporate subjects.[77]

Still, it was hard for the sailors to obtain compensation for their losses in Company service, even when these arose from battle with European rivals, for the practical reason that compensation required the merchants to actively disburse money. The families of sailors who died in Company service could make no legal claims beyond the dead men's wages and goods; anything more was discretionary, and the Company was reluctant to establish an expensive precedent. As Thomas Best's promises suggest, compensation for injuries was a gray area: maimed sailors had no legal claim on the Company, but they did have a moral claim, one the Company might or might not be persuaded to recognize.

Trinity House, the shipmasters' association, generally supported East India Company's sailors' claims to wages. In 1608, for example, nineteen Englishmen working in a frigate in the river of Surat were surrounded by Portuguese vessels and taken prisoner. They were carried to Goa, where, Nicholas Simonson recounted, most of them were "kept as prisoners by the space of fourteen months, and in that time were used very hardly being almost famished for want of meat and drink." Five of them died. Then, upon petition, a new viceroy let most of the survivors go to Lisbon on the carracks, though he retained three trumpeters for his service. Three of the Englishmen who survived the homeward journey were imprisoned again at Lisbon, while the rest were able to take ship for England. As the survivors trickled in, the governor of the East India Company, Sir Thomas Smith, was not sure what—if anything—it owed them or to those who remained in prison abroad, especially since the captured sailors admitted not fighting back against the Portuguese. Asked for guidance, the shipmasters of Trinity House decreed that the captives should be paid their wages through the time when their ship, the *Hector*, returned home, because it was not their fault they had been in the vulnerable frigate: "Had they not been sent out of [the *Hector*] for the benefit of the merchant, they might have come home in her if they had lived." This only applied to the men who had remained loyal, however: "Those who are now serving another nation voluntarily should be paid only up to the date of their capture." Similarly, in 1611, when the Company asked the Trinity House masters if they had to pay the wages of sailors of the *Union*, which had been wrecked close to home, fully laden, after most of its crew had died, the shipmasters advised that contrary to usual maritime practice, wages should be paid up to the date of the deceased sailors' deaths, and that the handful of survivors should receive their full pay "because they did their utmost, even though it was insufficient." Only deserters deserved no pay: loyalty, labor, and suffering entitled sailors to their wages.[78]

A few years later, the East India Company itself eagerly emphasized its seamen's patriotic sufferings. In 1619, as tensions between the English and Dutch companies erupted into open violence in Asian waters, the VOC captured several English ships and subjected their men to long and painful imprisonments. The Dutch capture of English ships created an uproar in England, especially since it took place shortly after the Dutch and English East India Companies had signed a treaty agreeing to share the East India trade between themselves. As the Company drummed up popular support against the VOC in England, it drew on sailors' narratives of suffering and national humiliation in an inflammatory printed tract.[79] Survivors were also asked to give depositions in the admiralty court, documenting Dutch cruelty and abuses, including slurs against the English royal family: Bartholomew Churchman, a master's mate, was allegedly punished for defending the honor of the queen, for example, after "a Dutch man . . . said she was a whore."[80]

The sailors had much to say about their own miseries and losses. Richard Roberts, quartermaster of the *Attendant*, recounted that when his ship and the *Solomon* had been captured by four Dutch ships near the Banda Islands, defeat in battle was only the beginning of a dismal ordeal. The English prisoners were brought first to the castle at Neira, where they were "kept . . . all in irons day and night" for five weeks. Then Roberts and twenty-four other Englishmen were transferred to one of the Molucca Islands, where they were kept guarded in a house for nine months, "being allowed no sustenance but a little rice and water . . . they were so much oppressed with hunger that if at any time they could entice a cat or a dog to come into the house amongst them they knocked them on the head and ate them, and [Roberts] did at times eat . . . two dogs and three cats." He was eventually brought back to Europe, having lost more than £24 in goods (clothing, bedding, pepper, benzoin, china dishes, and "stones to set in rings") and thirty months' wages. Thomas Hughes, quartermaster of the *Swan*, complained that he lost £63 in wages during his long imprisonment, as well as valuable trade goods. Many lost their lives as well. John Cook, who was taken on the *Swan* and imprisoned with twenty-four others at Amboyna (now Ambon) for about a year, reported that they were kept in harsh conditions after an escape attempt. "The Dutch apprehended them again and clapped them with irons where they remained in lamentable estate in great want of victuals, and [he] and five more were [chained] two and two in bolts with the shackles fast riveted." Nine or ten of the prisoners died.[81]

These wrenching narratives were politically useful. With James's support, the aggrieved merchants demanded restitution from the VOC, and they received it. It was not clear, however, whether the sailors could expect any part of the sums paid to the East India Company or any other recognition of their losses. According to custom, after all, seamen were not entitled to compensation when voyages ended in disaster. Hoping to gain from widespread outrage over Dutch aggression, a number of sailors and their relatives petitioned the Privy Council and Parliament for aid. Thomasine Powell, the widowed mother of young William Powell, appealed bitterly to the Privy Council, describing how her son, a sailor on the *Swan*, had been "most cruelly used, being stripped naked and despoiled of all such goods as he had . . . viz. nineteen bags of rice, two barrels of rack and one barrel of sugar besides his clothes and his chest . . . and afterwards was chained and kept miserably in slavery and captivity until his death." She had been "not only now deprived of her comfort in this life, but also utterly destitute of that benefit which by his careful endeavours and loving duty she might have been partaker of."[82]

To determine what the Company owed to the VOC's unhappy prisoners, Parliament asked the shipmasters of Trinity House for guidance. In May 1623, the shipmasters—including the veteran seamen Thomas Best and Robert Rickman—gave an answer, again, that was as favorable as possible to the seamen. They stressed the sailors' patriotic sacrifices: while the law provided little recourse for the injured seamen, "in conscience the case is different since the Hollanders offered the men wages to serve against the company, and when they refused, imprisoned them, kept them in irons and short of victuals, of which some died; 'more for their king they could not have done.' " The East India Company had by this time already paid the men one-third of their lost wages, and the masters of Trinity House strongly suggested that they should pay the whole. This, they conceded, was a matter not "of right" but of equity, in recognition of the sailors' sufferings in the English cause. As for the seamen's lost goods, however, there was no recourse, because the English agreement with the Dutch released the VOC from liability for private goods unless the petitioners could demonstrate that the VOC had received them.[83] Unsatisfied, the mariners continued to petition Parliament.[84]

Both the representative of the English state in Asia and a private commercial corporation, the East India Company was rife with contradictions. Its seamen, too, played dual roles: at times the Company cast them as English champions, participants in a patriotic national endeavor, but at others, they were treated as wage earners whose labor had been bought and paid for and to whom nothing more was owed. The Company shifted between these models—one hotly emotional, the other coolly financial—emphasizing the sailors' obligations while minimizing its own, yet it failed to impress its views on Company sailors. Eager to trade, determined to share in plunder and pillage, and anxious for compensation for their losses, the sailors used what leverage they had to press their own claims. Murmuring and mutinying, petitioning Parliament, and enjoying the sympathy of the shipmasters' guild, they insisted that the Company pay for their loyalty.

Allegiance and the English Nation

The national quality of the East India Company was complicated by the fact that at sea the Company's servants and the English nation were not entirely congruent. Some English seamen worked for the Company's rivals, while foreigners also served on English ships. This mismatch between the Company's national identity and its personnel was unavoidable and does not seem to have troubled the Company's London governors, who were open to hiring foreigners if the price was right. For the Company's sea commanders and overseas factors, however, it was a barrier to the national unity they strove to foster, and they doubted the loyalty of foreign recruits.

Like Christopher Evans, the *Hector*'s gunner's mate, some English sailors deserted the East India Company to work for its rivals—something Company officers considered tantamount to treason. Deserters stayed away from the VOC, perhaps because of the harshness of its discipline: punishments for serious offenses ranged from hundreds of lashes and enslavement to "gruesome" innovations "calculated to terrify the average sailor into obedience," while "a comprehensive system of fines and levies for a range of trivial offenses . . . seemed calculated to strip sailors of their earnings."[85] At Narasapur in 1614, Peter Floris, the Dutch-born factor in English service, shocked his English colleagues when he ordained that two Englishmen be punished for dueling by being keelhauled and then, in the Dutch style, "nailed with a knife through their hand[s] at the mainmast, and there to stand until they pulled it quite through their hands, and yet to lose six months wages besides." He remitted the punishment after a local port official and the English community intreated him on the men's behalf. The VOC could afford to be a ruthless employer, with strong state backing, soldiers at its command, and a workforce increasingly drawn from the German hinterlands and trafficked through the crimps known as soul sellers; but Dutch rule seems to have been more likely to produce deserters than attract them.[86]

Portuguese service was more appealing. Some East India Company sailors ran away "for fear of punishment," like Robert Clarkson, who had fled the *Dragon* in November 1612 and went to the Portuguese at Daman.[87] Others may have had more complicated reasons. Robert Drake, Thomas Foxe, and John Rose deserted the English ships at Surat in 1614 after making elaborate preparations, according to the captain, Walter Peyton. In addition to buying a dead merchant's silk clothing "so that they were furnished for their fugitive purposes, these fellows left letters in their chests, expressing the reason of their running away." Foxe was caught, but, as Peyton related, Drake and Rose "escaped away in a fisher boat which they found in the river, and went for Daman, where they were friendly entertained, afterward they writ letters unto some other of their consorts in our fleet, enticing them to follow their steps." Though the English officers tried to prevent any further desertion, three more Englishmen ran from the *Peppercorn* to Daman a few weeks later.[88] With Portuguese manpower stretched thin, English renegades like "William Johnson sailor of the *Darling*, and John Coverdale trumpeter of the admiral," who "ran away to the Portugal army" in 1611, were likely to find open arms, especially if they had experience in gunnery. Both English and Dutch sailors were thought more expert in artillery than the Portuguese, so much so that in 1616 when Henry Pepwell praised a Portuguese carrack's gunnery, he concluded that foreigners must be on board: "They behaved themselves with wonderful resolution; their gunners better than ever I knew before in Spanish or Portugal ships, which I verily believe were English and Dutch, seldom or never missing our hulls or sails."[89]

East India Company officers usually treated desertion harshly, doing their best to recapture and punish runaways. In Japan in 1621, for example, when some sailors fled toward Nagasaki to join the Portuguese, Cocks sent letters to forestall them, and "a barque of Japons, being sent after the runaways with speed, overtook them and kept them from proceeding forward." Six deserters were brought back, "most of them being double runaways and some felons, and therefore, by general consent, according to the martial law, [Cocks] condemned all to be hanged." Four of them were actually executed.[90] These harsh measures reflected Company officers' anxiety about desertion: sailors were well informed about Company dealings and plans, so runaways carried not only scarce skills but also valuable information to Company rivals. Other measures to encourage loyalty were gentler: debt bondage was common in the VOC, but Captain Saris was reluctant to record sailors' debts to English shopkeepers in the ship's book, a course he "held not fitting for that it might discourage the sailors finding themselves to have little credit, being a main occasion to make them runaways in foreign parts and leave the ship destitute." Men had to have more than the dreary satisfaction of clearing their debts to attract them home.[91]

Deserters' motives could be complex, and some eventually returned to English service. Thomas Herod's flight was partly prompted by the collapse of his marriage, for example. Promoted from master's mate to be

the master of the *Darling*, Herod sounded cheerful in a 1614 letter, sending news to the Company and asking that his wife be paid his wages.[92] A
different interlocutor writing to the Company gave a darker picture,
warning the merchants that Herod, among others, was busily lining his
own pockets at the Company's expense. The merchants planned to recall
him, but to no avail: Peyton heard that Herod meant to take his ship to
the Portuguese but "was prevented" and so "accomplished his fugitive desire in his person only, and fled to the Portugals." The Portuguese were
probably happy to have him: "They say he is an extraordinary fellow for
gunnery, God cut him short in his unnatural courses," Peyton groused.[93]
In 1619, after an unpleasant experience with the Inquisition, Herod resur-
faced in Japan via Macao, requesting to serve his nation once more.
Asked to explain his actions, he wrote a memorial explaining that he had
had just cause to depart and live with the Portuguese: the wrong done to
him on East India ships and the lewdness of his wife. Cocks allowed
Herod to join the English in Japan, where he remained until his death,
leaving his estate to his daughter in England "and to his wife two groats
or eight pence sterling, for that she should claim no part of his goods in
respect she married in his absence."[94]

In contrast, for the pilot William Adams, durable family bonds shored
up tenuous national loyalties. After about a decade spent guiding English
ships to Morocco, in 1598 Adams decided to test his mettle by joining a
Dutch fleet bound for the East Indies via the Strait of Magellan. The voyage was disastrous. Many men died of hunger in the strait, and the ships
became separated. A number of the survivors on Adams's ship were killed
in an ambush on Mocha Island off Chile, leaving them with "scarce so
many men left as could wind up our anchor." Eventually the two remaining ships made for Japan; only one ever arrived, and that with "no more
than six besides myself, that could stand upon their feet," Adams recalled.
Unable to return home, he amused the shogun Tokugawa Ieyasu by teaching him some mathematics, learned Japanese, and married a local woman.
Years later, Adams smuggled out two letters—one to the East India
Company and one to his English wife—with the help of an English sailor
serving the VOC, who brought them to the factor at Banten. In his letter
to the Company, Adams advertised his willingness to be of service to his
nation in Japan and his anxiety about his wife and children in England.[95]

When the Company later established a factory—a commercial outpost—in Japan, Adams repeatedly asked it to lend Mary Adams money on his account, and she lobbied the Company for aid as well. The merchants paid reluctantly, for they had their doubts about Adams's loyalty: John Saris thought him "a naturalized Japanner" whose "wish is but to have the Company bear his charges to his wife."[96]

Company officers recognized that some English seamen sailed honestly in Dutch service: like Adams and the sailor who had carried his letters, they were not deserters but simply worked for foreign employers. Rather than seeing these seamen as traitors, Company officers often valued them as potential sources of inside information. At a tense moment in Java, for example, Edmund Scot recounted that English Company men were about to board VOC ships "on business" when "some Englishmen of their fleet, with weeping eyes called to them, that they should not come" because the Dutch had orders to "kill the Englishmen they met with." VOC commanders sometimes strove to prevent these communications. In summer 1617, when the Dutch *Sun* reached Japan, Richards Cocks sought to speak with the Englishmen on board but found that they had been forbidden to talk with him: "There were four or five English men aboard the *Sun* . . . which, as it seemed, were afraid to make themselves known unto me; and one of them, a tall fellow, stood staring as if he had been aghast, and told me he was doubtful whether he might tell me he was an Englishman or no." A few days later, Cocks sent the Dutch-speaking Richard King on board, "and it fortuned the Englishmen found opportunity to tell him they asked the general leave to come ashore, to visit their countrymen." They had been denied, they said: their Dutch commander had told them "they held the English in these parts for their mortal enemies, and therefore forbade them to come to our house." Later, the shipmaster John Totten managed to speak at more length with one of the English VOC sailors and confirmed troubling rumors about VOC aggression toward the English on the Bandas. Even when they worked on rival ships, Englishmen were expected to help their countrymen.[97]

Company officers' attitudes toward non-English recruits were more ambivalent. Scots were also subjects of James I and were common on board, though Cocks seems to have found them especially mutinous. Even Cocks was willing to poach foreign sailors from the Company's rivals, however. In

July 1617 in Japan, he welcomed the disgruntled VOC employees who sometimes visited the English house in defiance of Dutch orders. On July 3, Cocks recorded: "There came two Japons to the English house, which came in these Dutch ships, and complain that the Hollanders will not pay them their wages according to promise, and desired, when our shipping came, if we had need of men, that they might be entertained, for that they would not serve the Hollanders any more, having been so badly dealt with for their six years' service now past." Two weeks later, "many Holland mariners came to the English house, complaining how they were misused and beaten like boys without form or reason." Still, Cocks thought it "doubtful how many will run away in the end."[98]

Suspicions remained about foreign workers' loyalty. Cocks was willing to employ Dutch sailors, but he disliked having to rely on foreign factors. In 1614, he relayed some news from the agent Lucas Antonison, noting sourly: "I have not one word in writing from any Englishman, there being none with him but an old surgeon and a mariner which can neither write nor read. . . . I wish our Company was served with Englishmen, for I doubt our Dutch factors will breed inconveniences."[99] The London merchants readily hired foreign sailors, but ship commanders often complained about them. William Keeling hated having Portuguese mariners on board his fleet. He wanted to land two of them before even leaving England, he said, "for sundry causes . . . justly causing my particular wonder that so wise a Company would entertain such unfit persons in voyages of this quality," but was prevented by contrary winds. He was still angry when he reached the Cape of Good Hope, where he left a letter for the Company warning that employing Portuguese men was "a ready way to betray all," and that "one of them shipped was a plotter to betray Captain Newport in the *Expedition*."[100] Two years later, Henry Pepwell chided the Company for hiring piratical Dutch mariners:

> Your Worships have also given entertainment to divers lewd and dissolute fellows, and amongst the rest to sundry Dutch, who being vagrant and fugitive persons are prone and ready to attempt any manner of villainy. . . . For being in the Road of Swally, myself not able to stir out of my cabin by reason of my late received hurts, most of the Dutchmen, combining themselves together with divers of our people, conspired to run away with our longboat, and so to have robbed and spoiled such frigates and junks as they

should meet and overcome, until, being better furnished with some shipping, they then determined to sail into the Red Sea, there to make what
havoc they could.

The plot had been uncovered, but the threat remained: "I did not use
such severe chastisement as the heinousness of the offense deserved . . .
because there were a great number of them, but . . . do watch my best
opportunity when I with most convenience may rid the fleet of such dangerous knaves." Sailors who were willing to serve their country's rivals
were, at best, of suspect quality, at worst a fifth column within.[101]

Hiring local sailors to make up for heavy mortality in the East Indies
was unavoidable, but English commanders doubted their skills and loyalty.
John Jourdain thought that "blacks . . . will serve to do ordinary work,"
while Arthur Spaight hired "black men" only when "forced" to do so.[102]
Asian seamen who were willing to undertake sea voyages to England were
probably desperate, and not the most skilled. In Japan, Saris was offered
the service of "divers vagrant people about town, which no doubt would
be willing to go, yet were not fit to be carried to sea; for that . . . they
would serve for nothing but to spend victuals." Saris later came to believe
that experience only made them harder to handle: "Indians" were "the
worse for being to England," he said, instructing a subordinate to "command them to all drudgery" and to deny them any relief if they refused.
Japanese seamen were thought to be especially "mutinous," and Cocks
complained about their demands for wages after voyages to England.[103]

In these early years, Asian sailors were hired as individuals rather than
labor gangs and seem to have lived on closer terms with English sailors
than would later be the case.[104] Their intimate knowledge of the inner
workings of English ships, their religious and cultural differences, and their
ability to speak local languages made them a potential threat for
Englishmen who wished to control local knowledge of Company doings.
At Mocha in 1612, for example, while thorny trade negotiations were under way, Saris wrote that a lascar called Moosoo "concluded with the
Indians aboard of his ship to run away, and if they could not get leave to
go ashore to swim aboard the junks which rid by us." These seamen were
returning home after a voyage to England, but Saris ordered them to be
locked up because they knew that his chief interpreter, Nicholas Boulton,

was an apostate who had converted to Islam and then returned to Christianity. Boulton had probably converted and acquired his languages while a captive in North Africa. Moosoo's intimate knowledge of Boulton's body left him "in fear to go ashore . . . doubting in regard he was circumcised he would betray him."[105]

When Saris's efforts to set up English trade on land at Mocha failed, he and Sir Henry Middleton fell instead to forcibly "trading" with the merchant ships from Gujarat. They sailed with their spoils to Java, where the lascars finally did get ashore and recounted what they had seen. When Saris conferred with the governor about customs duties, he found that "our swarts brought out of England had told him that we had stolen our cloth from the Gujarats and holy men of Mecca," and that the governor was unsure whether he could morally accept customs paid on such goods. To Saris's disappointment, the governor eventually decided that he could. In this case, the flow of information through lascar sailors had done no harm.[106]

Asian sailors who married English wives were expected to remain loyal to England and the Company, but they did not always comply. At Java in December 1612, Saris recorded indignantly: "Mumbarrick one of our Indian swarts married in England ran away notwithstanding the good usage he had, and the day before I bestowed a sack of pepper upon him to send to his wife. But for a small matter the Javans found him out again and sent him aboard where I gave the master order to keep him in irons till our setting sail." For Saris, Mumbarrick's marriage was cause to show him favor, but also to force him to remain on board and return to fulfill his familial obligations in England. For Mumbarrick himself, the Company's forcible barter with Gujarati ships in the Red Sea may have been too much to bear. He tried to run away twice more; the third time, at the Moluccas, in Saris's account, "he swam ashore in the night and was gotten to the Moors' houses, where he reported that we had robbed and spoiled the most of the holy men of Mecca, with other villainous speeches." To no avail: English sailors cutting wood in the forest found him, and he was forced on board again.[107]

Mumbarrick did not agree that marriage to an Englishwoman was supposed to anchor him in England; like three "Indians" who petitioned the Company in 1614 for permission to bring their English wives with them to the East Indies, he might have expected that *she* would travel with *him*. The women petitioned to go as well but were denied on the grounds that it was unfitting "for such women to go among so many unruly sailors in a ship." Still, realizing that "their wages are but small, whereby they are not able to maintain their wives and themselves here," the Company raised the "Indian" mariners' wages to twenty shillings a month "for the better encouragement of strangers."[108] Over time, however, the expense of men's families turned the Company away from encouraging marriage, and by the 1620s even Englishmen were sometimes explicitly denied employment because they were married. Indeed, seamen's wives frequently troubled the Company by petitioning for relief when their husbands were away, and after they were killed in Company service.[109] For Company merchants, these personal entanglements were an expensive inconvenience; they fostered sailors' loyalty but at too high a cost.

In its precarious early years, the East India Company conducted trade and diplomacy on a large scale and across huge distances. Facing daunting challenges, the London merchants strove for information, order, and predictability. For them, the Englishness of the Company seems to have lain in its royal charter and its competition with Portuguese and Dutch rivals rather than a community of interests and identity linking them and the sailors who manned their ships. It was more practical to think of the seamen as interchangeable wage laborers whose claims on the Company were strictly limited, and who could, if necessary, be replaced by cheaper foreign labor. At sea, however, the dangers and stresses of long-distance trade and violent imperial rivalry encouraged a more inclusive approach. Risking their lives in battle and against the far more potent enemy of disease, English sailors wanted to feel that their welfare mattered to their superiors. Emphasizing the Englishness of the East India Company's cause was a useful way to bring its disorderly subjects together, and Company captains preferred English or at least British seamen to foreigners whose allegiance always remained suspect. Appealing to their men's loyalty, Company commanders spoke a traditional language of care and comradeship, and they were under perpetual pressure to tolerate sailors' participation in trade. At sea, if not in London, nationhood underlay the company-state's internal cohesion.

As the East India Company expanded over the course of the seventeenth century, its appeals to English nationhood seem to have taken on a more marked racial tinge. Territorial expansion required soldiers, but those available were often of doubtful quality, poorly paid, and harshly treated. As Company rule became more authoritarian, it fanned fears of racial difference to reinforce racial and national solidarity.[110] In contrast, as we shall see, in the late sixteenth and early seventeenth centuries, when merchant companies were just beginning to send out trading voyages to unfamiliar places in the Americas, Africa, and Asia, they were more concerned with shaping foreigners' views of the English than with English views of foreigners.

CHAPTER SIX

ENGLISHNESS ABROAD

At anchor off Sierra Leone on September 5, 1607, the sailors of the East India ship *Dragon* put on a remarkable performance. While their captain, William Keeling, watched with "a Negro named Lucas Fernandes, who had lived at St. Jago in former time, and was turned Christian," the English seamen entertained them with "the tragedy of Hamlet." He was surely too polite to say so, but the Luso-African interpreter probably found the play tedious, and no surprise: though fluent in Portuguese and "very sensible and plentiful in Spanish compliments, both in speech and action, and very humane in his carriage," Fernandes spoke no English. To entertain his guest, Keeling could only draw on what he had: the seamen had been rehearsing *Hamlet* and *Richard II* while caught in the windless doldrums. During those long frustrating months as their fresh water dwindled and they grew drowsy with scurvy, their anxious captain had allowed them to amuse themselves with acting to keep them "from idleness and unlawful games, or sleep."[1]

While the seamen rehearsed their lines, the officers of the *Dragon* and the *Hector* had hunted through books of navigation, deciding at last to make for Sierra Leone because Drake and Cavendish had watered there decades before. They followed the path of the Elizabethan plunderers, but their style of cultural engagement could not be more different. Instead of burning towns and stealing rice, the East India Company captains and merchants were studiedly courteous, mindful of local sensibilities, eager to please. Reciting verse and striking attitudes for "a Negro," the sailors were enlisted in a new project, one that was becoming increasingly important as English merchants forged trading relationships with partners around the globe: they were not just acting in a play, they were performing Englishness.

As English imperial ventures shifted from plunder to trade and expanded beyond familiar limits, seafaring men encountered a wide variety of foreign peoples. Voyages in unfamiliar waters were tests of intercultural communication as much as technical skill. Heavily manned, with little cargo space, English ships stopped often for fresh water, food, wood, and information. While officers and merchants took primary responsibility for trade and diplomacy, all men on board participated in these repeated episodes of cultural engagement. Sailors cut wood and hauled water on land, while men with scurvy were brought there to recover. Seamen bartered with local people and served as "pledges," hostages for good behavior during trade. Local informants and trading partners provided critical aid when they told the Englishmen where to find water and sold them fruit, fowl, and livestock. Still, going on land was dangerous for English sailors. Establishing mutual trust despite language barriers and often without knowledge of one another's prior experiences and present intentions was a challenge for local peoples and travelers alike.

Building trust depended in part on convincing foreign audiences that the men in English ships were a strong but friendly people. English voyages were no longer individual predatory ventures; rather, in distant seas, they were increasingly set out by merchants with long-term interests in trading relationships. For those relationships to thrive, Englishmen had to communicate who they were to foreign interlocutors. When language barriers were impenetrable, sometimes projecting muscular friendliness was the best the English could do: commanders handed out trinkets, while sailors were enjoined to sing, dance, and play with locals. In Asia, where the English were just one of many merchant groups, East India Company merchants tried to gain their hosts' favor by projecting a specific image of Englishness, one that they thought distinguished them from the Spanish, the Portuguese, and the Dutch. Deriving the best value they could from their weakness, they sought to show that they were a civil people, respectful to the great and courteous to common folk. Sailors were essential to these performances of Englishness, not least because when they misbehaved they offended local sensibilities. In performances both formal and informal—athletic competitions, martial displays, and concerts, for example—they were subject to local scrutiny.

For the sailors themselves, these performances must often have been uncomfortable. This new courteous, self-disciplined Englishness was far removed from the aggressive rapacity that had been fostered by the war with Spain and by endemic maritime violence thereafter. Indeed, as polished cosmopolitans, English seamen left much to be desired. Though their survival sometimes depended on getting along in foreign cultures, they failed at least as often as they succeeded. They were protective of their honor and fond of unguarded festivity. They took offense when conciliation was more wise; they were fearful and quick to resort to violence; they pilfered local people's things; and they succumbed easily to unfamiliar illnesses, potent drink, and strange drugs.

Sometimes sailors' performances were wholly involuntary. When their men abused local people, English commanders gratified the victims by publicly punishing the transgressors. The displays of Englishness forced on English sailors by their enemies were even more humiliating and dangerous. Venturing into places where other powers held sway, East India Company merchants could not always control the script. Captured by Ottoman forces or by the VOC, English prisoners were sometimes displayed to local audiences in spectacles of shame, triumphs intended to teach observers that they were a negligible nation, subject to their captors' might. The conflicted ways in which sailors performed Englishness for foreign eyes illustrate the psychic costs of the turn from plunder to commerce for seafaring men. They had come a long way from fighting crocodiles, a long way from taking what they liked and doing as they pleased.

Vulnerability and Violence

English sailors' work often took them on shore. In this early period when there was hardly anything in the way of established routes, suppliers, and factories, the English had to procure supplies and information as well as trading opportunities from peoples who were strange to them, often the subjects of formidable foreign empires. The quantity and intensity of these contacts stand in stark contrast to the wind-swept isolation in which we tend to imagine that sailors led their lives. While studies of encounters focus on settlers and elite travelers, most English people who engaged with non-Europeans in the early seventeenth century were sailors, transient laboring men who often lacked the bookish knowledge that shaped elite travelers' perspectives on cultural difference, but whose personal and collective experiences endowed them with a rich set of expectations and anxieties.

The surviving journals and accounts of the doomed voyage of the East India Company ship *Ascension* in 1608–1609 provide a vivid illustration of the urgent physical needs and fears that shaped English seamen's frequent encounters with foreign peoples, both before and after the ship was wrecked at Surat. From early on, constant shortages of fresh water drove the *Ascension* and its consort, the *Union*, to foreign shores. Although the commander, Alexander Sharpeigh, had been instructed to sail directly to Madagascar before putting to land, the ships sought supplies both on the Canaries and on the Cape Verde Islands, where the cape merchant John Jourdain reported that some "Negroes" spoke to the English in Portuguese and offered them goats, but showed them no water.[2] Fortunately, the ships were able to reach their next landfall, at "Saldania," as they called the Cape of Good Hope, where they were obliged to stop because so many sailors were suffering from scurvy. There too they depended on the cooperation of local people: to cure their sick men, they needed to put them on land and procure fresh food, and at the Cape the only practical way to acquire fresh food was to buy it from Khoekhoe herders who had been trading with European seamen for more than a decade.

The Khoekhoe spoke a click language that the English could not even mimic, and the entrails that some of them wore around their necks offended English sensibilities. Nonetheless, trade with the Khoekhoe was essential to the English sailors' health, and they tried to give them "as much content" as they could. According to Jourdain, when the Khoekhoe drove away cattle they had sold to the English, Company officers paid up "without giving any foul language, for fear lest they would bring us no more."[3] Fearing attacks, the English constructed an earthen bulwark to protect themselves while building their pinnace, but they made themselves as congenial as possible. The herders had no boats, so when the sailors slaughtered seals on a nearby island to make oil for their lamps, they gave the Khoekhoe the carcasses as well as a boatload of penguins, Jourdain continued, "to give content to the Saldanians, they much rejoicing at our coming, making a great feast amongst themselves." The steward, Robert Coverte, who later published an account of his adventures, recorded with disgust that when the Khoekhoe found the seal carcasses, "these people have taken them up and eaten them, when they have swarmed with crawling maggots." Still, the sailors were happy to trade with them for ostrich eggs and feathers, and porcupine quills.[4]

The *Ascension* was separated from the *Union* and the pinnace when rounding the Cape, and by the time it reached the Comoro Islands, the Englishmen were desperate for water again. They were frightened of the islands, though: in 1591, Englishmen who had gone ashore at the Comoros had been attacked, and most of them had been killed. Sailors from the *Ascension* rowed uneasily toward the shore, afraid to land among the beckoning people. Instead, they spoke with equally nervous fishermen, who told them truthfully that there was little water on the islands. The Englishmen decided to send a delegation to the ruler regardless. At first the sailors were eager to go along, hoping for tips from Comoran nobles, Jourdain recorded; "but when we came to the shore, those which were desirous to have the credit to carry the present, seeing so many people armed on land, had no great stomach to go aland." The Comorans and the English soon agreed to exchange hostages: two Comoran "pledges" climbed into the English boat to guarantee Jourdain's safety as he went alone to give his compliments to the sultan.[5] After an exchange of gifts, a banquet, a trumpet fanfare, and many ceremonies, the Comorans treated the English with great courtesy, allowing them to cut wood, selling them plantains, hens, goats, and coconuts, and offering to share what little water they had.[6] Though Jourdain remained suspicious of their motives, two sailors expressed nothing but gratitude for this unexpected kindness. Coverte, the steward, was dazzled by their perfect manners, commending them as "civil, kind, and true hearted to strangers," as well as having "a very civil government amongst them." The boatswain, Thomas Jones, who later wrote an account of his travels, reported gratefully: "We were used of the king and people, with all the kindness that might be."[7]

The *Ascension* was still in desperate need of water when it left the Comoros, and it stopped next at Pemba in the Zanzibar archipelago, where events took a deadly turn. On land, the Englishmen met people who told them that they were welcome—but only if they were Portuguese. Jourdain claimed they were, but the imposture must have been obvious. While mariners were filling the casks, a nobleman sought to lure them inland, promising them a better source of water in the woods. The English remained wary, especially after a sailor sent inland with a message reported seeing men in Portuguese attire. Still, when the nobleman invited the English to come and fetch a gift of oranges and lemons, it seemed rude to decline, and young Edward Churchman volunteered to go. He never returned.[8] Soon thereafter, the sailors filling casks at the water's edge were attacked, and the boatswain's servant was killed before the others managed to escape. The Englishmen went ashore the next day with a truce flag, hoping to negotiate Churchman's return, but when no one came to speak with them, they were obliged to content themselves with giving their dead countryman a proper burial.[9]

Although they had known they were in hostile territory, the English sailed away from Pemba feeling ill-used, and when they took three small boats carrying merchants returning home from Mombasa shortly thereafter, they were in a vindictive humor. The crew suspected some of their prisoners of being Portuguese because of their "pale and white" skin, "yet being asked, what they were, they said, they were Moors, and showed us their backs all written with characters." The Englishmen angrily told their captives "how treacherously their countrymen of Pemba had dealt with us . . . whereat they were much dismayed," and they were even more frightened by the threatening gestures of the shipmaster. At this tense moment, the sailors noticed that the Zanzibari pilot was armed;

when they tried to grab his knife, he screamed and struck at them. Panicked, the merchants of Pemba drew their knives—or so the English sources report—but they were massacred by the English sailors, who "took such arms as were next hand and began to kill as fast as they could." In his printed account, Coverte argued that they acted "for the safeguard of our lives." He did not mention—perhaps he was ashamed to remember—that a little boy and "a maid of some eight years old" were the only survivors, except for some who swam to land. The frantic little girl jumped overboard three times "when she saw her mother drowned," so that the sailors "had much ado to save her." But if rescuing the child they had orphaned gave the mariners occasion to examine their consciences, they soon got over it. Once the slaughter was complete, "the sailors made pillage" of the rich merchandize in the boats.[10]

Soon thereafter, the *Ascension*'s men found relief on the uninhabited Seychelles. With ample water and fresh food, they were able to relax as they had not done in months. Under the circumstances, a few odd crocodiles were a small inconvenience. "These islands seemed to us an earthly paradise," Thomas Jones remembered. Sailing on, they briefly considered going on land at Malindi on the Kenyan coast, but a mariner who swam ashore was frightened by an armed man, and so they continued on their way. At Socotra, they met with Gujarati merchants bound for the Red Sea, who gave them news of English affairs in Surat and happily joined company with the powerful *Ascension* for the voyage to Aden, lending them a pilot and coming on board "to pass the time." These cosmopolitan merchants even "heard prayer" when the English conducted their services, and were "very attentive," the factor William Revett recorded.[11]

The *Ascension*'s time in the Red Sea proved frustrating for the ship's sailors. At Aden, an arid Ottoman outpost where a few "Turks"—mostly renegades, according to Jourdain—ruled a conquered Arab population, Jourdain and Sharpeigh at first met with courteous entertainment, then found themselves the prisoners of their hosts, who urged them to land their trade goods without delay.[12] Most of the sailors stayed on board, although Coverte went ashore to cook for his masters. After much wrangling over fees and rights, Jourdain traveled to Sana'a to appeal directly to the pasha, while the ship sailed to Mocha, a much larger center of trade. There the *Ascension*'s pinnace—which had finally reappeared, minus its murdered master—was repaired on land by a number of English sailors who spent three weeks there (very imprudently given the precarious status of the English, Jourdain thought). Still, the sailors must have enjoyed the interval, and several surely slipped away to go to the market, where they found "apricots, quinces, dates, grapes abundance, peaches, lemons, and plaintains great store," which Coverte "much marvelled at."[13]

Having done very little business at Mocha, the *Ascension* stopped once more at Socotra. There, with the aid of a polyglot Jewish passenger, the Englishmen spoke with the sultan; he sold them water and spoke with them at length about English affairs at Surat, being well informed by "Gujarats of good credit." Finally the *Ascension* sailed for Surat, but—lacking a local pilot—came instead to Mua (Mahuva) on the opposite side of the gulf. As usual, the sailors bought food and sought news, and they also took on a Hindu passenger, who suggested that they wait for a local pilot before crossing to Surat. According to English sources, the *Ascension*'s Dutch master arrogantly refused, a decision that was to doom the ship.[14]

In September 1609, sailing toward Surat, the *Ascension* struck ground and lost its rudder. As the master cursed, the lurching ship hit the skiff and split it in two. The sailors promptly hauled it on board for repairs, but they were clumsy with fear. That black night was spent in prayer and the following day in frantic labor, as some men pumped the *Ascension*, "yet all in vain, for the water came in much faster than they were able to free it," while others strove to repair the skiff and to make the longboat's sides higher so that it would be able to carry more weight. The boats were not thought big enough for everyone, and fearing that the officers would take the ship's treasure and abandon them, the sailors mutinied, standing "on the pump with half pikes, swearing that they would kill the first that should set hand to put in any chest of money." At this point, it seems that Sharpeigh opened the chests of treasure and "bid the company take what they would." Laden with silver, the mariners scrambled into the boats. As Jourdain gripped the ladder, Coverte clung to his back, "so laden with money . . . that he could not hardly go." When the merchant protested, the cook answered "that now there was no respect of persons, that it was every one for himself." Astonishingly, most and perhaps even all of the crew managed to huddle in the skiff and the overladen longboat—about seventy-five men in all, including the two passengers. Many of them were richer than they had ever been in their lives.[15]

In the middle of the night, the bedraggled survivors in the longboat organized themselves as well as they could, with those around the sides holding up a sail to keep out the surf, others bailing, and, Jourdain related, "the rest all stowed one upon another. In this manner we put off from the ship, singing of psalms to the praise of God, leaving the ship as yet standing, with her yards across and the flag atop, to our great griefs." At length they rowed into a river, in full sight of four Portuguese frigates, who to their amazed relief did not pursue them, apparently not recognizing them as Europeans. Friendly bystanders on the riverbank urged them to row farther for fear of capture, so the Englishmen continued on until late in the evening, when finally they dared come ashore, in Jourdain's words, "to stretch our legs, being a fair moonshine, giving God thanks for our delivery."[16]

Famished and exhausted, the sailors sent their Jewish and Hindu passengers in search of help. A "poor man" came to their rescue, agreeing to bring two or three of them to speak with the local governor, while the rest huddled by their boat, waiting for the tide to come in. They were frightened by the approach of twenty armed men, but met with no harm. Unarmed, exhausted, and hungry, they told the headman their story through an interpreter who spoke Portuguese, and, Jourdain related, he "seemed to be very sorrowful of our distress, and gave us very comfortable words, saying that the loss of our goods was nothing in respect of our lives, which [it had] pleased God to lend us and bring into a good country that wanted nothing, where we should find many friends." The Englishmen were terrified that they would be betrayed by their rescuers, for they were helpless foreigners with a great deal of money. When they eventually arrived at the governor's seat in the town of Gandevi, however, the governor welcomed them warmly, "entreating us," Jourdain wrote, "to rest ourselves while they made ready such victuals as was to be had, which was rice with butter and fruit, for the Governor is an Abramane, who doth never eat of any live thing, and therefore he prayed us to pardon him, that it was against his law." The starving men were not likely to turn up their noses at vegetarian fare. After a night's rest, the sailors consumed a delicious breakfast of "rice, bread, cakes, and fruits of divers sorts and sweetmeats," and they set off for Surat, some on foot, others riding on bullocks, horses, and palanquins. Gratefully, they offered the governor two hundred *reales,* which he courteously refused, asking instead for "something from our country" when the English ships came in.[17]

During their journey, the English mariners continued to be treated "with great kindness" by the people they met, both Hindu and Parsi. They recovered their spirits, "well refreshed with a kind of drink of the palmita tree called taddy," and began to quarrel among themselves: some of the men, in particular the steward, were no longer willing to defer to the captain's authority. With the money they had saved from the wreck, the sailors were no longer dependent on their officers, who were in any case unable to maintain them. At length they reached a cistern and some tombs surrounded by mango trees about a league from Surat, where they were told to stay. The merchant William Finch came there from Surat to meet them and to tell them of his efforts on their behalf. After a pleasant night "under the green trees," the Englishmen received gifts of "eating things" and were told that they should go to a village about two miles away, because the Portuguese would dislike their presence in the town. "But our unruly company began to be in a mutiny amongst themselves," Jourdain wrote, "some were content to go, but the most part would stand upon their guard and would not go to any other place to have their throats cut; that they had rather die where they were than to go to a worse place." After the many dangers they had passed through, their leafy refuge amid the tombs must have seemed a blessed asylum. Although they had been treated kindly so far, they half expected that the fair words they had met with were only meant to lure them into a murderous ambush.[18]

The merchants eventually persuaded the mulish sailors to move, and at the village they recovered from their anxiety with the help of "palmita drink and raisin wine." Then they "fell to lewd women, which went thither to that purpose, that in short time many fell sick and others in their drink fell to quarreling one with another." Their drunken disorders created a minor crisis when "in his valour" a seaman named Thomas Tucker assaulted a calf, causing great offense. Finch came from Surat to make amends, which he did by having Tucker whipped until local people decided he had had enough.[19]

Despite the hospitality of the people, the sailors' prospects were dismal. There was no secure English presence at Surat and no immediate hope that other English ships would arrive. The men refused to obey Sharpeigh, who was seriously ill; their chosen leader, the merchant William Revett, soon died; and the Dutch shipmaster was so hated that one sailor stabbed him in the chest. Most headed first toward Agra, the Mughal capital nearly seven hundred miles away, but as death and illness ravaged the group, "some went to one place, and some to another, and some back again for Surat," "every one following his own course as long as the money lasted." Straggling, the men fell victim to the flux, strong drink, and stronger drugs. John Johnson died "with eating opium betwixt Cambaya and Surat." His money was promptly pocketed by the loathed master, Philip de Grove, angering John Jourdain, who "purposed to have it from him to give to other poor men which wanted." The shipmaster set off secretly for the Dutch factory at Masulipatnam, but he reportedly died before reaching his destination.[20]

A few sailors saved themselves by finding new patrons. The boatswain, Thomas Jones, was at loose ends when he met the Jesuit Emanuel Pinheiro, who promised to send him back to Europe. He and several others traveled to Goa, eventually taking ship in the carracks for Lisbon.[21] They may have converted and were flagged by an English diplomat in Lisbon as "very malicious fellows" who should be watched closely.[22] Rather than going to the Portuguese, the sailor William Nicols decided to embark on a Dutch ship at Masulipatnam if he could. No other Englishmen wished to go that way, and so Nicols decided to join three Jewish traders, though he later recounted that he hated and feared them: "I thought, if I travelled with any money the dogs would cut my throat. So I made away with all my money, and attired myself in the habit of a Turk, and took my journey with those dogs, without any penny of money in my purse: and travelling with them, four months, had nothing to eat but only such food as the Jews gave me, and many times when I was hungry they would give me no meat, so that I was enforced to eat such meat as they gave their camels." After a long journey, they eventually arrived at Masulipatnam on the southeastern coast of India, where Nicols was delighted to find the Dutch factory and entered VOC service, ultimately arriving at Banten in September 1610. He was still there when his account was recorded by Henry Morris "from his mouth" (Nicols "could neither write nor read") about two years later.[23] Four other English sailors later followed Nicols toward Masulipatnam, and at least one of them made it, since he was found in Banten by Captain Saris in November 1612. This man, Herman Lane, a "turbulent" and "disordered fellow," offered to sign on with Saris for his voyage to Japan, but when Saris refused to pay his back wages he changed his mind.[24]

Meanwhile, the steward, Robert Coverte, and John Frencham latched onto the purser, Joseph Salbank, and the three of them journeyed to Agra. They survived by appealing to local authorities for aid. According to Coverte's account, at Burhanpur, he and Frencham "went to crave the general's pass, to go to the Great Mogol." This "great general," the emperor's viceroy in Gujarat, asked them if they "would serve him in his wars," but the mariners begged off, explaining that they "were poor distressed merchants, that had been shipwrecked" and, Coverte wrote, "had wives and children in our country, to whom we must of necessity go." Armed with the viceroy's pass, Coverte, Frencham, and Salbank set off for Agra, traveling most of the way with merchant caravans and pretending that they were on important business. Finally, in December, they reached Agra, where they were met by William Hawkins, who took them to the emperor, "as it is the custom and manner of the country." Following local etiquette, the travelers offered the best presents they could afford to Jahangir, who apparently received them graciously.[25]

The trio spent more than a month in Agra, where they admired court entertainments, bazaars, and imposing monuments, and were censured for their loose conduct: Hawkins's sole comment on the *Ascension*'s men in Agra was that he "could have wished of better behaviour, a thing pried into by the king."[26] Then the three Englishmen once more prepared to depart. Hoping to obtain a safe-conduct for England, they "went to the king and craved his pass." Again they were invited to stay and enter Mughal military service, and again they "humbly excused" themselves and were granted a pass. After also begging letters of recommendation from the chief Portuguese priest at Agra, the three Englishmen and two others set off to travel homeward along the Silk Road.[27] Salbank split off on the way, and two more appear to have died, but after almost a year, Coverte and a companion finally arrived at Aleppo, where they were relieved by English merchants before traveling on to Tripoli and boarding an English ship bound for Dover. As "Captain Robert Coverte," the enterprising steward then published a narrative of his adventures.

Three more English sailors were still in Surat when the next English ship arrived in 1611 and were able to get on board, circumventing a Portuguese blockade.[28] As for the rest, if survivors remained in India, they probably became gunners, for Jahangir was always ready to employ European soldiers. At least one entered Mughal service: when an East India Company fleet anchored off Surat in the winter of 1615–1616, the commander, William Keeling, noted that "Charles Clarke, one of the *Ascension*'s company and hath ever since served the Mogol in his wars, came now down . . . purposing [to travel] home." The following October, Sir Thomas Roe promised Jahangir's secretary to procure "two gunners out of our fleet to serve him in this year's wars for good pay, which courtesy he would take very kindly and requite it." If nothing else, English seamen's ability to kill retained its value in translation.[29]

Familiar Strangers

Over time, English sailors gained more experience of foreign peoples, but familiarity did not necessarily lead to understanding. Two sites of cultural contact, the Cape of Good Hope and Japan, show how English seamen's status as poor, young, laboring men shaped their reactions to the peoples they encountered and their ability to engage with them. In both places the English generally enjoyed healthy climates and (at least for a time) peaceful commercial relations, though to their eyes the Khoekhoe of the Cape were unquestionably savage and the people of Japan were clearly civil. In both places, the sailors made sense of foreign ways through their experience of English social hierarchies, which often led to misunderstanding.

When early seventeenth-century English sailors looked at the Khoekhoe, they saw people who ate filthy garbage that was fit for dogs rather than men: "very brutish or beastly people, especially in their feeding," as Robert Coverte put it.[30] Disgust at Khoekhoe dietary practices seems to have been at the heart of their judgment, rather than concerns about sexuality.[31] English sailors were not conservative about trying new foods, but rotten meat was beyond the pale, not because it was unfamiliar but because they encountered it all too often. In a period in which preserving meat was difficult, poor laboring people both on ships and on land rejected spoiled food in terms that defended their standing as dignified human beings. Rotten meat or fish might be described as "not fit to be eaten of by any Christian man or woman" or, more sweepingly, as "too bad to give a dog."[32] The English could not speak with the Khoekhoe or read the status cues encoded in the grease rubbed on their skin, so they may not have realized that their large herds were not held in common, and that some of the herders were very poor.[33] What could they make of people who seemed so rich in cattle yet willingly ate things Englishmen rejected as unfit for human consumption?

Nonetheless, the seamen had no doubt that the Khoekhoe were people. Their speech was strange, but it was clearly speech, and the Englishmen did try to learn some of it, though they failed: "Their language is very hard to be pronounced by reason of a kind of clacking with the tongue, so that we could not learn one word of their language."[34] Moreover, as English sailors became more familiar with the Cape's inhabitants, they grew to recognize Khoekhoe individuals, giving them names to remember them by. Anthony Marlowe recorded in 1607: "Among the rest of the Indians was one which the General knew to be the honestest of them all (as afterward he proved himself to be) and the likeliest man to do us good, to help us with cattle. . . . This man our people in voyages past had named Roswell." Later on, two more leading Khoekhoe men came down, "whom our men also in times past had given names unto. The one was called Dixon, the other Deverell, who the General also knew and used very kindly and gave them two pieces of iron between them." They may well have been named derisively after unpopular officers: a Robert Roswell was steward of the *Hector* in 1607, and a William Dixon had been purser of the *Dragon* on a 1601 East India voyage.[35] Still, the seamen recognized familiar faces in the crowd.

In 1614, English sailors became more intimate with Khoekhoe individuals when they abducted two men to bring to England. One of them, a man called Coree, survived and spent six months in London before he was returned to the Cape, where he was supposed to serve as an interpreter and cultural broker. As a commercial strategy, this was a failure.

One irate merchant complained that Coree had learned far too much about the abundance of metal in England: after his return to the Cape the Khoekhoe demanded higher prices for their cattle. Another concluded venomously that he ought to have been "hanged in England or drowned homeward." In the months that Coree spent living with sailors on English ships, a sort of mundane friendliness seems to have developed, however, and in 1615 Walter Peyton recorded that Coree took some of the sailors to visit his village, which Peyton described in homely terms: "Coree carried of our people who desired to see the country and showed them his house, wife and children at a town distant from Saldania eight English miles, containing about one hundred housen or small cottages."[36]

Despite these tentative gestures, an unbridgeable gulf separated the English and the Khoekhoe. No English boy was ever left at the Cape to learn the language, and no sailors ran away there. Instead, when some expendable convicts were put on shore in 1615, the sailors pitied them as men expelled into the wilderness. Peyton recorded that "these miserable men" were sent "on shore, with each man something for his own defense, both against the wild beasts or heathenish people amongst which they were to be left," as well as food and "some wine and strong waters which in charity was bestowed of [sic] them by sundry well disposed people in our fleet." No one seems to have expected the convicts to assimilate into Khoekhoe society, and indeed they retreated to a small island off the shore. Within a short time, all were dead or back in Europe.[37]

The sailors' reaction to Japan was altogether different. At the Cape even seemingly well-off people appeared to be driven to starvation, but in Japan even poor seamen could behave as though they were rich. The first English ship to reach Japan, the *Clove,* arrived there in 1613 and stayed at Hirado for several months. During that time, the lords of Hirado hospitably received the English as exotic curiosities and potential sources of goods and revenue, and the captain, John Saris, and the cape merchant, Richard Cocks, did their best to ingratiate themselves with their hosts. While Saris and Cocks gave out gifts left and right and admired courtly Japanese entertainments, the *Clove*'s sailors eagerly familiarized themselves with Hirado's brothels and drinking places.

In early Tokugawa Japan, prostitution was widespread: women's bodies could be characterized as assets, and selling them was legal, socially acceptable, and an important sector of the economy. Most prostitutes were indentured servants who worked to support their parents, and, before the status orders of the mid-seventeenth century, husbands could also sell access to their wives' bodies.[38] For the sailors of the *Clove*, being able to purchase legal sexual rights to women's bodies must have been remarkable. Prostitution existed in early modern England, of course, but there it held the double stigma of sexual sin and economic disorder. In a country in which poor people were supposed to marry late, if at all, enforcing premarital chastity was an economic objective as well as a reflection of Christian morality. As paupers strained parish resources, magistrates sought to restrict the illicit sexual unions that produced poor children, whipping mothers, fining fathers, and imprisoning prostitutes in houses of correction. Bachelor sailors could, no doubt, find bawdy houses in early modern London, but they were in theory expected to remain chaste, like apprentices and servants.[39] In early modern Japan, in contrast, abortion and infanticide were more widely accepted, and population control was less dependent on chastity.[40]

English sailors may have been surprised by these aspects of Japanese society, but they were not necessarily appalled: licit prostitution offered them an intoxicating taste of masculine privilege that was generally denied to poor English bachelors. In their journals, Saris and Cocks both complained at length about the resulting problems with discipline. To pay for their mistresses, for example, two sailors stole goods from the hold in August 1613. Later that month, the shipmaster decided to send the East India commodities on shore "because our men begin to fitch and steal, to go to taverns and whore-houses." In September, emboldened by drink, the sailors increasingly adopted aristocratic methods of settling their differences, ending arguments that began in drinking houses and brothels by dueling in the fields. One man was killed, another severely injured.[41]

There is no evidence that the sailors were able to see Japanese prostitutes as dutiful daughters rather than lewd whores. If, however, they got to know Japanese women well enough to quarrel about them, perhaps they also learned other things. The factors who remained at Hirado gained valuable knowledge from their consorts, and similar exchanges may have taken place among the seamen. One sailor was so close to a woman that after he left and she became pregnant, the cape merchant assumed that it was his child, disapprovingly recording: "James Turner, the fiddling youth, left a wench with child here, but the whore, the mother, killed it so soon as it was born, although I gave her two taels in plate before to nourish it because she should not kill it, it being an ordinary thing here."[42]

All in all, sailors' interest in Japanese culture appears to have been enthusiastic but superficial. When a few sailors accompanied Saris on a trip to Edo, they passed by an enormous copper Buddha and "went into the body of it, and hooped and hallowed, which made an exceeding great noise," before adding their own scratches to the "many characters and marks made upon it by passengers." At least one seaman thought Japanese magic was worth a try: "being in his pots," the surgeon paid a conjuror to tell him when his commander would return and "heard a voice answer him from behind a wall."[43] In 1616, a seaman of the *Hosiander* stole a number of things "to give to whores" and then, shockingly, tried to convert: "And that which was much worse, he went and cut his hair after the pagan fashion, thinking to turn pagan; which he could not do here, although he would. Yet there wanted no good will in him." John Hawtery probably only had a vague idea of what Japanese religion was, but he knew he liked it.[44] As seamen translated foreign practices into familiar meanings, deeper understanding fell by the wayside.

Trade, Trust, and Englishness

Examining cultural encounter through the experiences of merchant sailors provides us with a new perspective on the old question of how global travel shaped the development of English identity. Despite the long shadow of Edward Said's argument that in colonial contexts English people and other Europeans imagined "Others" as opposite and inferior to their own emerging identities, for the precolonial period scholars have increasingly recognized English travelers' need to come to terms with the real existence of foreign peoples, who were often dauntingly powerful. From the Ottoman Empire to the New World, others might be regarded with curiosity, admiration, disgust, hatred, or fear, but they could not be imagined into subjection.[45] How, then, was English identity shaped by pre-imperial global encounters? Empire—as an aspiration, not a reality—remains one avenue of exploration. Gerald MacLean thus characterizes the dominant English attitude to the Ottoman and Mughal Empires as "imperial envy": diplomats and merchants struggled to reconcile their fantasies of power with the everyday humiliations of being treated like marginal outsiders.[46] Even in their dreams, however, sailors were unlikely to see themselves as masters of empire. For them, Ottomans and Mughals were potential patrons, not imagined rivals.

The urgent demands of cross-cultural trade provide an alternative path. Following the pioneering work of Philip Curtin, studies of premodern cross-cultural trade have stressed the importance of trading diasporas in establishing and maintaining commercial links between different peoples and parts of the world. Initially, these studies had more to say about the internal dynamics of trading diasporas than about trade across cultural lines.[47] More recently, however, scholars have turned increasingly to the factors that shaped trade *across* cultural boundaries, including the development of shared commercial procedures and practices, tit-for-tat reprisals, and collective reputations for trustworthiness.[48] In the Mediterranean, as we have seen, these factors did indeed shape the development of English trade with Ottoman subjects, driving Levant Company efforts to regulate the behavior of English seamen. Farther afield, where English traders were still unfamiliar, their efforts to establish their collective reputation took on particular importance.

Encountering foreign peoples in trading contexts prompted the construction of English identity, in fact, because Englishmen were obliged to explain themselves to foreign audiences. Traveling abroad in search of commercial opportunities, they expected to find peoples, or "nations," with identifiable collective characteristics: true-hearted or crafty, kind or cruel, honest or thievish. They expected, too, that foreigners would see *them* as a "nation," a particular sort of people, and attempted to present themselves in the best possible light. Their self-representations varied depending on circumstances and met with mixed success, but by and large, early English merchants sought to present themselves as courteous and friendly people, while also stressing that they were the subjects and representatives of a distant but mighty sovereign.

This image of Englishness was strategically designed to foster peaceful and profitable relationships, to be sure, but it was not only a mask.

Performing an identity was a way of inhabiting it. For the leaders of English expeditions, courtesy was closely aligned with contemporary ideals of restrained and self-disciplined manhood, and it provided a flattering means of interpreting their engagement with the world at a time in which raw English power was highly circumscribed. This "cosmopolitan" style of global expansion became a way of life for intellectually curious practitioners, as Alison Games has shown.[49] For ordinary sailors, meanwhile, voluntary or involuntary performances of courteous Englishness carried powerful messages about who they were, and their role in the world.

Courteous Englishness became more prominent in the trading initiatives of the early seventeenth century, but it had also been practiced earlier when English travelers were focused on trade rather than plunder. How it was performed depended on the situation. In early Arctic expeditions, when language barriers impeded direct communication, sailors simply acted out friendship: they sang and danced for native audiences and played games with them. On Frobisher's first voyage to Baffin Island in 1576, for example, the English first brought one man onto their barque, the *Gabriel,* gave him food and drink, and then put him on shore. This persuaded more men and women to come with gifts of fish and meat to visit the ship, where, according to George Best, who wrote an account of the voyage, they showed off by climbing in the rigging "after our mariners' fashion." The English sailors seem to have been proud to demonstrate their skills for this new audience, and the Inuit were likewise eager "to shew their agility" in friendly competition that displayed their strength.[50] Play allowed the men of both groups to explore one another and establish trust. The sailors also sang for the Inuit; as Best later wrote, "They delight in music above measure, and will keep time and stroke to any tune which you shall sing, both with their voice, head, hand and feet, and will sing the same tune aptly after you. They will row with our oars in our boats, and keep a true stroke with our mariners, and seem to take great delight therein."[51] We are not told whether the English sailors also tried to mimic Inuit feats of skill or strength, but they may well have done so. The Inuit and the English also traded together: in Best's account, the Inuit "exchanged coats of seals, and bears' skins, and such like, with our men; and received bells, looking glasses, and other toys, in recompense thereof again."[52]

In 1585, when John Davis of Sandridge and his men were seeking the Northwest Passage in two barques, the *Sunshine* and the *Moonshine,* they also encountered Inuit and tried to attract them with what must have been a comical display. Davis wrote: "When they came unto us, we caused our musicians to play, ourselves dancing, and making many signs of friendship." When an Inuk ventured on shore from his kayak, they threw him their "caps, stockings and gloves, and such other things as then we had about us, playing with our music, and making signs of joy, and dancing." The next day, the Inuit danced and played in turn, and both parties engaged in trade. The following year, Davis found the same group, and the English sailors and the Inuit competed in feats of manly prowess: "I was desirous to have our men leap with them, which was done, but our men did overleap them: from leaping, they went to wrestling; we found them strong and nimble, and to have skill in wrestling, for they cast some of our men that were good wrestlers." These competitions were repeated the next day: after the Inuit helped the Englishmen launch their pinnace, Davis related, "our men again wrestled with them, and found them as before, strong and skillful." Another account of the voyage mentions a different group of Inuit inviting the Englishmen to play football, whereupon "some of our company went on shore to play with them."[53]

From the point of view of their commanders, sailors' performances of friendship were strategic, designed to help Englishmen collect information about local people's strengths and weaknesses, knowledge, and commodities. For some sailors, however, the distinction between strategic performance and true friendship was less clear. The intense violence that came to mar early encounters with Inuit in the Arctic stemmed in part from English anger at Inuit "betrayal"—anger that reveals the depth of the sailors' emotional engagement in their own performances. On Frobisher's voyage, the sailors became all too trusting, taking seeming friendship for reality, according to George Best: "After great courtesy, and many meetings, our mariners, contrary to their captain's direction, began more easily to trust them."[54] After an Inuk visited the English ship, five sailors were supposed to return him to his people without putting themselves at risk. The shipmaster wrote, "The Captain and I willed five of men to set him a shore at a rock, and not among the company, which they came from," but "their willfulness was such, that they would go to them, and so were taken themselves, and our boat lost."[55] The Englishmen never found out what had happened to the five, and their attempts to rescue them led to repeated abductions of native people and deadly violence.

Davis's men had a different problem: their honor was offended by what they saw as Inuit thievery. Davis and the sailors agreed that the Inuit took whatever was left lying around, but whereas Davis regarded this as "an occasion of laughter, to see their simplicity," the sailors were "grieved." They suspected—and they may have been right—that by tolerating petty theft, they had convinced the Inuit they were a weak and foolish people. When the Inuit began to sling stones at the sailors after nightfall, the humiliation became intolerable. As Davis recalled, "Our mariners complained heavily against the people, and said that my lenity and friendly using of them gave them stomach for mischief: for they have stolen an anchor from us, they have cut our cable very dangerously, they have cut our boats from our stern, and now . . . with slings they spare us not with stones of half a pound weight: and will you endure these injuries? It is a shame to bear them." After his initial forbearance, Davis also "grew to hatred." After shooting at but missing the Inuit, they managed to take a captive, hoping to exchange him for their missing anchor. When the wind changed, their negotiations were cut short, and they sailed away with their unfortunate prisoner.[56]

These staged friendships were fragile, so to prevent seamen from shattering them through rudeness or theft, English commanders sometimes inflicted ostentatious punishments on their own men for real or perceived offenses. One such sufferer was a sailor who accompanied Captain Christopher Newport on a voyage of reconnaissance up the James River in Virginia in 1607. When the Englishmen spoke with local *weroances*, they were anxious to make themselves agreeable and to demonstrate their respect for their hosts. Suspecting that one of his sailors had jostled an Indian, Newport immediately "sent for his own man, bound him to a tree before King Arahatec, and with a cudgel soundly beat him."[57] In the same year, when the ships of the third East India Company voyage were at anchor off Sierra Leone—the same visit during which the sailors performed *Hamlet*—a trumpeter strayed off and was taken prisoner. The next day, the coastal people angrily beckoned the Englishmen to come on shore, where one African man showed them eleven sticks and, in the words of the factor Anthony Marlowe, "with a little broken Portuguese which he spake, much lamented to him as though some great injury had been offered to them by some of our people." Anxious to resolve the mystery and reclaim their lost man, the English officers invited some Africans on board and tortured several sailors in their presence: "Some were at the main capstan with weights about their necks, and others suspected, threatened with the like." Finally, an elderly sailor and his accomplices confessed to stealing two brass basins and other things, and the goods were restored to their owners: "One of the offenders was ducked at yard arm, and the others chief in fault [punished] at the capstan before the Negroes' faces, to their great content and credit to our nation's justice ... the Negroes which were aboard did declare to their fellows of these parts of the good justice they had found, and what punishment was inflicted upon those that wronged them."[58] When language barriers loomed, inflicting pain on their own people was a vivid way for English commanders to prove their goodwill and their "nation's justice."

English performances of courtesy, good government, and strength were explicitly national in the Indian Ocean world. There an array of traders from different lands and ethnic groups had long circulated among bustling port cities. To obtain permission to join them, English merchants were obliged to explain who they were, how they were different from other European traders, and why they ought to be allowed to establish factories. They hoped to show that they were "a nation of friendly and honest disposition," unlike the "proud and unfaithful nations" of their European rivals. In part, these overtures consisted of formal delegations and gift-giving rituals in which English representatives' desire to prove their sovereign's greatness conflicted with the London merchants' reluctance to waste money on ostentatious displays.[59] However, English performances were also national in the sense that they sought to demonstrate that the English were a certain sort of people—and in these, sailors played important roles.

Proving English respectability was an urgent task when rivals were eager to tarnish the reputation of the English nation. William Hawkins related that in 1610, when enemies at court told Jahangir "we were a nation, that if we once set foot, we would take his country from him," Hawkins tried to convince him that "we were not so base a nation." In

1615, when English traders arrived at Jambi in Sumatra in the pinnace *Assistant*, the ruler told them they could not have a house there because "he had heard evil of us and our nation both by the Hollanders and the Portingals . . . that we were a rude and ungoverned nation, given to drunkenness and abusing of women, quarrelling, fighting, and such like." To the merchants' mortification, shortly thereafter the *Assistant's* mate, Robert Burges, came on board "very drunk, having abused himself in running after the Javas' women, and fighting and wrangling with the Chinas . . . and made an uproar in the ship that all the town wondered at us." The factor Richard Westby feared "we shall hardly recover the shame and discredit he hath done to the Worshipful Company and to our nation." If sailors performed Englishness correctly, good relations might follow; if they gave offense, the entire English nation risked being blamed. Small wonder that when Company ships arrived at Banten, their commander proclaimed a set of rules for their "good demeanour."[60]

One problem, according to Company factors, was that Portuguese Jesuits defamed the English as a nation of pirates and thieves. In Japan, for example, Saris wrote that "our English nation hath been long known by report among [the Japanese], but much scandaled by the Portugals Jesuits, as pirates and rovers upon the seas, so that the naturals have a song which they call the English *Crofonia*, showing how the English do take the Spanish ships . . . with which song and acting they terrify and scare their children." In 1613, when the governor of Surat told the factor Thomas Kerridge he thought the English "were not merchants" but came in search of plunder, Kerridge implored him "not to believe those prattling, juggling Jesuits but credit rather the experience their own people had of us." Two years later, Kerridge complained that the "Viceroy of Goa" had written to Jahangir "very basely of our nation, terming us thieves, disturbers of states and a people not to be permitted in a commonwealth." Other Company factors reported from Isfahan in 1617: "This prince and people . . . by our adversary, the Portingal, are informed that we are such as trade not, we are not merchants but thieves and sea-robbers, who under pretense of merchandizing do entrap and despoil the ships and subjects of the princes of India and the Southern parts."[61]

The English nation's reputation for maritime aggression was not all bad, of course: it emphasized the strength of their shipping. When

Sir Henry Middleton captured Surat shipping in 1612 after he was denied permission to trade, for example, his show of force—along with Thomas Best's dramatic victory over a larger Portuguese fleet close to Surat later that year—helped the English obtain Mughal trading privileges. Company factors remembered the value of violence when Sir Thomas Roe was struggling to assert himself at Jahangir's court in 1616; they urged him to seize Mughal ships and hold them hostage.[62] Brutal tactics eroded hard-won English respectability, however. When Henry Pepwell took a boat of Surat, apparently thinking it Portuguese, Roe lamented: "Nothing more afflicts me than to hear the scandal of our nation by brutish disorders, and I cannot conceive how the chiefs can any way excuse it. I am sure we will suffer for it."[63] Moreover, English resident factors' vulnerability to reprisals meant that maritime violence had to be carefully controlled. Even the interloper Edward Michelborne had been mindful of the danger he posed to Company factors when he sailed to the Indian Ocean in 1604–1605 on a predatory voyage with a royal license that allowed him to infringe on the Company's charter. He avoided plundering Banten shipping for fear of the "injury he might do to the English merchants that had a factory in Bantam at that present," attacking a Chinese junk instead. Even this was not safe, however: Michelborne's navigator, John Davis of Sandridge, heard "that our English merchants in Bantam were in great peril . . . because we had taken the China ship, whereby the king of Bantam had lost his custom."[64]

While the East India Company's directors were not always averse to violence against Asian shipping, they were adamant that predatory English interlopers had to be suppressed to protect the honorable reputation of the English nation and guard against damaging reprisals. Faced by the possibility of a predatory Irish East India Company in 1614, for example, Company merchants complained that they would bear the losses: "The English nation having attained an honourable report in those parts and known to proceed in peaceable manner like merchants, these going forth now only with powder and shot, can be no other than pirates, to rob and spoil the country people, which must necessarily bring a great scandal and be a great dishonour unto this nation." They objected just as violently to news that Englishmen were "combining themselves with Frenchmen" to get a French commission, saying: "It may well be suspected their purpose is rather to behave themselves as pirates, than merchants, to the great scandal of this whole nation, and apparent damage unto the trade now driven into those parts by the said Company." Their logic was that the victims of these pirates would not distinguish between English, Irish, and French East India Company ships. Indeed, it seems that these new companies would have been funded by English merchants and their ships crewed largely by English sailors; their Irish and French names were purely formal, designed to sidestep the East India Company's patent, the merchants implied.[65]

Similarly, when Lord Rich and the ubiquitous Filippo Bernardi sent two English warships to the Indian Ocean with letters of marque from the Duke of Savoy, Company commanders who came across the warships attacking a ship belonging to Jahangir's mother assumed that their commissions would mean less to the Mughal victims than the nationalities of the crew. They were able to rescue the Mughal ship and to detain the warships and their men, to Martin Pring's fervent relief. He wrote to the Company in London: "I praise God with all my heart that we lighted so on them, for if they had taken the junk and known to be English (which could not long have been concealed), all your goods in this country could not have made satisfaction according to their desire (and that is commonly their law in these cases)."[66] In the Company's ensuing legal battle with Rich, the governors stressed "the dangers that had been like to have befallen by the act of my Lord Rich his ship and Philip Bernardi's, in surprising the rich ship appertaining to the grand Mogol's mother, to the hazard of themselves, of all our people, utter disgrace of our nation, and final overthrow of all trade in those parts."[67] Indeed, for non-European rulers, national reprisals were a powerful tool that cut through European legal obfuscations and drove vulnerable merchant corporations to lobby for the regulation of predatory seamen and their backers.[68]

Countering accusations of piracy, the English struck back against their Portuguese and Jesuit detractors, accusing them of sinister designs and underlining Protestants' differences from Roman Catholics. As Richard Wickham related in 1615, when the Jesuits were banished from Japan, the priests complained that the English "were the cause thereof, saying that they never were in disgrace until we came hither." Wickham thought their own "subtle dealings and covetous practices" were the real cause, but he conceded that "as occasions offered, we have done the Jesuits little credit here." Negotiating for the renewal of English trading privileges in Japan, Richard Cocks was at pains to show that while, as he put it, "the English nation were Christians," the Jesuits were "not such as we were; for that all Jesuits and friars were banished out of England before I was born, the English nation not holding with the Pope nor his doctrine."[69]

Explaining what Protestants were *not* proved easier than describing what they *were*, however. In Southeast Asia, where Islam and Catholicism were both spreading, English Protestants found their readiest trading partners among Muslims, and they tended to elide the differences between their faith and that of their interlocutors. An English account claims, for example, that the sultan of Aceh asked twelve men on Lancaster's early voyage to the East Indies to sing psalms: "And when the general took his leave, the king said unto him: Have you the Psalms of David extant among you? The general answered: Yea, and we sing them daily. Then said the king: I and the rest of these nobles about me will sing a psalm to God for your prosperity; and so they did, very solemnly. And after it was ended, the king said: I would hear you sing another psalm, although in your own language. So, there being in the company some twelve of us, we sung another psalm."[70] English sailors even participated in explicitly Muslim festivities. In November 1612, John Saris recorded that the governor of Banten sent to him and other English captains "desiring them to send their men ashore with their furniture because it was the end of their Lent." The English captains complied: roughly half the sailors from the *Clove, Hector,* and *Solomon* went on shore in their best finery to parade in military array in celebration of Eid al-Fitr, "which gave [the governor] good content." The account in *Purchas* noted with satisfaction that "the Flemings denied him: it was for the breaking up of the Mahometans' Lent," implying that Dutch arrogance gave the more accommodating English a chance to demonstrate their superior goodwill.[71]

In the earliest years of the East India Company, differentiating the English from the Dutch was particularly difficult: merchants rather than missionaries, Christians but not Catholics, the two nations had much in common. The most salient difference was that the English hailed from an ancient kingdom, while the upstart Dutch had rejected their sovereign. Even here, however, English observers worried that hostile rivals blurred the lines. At Agra, Kerridge lamented that the Jesuits "shame not to say, we are a people rebelled subjects to their king, and make us and the Hollanders as one." The Dutch themselves allegedly passed themselves off as English on occasion: in Japan, Saris described the arrival of a junk from Siam "wherein was said to be Englishmen, but proved Flemings. For that before our coming, they passed generally by the name of Englishmen." At Banten, similarly, the Dutch "usurp[ed] our name at their first coming thither to trade," according to the factor Edmund Scot.[72]

It is not clear that Dutch merchants really claimed to be English; more often, on early voyages they presented themselves as subjects of the "king of Holland," as they grandiosely styled the *stadhouder* Prince Maurits.[73] Nonetheless, in Java Scot was deeply concerned about confusion between the two nations, and perhaps with reason, because the behavior of the VOC sailors and soldiers left much to be desired. In Banten, a sprawling, multiethnic, and lightly policed city, the tiny English community had to seek not only the favor of the governing elite but also the toleration of the plebeian people among whom they lived: street violence and arson were significant threats. The "rude and disordered" demeanor of the Dutch was thus a serious problem; making the English sailors behave civilly toward local people would be useless if Dutch abuses tarnished their reputation. As Scot related, in 1603 "there was much falling out between the Flemings and the country people, by means of the rude behavior of the Flemings, and many of them were stabbed in the evenings: and at that time the common people knew us not from the Flemings, for both they and we were called by the name of Englishmen . . . and as we passed along the street, we might hear the people in the market, railing and exclaiming on the Englishmen, although they meant the Hollanders, wherefore, we fearing some of our men might be slain instead of them, we began to think how we might make ourselves known from the Hollanders."[74] Monarchy played a central role in this project. The English could truly claim to be a well-governed people, subjects of a famous monarch, unlike the "Hollanders" who "had no king, but their land was ruled by governors." This, the English hoped, would allow them to contrast their well-governed behavior with Dutch disorder. According to Scot's account, the English factors and sailors in Banten ostentatiously celebrated Elizabeth's accession day. All the Englishmen wore "scarves of white and red taffeta, being our country colours," with a gold fringe for the merchants, and on November 17 they flew their banner and put on the best parade they could: "With our drum and shot we marched up and down within our own ground, being but fourteen in number, wherefore we could march but single one after another, and so plied our shot, and casting ourselves in rings and esses." According to Scot, Javanese nobles noted the difference between the true Englishmen and the Dutch, who had not joined the celebrations. That afternoon, to attract still greater audiences, the English sailors and servants were sent "to walk abroad the town, and the market, whereby the people might take notice of them." With the English so few and so vulnerable, even the opinion of common children was worth recording: "Ever after that day, we were known from the Hollanders, and many times, the children in the streets would run after us, crying, *Oran Engrees bayk, oran Holland Jahad*, which is, the Englishmen are good, the Hollanders are naught."[75]

Sailors may have enjoyed parades and celebrations designed to show foreign audiences that they were the subjects of a mighty sovereign. When Sir Thomas Roe landed at Surat to journey to Agra as ambassador to the Mughal Empire, the sailors provided suitable pomp, with "four score men in arms with shot and pike ready ordered upon the sand in ranks," the ships decked out in the finest streamers and ordnance booming. James's coronation day was celebrated in Japan with guns and flags, which, Saris wrote, "the naturals took great notice of, the king much commending our order in remembering our duty." Good government also meant strict justice, however: English sailors who injured local people could expect severe punishment. In Japan in 1621, an English sailor named William Barker got drunk in a carpenter's house and "would have lain with a woman perforce, and against her will took four rings of silver off her fingers, and drank two *mas* or 12*d*. in wine, and in the end would have gone away and pay nothing and carry the rings along with him." When the "good wife of the house laid hands on him, he did beat her." The neighbors seized the Englishman and alerted the cape merchant, Richard Cocks, to his offense. Cocks restored the stolen property, made the miscreant pay for the wine, and had him savagely beaten: "first sixty lashes with a whip, and then washed in brine, and after, forty more lashes."[76]

Cultural performances were less painful for English sailors, though they may have been uncomfortable. To prove themselves eager to please, Company captains and factors directed the seamen to sing, dance, play music, and parade around for foreign rulers and notables. When the *Consent* visited the Molucca Islands in 1608, a ruler "was very merry, and much desired dancing," so "some of our men danced before him, who was well pleased, both at their dancing and music." John Saris invited the Muslim ruler of Mohéli on board the *Clove* "and entertained him with a noise of trumpets, and a consort of music, with a banquet." When two young notables from Nagasaki visited the English house at Hirado in 1613, the carpenter, Richard Frobisher, and the master's mate of the *Clove* happened to be there and played an impromptu concert.[77]

Some seamen may have balked at these command performances; others were probably proud of their talents and their complaisance. The navigator John Davis of Sandridge took pride in the courtesy of the English, for example, depicting their Dutch rivals as an altogether cruder and less manly people, and implying that good manners and courage went hand in hand. After serving as a pilot on an early Dutch expedition to the East Indies, he regaled his English audience with an unflattering depiction of the voyage. Celebrating their passing the Abrolhos, Davis wrote, the Dutch drank so much that even commanding officers were "both lawless and witless." At Saldania, they alienated the Khoekhoe by offering them "some rude wrong," then "fled before them like mice before cats, throwing away their weapons most basely" when they were attacked, even though their assailants were armed with nothing but "hand darts." The Dutch commander sent them weapons and armor, Davis related, "but there was neither courage nor discretion . . . we were in muster giants, with great armed bodies, but in action babes, with wrens' hearts." When Davis and another Englishman tried to "order these fellows," they refused and "ran to the pottage pot, for they swore it was dinner time." Eventually they retreated to the ship, "only leaving our great mastiff dog behind us, who by no means would come to us. For I think he was ashamed of our company." On Madagascar, the Dutch "greatly abused the people": the commander "took one of them, bound him to a post, and shot him to death, with other shameful disorders." Near the Maldives, they took a boat in which "a gentleman and his wife" were traveling. Davis was struck by the nobility of the man: "His behaviour was so sweet and affable, his countenance so modest, and his speech so graceful, as that it made apparent show he could not be less than a noble-man." Over the husband's objections, the Dutch *baas* barged onto the boat to see the wife, who "sate with mournful modesty," ignoring the intrusion as best she might.[78]

Davis's comparison of the "princely" Maldivian passenger to the crude Dutch commander stressed the ways in which the Dutch allegedly failed to live up to early modern English ideals of masculinity. Self-mastery was at the core of manhood in English prescriptive texts: by mastering themselves, men—especially elite men—earned authority over others, such as women and boys, whose less temperate bodies and minds prevented them from exercising self-control.[79] In Davis's narrative, the Dutch seemed to lack the requisite qualities of reason, discretion, courage, and grace. The Maldivian nobleman, Davis himself, and his English companion were able to act advisedly and resolutely, and to show courteous consideration for other people. Where the Dutch were concerned, however, even the highest-ranking officers failed to pass the test. Instead, they were driven by baser instincts and appetites: hunger, thirst, fear, and lustful curiosity.

In practice, of course, Englishmen on East India ventures were no strangers to base appetites: factors as well as seamen often led loose lives, amply chronicled in the backbiting letters they sent home to London. Yet Davis's contemptuous portrait found echoes in English descriptions of Dutchmen abroad in the following decades. When William Keeling told a messenger from a Dutch commander "that if he were a gentleman, he would not permit his base people to abuse me as I walked among them," he was startled to be told that the commander was not a gentle-man but "a weaver." Dutch drunkenness was a frequent theme: though Englishmen certainly drank heavily, they claimed to be shocked by Dutch excesses. At Ternate, an English observer claimed in 1604, "the Hollanders are not beloved of the country people. The cause is their manifold disorders in their drunkenness, against men, but principally against the women."[80] In Japan, Richard Cocks wrote: "It is strange to see the unruliness of these Holland mariners and soldiers, how they go staggering drunk up and down the streets, slashing and cutting of each other with their knives, like mad men." In 1621, when "the unruly mariners of the Hollands ships, being drunk, did ride over children in the streets and slashed and cut Japons," two were summarily executed by Japanese authorities.[81] Cocks thought the Dutch drank so much that they completely lost their reason. They also drank, according to English critics, to avoid facing danger with manly fortitude. When an English seaman was sentenced to death for the murder of a Dutchman in Japan, he made a moving speech about resisting temptation, took the sacrament, and was hanged with decorum in front of a morose audience, dying "very resolutely." A few weeks later when a Dutchman was similarly condemned to die for the murder of an Englishman, English observers noted contemptuously that rather than making an edifying end, the man was "first made . . . so drunk that he could scarce stand on his legs," after which the "Hollanders" cut off his head. Similarly, an account of the 1623 Amboyna massacre contrasted the manly piety of the English victims with the rudeness of their captors. Knowing that they were to be executed the following day, the English "spent the rest of the doleful night in prayer, and singing of psalms, and comforting one another; though the Dutch that guarded them offered them wine, bidding them drink lustick and drive away the sorrow according to the custom of their own nation in the like case, but contrary to the nature of the English."[82]

Dutch observers did not agree that the English were a more manly nation, to be sure. While Englishmen criticized Dutch rudeness, a contemporary Dutch merchant cast the English as a fiery but fundamentally precious people, in implicit contrast to the plain-spoken and hard-working Dutch: "The English are a clever, handsome, and well-made people, but, like all islanders, of a weak and tender nature. . . . They are full of courtly and affected manners and words, which they take for gentility, civility, and wisdom. . . . The people are not so laborious and industrious as the Netherlanders or French, as they lead for the most part an indolent life."[83] Rude violence or hard-headed realism, manly courtesy or foppish weakness—all depended on the eye of the observer. For the English in Asia, valorizing courtesy allowed them to imagine and portray themselves as culturally superior despite their material inferiority. With more firepower and manpower at its disposal, the VOC did not have to worry as much about social niceties, although some VOC commanders thought their men's behavior reflected badly—and falsely—on the Dutch nation.

Governor Reynst complained to the Heren XVII—the directors of the VOC—in 1615 about the negligence, drunkenness, and debauchery of the men sent to the East Indies, and in 1621 Jan Pieterszoon Coen, the governor-general of the Dutch East Indies, lamented that some behaved "worse than witless animals, causing horror and scandal in many of the Indians, who having never seen better, think that our whole nation is similarly godless, mindless, and unmannerly." Though many of the "Hollanders" were not Dutch at all, their drunkenness and undisciplined behavior were "major scourges for the VOC, scourges that profoundly shaped Javanese perceptions of the Dutch," according to Romain Bertrand.[84]

Dutch disorder did not prevent the VOC from being more successful than the English East India Company, of course: with strongholds like Batavia, the Dutch could dispense with the toleration of local people. For the English, too, performative courtesy was a means to an end rather than an end in itself; it was summarily abandoned when violence promised better results or when the prospective victims were defenseless. Edmund Scot, who orchestrated the elaborate parade for Elizabeth's coronation day in Banten, also sadistically tortured a Chinese arson suspect to death, secure in the knowledge that Javanese elites were indifferent to the man's welfare. Company ships did indeed attack Asian ships—such as those of Dhabol in the early 1620s—that lacked the protection of a powerful ruler. Moreover, cross-cultural trust did not depend solely or even primarily on personal or national trustworthiness. The fact that the English were vulnerable on land but strong at sea while Asian elites were the reverse tended to produce what Ashin Das Gupta termed a "balance of blackmail" that inhibited abuses on both sides. As in the Mediterranean, the silent threat of retaliatory violence underlay seemingly peaceful trade.[85]

In addition, foreign audiences may not have understood or cared much about sailors' and merchants' behavior. In most cases, successful trading relationships depended more on the availability of interested partners than on English self-representations. Lords and princes often welcomed foreign merchants because of the wealth and potential military aid they brought with them, regardless of who they were. In Hirado, the ruling daimyo family wanted English and Dutch merchants to make their bases there rather than in another domain. In Japan more generally, during the

reign of Ieyasu the Tokugawa regime was diplomatically isolated and received marginal embassies warmly—a practice that would alter, as VOC
representatives were dismayed to discover, once the regime gained a
stronger diplomatic footing. Javanese aristocrats may have regarded
European merchants as a necessary evil rather than as men of honor,
men whose thirst for gain and crass ignorance of rudimentary social conventions betrayed their base, even diabolical origins. Still, these nobles
appreciated trade's pecuniary benefits and the help Europeans could supply in regional power struggles.[86]

When the English were welcomed, then, it was not necessarily because
they had convinced local audiences that their nation was worthy of respect and trust. To begin with, the message that the English were simultaneously strong and courteous was not easy to impart: as in the Arctic, the
problem of appearing friendly but not naive bedeviled English travelers.
John Jourdain wrote disgustedly that "the Turks themselves say: 'If thou
wilt have anything of an Englishman, give him good words and thou
shalt be sure to win him.' " Cultural differences also made it hard for the
English to guess how they might be perceived and to respond appropri-
ately. Seeing themselves as a cleanly people, they were slow to realize that
Southeast Asians thought otherwise, like the people at Tiku who refused
to buy salt from them because of rumors that "the English do their needs
in the salt."[87] More broadly, the paucity of contemporary descriptions of
the English—and of Europeans in general—testifies to their marginality
and unimportance in the eyes of Asian elites. Sir Thomas Roe fondly believed that Jahangir treated him—and by extension, his sovereign and his
nation—with special respect and favor, but Jahangir's own memoirs suggest otherwise: for him, European nations were different varieties of
Franks, all handy as purveyors of exotic commodities and natural curiosities but otherwise insignificant.[88] Ordinary people may have been even
less informed about or less interested in the fine distinctions between different varieties of foreigners. In Japan, for example, on his trip to Edo,
Captain Saris reported that Japanese boys mistook the traveling
Englishmen for Koreans—the foreigners they had heard of.[89] In the end,
those most profoundly affected by performances of Englishness may have
been the English sailors and merchants themselves.

Staging Humiliation

English people did not always get to choose how their nation was presented to foreign eyes. In Asia, they hoped to show that they were both courteous and strong, desirable partners who could provide effective military support in local conflicts or against other Europeans. At times they were indeed useful allies, most notably in 1622 when Company ships partnered with Persian forces to capture Ormuz from the Portuguese, gaining trading privileges as well as plunder. At others, however, English forces were too weak to accomplish their aims. When English sailors were taken captive, they were sometimes forced by their victorious enemies into performances of abject humiliation. These spectacles terrified and shamed the captives themselves, but their real object was to enhance the victors' power by intimidating local audiences.

At Sana'a in 1610, for example, English sailors were forcibly enlisted in Ottoman imperial propaganda. East India Company efforts to establish a factory at Mocha at the mouth of the Red Sea were strongly opposed by Ottoman governors: Red Sea traffic was too valuable to be shared with outsiders, and the sailors' "uncivil behaviour . . . as pissing at the gates of their churches, forcing into men's houses to their women, and being daily drunk in the streets," provided convenient grounds for harsh measures.[90] When the sailors of the *Trade's Increase* were taken prisoner by the authorities, they had no choice but to exemplify Ottoman power and English humiliation. Sir Henry Middleton reported that he and his men were marched from Mocha to the seat of Ottoman rule at Sana'a, exhibited along the way as captives, with "multitudes of people standing all the way gazing and wondering at us." They arrived there in elaborately choreographed misery, "caused to go one by one in order, a pretty distance one from the other, to make the better show; our men had their gowns taken from them, and were caused to march afoot in their thin and ragged suits." The English trumpeters were commanded to play but, Middleton recorded with bleak satisfaction, he "forbade them." The point of the spectacle was presumably to discourage local resistance to Ottoman rule, intimidating potential supporters of the insurgent Yemeni imam al-Mansur al-Qasim, but these performances of powerlessness also left the Englishmen themselves shaken to the core. One boy fainted in fright, according to Middleton, when the English commander was taken before the pasha; he later died. Another youth, left behind on the trip when he fell ill, had converted to Islam by the time the Englishmen found him again. In tears, he told them that he had thought they were all dead.[91]

At the center of the spice trade, meanwhile, VOC agents sought to increase their control of the market by persuading and coercing local rulers to grant the Dutch nation sole rights to purchase spices. As part of this strategy, VOC commanders turned from eliding Dutch national differences from the English to underlining them. Dutch characterizations of the English nation for local audiences came to center on its military weakness, a serious vulnerability for the English East India Company. In violent confrontations between English and Dutch actors, defeated English sailors and merchants were often taunted and mocked in front of local audiences. In Banten, for example, where the Company and the VOC maintained a tense coexistence, English sailors were vulnerable as they wandered around in ones and twos, drinking in the same arrack houses that served VOC soldiers. In 1616, John Jourdain recorded that common English and Dutchmen began arguing at an arrack house, with painful results: "A Dutch soldier drew his sword upon two of them of our men; and they running away, because they had no weapons, the soldiers following after them with their swords drawn met with two more of our Englishmen, who in peaceable manner persuaded the Flemings to be quiet; but they without regard fell upon them, and cut three of our men in such a manner as that all men had thought they had been slain." To add insult to injury, the aggressor went "walking in braving manner, the more to aggravate our griefs," back and forth in front of the door of the English compound. Walter Peyton complained bitterly about the aggression of the Dutch: "They threaten to pull our people out of the factory by the ears, and sometimes quarrel with them in the streets, otherwise imprison them at their own pleasures . . . to bring our nation in disgrace with the Pangeran of Bantam."[92]

In the Banda Islands, as Alison Games has shown, Dutch efforts to defeat and publicly humiliate the English took on special intensity.[93] There, in the face of VOC monopoly claims, English agents struck a formal political and military alliance with Bandanese opponents of VOC hegemony. Like the Dutch, the English expected monopoly rights in return for military support, and the alliance was sealed by the surrender of the islands Ai and Run to James I—but culminated in disastrous defeat.[94] During this struggle, the Dutch orchestrated spectacles of English weakness to discourage Bandanese resistance. Peyton wrote in 1616 that VOC soldiers pulled down the English colors "so disgracefully as they could and abused our people, more like heathenish pagans than Christian neighbours, putting halters about their necks and led them through the town with an hourglass before them, publishing withal, that they should be hanged as soon as the glass was run out." When the English *Swan* was captured in 1617, its sailors were brought to the VOC fort at Neira, with the Dutch "much glorying in their victory, and showing the Bandanese their exploit, in the great disgrace of the English . . . saying that the king of England might not compare with their great king of Holland, and that one Holland ship would take ten of the English ships, and that Saint George is now turned child." Some English sailors got the message too: a handful of hungry, mutinous seamen surrendered the *Defence* to the VOC.[95]

Later, captive English seamen were carried to other VOC forts, partly for security, but also to display their defeat more broadly to local people. In 1617, a factor at Makassar wrote to his colleague at Banten that a Javanese shipmaster told him "that the Hollanders had brought in a ship to Amboyna at his being there 40 or 50 Englishmen from Nero Castle, and kept them in irons, so that the men were lame, and allowed them but one cake of bread a day for a man and a little rack; so that the men seemed to him to be starving, h[aving] nothing left them but skin and bones; and that the Hollanders, vaunting of their former enterprise, said to him that if there were but one ship of them, they alone would fight with ten English ships, giving the English the worst language they could, wishing him to beware of the English."[96] After the VOC captured several English ships in 1619, more English sailors were degraded in front of local audiences. George Jackson of the *Attendant* reported that the Dutch trampled on the captured English colors in front of the Bandanese on Neira and sent some English sailors "in their ships prisoners to show in triumph to the blacks at Amboina, the Moluccas, the Manilas, and Japan." Later, after the VOC captured the *Sampson,* Jackson himself and the steward, Marmaduke Stevenson, were brought on board where, Jackson claimed, they were exhibited in chains: "The Dutch did show the

Orankays, blacks, and Malays in what sort they did tyrannize over and use the English keeping them in irons and slavery."[97] Bartholomew Churchman, who had risen in the ranks to be a master's mate, affirmed that the Dutch called them "slaves to the king of Holland," saying they "should all be sent to the Moluccas to row in their galleys, and so be kept bond-slaves under them during our lives." Men of the VOC "pissed and ( )" on Englishmen kept prisoner under a grate, so that they "were broken out from top to toe, like lepers," he recalled angrily, using language too coarse to be printed. "They have taken our men, and without any cause have stripped and whipped them openly in the marketplace," the sailors complained; "they have also beaten up their drum, and called the blacks together to see it done." Some captured English sailors alleged that they were confined in cages and carried from port to port, while the Dutch cried: " 'Behold and see, here is the people of that nation, whose king you care so much for. But now you may hereby plainly behold how kindly we use his subjects,' making them believe, that Englishmen were their vassals and slaves."[98] These English sailors were unwilling conscripts in a theatrical performance of Dutch superiority, their starved and chained bodies exhibited in spectacles designed to warn local people not to challenge Dutch restrictions on the spice trade.

These passionate allegations were made in London at the behest of the English East India Company in a highly publicized conflict with the VOC. Their broad outlines are credible nonetheless. The spectacular Dutch humiliation of English bodies for audiences of "blacks and Malays" made good sense in Southeast Asia, where Dutch commanders probably saw it as a cheap and easy way to discourage local resistance to the VOC's increasingly coercive imperial expansion, and an effective way to counter English claims about their nation's desirability as a trading partner and ally. It was only in Europe that the propaganda value of the incidents was reversed. For the captured sailors themselves, meanwhile, the fact that "blacks" observed their degradation only deepened their humiliation.

In pomp and in pain, English sailors embodied their nation for foreign eyes. In the interests of cross-cultural commerce, English representatives strove to present their nation as an attractive and reliable trading partner: their foils were rival Europeans, not "natives." Rather than being the passive objects of the English gaze, non-Europeans were imagined as critical observers; their opinions mattered because in its vulnerable early stages English trade could not hope to succeed without their cooperation. In the Indian Ocean, as we have seen, English merchants and commanders tried to convince local people that they were a particularly courteous nation, respectful of foreign traditions and sensibilities. They may even have believed it, though indiscriminate violence and plunder had been characteristic of English maritime expansion only years before. For the English sailors who embodied this new way of being English, the contrast must have been striking, and it is hard to know how seriously they took their new identities. Manly courtesy was all very well, but for many of them the useful core of Englishness was probably something closer to national solidarity: claims to reciprocity and consideration from their officers and employers, to help and friendship from countrymen in distant lands and seas, and, increasingly, as English seamen were captured by hostile foreigners, to help from the state. The Dutch mocked King James and claimed he could not protect his subjects, Bartholomew Churchman testified. Would the Crown prove them wrong?

CHAPTER SEVEN

SAILORS AND THE STATE

In the Mediterranean, some Englishmen were exhibited to foreign eyes not as a spectacle but as commodities for sale. English sailors had been enslaved there periodically since the late sixteenth century, but by 1620 the auction of English captives in North Africa was becoming routine. John Rawlins, the master of a Plymouth barque captured in November 1621 close to Gibraltar, remembered the humiliating publicity of being sold at Algiers: "The soldiers hurried us, like dogs, into the market, where, as men sell hackneys in England, we were tossed up and down to see who would give most for us. And although we had heavy hearts and looked with sad countenances, yet many came to behold us, sometimes taking us by the hand, sometimes turning us round, sometimes feeling our brawns and naked arms, and so beholding our prices written in our breasts, they bargained for us accordingly, and at last we were all sold, and the soldiers returned with their money to their captains."[1] Shaven, stripped, and exhibited in the slave markets of Tunis, Algiers, and Salé, merchant sailors were transformed into commodities. Sometimes they were "crammed like capons, that [they] might grow fatter and better for sale." Sometimes potential buyers peered into their mouths, "for they know that they who have no teeth, cannot eat; and they that cannot eat, cannot work."[2] The exhibition of English bodies in North African slave markets was not designed to make a statement about Englishness; instead, it served the practical purpose of allowing buyers to assess captives' value. Still, for English slaves, ties to their homeland were all they had: without being redeemed, they were unlikely to regain their freedom.

Redemption never came for Rawlins. Instead, he was purchased by an English renegade in partnership with two Muslims to become part of the crew of corsair ship manned by "sixty-three Turks and Moors, nine English slaves and one French, [and] four Hollanders that were free men" for an Atlantic cruise. The captain, shipmaster, one of the gunners, and several more were English-born converts to Islam. As the voyage proceeded, he recounted, Rawlins cautiously gained the confidence of the other slaves, the free Dutchmen, and even of some of the renegades. Once the capture of another English ship increased the proportion of potential rebels, he and his allies struck, using their superior knowledge of the sailing ship's balance and guns to defeat the Muslim soldiers, methodically slaughtering all the prisoners save the repentant English renegades. Victorious, the Christians cleared the corpses from the deck, sang a psalm, and sailed home to Plymouth.[3]

Rawlins must have known how rare such escapes were: most enslaved English sailors seem to have died in captivity, as he might have done if he had been unable to free himself.[4] Dedicating his narrative to the Lord High Admiral, the Duke of Buckingham, the mariner made a bold plea for reciprocity, calling attention to English sailors' vital contributions to their country's prosperity and safety: "By such men as myself, your Honour must be served, and England made the happiest of nations. For though you have great persons and more braving spirits to lie over our heads and hold inferiors in subjection, yet are we the men that must pull the ropes, weigh up the anchors, toil in the night, endure the storms, sweat at the helm, watch the biticle, attend the compass, guard the ordnance, keep the night hours, and be ready for all impositions."[5] Would the king and his ministers requite sailors' pains? Seamen knew their worth, but for Rawlins their value to the state was still a question.

For all Rawlins's bitter doubts, the English state did indeed value its seafaring subjects. It could hardly do otherwise: the kingdom's safety depended on the same seamen who served on private warships and merchant vessels. They were also essential to England's imperial projects: despite the learned dispute between Selden and Grotius over English territorial waters, dominion over the seas was not a matter of demarcating space but a question of setting ships and men afloat.[6] Accordingly, the English state generally followed a "maritime" policy of supporting shipping and favoring seamen. When it could promote the interests of English sailors without too much expense or effort, it did so. All kinds of maritime offenses could be overlooked: pirates were pardoned and mutineers were treated gently so as not to waste useful seafarers and to encourage them to return home. In wage disputes between sailors and their merchant employers, the High Court of Admiralty could be remarkably considerate of sailors' rights, not wishing to drive men from the sea. More broadly, however, the state's ability to retain the service and loyalties of English sailors was limited. Foreign rulers were eager to recruit English seafaring men, and proclamations alone could not stem the flow of English labor and expertise abroad. Moreover, despite its pragmatic care for sailors' well-being, the early Stuart state buckled when it came to expensive challenges like protecting its seafaring subjects against foreign threats, regularly paying sailors in the navy, and providing them with adequate supplies and medical care. The state's financial and institutional weakness left hundreds of Englishmen in captivity, and for sailors, serving in royal ships was a quick road to destitution.

Sovereigns of the Seas

Fearsomely armed and lavishly gilded, the *Sovereign of the Seas* was launched in 1637, the pride of the royal fleet. The ship symbolized a far-reaching claim to the sovereignty of the seas, a claim that Charles I, like his father, considered to be an ancient part of the English royal prerogative.[7] The claim to dominion over English territorial waters was justified in print with antiquarian appeals to precedent, but in practice it depended on access to the ships and sailors who alone could make maritime sovereignty a reality. To the irritation of the early Stuarts, the teeming waters off the English coast were to all intents and purposes possessed by the Dutch herring busses that had long been allowed free access to

"English" fish. No amount of erudition could dislodge such a well-guarded fleet.

Elizabeth, an energetic proponent of the freedom of the seas, had remained deaf to John Dee's assertions that the fisheries in English territorial waters belonged to the Crown, but English maritime policy changed under James VI and I. In Scotland, territorial waters had a more distinct meaning than in England, and in the years after James's accession to the English throne, circumstances encouraged the king and his advisors to take a more Scottish view of the seas around England.[8] The Dutch United Provinces had been an ally in the war with Spain, but with the advent of peace the commercial rivalry between the English and the Dutch became hard to ignore. Dutch ships increasingly ruled the waves, and they did so, it seemed, because of the wealth they extracted from British waters. Sir William Monson warned: "It is the fish taken upon His Majesty's coast of England, Scotland and Ireland that is the only cause of the increase of shipping in Europe, and he that hath the trade of that fish becomes mightier than all the world besides in number of shipping." This state of affairs could no longer be tolerated, argued Sir Nicholas Hales, and he advocated that the Dutch be obliged to pay for the wealth they extracted from James's seas and access to his harbors. For James, the idea of adding to his own revenues at Dutch expense was naturally attractive, and in 1609 the Privy Council decided that the king could indeed require Dutch fishermen to obtain licenses to fish in British coastal waters.[9]

Asserting sovereignty over the Sea of England was one thing; inducing the Dutch to recognize it was another. While James eagerly sought to bring Dutch diplomats to the negotiating table, they as resolutely avoided the subject, explaining that they had no authority to address the subject—authority their masters were careful to deny them.[10] While Dutch envoys hemmed and hawed, little could be done: the Royal Navy was decayed, and the herring busses were well protected by Dutch men-of-war. Still, simmering tensions might have come to a boil had not circumstances intervened to remind the Protestant states of what they had in common: in 1610, the English plan to tax the Dutch fishermen was temporarily suspended after the assassination of Henri IV. In 1617, tensions rose again when a representative of the king tried to demand fees from the herring fishermen and was summarily taken into custody by the captains of

Dutch warships. The outbreak of the Thirty Years' War made England and the United Provinces set their differences aside, however.[11]

The Stuarts did not abandon their claims to the Sea of England, but its exact demarcations were left cautiously undefined. When beleaguered naval commanders asked where, exactly, they were supposed to force foreign ships to pay homage to the English flag, they received cryptic answers. In 1635, for example, Sir Edward Coke informed a frustrated admiral that "His Majesty's seas are all about his dominions, and to the largest extent of those seas."[12] The truth was that English commanders should claim dominion when they could but avoid confrontations they were likely to lose. The sheer impracticality of controlling expansive territorial waters would eventually result, of course, in the formulation of the eighteenth-century consensus that territorial waters should be bounded by the range of guns set on land, a distance at that time of about three miles. Legal disputes about maritime sovereignty remained unsettled in the seventeenth century, but it had already become clear that projecting power at sea was fundamentally not a matter of demarcating space but of peopling the sea. States with large fleets projected power wherever their ships went; those without them could not.

Fishing for Seamen

In the sixteenth and seventeenth centuries, England's sea defenses were its main bulwark against foreign invasion, and seamen were critical to the kingdom's security. Unlike armies, which could be quickly formed out of conscripts, civilian militias, and ready-made mercenary units, navies depended on the availability of ships and skilled sailors. Ships simply could not be sailed by novices. Lacking the resources to maintain a large permanent navy, English monarchs relied on their ability to impress merchant ships and mariners into national service when imminent threats loomed. Elizabeth and her successors subsidized the building of large, warlike private ships, but increasing the supply of sailors was more complicated.[13] The challenge was to ensure the training and employment of thousands of seafaring men without having to pay for it.

From the mid-sixteenth century, prohibitions on importing wine in foreign bottoms and especially the promotion of fishing were favored solutions to this problem. Already in 1548 William Cecil had sought to stimulate the English fishing industry through the institution of "political lent," days on which the consumption of flesh was forbidden on pragmatic rather than spiritual grounds. In addition to certain holy days, Friday and Saturday were established as regular fish days, but these measures proved insufficient: in 1563, at a low point for English shipping, Cecil concluded that "some other thing must be provided to increase the navy and to multiply mariners," since building ships with no mariners to man them was no better than to set up suits of armor on stakes "and to provide no people to wear it."[14] Wednesday was made another fish day, and English subjects were forbidden to buy fresh herring from foreigners. Still, English coastal fishing lagged.[15] In 1580, Robert Hitchcock argued that more aggressive measures were needed to make the English herring fleet competitive, thus providing employment at sea and on land and giving the state a wellspring of ships and sailors. He proposed an organized effort to raise funds to set out four hundred herring busses, built in imitation of the Dutch, with warships to protect the fleet. By these means, he suggested, the idle vagabonds who plagued the kingdom would be transmuted into "nine thousand mariners more than now presently there is, to serve Her Majesty's ships at all times if need be." Hitchcock's plans were praised by John Dee, but nothing came of them.[16] Instead, the war with Spain and the privateering boom muted English concerns about promoting shipping: war proved an excellent nursery of seamen.

After the war, printed schemes for the creation of an English herring fleet emerged once again. The growing belief that Dutch fishermen were expropriating British wealth gave these pamphlets a bitter edge. In 1614, Tobias Gentleman complained bitterly about the way Dutch herring fishers reportedly mocked English fishermen "for being so negligent of our profit, and careless of our fishing . . . saying, *Ya English, ya zall or oud scoue dragien*, which in English is this: You English, we will make you glad to wear our old shoes." The idea that the Dutch treated English coastal waters as a "gold mine" led several enthusiasts to push for major investments in the fishery, promising the usual rewards: profits for investors, customs and honor for the Crown, employment for the poor, wealth for small ports, and an increase in shipping and mariners. A year later, Edward Sharpe provided a detailed account of the expense of building a herring buss, arguing that an enterprising investor could rapidly recoup his costs. While some promoters suggested that the field was ready for individual enterprise, others recognized that a viable herring fleet would require naval protection and suggested taxing the herring catch to cover the expense.[17] There were even concrete attempts to imitate Dutch methods: Dutch fishermen were enticed to settle on the Hebrides in 1623, and in 1631 Charles I chartered a herring company to be based there. Yet the barriers were high: Dutch success was founded on strict centralized regulation, state protection, and a well-integrated industry, and specialized skills proved difficult to acquire. Even when European competitors faithfully imitated Dutch methods, they struggled to match their success.[18]

Fortunately, English fishermen's achievements were as brilliant in Newfoundland as they were mediocre in coastal waters. Drawing on their long experience fishing for cod near Iceland, their numbers at the Great Banks of Newfoundland increased dramatically in the late sixteenth and early seventeenth centuries. While French fishing at Newfoundland continued to outpace English activities, English ships increasingly replaced their Iberian competitors. Roughly fifty English ships visited Newfoundland in 1578, one hundred in 1594, and many more by the 1620s. Thousands of men were involved; according to Richard Whitbourne, in 1622 more than five thousand seamen manned the roughly 250 ships that sailed for Newfoundland.[19]

Elizabeth's hostilities with Spain favored the development of Newfoundland fishing. At the time, the Great Banks attracted little attention from lettered people; for aspiring English imperialists, chilly Newfoundland may not have been the most luscious of fruits, but at least it seemed to be within reach.[20] In 1577, Sir Humphrey Gilbert proposed to Elizabeth that he could "annoy the king of Spain" by seizing Spanish, Portuguese, and French ships there. This being done, he argued, "they will never be recovered to the like number," and while foreigners were rebuilding their ships, the English could move into the vacuum.[21] Though a first expedition foundered, in 1583 Gilbert anchored at St. John's and formally took possession of the place in front of a bemused audience of English, Portuguese, Spanish, and French fishermen. Though Gilbert's voyage had little impact, in the following years English aggression upset the rough-and-ready multinationalism of the fishermen's seasonal settlements.

In 1582, a Southampton merchant sponsored a raid on Portuguese fishing ships, and in 1585, after the Spanish embargo on English shipping, Bernard Drake captured sixteen Portuguese vessels.[22] More attacks followed. Though English fishermen benefited in the end, there is little evidence that they promoted the privateers' attacks on foreign fishing ships. Newfoundland men were intensely competitive, but they competed as ships' companies for the best landing spots, not for national supremacy. Every year, English ships braved storms to race across the Atlantic at the earliest possible moment each spring, because the first ship to arrive could claim the best spot, and its master would be "admiral" for the year. In 1595 one of these admirals, William Purfay, even gave French ships passports in hopes of protecting them from the privateers, but in vain.[23] Privateers' attacks on Iberian ships imposed national divisions onto a space where borders had meant less than cultural groupings.[24]

While English attacks damaged Iberian Newfoundland fishing and whaling communities, the relentless exactions of the Spanish Crown played a more serious role in undermining their prosperity, opening the way to a broad expansion of French and English fishing. The Portuguese Crown had long been well aware of its dependence on seamen's and merchants' voluntary involvement in naval enterprise, seeking to allure them with privileges rather than to force them, but this policy altered during the Iberian Union, under the pressure of war.[25] The Spanish government relied heavily on Portuguese and Basque seamen and ships for naval needs, and Newfoundland-bound ships were repeatedly barred from sailing, impressed instead into royal armadas. Investors lost their capital and men lost their lives, while wages and compensation for lost ships were paid achingly slowly, if at all. Ongoing Spanish involvement in warfare with France, England, and the United Provinces stifled the Basque mariners' ability to recover, and by the early seventeenth century, cod arrived in Spain mostly in foreign ships.[26]

For England, this was a success story. The Newfoundland fisheries spurred shipbuilding and the training of seafaring men, serving along with the Newcastle coal trade as one of England's two major "nurseries of seamen" after the end of the privateering war. Fishing vessels and colliers were both unusually accessible to novices. Though there were plenty of poor men looking for work in the hard years around 1600, they could only become sailors if they found masters willing to take them on, and this was no simple matter. To keep costs down, merchant ships were manned by as few sailors as was consonant with safety and efficiency, and merchants were reluctant to pay for novices' training. As Robert Kayll explained: "In the ships that voyage to the southward, or otherwise, far out of the kingdom, there is no owner, or master, that will ordinarily entertain any landman, be he never so willing, as being bound by their charter-party to the merchant, as they say, not to carry but sufficient men, and such as know their labour, and can take their turn at the helm, top, and yard." Beginning sailors could only hope to find employment if they had already learned the ropes in fishing boats or on the Newcastle colliers that hugged the coast. Indeed, there was no need of oceanic expertise to find work on a Newfoundland vessel. The ships carried more men than necessary to sail to and from the Banks because there was plenty of work for beginners do to in small boats or splitting and drying fish on the shore. Richard Whitbourne estimated "that most ships which trade thither yearly a-fishing, do commonly carry in them every fifth person that was never at sea before, or such as have but little understanding in their compass; neither knowledge of sea terms, or what to do in a ship." Since shares made up a large proportion of fishermen's renumeration, the monetary cost of hiring novices was, like the risk, comparatively slight.[27]

Once beginners had gained some experience on colliers or fishing vessels, they might be hired, a few at a time, on merchant ships. Kayll thought Muscovy-bound vessels could take three or four beginners on a ship, and four or five of the twenty-three or so men on ships sailing to the Mediterranean might be relatively inexperienced. New sailors were thus always being trained, but the process took time and depended on the capacity and composition of English shipping. According to Kayll's estimates, the Levant routes commonly produced 140 new able seamen a year, while the western Mediterranean contributed forty new sailors annually. In contrast, the hundreds of colliers that endlessly fed London and other markets' appetite for energy bred at least two thousand seamen a year, while fifteen hundred emerged from the Newfoundland ships, and others from the Iceland fishing fleet. It was clear, Kayll concluded, "that . . . our coal excepted, our especial employment, nourishment, and increase of seamen, is even in this foreign fishing."[28]

English observers tended to assume that the ocean was an inexhaustible source of fish but that sailors, a renewable though limited resource, had to be carefully fostered. The value the state placed on the Newfoundland fishery even impeded the establishment of a colony there. Worried that colonists would seize the most desirable drying locations on shore, in 1618 West Country fishing merchants reminded the king of their industry's critical importance for English prosperity and security. Because of the Newfoundland fishery's unquestioned role as a nursery of seamen, the colonial Newfoundland Company was unable to convince the Privy Council that its interests were also those of the kingdom, and it was ordered to respect the fishermen.[29] The value of "foreign fishing" long remained an article of faith for those concerned with England's security and prosperity. Even when naval manpower shortages loomed in the decades after 1688, Parliament was careful to protect the Newfoundland fishery from the impact of impressment.[30] State power depended on a vibrant *private* shipping industry: there could be no dominion at sea and no safety at home without ships to venture forth and men to sail them.

Sailors and the Law

Training seamen was essential, but retaining them was important too. On James's accession, his new kingdom enjoyed an enviably vibrant population of skillful deep-sea sailors. In his assessment of English capabilities, the Venetian ambassador Nicolò Molin noted that despite its small and decayed navy, "England is as well supplied as any country with artillery, powder and arms, and, more important still, is full of sailors and men fit for service at sea."[31] But while skillful and experienced seamen were the kingdom's best defense, they were apt to wander. As we have seen, warlike English sailors were recruited by the United Provinces, Spain, and an array of Mediterranean princes, while others became independent pirates. In its response to this problem, the state was limited to policies that were cheap for the Crown, such as royal proclamations, although the frequency with which sailors were commanded to leave foreign service suggests that these had limited effect. Other measures were more costly, but the burden was borne by foreign and English merchants: pirates were pardoned more often than they were hanged, and sometimes admiralty judges put their thumbs on the scales of justice, hoping to keep English shipping attractive to the seamen who supported the kingdom's security and prosperity.

With warlike sailors still plentiful in the years after the 1604 Treaty of London, English statesmen were more concerned about stopping English seamen from strengthening foreign rulers than about an absolute shortage of maritime manpower in England. In 1607, worried about Tuscan recruitment of English seamen, Henry Wotton warned his superiors about "the dangerous consequence of the example given herein to other princes who have better harborage and commodity to employ our shipwrights and sailors and sea captains, and finally, the communication (that will ensue upon it) of our shipping and maritime knowledge (His Majesty's principal strength) with foreign nations." The Grand Duke of Tuscany was "not only entertaining, and fostering, and employing of fugitives and pirates, but by his inviting and alluring of them also thither ... the like practices tending towards the setting up of some better navigation than hath before been seen in the Mediterranean." Indeed, Ferdinand used his Englishmen to send a 1608 expedition to the Amazon River, far from the usual haunts of Tuscan shipping.[32]

As the English Atlantic pirate community flourished between roughly 1608 and 1614, its members were recruited by Mediterranean princes eager for fighting seamen. Though in law pirates were conceived as *hostis humani generis*, in practice they were often courted: by pardoning a dangerous pirate, a ruler could simultaneously protect his own shipping, tax the pirate's spoils, and enjoy his service. Working for the grand duke, for example, the playwright-turned-pirate Lording Barry offered a Tuscan pardon to the pirates at Mamora. By July 1611, his efforts had borne modest fruit: the Venetian resident at Florence reported that three English pirate captains had arrived there and converted to Catholicism. They had left their ships at Mamora, however, because most of their men were unwilling to enter Tuscan service: "It is doubtful whether they will leave that place where they have freedom to prey on friends and foes alike, nor do they desire to share their booty with the Grand Duke."[33] The Duke of Savoy, who pardoned Peter Easton, was also eager to acquire seafaring subjects at Mamora, though his unfortunate agent arrived there too late, shortly before a successful Spanish assault permanently deprived the

English pirates of their base.[34] Trumpeting his loyalty to James while also underscoring his fame, the pirate admiral Henry Mainwaring boasted of all the pardons he had allegedly rejected from potential patrons: "The Duke of Medina sent to me that, if I would deliver up Mamora to the King of Spain, that I should have a great sum of money . . . and good entertainment if I would command in the King's ships. The Duke of Savoy sent me my pardon. The Duke of Florence sent me my pardon. . . . The Dey of Tunis ate bread and salt and swore by his beard . . . if I would stay with him, he would divide his estate equally with me and never urge me to turn Turk."[35] Mainwaring never accepted a foreign pardon, but after the loss of Mamora, a number of the English pirates did indeed enter the service of Mediterranean princes, as we have seen.

James was reluctant to lure the English Atlantic pirates home with pardons, but he had little choice. No practical naval alternative presented itself: even assuming a fleet could locate the pirates, it would take considerable time to set out a strong enough force. In 1611 the Lord Admiral was reluctant to send out the one available warship to a probable defeat.[36] On the southern coast of Munster, where the pirates engaged in mutually profitable trade with English settlers, officials were none too anxious to capture the miscreants, and even when they did, until 1613, imprisoned pirates had to be sent to England to be tried. Under these conditions, even the merchants who had suffered at the pirates' hands lobbied for a general pardon, considering it the surest means to reclaim their lost goods.[37] When some of the pirates offered to surrender in return for a pardon, the Privy Council took the offer seriously, despite James's scruples: "A council has been held on the subject, and a diversity of opinion was manifested; the king declared his conscience would not allow him to grant impunity so easily to such a ruffianly race who had done so much mischief in the ocean and in the Mediterranean, but that he must find out some way more consistent with his honour and his conscience to compel these and all the others as well; on the other hand the majority of the Council approve of accepting the pirates' proposals in the hope that their example would help as an incentive to others, or at least reduce their numbers and make them less capable of resistance."[38] The United Provinces, whose ships suffered heavily at the English pirates' hands, were willing to take strong measures if their warships could be allowed to pursue the pirates into Irish harbors, but allowing a Dutch naval force to attack English subjects in James's territorial waters clashed with his ongoing efforts to persuade the Dutch to respect British maritime sovereignty. Ultimately, however, James pursued both lines of attack, enticing the pirates home with pardons and menacing them with Dutch naval force.[39]

In the short run, carrot and stick both failed: the thirteen pirate ships that had been anchored near the Irish coast sailed away before Captain Roger Middleton arrived with a royal pardon or the Dutch fleet could assault them. Middleton persisted in his mission, however, even following the pirates to Mamora, where he eventually persuaded several pirate companies to accept the king's pardon.[40] Amazingly, once the repentant pirates were waiting off the coast of Ireland for the final terms of the pardon, the Privy Council sweetened the deal, allowing them to keep their ill-gotten gains. The government appears to have feared that otherwise the pirates would seek the protection of the Grand Duke of Tuscany, for there had been persistent rumors to that effect.[41] This remarkably generous policy became standard. When Captain William Baugh arrived in Ireland in September 1612, the Privy Council wrote that it would make out "pardons for himself and his consorts . . . as soon as possible."[42] The following year, William Marlett was employed to carry a pardon to Gilbert Roope and other pirates, and for the rest of the decade pirates continued to be offered pardons.[43] However much it may have galled the king, pardoning pirates had the great merit of bringing stalwart fighting seamen back into the English fold and denying them to other maritime powers.

Unfortunately, the ease of obtaining pardons also encouraged seamen to become pirates. Henry Mainwaring—himself a pardoned pirate—advised the king to adopt a more ruthless stance: "To take away their hopes and encouragements, Your Highness must put on a constant immutable resolution never to grant any pardon . . . for if Your Highness should ask me when those men would leave offending I might answer, as a wise favourite did the late queen, demanding when he would leave begging, he answered, when she would leave giving; so say I, when Your Highness leaves pardoning." Mainwaring thought that severe punishments were required, though he believed that captured pirates ought to be enslaved, not hanged, since "the state may hereafter want such men, who commonly are the most daring and serviceable in war of all those kind of people.' " In fact, even pirates who were captured or who surrendered without negotiating pardons tended to go free; as Mainwaring noted disapprovingly: "The common sort of seamen, even those that willingly and willfully put themselves into these courses, are greatly emboldened by reason of a received opinion and custom that is here for the most part used, that none but the captain, master, and it may be some few of the principal of the company shall be put to death."[44]

Hangings were indeed rare; executions did take place, but they seem to have been sporadic and arbitrary. In a striking miscarriage of justice, when Sir William St. John captured Captain James Harris and his men in 1609, four members of Harris's crew who had been with him for only a few weeks were sent to London for trial with him, while the veteran pirates "were sent ashore . . . and let go whither they would." The new recruits—including a fisherman and a husbandman—were hanged, despite having never robbed a ship.[45] St. John may have agreed with Mainwaring that it was better to keep experienced seamen alive for the navy than to waste them on the gallows. Unfortunately for some of these pirates, the Dutch were less solicitous. When the Irish Captain Myagh arrived at Crookhaven for pardon negotiations in 1614, a Dutch naval squadron unceremoniously blew up his ship in an act of "outrageous murder," according to a scandalized survivor.[46]

In most cases, pardoned pirates probably went back to work as sailors, since by the time the pirate captains and royal officials had skimmed off their shares of plunder, little remained for the common men. The fortune amassed by Baugh's fleet seems to have melted away after the ships reached Ireland. As the resentful crew watched, Baugh—eager to ingratiate himself with the colonial elite and marry a local gentleman's daughter—handed out armfuls of "holland, taffeta, garters, ribbons, and many other things daily at his pleasure." He told the company that "all he gave should be out of his own shares," but they did not trust him and, like true litigious Englishmen, went to law to recover their rightful part of the plunder.[47] St. John was accused of taking many valuables from the pirates. The gunner's mate, William Pyborne, complained that when he went on board the *Lion* to fetch his chest of ambergris and linen, he found it empty, and that he had even been prevented from carrying his bed away. What was more, St. John immediately pressed him into the royal ship *Speedwell*.[48] Still, pirates probably kept more than they admitted in court. Henry Orenge, a master in Baugh's fleet, seems to have successfully concealed a number of precious stones from Baugh and the authorities alike. When an acquaintance met him on the street in London "and asked him how he did and how the world passed with him," Orenge allegedly replied "that he was come home poor but ... had some stones." He boasted to other friends: " 'Though he seemed poor he would be merry with his friends one of these days, for,' he said shaking his breeches by the waistband, 'that although they seemed to be but a poor pair of breeches, yet they were as rich as any breeches the king wore.' " Questioned closely in early 1613 about these suspicious statements, the pirate audaciously explained that he only meant that he "had two stones in his breeches that he would not lose for a great deal of money."[49]

The Jacobean state's lenient approach to English piracy preserved the lives of seamen who went on to serve English interests in other ways. Some, like Walsingham, Pyborne, and of course Mainwaring himself, served in the navy. The Cornish surgeon Richard Len, who had been serving in the Earl of Thomond's company in Ireland, went to sea with the pirate Captain Baugh for a year, then, pardoned, immediately became surgeon of the naval ship *Speedwell*.[50] Ex-pirates also appear in the records of the East India Company. Indicted for the spoil of the *Balbiana* in 1604, Cornelius Billing died master of the East India Company ship *Darling* in 1613.[51] Peter Easton's surgeon John Neve served on the *Globe*.[52] The trumpeter John Simnell, who sailed with the renegade John Ward out of Tunis and was left there as a hostage by Richard Bishop in 1608, gave evidence about VOC aggression in the Indian Ocean twelve years later.[53] Nicholas Haydon, a pirate boy reprieved from the gallows around 1606, "was lamed in one leg" when the VOC captured the *Sampson* in 1619.[54] Some former pirates were still active seamen when Charles I caused a general muster of sailors to be made in 1629. Baptist Ingle had joined Captain Stephenson at Mamora after the pirate captain heard the boy play his whistle and took "a liking of him." Along with his captain, Ingle was pardoned around 1612 and came to Ireland, where he broke "up one of the company's chests and stole away near one hundred pounds and ran therewith away from the ship." By 1629 the pirate youth had become a respectable master's mate.[55]

Jacobean courts' favor extended to other criminal seamen as well. On merchant ships, mutiny was not yet a felony and carried no severe legal consequences. The state could even wink at murder when sailors carried valuable navigational knowledge.[56] This was the case, famously, in the 1611 mutiny that led to the death of Henry Hudson. The sailors who abandoned Hudson and his supporters in a small boat in the Arctic had some justification, to be sure; after the long winter that had exhausted their stores, they had entered uncharted moral waters.[57] Still, they had expelled their commander and eight other people into the wilderness, leaving them to their deaths. Remarkably, back in England these seamen escaped hanging and even received their wages for the voyage. Their rare knowledge of northern waters may have saved their lives: under questioning, the surgeon Edward Wilson certainly suggested that their experience was valuable. Asked whether the Northwest Passage existed and could be found, he replied that it could "be easily discovered if such may be employed as have been acquainted with the voyage and knoweth the manner of the ice."[58] At least one of the eight survivors did return to the Arctic: Robert Bylot, who piloted the *Discovery* to Ireland after the mutiny, sailed four more times to explore the cold Northwest, most notably with William Baffin in 1615 and 1616. The following year, after the North-West Passage Company's interest in exploration had cooled, he and six more were belatedly indicted for murder, but only four were tried and all were acquitted.

The admiralty judges may also have been sympathetic to the impossible situation in which Hudson's seamen found themselves. As George Steckley has argued, these judges were not agents of capital who promoted merchants' interests over those of maritime workers. Rather, when investors and seamen contended over the allocation of profits and losses, they tended to support labor. The admiralty court's structure was well adapted to the needs of mobile seamen: suits were not bound to the common law terms but could proceed at any time; sailors could share legal expenses by joining together to sue for their wages; written depositions were used so that litigants were not obliged to stay in town during the proceedings; and sailors could sue *in rem* to seize ships and cargoes rather than having to sue individuals who might be bankrupt or absent. Moreover, Steckley has found that admiralty judges favored sailors who sued for their wages. When merchants and masters sought to change voyages' routes over sailors' objections, the sailors refused to comply, and their employers withheld wages, the seamen who sued at admiralty were likely to be awarded their full pay. The rule that sailors were only paid up to the last port of call was not always enforced: in 1609, the admiralty judge Richard Trevor ruled that the sailors of the *Prosperous* were due wages up to the day when their ship was captured by pirates. In a variety of seventeenth-century cases in which employers docked seamen's wages for misbehavior—pilfering, incompetence, disobedience, desertion, and so on—admiralty judges generally reduced the severity of the punishments or even canceled them completely. "Only evidence of utterly careless performance . . . could provoke a judge to deny all wages." Indeed, in the early years of the seventeenth century, sailors who went to law for their wages almost always won. In a sample of forty-seven cases, they were awarded full wages more than 90 percent of the time.[59]

Admiralty judges' tenderness for seamen's interests probably resulted, as Steckley argues, from their desire to keep English shipping attractive to mariners. While individual verdicts rarely include evidence of judicial reasoning, this concern emerges clearly in several mid-seventeenth-century treatises defending the civil law against the encroachment of common lawyers. Richard Zouch warned that weakening the admiralty courts "must needs more weaken the shipping of the kingdom, than divers ordinances and constitutions intended for the maintenance thereof can possibly advance the same." If a sailor cannot obtain his wages, he "in consequence must betake himself to some other course of life." "It is considerable what justice the poor mariner could expect, or should be like to have," John Exton noted cuttingly, "if the determination and adjudication of their wages should be left unto merchants and owners of ships . . . out of whose freight the same ought to be paid, and would be as it were parties in all causes of that nature." "If the merchant should sit to judge the mariner, in time, the company of poor mariners might be severely dealt with, and kept with such short wages by the merchant, at whose pleasure and command he is, that he will not care to serve, and so navigation may be quite lost," John Wiseman warned. Exton agreed: it "would be a means to dishearten and discourage all mariners for serving in English bottoms, whensoever employment should be offered them elsewhere."[60] Without fair wages, English sailors would either leave the sea or, as aggrieved seamen pointed out in a 1628 petition to Parliament, "leave their native country to sail out of foreign parts, to the weakening of ourselves and strengthening of them," two dangerous outcomes for English commerce and security.[61] For their own good and for England's safety, then, merchants and shipowners had to be obliged to deal fairly with the men who sailed their ships.

Protection

For the state, as we have seen, seamen were an indispensable national resource. For sailors, the state was a valuable resource too. Allegiance entailed rights as well as obligations, and English sailors were often anxious to affirm their loyalty. None were more desperate for their sovereign's aid than the unfortunate seamen captured by hostile powers abroad. When captives appealed to the state for protection, however, they met with uncertain success. The state could pardon pirates and favor sailors in wage lawsuits, but effectively interceding abroad was a far greater challenge.

English seafarers captured in the Caribbean regularly appealed to their sovereign for help. The 1604 peace treaty between England and Spain had left the question of Spain's sweeping claims to American territory unresolved: the gap between the two kingdoms could not be bridged, yet the problem was too minor to stand in the way of a treaty. James was willing to prohibit his subjects from trading to specific ports in Spanish America, but he remained blandly noncommittal about plans for settlement in Virginia as well as the right of Englishmen to sail through Caribbean waters, while Spanish officials took a hard line with interloping English ships. When English prisoners in the West Indies were not summarily put to death, they became the subjects of tense negotiations. They were not, however, "merely counters in a diplomatic tussle." They could not afford to suffer in silence: those who did not publicize their plight might swiftly disappear, like the company of the *Castor and Pollux* in 1605.[62] Moreover, while James quietly supported the establishment of a plantation in Virginia against Spanish opposition, he had good reason to accept the usual Spanish explanation that captured English mariners had been up to no good: leaving them to their fates was the path of least resistance. As a brief sketch of the situation in Salisbury's papers notes, "for the avoiding of the occasion whereby to call into the general question of the Indias and our trading thereinto, it might be better to leave these prisoners to their fortune than by bringing it into question to stir up some greater inconveniences."[63] If the mariners hoped for freedom, they and their friends would have to convince the Crown that they were innocent victims of Spanish cruelty.

Knowing how vulnerable they were to attacks on their character, English prisoners presented themselves as faithful subjects, the deserving objects of royal protection. The captured factors William Squire and Thomas Tile took this line when they wrote to Salisbury: "We are poor merchants, and neither rebels nor pirates . . . we went forth in the true estate of merchandize . . . we have committed no stubbornness nor disobedience against the king of Spain's subjects." When their merchant ships had been commanded to strike by Spanish galleys, they had faced an impossible choice: "If we yield and depend upon their friendly promises we lose our goods and are made slaves, if we make any resistance we are all thrown overboard, as they did in this voyage to a ship of Mr. Edwards of London, which they took at Margarita and threw all the men overboard, saving three, which certain days after were put to death by the general's order, so that none escaped but one boy, which a captain begged to serve him." They themselves had yielded, they said, and were imprisoned and the sailors "committed to the galleys chained and shaved."[64] Adam Tanner and other mariners who escaped the galleys represented Spanish cruelty in even starker terms, alleging that Don Luis Fajardo and his men "used us in most slavish and barbarous manner scant allowing unto us food to maintain life, neither apparel to cover our naked bodies. Albeit we strived in those base and servile offices we were employed in, to give them all content (yet such was their malice to us) that the fairest word, that at any time they did give us, was to bid us, come dog, or go devil, and to make a jest of our miseries committing us every night for the space of twenty days or more at their pleasure after great and extreme labour all the day to the stocks at night." Entreating Salisbury to secure the release of the rest of the men "for the relief of their poor wives, children, and families," the mariners noted darkly that English colors and King James himself had been shamefully reviled by the Spaniards, with words "not fit to be uttered (which did more grieve us than all our miseries)." In short, the sailors suffered because Fajardo hated and despised their nation, not for any crime they had committed.[65] Meanwhile, the sailors' miseries reached deep into English families, as the wives of the prisoners declared in their own petition. As the men suffered "intolerable pains and penury with grievous irons upon them," their wives, who had "long hoped of the happy and prosperous return of their distressed husbands," were left with "their poor children, ready to famish for want of harbour and relief."[66] Their petitioning campaign bore fruit when, after diplomatic intervention, the prisoners were released.[67]

Honor and compassion moved the Crown to aid its distressed subjects, but concern about English navigational expertise was probably also a factor. The captured pilot John Stoneman claimed that his skills and knowledge of the North American coast were eagerly coveted by his Spanish captors. Stoneman had sailed along the coast of North Virginia in 1605 with George Waymouth and served in 1606 as pilot of the *Richard*, bound for Virginia. Sailing through the Spanish Caribbean, disaster struck when, blinded by fog, the Englishmen blundered into the midst of a Spanish merchant fleet. They and two Etchemin men who had been kidnapped on the coast of Maine the year before were promptly taken prisoner and dispersed among the fleet, which continued on to Spain. Luckily for the prisoners, some of the ships lost their way; one ended up in Bordeaux, where the Englishmen were promptly released and made their way home to tell their story.

Stoneman had nothing but scorn for Spanish navigators, whom he accused of "wilful negligence or simple ignorance"; he reported that the ship on which he sailed had arrived at Sanlucar only because he helped the hapless Spanish pilot set a course. Stoneman's expertise allegedly attracted much attention in Spain. The president of the Casa de la Contratación, Stoneman wrote, "did often earnestly examine me of the manner and situation of the country of Virginia, together with the commodities and benefit thereof." He refused to share his knowledge or to enter Spanish service: "The Spaniards were very desirous to have me to serve their state, and proffered me great wages, which I refused to do, affirming that this employment which I had in hand was not yet ended until which time I would not determine any. Then the Alcade major of the Contractation House and divers other merchants persuaded me to make them some descriptions and maps of the coast and parts of Virginia, which I also refused to do." The Spanish authorities were angered by Stoneman's obduracy, and he recounted that he was warned that he would be tortured if he would not speak freely: "They resolved to bring me to the rack and torment me, whereby to draw some further knowledge by confession from me, before any discharge might come for us." The pilot, who at that point was out on sureties, fled with two companions from Seville to Lisbon, where he boarded an English ship and sailed for home.[68]

The mariners of the *Richard* who returned home and their backers were successful in arousing official concern for the remaining prisoners. Salisbury was particularly incensed by the fact that the *Richard*'s men had been harshly treated despite the fact that they were going "but to a place formerly discovered by us, and never possessed by Spain."[69] The English government mounted a vigorous effort to secure the release of the prisoners, but with scant success. In May 1608, the men were sent to the galleys, although the diplomat Nevill Davies was able to secure the release of four boys and one surviving Etchemin. In July, the ambassador to Spain, Sir Charles Cornwallis, wrote: "For the prisoners sometimes at Seville, and now in the galleys in St Lucar, I . . . have now less hope than ever." Only after months of hard labor, in November, were the surviving men unexpectedly released.[70]

Spanish severity was harsh but largely avoidable for English sailors who kept well away from the West Indies; for most seamen, the corsairs of Algiers, Tunis, and Salé posed a far greater threat. By hastening the North African corsairs' acquisition of ocean-going ships and guns, the English and Dutch pirates who traveled to Tunis and Algiers in the early seventeenth century had altered the geography of maritime power. With the help of these renegades as well as Moriscos expelled from Spain, North African corsairs quickly mastered the use of sailing ships that could withstand the Atlantic. Soon slaving corsairs were snapping up small English vessels in the western Mediterranean, the Atlantic, and even off the English coast. In early 1617, merchants representing the West Country and the major merchant companies petitioned the king for "securing His Majesty's subjects . . . otherwise the strength of them doth daily increase as almost no ship is able to trade in safety." Two years later, the Privy Council estimated that more than three hundred ships had been taken with their cargoes "besides the captivating of many hundreds of His Majesty's subjects, to the utter ruin of themselves, their wives and children, and the impoverishing and weakening of these his realms and dominions."[71]

These attacks on English shipping touched the interests and the honor of the Crown, but it was hard to mount an effective response. In accordance with his usual diplomatic approach, James first complained to the Ottoman sultan about Algiers and Tunis, but with scant success.[72] As the grand vizier's deputy informed the Venetian bailo a few years later, the Ottoman regime took the view that "the fault lay with those who introduced these pirate bertons at Tunis and Algiers, who were English, French and Flemings." These European renegades "taught the people of Barbary, who before that time had not known what bertons were."[73] In any case, the corsairs were beyond the effective control of Istanbul.

That James and his advisers then began to plan a naval expedition against Algiers illustrates the severity of the problem and the value they placed on English shipping, trade, and mariners. This was not a regime that undertook naval mobilization lightly. Nor, as it turned out, could it do so successfully. The Crown was committed to protecting its subjects, as David Hebb has shown, yet manifold challenges barred the way.[74] Initially, James hoped to secure Spanish and Dutch cooperation against the corsairs, but negotiations dragged on, stymied by Dutch distrust of Spain and by internal political turmoil. On the English side, Crown administration proved wanting, and fundraising for the expedition was soon mired in bickering and delay as the corporations and towns tasked with contributing money complained and dragged their feet. It was two years after James's initial resolution before an English fleet set sail to Algiers in 1620, and even then, though the fleet carried local experts like the reformed Robert Walsingham and had secured access to Spanish ports for revictualing and repairs, victory remained stubbornly out of reach. The element of surprise was long lost; the English fleet lacked galleys; contrary winds and rains frustrated an attempt to burn the ships in the harbor; and it became clear that successfully blockading the port would be a matter of months or years, not weeks. Bedeviled by short supplies, sick men, and late reinforcements, the fleet's commander, Sir Robert Mansell, gave up hope, while in Westminster the huge expense of maintaining the Mediterranean fleet prompted the Privy Council to recall it to England.

A great deal of money had been spent, only a handful of captives had been released, and the corsairs of Algiers were as active as ever. In his misery, John Rawlins—whose small ship was captured in this period—had plenty of company. In early 1622, Richard Ford, a seaman left in Algiers by Mansell to keep a register of English captives, begged James "to consider the distressed and miserable estate of Englishmen here." Scores of ships had been taken, Ford lamented, and five hundred men and boys carried to Algiers: "The young men and boys they force to turn Turks, two ships' companies they put to the sword being to the number of seventy and some they have thrown overboard and sold in other parts of Barbary as at Salé, at Tetouan, at Tunis, and some few in other places and now they are sending some for the Levant, so that I doubt the one half will never see their countries again."[75] The following year, when crowds of poor women "petitioned to the king, for the relief of their husbands, now captives in Algiers and Tunis," the secretary of state turned to Nicholas Leate of the Levant Company for advice. As Leate wrote, he too had been much struck by "the importunities of the mariners' wives . . . every day crying out upon the Exchange and at my house and others . . . many of them in desperate and miserable case, wanting bread to relieve them and their children." He stressed the urgency of the matter. If action was not quickly taken "for the redeeming of those poor captives, His Majesty's subjects, both English, Scots, and Irish being with those lately taken above a thousand persons . . . these His Majesty's subjects, being void of all hope to be redeemed, it is to be feared, will either turn Turk or desperately attempt some mischief against this nation." Leate meant that captive seamen would help their captors "come into the Narrow Seas and take our ships here at home for some of them have protested that much." If their sovereign failed to help them, the embittered sailors would turn their knowledge and skill against their nation.[76]

The Crown was already pursuing a diplomatic solution: shortly after the failure of the Mansell expedition, Sir Thomas Roe had been sent to Istanbul. By 1624, with the assistance of Ottoman officials and generous bribes for the pashas of Algiers and Tunis, Roe forged a fragile peace with the two regencies, and a new consul in Algiers, James Frizell, did indeed help English captives return home. Money again proved a sticking point, however. Seeking compensation for his expenses toward liberating English seamen, Frizell met with a cold shoulder from the Levant Company—despite his concern for the mariners, Leate was reluctant to put up funds—and foot-dragging from the Privy Council. The corsairs themselves were hostile to an agreement that restrained their enterprise without full compensation, and by the end of 1626 the peace had disintegrated.[77]

Meanwhile, ships from Salé, the Moroccan enclave controlled by Morisco pirates, increasingly appeared off the West Country. These slavers targeted sailors themselves, attacking small, weakly defended vessels and terrorizing local ports. In April 1625, two abandoned fishing boats were found floating at sea, the Plymouth mayor anxiously informed the Privy Council. One escaped fisherman told a harrowing story: the men had been captured by a small Salé barque manned by "nine Dutchmen, six Turks, and three Moors, and one of them a black Moor," the last of whom had compassionately "unloosed his hands," allowing him to creep to the side and jump overboard into a boat. Pleas for naval protection came from Cornwall too: "The Turks are upon our coasts have taken divers ships, they only take the men to make slaves of them."[78] The slavers took "His Majesty's able-bodied subjects . . . other booty they looked not for." When Salé men, including "four . . . English and five Flemish renegadoes, besides thirty Turks and Moors," took a Newfoundland-bound ship, they "did take out of her the said master and seventeen others of her choicest men, all which . . . they chained" and stowed in the hold.[79] The mayor and bailiff of Weymouth lamented to the Privy Council in May that the Salé slavers treated their captives "worse by much, than they were wont to be used in Algiers . . . setting their ransoms so high and great, as they and their friends are not by any means able to defray or raise the same." In July, a returned Scottish captive said there were six hundred English slaves at Salé.[80] The following year, Trinity House officers estimated that in all between twelve hundred and fourteen hundred English subjects had been taken by Salé ships.[81]

Urgently requesting naval assistance to clear the coasts of pirates, coastal magistrates stressed the fact that the captured seamen were valuable to the Crown as well as to their unhappy families. Because of the Salé slavers, "His Majesty loseth his customs, and is deprived of many good and serviceable subjects, the whole country is debarred from their trade, and thereby utterly impoverished, the kingdom is weakened, and a great number of women and children are bereaved of their husbands and fathers, whose woeful complains do daily fill our ears," the Grand Jury of Devon wrote. "Within these two years they will not leave His most excellent Majesty sailors to man his fleet," warned the mayor of Poole.[82] These arguments held weight: Buckingham did indeed send warships to patrol the coasts in June 1625.[83] In addition, in 1628 John Harrison sailed to Salé with a commission to negotiate peace. In exchange for arms, money, and some Muslim prisoners, he obtained the liberty of more than two hundred English captives and a few years of relief from attacks by Salé ships.[84]

Ultimately, however, the ravages of corsairs from Salé and resurgent Algiers had no economical solution. With little vulnerable merchant shipping to defend and, in the case of Algiers, a highly defensible base, the corsairs were in an enviably strong position. Ransoming English subjects only encouraged further attacks, and at about £40 per man, the potential expense was huge. Buying peace with money and arms was both dishonorable and costly. War had no guarantee of success, as Mansell's failure had shown, and paying for it was a daunting challenge. The Crown's regular revenues were wholly inadequate, and the rich merchants of the Levant Company preferred to provide for their own defense by hiring "extraordinary good ships the best we can procure" rather than sharing in the high costs of naval ventures, while the small shipowners whose ships were the most vulnerable were the least able to pay.[85] Committees were convened and reports were drafted, but without stronger naval power, little could be done. Only when Ship Money revenues made the 1637 expedition against Salé possible would the Royal Navy mount a successful attack on a pirate stronghold.[86] Faced with the threat posed by the corsairs, both subjects and sovereign recognized the importance of the bond between them, but the state was better at inventing ceremonies for the reincorporation of former captives than at projecting naval power thousands of miles away.[87]

The Crown's real difficulties did little to assuage the desperation of enslaved sailors and their families. Small wonder that some captives took matters into their own hands, mounting savage revolts on shipboard. In 1625, for example, five slave sailors (three English, one Dutch, and one French) cut the throats of about twenty Salé corsairs during the night and then took control of the ship by training its ordnance against the other Muslims and renegades. After their former captors surrendered, the Christian victors put them in irons and tried to sell them on the nearby Canary Islands. When the ship was denied entrance to the Canaries, the sailors simply threw most of the surviving prisoners "overboard into the sea."[88] Such victories were rare, however. For the coastal fishermen and sailors who were taken to the Maghreb, enslavement was probably even more traumatic than it had been for the ocean-going English seamen captured in the Mediterranean in earlier years. Stumbling up from the lower decks, blinking in the glaring sunlight, these prisoners would have to accommodate themselves to a profoundly alien world, one without parents, wives, children, or the modest comforts of home. With little knowledge of the region and weaker access to maritime credit networks, their chances of redemption were surely slimmer. English redemption efforts remained sporadic and haphazard: lone wives could gather charity, and funds were also raised at times in local and even national efforts, but it seems unlikely that more than a minority of captives saw their homes again.[89]

Service

In 1625, when Charles I succeeded his father, the demands of war combined with corsair attacks to strain the relationship between seamen and their sovereign. The new king's aggressive foreign policy depended heavily on maritime labor. In spring 1625, sailors—"the ablest and sufficientest mariners and seafaring men . . . not loose and unskillful poor men"— were pressed into service in great numbers for the expedition to Cadiz, and ambitious naval ventures were repeated in the following years.[90] In warfare, as in the captivity crisis, the Crown's desire to cherish its seafaring subjects outstripped its capacity, resulting in widespread misery and unrest.

When they were pressed into royal service, English sailors brought the expectations they had developed in private shipping to the navy. In some ways, of course, naval service was unique; few doubted that sailors could be required to serve their sovereign in times of war. Yet sailors expected the relationship to be reciprocal: they had rights—to victuals and pay—as well as obligations, and they even expected to be able to refuse unpopular orders. When, as part of Charles's initial alliance with France, English ships were supposed to be loaned to French service, the sailors suspected that they would be deployed against Huguenot rebels rather than the shared Spanish enemy. They stubbornly refused to obey French orders, swearing "they [would] be hanged or thrown overboard before they [would] ever do it."[91] For Charles and Buckingham, the sailors' mutinousness provided useful political cover. They sent official orders that the English ships were to be handed over to the French admiral as soon as possible, while unofficially the English admiral was told that "the king and all the rest were exceedingly glad of that relation which he made of the discontent and mutinies of his company," and that if necessary, "his men should take him prisoner and bring away the ship." The delays continued until Charles was assured that Cardinal Richelieu had made peace with the rebels—although this proved too soon, since the ships were indeed used against the Huguenots.[92]

Early modern structures of command could accommodate negotiation and compromise, but the Stuart regime's inability to supply its fleets strained the bond between the monarch and his seafaring subjects to the point of collapse. This failure resulted from institutional weakness and lack of money, not from the state's refusal to recognize its obligations toward the seamen. While the king's love for his sailors was probably always fairly abstract, Charles's government never questioned their customary allotments of food; nonetheless, it consistently fell short in providing them. The miserable end of the Cadiz voyage set a pattern that would often be repeated. Returning home after the failed assault, the old Elizabethan privateer Michael Geere wrote sadly to his son that he had one hundred sick men, fifty-nine dead, not ten able to do any service: "I grieve to write of many other abuses as in our victuals, our flesh cut at half the king's allowance, and that so stinks, that I presume hath been the cause of the death, and sickness, which is amongst us. No dog of Paris Gardens, I think, will eat it." When the ships finally straggled back to England, Sir William St. Leger reported that the surviving soldiers were too weak and sick to be moved, and in urgent need of clothing: "The state they now stand in is most miserable. They stink as they go, the poor rags they have are rotten and ready to fall off if they be touched." The sailors were just as sick as the landsmen.[93]

The expedition was over, but there was no respite. In the years that followed, the Crown continued to make heavy demands on English seamen, pressing continually while reeling from financial crisis to crisis. The low rate of pay in royal service was a glaring problem, Sir Edward Cecil wrote to Sir John Coke: "The chief thing wherein we hope to do His Majesty's service is to have his mariners better paid . . . for as His Majesty's pay is now, all good sailors fly his service both in the kingdom and out of the kingdom, and serve rather his enemies than otherwise . . . it were a great policy (in my poor judgment) to cherish them and breed them with as much care as may be." The poorly paid sailors on the Cadiz voyage had hated their work, "their ordinary talk being that His Majesty presses them, and gives them so little means that they are not able to live on it, and that it were better to be hanged or serve the king of Spain, or the Turk, than His Majesty."[94] The Privy Council knew that sailors had to be encouraged and could not be simply forced, and proposals were made and eventually implemented in 1626 to raise the pay of naval seamen, while Admiralty secretary Sir Edward Nicholas proposed that sailors on naval ships be granted much of the value of captured men-of-war.[95]

In practice, however, sailors could still not obtain their pay; they were short of food and drink, clothing, and shoes. The only way to obtain their wages, it seemed, was to mutiny, petition, or desert. Informed in late June 1626 of the "tumultuous and disorderly manner of certain mariners and seamen abandoning His Majesty's fleet," the Privy Council ordered that the deserters be intercepted and brought back to Portsmouth, "where they shall with all convenient expedition, have payment of such monies as are due into them for their wages." Three weeks later, the sailors—still unpaid for eighteen months and deeply in debt—were called before the paymaster, only to be told that he could pay them for just fifteen months, and that they were to go to sea again in a week. "Then was their case desperate without some provision for their clothes and for their poor families," they lamented, petitioning for relief.[96] Emboldened by despair, unpaid mariners flocked to London, where John Pory saw "some twenty . . . take the Duke's [Buckingham's] coach horses by the head and stay his coach," demanding redress.[97] By August, sailors were escaping to the Isle of Wight to avoid the press, hiding in the woods—and even when they could be found, "to press men is almost in vain. They regard it not and will not repair to the ships." The fleet lacked a thousand men, Captain Richard Gyfford concluded.[98]

These disorders continued as the state eked out its resources to keep the fleet together while a double war with France and Spain strained them to the utmost. In September two hundred sailors converged "tumultuously at the Duke's house at Chelsea for pay." Days later, Buckingham "was so hotly encountered by the sailors . . . that he was since fain to set a guard about his house." In a royal proclamation, the king commanded all "disorderly" mariners and soldiers to leave London and the court, and to "return to the places from whence they came."[99] Obedience could not be expected of starving men, however. In London, a December newsletter recounted, "here was some three hundred sailors come up for their wages, which this other day brake ope the great gate of Sir William Russell, Treasurer of the Navy, and would have plucked him out by the ears had he not given them fair words. Since his house hath been guarded with pikes and muskets, and my Lord Treasurer at Clerkenwell with halberds."[100]

On shipboard, "the common sailors grow insolent for want of victuals," refusing orders, Captain Sir John Watts reported around same time. He hoped to tame the mutinies by punishing their leaders "severely." Other mutinous seamen forced their ships to sail home because they had no food, signing their names "in a round and circular form that so none might appear for a ringleader, but if any suffer, they will go to it, as themselves say, One and All, One and All."[101] In January 1627 the men of the *Vanguard* petitioned the commissioners of the navy, explaining that they had gone ashore because they were cold and hungry, and were obliged to go into debt to keep themselves alive, asking for redress and their wages, "which will be to the great encouragement of the petitioners (and other His Majesty's servants who by the like occasions are forced to avoid and distaste His Majesty's service."[102] It was more effective to go directly to the king: according to newsletters, "some hundreds of sailors went for their pay to Whitehall" in early February. When Charles sent them a message promising redress the next day, they thanked him joyfully, but later at Tower Hill they made their own grim promise: "if they had it not . . . the Duke should lose his head."[103] Some money was distributed, but as the war dragged on, so did the sailors' miseries.

In March, rioting sailors were "again busy at London," threatening to destroy York House. Begging Buckingham for supplies, Sir Henry Mervyn wrote that the sailors "by reason of want of necessary clothing are become loathsome to themselves and so nastily sick . . . that they are not only unfit to labour, but to live withal."[104] A slow-moving disaster became a crisis after the catastrophic failure to lift the siege of Île de Rhé and rescue the Huguenot rebels. Only three thousand men returned of a force that had numbered eight thousand, and they were in a shocking state. Reporting to their superiors, appalled naval commanders struggled to put their thoughts into adequately respectful words. Too ill to manage a pen in November 1627, Sir Allen Apsley burst out: "My soul even melts with tears to think that a state should send so many men and no provision at all for them." In December, Mervyn wrote: "I protest to God unless my Lord take it speedily into consideration the king will have more ships than sailors . . . you would be of the same mind if you saw the more than miserable condition of the men, who have neither shoes, stockings, nor rags to cover nakedness. . . . [F]aster than we can supply fresh men we send away the sick, and all the ships are so infectious that I fear if we hold the sea one month we shall not bring men enough home to moor our ships. You may think I make it worse, but I vow to God I cannot deliver it in words."[105] By this point, the arrears in seamen's wages amounted to almost £62,000. At Portsmouth, Watts explained, "they come to me in companies showing their want of apparel and hose and shoes demanding of me what they shall do, having been in His Majesty's service ten months without pay."[106] About two weeks later, Watts wrote nervously that the pay for the sailors had not yet come, though he expected it at any moment. A week later it had still not come.[107] Meanwhile, the sailors suffered: naked and exposed as they were in bleak midwinter, "their toes and feet miserably rot and fall away piecemeal mortified with extreme cold," Mervyn lamented. On January 14, the sailors' frustration boiled over: they flooded ashore "in a mutinous manner intending to go up to London," and Watts was only able to pacify them with a combination of violence and promises. He wrote the following day that he had vowed to discharge them if they were not paid by the 20th.[108]

As the war went on, sailors continued to mutiny. Some commanders advocated taking a hard line with mutineers, like the Earl of Denbigh, who advised that a ringleader ought to be executed "to deter the loose and disorderly number from presuming that they shall hereafter work any advantage to themselves by other means than submission." Others agonized over the state's failure to provide for its men, like Mervyn, who wrote to Nicholas: "The shore affords a soldier relief or hope, the sea neither. Now with what confidence can punishment be inflicted on men that mutiny in these wants? My lord be pleased to judge impartially what scandal these neglects must throw upon your lordship here at home. . . . These neglects be the cause that mariners fly to the service of foreign nations to avoid His Majesty. My lord let not your eye that looks on the public good overlook this mischief, for without better order His Majesty will lose the honour of his seas, the love and loyalty of his sailors, and his Royal Navy will droop."[109] Indeed, it became difficult to man the fleet. Sailors recognized that they had an obligation to serve the Crown, but not under these appalling conditions. They violently resisted impressment and "ran away in troops."[110] Complaints of the "great want of seamen in the fleet" became endemic, and the government was obliged to use landsmen in their stead and to employ ships with much less than their usual complement of sailors.[111] These were critical problems, but there was little money to be had, even though Charles had sold Crown jewels and adopted controversial fiscal expedients. In May 1628, after he was accosted by a crowd of armed mariners, Buckingham pleaded yet again with the sailors for patience: "I have done more for you than ever my predecessors did. I procured the increase of your pay to a third part more than it was. I have parted with mine own money to pay you, and engaged all mine own estate for your satisfaction."[112] Assembling yet another fleet, he was stabbed to death at Portsmouth three months later by a soldier who had survived the Rhé expedition. The Huguenots would go unrescued; the wars could not be won. Without money and without an adequate administrative structure, the state had failed its fighting men; pushed well beyond their limits, they would necessarily fail the state.

While the sailors were rioting on their ships, in port, and in London, members of the House of Commons protested too, but they were outraged by royal power, not by royal weakness. In the 1628 Petition of Right, the grievances of the seamen had little place. Complaining about unlawful wartime taxation, the politicians defended the rights of English property owners; they cast English sailors and soldiers as burdens on the people rather than members of the nation: "Inhabitants against their wills have been compelled to receive them into their houses, and there to suffer them to sojourn against the laws and customs of this realm, and to the great grievance and vexation of the people. . . . They do therefore humbly pray your most excellent Majesty, that . . . your Majesty would be pleased to remove the said soldiers and mariners, and that your people may not be so burdened in time to come." Yet for seafaring men, the relationship between subject and state was both intimate and critical. No one paid more heavily for the military aspirations of the Crown or for Parliament's paralysis. No one depended more on state power, both for sustenance and for protection against their enemies, who now included privateers from France and Dunkirk as well as slavers from Salé and Algiers. Petitioning and rioting, sailors and their wives and widows organized in their hundreds and thousands, demanding that the Crown fulfill its obligations to its subjects. Unfortunately for them, setting out a navy that could effectively project power abroad and take reasonable care of its men required vast amounts of money and a sound institutional structure. Under Buckingham the navy was making organizational strides, but money remained in woefully short supply.[113] For seamen held captive in North Africa or shivering on royal ships, the limitations of the early Stuart state were a personal tragedy.

EPILOGUE

The late 1620s were terrible years for many English sailors. While English privateers again took to the seas in wars against Spain and France, plunder did not define the war experience as it had in the Elizabethan period: a far greater proportion of English seamen sailed in merchant and fishing ships that were vulnerable to attack by pirates and enemy privateers.[1] Yet despite the miseries of Charles's early years, in the 1630s recovery was swift. Collapse called for reformation, and the navy made advances under the king's watchful care. The disasters of the 1620s made it clear that regular revenues and a more coherent structure would need to replace the fiscal expedients and public-private partnerships of the past if England was to compete with other European navies at sea. With regular infusions of Ship Money, the royal navy was rebuilt; it achieved few glories in the 1630s but did establish a consistent presence in the Narrow Seas between England and the coasts of northern France and the Netherlands.[2] Complaints about Salé pirates off the coast of the British Isles lessened, and a moderately successful expedition to Morocco was actually carried out in 1637.[3] Progress was slow but real.

Moreover, the Thirty Years' War created just the sort of unsettled conditions that most favored English shipping. England's well-armed neutral merchantmen took over a large part of the carrying trade from the Dutch, transporting essential cargoes across violent seas. English shipping boomed: by 1635, English tonnage had grown to at least a hundred and fifty thousand tons, and a disproportionate part of the increase was in larger vessels of more than a hundred tons. Shipowners prospered, and so did seamen, who were in short supply and used their increased bargaining power aggressively, petitioning, suing, and agitating for their rights. During the war years of 1625–1630, wages for common seamen had risen from roughly sixteen or seventeen shillings a month to twenty to twenty-four shillings. They dipped briefly with the coming of peace, but recovered by 1633 due to strong demand, setting a new record high for peacetime wages.[4]

By the 1630s, the basic elements of English maritime power had been set: thriving fishing and coal-shipping industries, a large merchant fleet, global trade routes, and a standing navy. Although piracy and maritime disorder would remain serious problems, by and large the vexed transition from a freewheeling, predatory mode under Elizabeth to a more disciplined commercial and colonial orientation was complete. In that transition, moreover, seamen's dogged defense of their interests had helped ensure that the new maritime world worked, more or less, for sailors too. Their successes were due to their determination, but also to the peculiar circumstances that shaped English maritime expansion: the long Elizabethan war that left English ships and sailors primed for battle, the private nature of English sea empire, and England's heavy dependence on sea defenses. Relying on its sailors for protection as well as transportation, the early East India Company was never able to exert the kind of hegemonic control over its seamen that was characteristic of the VOC, for example, and out of concern for security the state often favored sailors at the expense of merchants' profits. English sailors' scarce skills in navigation and gunnery strengthened their hand in labor negotiations, and their centrality to maritime trade and national security gave them valuable leverage, making going to sea more attractive. As English tonnage expanded, then, so did sailors' numbers: in the century after 1580 the population of English sailors roughly tripled, reaching around fifty thousand, about 1 percent of the population.[5] Enshrining the state's long-standing concern for English shipping, the 1651 Navigation Act protected what was already a vibrant industry; it did not call it into being.

In the later seventeenth and eighteenth centuries, when English ships arrived at distant destinations, they increasingly anchored at familiar ports: the strange became routine. Sailors' work became routine as well, and in the long eighteenth century their status seems to have slowly decayed. After continuing to rise into the 1670s, for example, peacetime wages for common sailors stagnated for the next hundred and fifty years at about twenty-four to twenty-five shillings a month, little more than what their predecessors had enjoyed during the 1630s.[6] In part, this may have been because the rise of the English fiscal-military state altered the conditions described in this book. As the navy grew in size and power and men-of-war became increasingly distinct from merchant ships, convoys and passes made sea travel safer for sailors, passengers, and merchants' goods.[7] Merchant sailors gradually ceased to be fighting men, losing the leverage their force of arms had given them. In the navy, sailors' wages were increasingly paid on time, but the rise of parliamentary power did little to secure the liberties of British seamen, and impressment became more violently coercive.[8] Maritime discipline became harsher, especially in the navy.[9] In the early seventeenth century, sailors rarely felt the lash; by the late eighteenth century, naval seamen complained that only they and slaves were flogged: their identity as free white men seemed precarious. So did their Englishness: already by the later seventeenth century, seafaring men were seen as alien to the nation rather than central to it, prompting Anglican outreach to this suspect but essential population.[10] When the security and prosperity of the British Empire depended so heavily on sailors' unfree labor, it seems to have become harder for their social superiors to think of them as true Englishmen. In 1776 a gentleman wrote that in sailors' neighborhoods "a man would be apt to suspect himself in another country."[11]

The swift rise in the number of English sailors that took place between 1580 and 1680 was not repeated in the following century or so. As conditions worsened and wages stagnated, the population of seafaring men stagnated too; further expansions in shipping depended on more efficient manning, with heavier workloads for ships' crews.[12] Still, the negative impact of these changes on the lives of working seamen should not be exaggerated. Enslavement ceased to be a serious danger, for example; instead, English sailors served in large numbers on Atlantic slave ships. Though slave ship sailors shared in the high mortality of their victims and were themselves often trafficked and brutally treated, they surely preferred to be crew rather than cargo.[13] In addition, the decrease in lethal violence between merchant ships and their attackers may have meant more for the sailors working on them than the rise in disciplinary violence aboard ship, and if the navy became more efficiently coercive, it also learned to feed, clothe, and pay its men, while in wartime the scarcity of merchant sailors sent wages to stratospheric heights. On most merchant ships, too, the scale and brutality of disciplinary violence was limited even in the eighteenth century: custom was fiercely defended, and change was slow.[14] In terms of sailors' standing as men of honor, however, something seems to have been lost.

This was all well into the future. The 1630s were good years for English sailors, but for the men of the transitional generations considered here, life was drawing to a close. Most were dead already, of course: "Of so many, so few grow to gray hairs," as Hakluyt had written.[15] In their line of work, even notable survivors eventually ran out of luck. Alexander Cole had survived Cavendish's disastrous last voyage on the *Desire* in 1592, dabbled in trade and plunder in Guinea and the Mediterranean in 1599, and returned alive on the *Hector* on the East India Company's first voyage. He shipped out for Asia again and drowned in Table Bay at the Cape of Good Hope.[16] The navigator John Davis of Sandridge sought the Northwest Passage, braved mutiny and storms in the Strait of Magellan, and sailed to the East Indies on both Dutch and English ships. He met his death in 1605 near Singapore at the hands of Japanese pirates.[17] Fevers, fluxes, accidents, shipwreck, and violence claimed countless others: these were dangerous times, and theirs was a dangerous profession. Those who were still alive and visible in the records in the 1620s and '30s had often found quiet harbors in their old age. The pirate commander Peter Easton may still have been living in the 1620s in Savoy, where he had been made a marquis. Anthony Knivet was working for the Royal Mint; he had probably forgotten his Brazilian languages, if not the hardships of captivity.[18] Joshua Downing had become a naval administrator.[19] The one-armed reformed pirate Robert Walsingham was living in Stepney in the late 1620s, an elderly but still formidable neighbor, one to whom people came running for help to stop a drunkard from beating his wife.[20] New sailors replaced the men who had first sailed English ships across the world's oceans, but those early seafarers had left their mark. Piratical and hapless by turns, grasping for gain and struggling for survival, they had set England's course for empire.

NOTES

Abbreviations

BL:	British Library
Cal. SP East Indies:	*Calendar of State Papers Colonial, East Indies, China and Japan*
CP:	Hatfield House Archives, Cecil Papers
CSPD:	*Calendar of State Papers Domestic*
CSP Ireland:	*Calendar of State Papers, Ireland*
CSP Venice:	*Calendar of State Papers Relating to English Affairs in the Archives of Venice*
EIC:	English East India Company
HCA:	The National Archives, High Court of Admiralty
IOR:	India Office Records
Letters Received:	William Foster, ed., *Letters Received by the East India Company from Its Servants in the East* (London: Sampson Low, Marston, 1896–1902)
LMA:	London Metropolitan Archives
PC:	The National Archives, Privy Council
Peyton, *Expedition* MS:	Walter Peyton's *Expedition* journal, 1614–1617, BL Add MS 19276
Purchas:	Samuel Purchas, *Hakluytus Posthumus, or, Purchas His Pilgrimes* (Glasgow: James MacLehose and Sons, 1905–1907)
Saris, *Clove* MS:	John Saris's *Clove* journal, 1611–1613, BL IOR/L/MAR/A/XIV
SP:	The National Archives, State Papers
VOC:	Dutch East India Company, or Vereenigde Oostindische Compagnie

Introduction

1. William Strachey, "A True Reportory," *Purchas* 19:10, 13, 27–28, 42.

2. Robert Walsingham, 1599: HCA 13/34 fol. 57.

3. Francis Magner, 1606: HCA 13/38 fols. 45v–48v.

4. Cuthbert Appleyard, 1612: HCA 13/98 fol. 7v.

5. *A Fight at Sea;* Robert Walsingham, 1618: HCA 13/48 fols. 175–76v.

6. In 1622 he was briefly imprisoned in the Tower after the unsuccessful expedition to Algiers, when "ill satisfied of that service . . . he began to prattle of returning to his old occupation." Chamberlain, *Letters,* 2:433. Walsingham commanded a ship in the Cadiz expedition (SP 16/111 fol. 4) and was still active in 1633 (SP 16/251 fol. 80).

7. Satow, *Voyage to Japan,* 159.

8. His children seem to have disappeared, but his maidservant Judith converted and eventually married a mestizo in Macao, while his wife, Joan, was exchanged for Portuguese prisoners in 1625 and returned to petition the East India Company for Frobisher's back wages. Mundy, *Travels,* 3:141–2; BL IOR/B/11 fol. 160v, 25 Oct. 1626.

9. *Purchas* 19:51.

10. Andrews, "Cecil and Mediterranean Plunder," 532.

11. Mancke, "Negotiating an Empire," 252.

12. Stern, "Bundles of Hyphens," 21.

13. See Withington, *The Politics of Commonwealth.*

14. Stern, *The Company-State.*

15. See Hindle, *On the Parish?* 7.

16. Morgan, *American Slavery, American Freedom,* 126–29; Beckles, *White Servitude and Black Slavery,* 5–11. More recently, in *Freedom Bound,* Tomlins has argued that the importance of indentured servitude has been exaggerated, but he excludes the West Indies from his analysis.

17. Swingen, *Competing Visions of Empire,* 12–16; Johnson, *Nova Britannia,* sig. Dv.

18. For English Indian slavery, see Goetz, "Indian Slavery," 62; Newell, *Brethren by Nature.*

19. Swingen, *Competing Visions of Empire,* 20–31.

20. See Newman, *A New World of Labor,* 17–35.

21. It was not always clear, of course, *where* they belonged. Conflicts about pauper settlement underscore the power of claims to poor relief. Hindle, *On the Parish?* 207–8, 300–337.

22. Andrews, *Trade, Plunder, and Settlement,* 16; Rodger, "Guns and Sails," 96; Appleby, "War, Politics, and Colonization," 77.

23. See Benton, *A Search for Sovereignty,* 2.

24. Raleigh, *Judicious and Select Essayes,* 20; Mancke, "Early Modern Expansion," 233. See also Mishra, *A Business of State,* 12–13.

25. See also Chaudhuri, "The Portuguese Maritime Empire," 63.

26. Appleby, "War, Politics, and Colonization," 68.

27. Benton, *A Search for Sovereignty,* 3.

28. For sailors and mercantilism, see McCormick, "Population," 28–30.

29. Hawkins, *Observations,* 15.

30. See Fury, *Tides in the Affairs of Men*, 1.

31. Linebaugh and Rediker, *The Many-Headed Hydra*, 17, 22–26.

32. For runaway servants, see Morgan, "The First American Boom," 196; Kupperman, *Settling with the Indians*, 118–19, 139, 157–58, 173.

33. See Rediker, *Between the Devil*. For a more consensual view of eighteenth-century shipping, see Vickers, *Young Men and the Sea*.

34. Swingen, "Labor," 58–9.

35. See Greenfeld, *Nationalism*; Helgerson, *Forms of Nationhood*; Suranyi, *Genius of the English Nation*; Collinson, "This England"; Brennan, *Patriotism, Power and Print*; Kidd, *British Identities before Nationalism*.

36. See Dursteler, *Venetians in Constantinople*, 61.

37. Indeed, the sea has classically been taken as a space that broke down national attachments in favor of broader class consciousness because of the highly technical and regimented nature of sailors' working lives. See Rediker, *Between the Devil*.

38. Colley, "Whose Nation?" 109.

39. Seeking the lost Roanoke colonists, the men of the 1590 expedition sounded "many familiar English tunes of songs" to let them know they were friends. Quinn, *Roanoke Voyages*, 2:613.

40. See for example García-Arenal and Wiegers, *A Man of Three Worlds*; Davis, *Trickster Travels*; Subrahmanyam, *Three Ways to Be Alien*; Ghobrial, "The Secret Life of Elias of Babylon."

41. For the history and operation of the High Court of Admiralty, see Appleby, *Calendar*, ix–xviii; Marsden, *Select Pleas*, 2:xi–lxxxviii.

42. See Blakemore, "The Legal World of English Sailors," 105–8.

43. Ralph Lee, 1591: HCA 13/29 fol. 244v.

44. Steckley, "Litigious Mariners," 325.

45. See for example Andrews, *Elizabethan Privateering*; Senior, *A Nation of Pirates*; Rediker, *Between the Devil*; Fury, *Tides in the Affairs of Men*; Appleby, *Women and English Piracy*.

46. See Fuller, "Arthur and Amazons"; McJannet, "Purchas His Pruning"; Carey and Jowitt, *Richard Hakluyt and Travel Writing*.

47. Barbour, *The Third Voyage Journals*, 2, 19–20.

Chapter 1. A Plundering People

1. William Lane, 1593: HCA 13/30, fol. 151.

2. Rodger, *Safeguard*, 279–80.

3. William Cradell, 1592: HCA 13/29 fol. 341r and Stephen Michell, 1591: HCA 13/29 fol. 235r.

4. See for example William Bendes, 1592: HCA 13/29 fols. 290v–94r.

5. Harry Towers, 1592: HCA 13/29 fols. 289v–90r.

6. William Cradell, 1592: HCA 13/29 fols. 340r, 342r; Parish register, St. Dunstan's, Stepney: LMA P93/DUN/264, fol. 19v.

7. Kassell et al., "CASE6082," *Casebooks of Simon Forman;* Harris, ed., *Trinity House of Deptford Transactions,* no. 39.

8. Harris, *Trinity House of Deptford Transactions,* no. 39; "The relation of Master John Wilson . . . returned into England from Wiapoco in Guiana 1606," in *Purchas* 16:342; *Letters Received* 2:184; Benedict Cradell, 1626, LMA DL/C/230 fol. 92v.

9. See Andrews, *Trade, Plunder and Settlement,* 64–75; Hair and Alsop, *English Seamen and Traders in Guinea.*

10. Burwash, *English Merchant Shipping,* 100, 148, Davis, *Rise of English Shipping,* 1–2, 7.

11. Burwash, *English Merchant Shipping,* 42, 61.

12. See Andrews, *Elizabethan Privateering,* 16.

13. For the belated development of English navigation, see Waters, *Art of Navigation,* 78–123.

14. Rodger, "Guns and Sails," 86–87. Only by capturing hundreds of Dutch ships in the mid-seventeenth century Anglo-Dutch War would England finally diversify its merchant fleet to include more cheap carriers. Davis, *Rise of English Shipping,* 50–51.

15. Madox, "Diary," 197–98; Hawkins, *Observations,* 114–15.

16. Walker, "Diary," 314; Hawkins, *Observations,* 113.

17. Madox, "Diary," 176; Hortop, *Travailes,* 8, 10, 20–21.

18. Hawkins, *Observations,* 50; John Sparke, "Voyage made by M. John Hawkins," in Hakluyt, *Principal Navigations,* 2nd ed., 3:507.

19. Hawkins, *Observations,* 86–87.

20. Walker, "Diary," 289–89; Madox, "Diary," 200.

21. Hawkins, *Observations,* 113; Walker, "Diary," 314.

22. Walker, "Diary," 317 and 313; Madox, "Diary," 176–77.

23. Hawkins, *Observations,* 112; Walker, "Diary," 315.

24. Walker, "Diary," 307; Fenton, "Journal," in Taylor, *Troublesome Voyage,* 103. A few years later, the men on the Earl of Cumberland's expedition also fought and killed a crocodile, a "great foul monster whose head and back was so hard that no sword could enter it." See John Sarracoll's narrative, BL Lansdowne MS 100/3, fol. 26v, and the Red Dragon Logbook, Huntington Library, San Marino, CA, HM 1648, fol. 20v.

25. Hortop, *Travailes,* 11–12.

26. Walker, "Diary," 320; Hawkins, *Observations,* 69–70.

27. Madox, "Diary," 162.

28. Taylor, *Troublesome Voyage,* 234; Donno, *An Elizabethan,* 38.

29. Jobson, *Golden Trade,* 149, 88–89.

30. Alsop, "Tudor Merchant Seafarers," 76.

31. John Sparke, "Voyage made by M. John Hawkins," in Hakluyt, *Principal Navigations,* 2nd ed., 3:503.

32. Heywood and Thornton, *Central Africans,* 12; Wheat, *Atlantic Africa,* 48–50; Sparke, "Voyage made by M. John Hawkins," in Hakluyt, *Principal Navigations,* 2nd ed., 3:504.

33. Hortop, *Travailes*, 8; John Hawkins, "The third troublesome voyage," in Hakluyt, *Principal Navigations*, 2nd ed., 3:522. In another case, Hakluyt edited out moral doubts about English violence; he may have done so here. See Palmer, "Early English Travel Anthologies."

34. For relations between the Portuguese and the Imbangala, see Heywood and Thornton, *Central Africans*, 94–95 and 114–16. For Imbangala cannibalism, see Thornton, "Cannibals, Witches, and Slave Traders," 287–89; Miller, "Significance of Drought," 26–27.

35. Purchas published an account of his travels in *Purchas His Pilgrimage* in 1613 (vol. 3, bk. 7, chaps. 9 and 10), and a first-person narrative transcribed by a third party in *Purchas His Pilgrimes* in 1625. To the extent that his account can be checked against other sources, historians of Angola and Loango consider Battell a reliable observer, though not good at estimating numbers. See Vansina, "On Ravenstein's Edition," 337.

36. "The strange adventures of Andrew Battell," in *Purchas*, 6:377–78.

37. *Purchas*, 6:379–81.

38. *Purchas*, 6:381–83.

39. *Purchas*, 6:385–87. The migratory Imbangala allegedly killed their infants, reproducing themselves instead with older enslaved child soldiers. See Heywood and Thornton, *Central Africans*, 93.

40. Translated from Latin by E. Donno. Madox, "Diary," 173, 186.

41. Francis Petty, "Voyage of Thomas Candish," in Hakluyt, *Principal Navigations*, 2nd ed., 3:803; "Worthy and famous voyage of Master Thomas Candish," in Hakluyt, *Principal Navigations*, 1st ed., 809. The second edition account downplayed the English aggression recounted in the first edition.

42. John Sarracoll's narrative, BL Lansdowne MS 100/3, fol. 26r.

43. Andrews, *Trade, Plunder and Settlement*, 247–48, 224.

44. See for example Haigh, *English Reformations*, 286–90.

45. Hortop, *Travailes*, 22–23.

46. Schwartz, *All Can Be Saved*, 129.

47. Library of Congress MSS, G. R. G. Conway Collection, "Englishmen and the Mexican Inquisition, 1559–1577," 2:77–118, transcribed from AGN Inq. t. 56.

48. Hakluyt, *Principal Navigations*, 2nd ed., 3:482.

49. See Rodríguez García, "Signs of the Other"; Fuchs, "An English *Picaro*"; Helgerson, " 'I Miles Philips.' "

50. Hortop, *Travailes*, 31.

51. BL Sloane MS 61, in Temple, *World Encompassed*, 97.

52. Taylor, *Troublesome Voyage*, 236, 220.

53. Madox, "Diary," 143–44, 151, 196–97.

54. For the enslavement and destruction of coastal Indian communities, see Sá, introduction to *Admirable Adventures*, 11–16.

55. They were familiar with French traders.

56. "The admirable adventures and strange fortunes of Master Antonie Knivet," in *Purchas*, 16:183, 203, 210, 244. Cavendish had taken Christopher off a Manila galleon in 1587. For his reception in England, see Massarella, *A World Elsewhere*, 48.

57. HCA 13/34 fols. 408v–9, 395v, 403r.

58. HCA 13/35 fols. 298r, 454v, 359r.

59. Fortunately, he fell into a boat. John Bessire, 1594: HCA 13/31 fol. 71v.

60. Nicholas Barentson, 1592: HCA 13/30 fols. 53v–54r.

61. Olaert Adrianson, 1592: HCA 13/30 fol. 54v.

62. Reiner Reinerson, 1591: HCA 13/29 fol. 53r.

63. William Johnson, 1595: HCA 13/32 fol. 15r.

64. Andrews, *Elizabethan Privateering*, 11–15.

65. Andrews; "Cecil and Mediterranean Plunder," 532; Rodger, *Safeguard*, 343.

66. Rodger, *Safeguard*, 273–74.

67. Andrews, *Elizabethan Privateering*, 34, 128.

68. The terms "letters of reprisal" and "letters of marque" were used indiscriminately in this period. See Andrews, *Elizabethan Privateering*, 4; Marsden, *Documents Relating to Law*, 1:xxvi; Rodger, *Safeguard*, 199–200.

69. Carey to Walsingham, 25 June 1585, SP 12/179 fol. 80v.

70. For high mortality rates and low pay in the Elizabethan navy, see Rodger, *Safeguard*, 316, 500.

71. Andrews, *Elizabethan Privateering*, 46.

72. Andrews, *Elizabethan Privateering*, 67–70, 104–9.

73. James Steward, 1602: HCA 1/46 fol. 10.

74. Andrews, *Elizabethan Privateering*, 87.

75. Nicholas Brown, 1600: HCA 13/34 fol. 234v; James Harvey, 1601: HCA 13/35 fol. 205r.

76. William Roberts, 1593: HCA 13/30 fol. 260r; Robert Harwin, 1595: HCA 13/31 fol. 230v.

77. Andrews, *Elizabethan Privateering*, 41–42.

78. HCA 13/31 fols. 31v–32r, 43v.

79. Andrews, *Elizabethan Privateering*, 75; *Purchas*, 16:179, 180, 182.

80. Then Locke fired at the enemy until his overheated musket "went off of itself," killing Keyball. John Estridge, 1592: HCA 13/30 fol. 108v.

81. Thousands of English seamen reported living in Stepney, Wapping, Shadwell, Ratcliffe, St. Katherine's by the Tower, or simply London.

82. In the French encounter, none of the participants knew that Le Havre had made peace with Henry IV and no longer supported the Catholic League. Roger Crampton, 1594: HCA 13/31 fol. 109r; Clement Vanefeld, 1600: HCA 13/34 fol. 329v.

83. "Skite," a dialect borrowing from Dutch, has the same meaning as the more familiar English term. HCA 13/36 fol. 218r; 13/31 fol. 67r; 13/32 fols. 355r–56.

84. Cornelius Peterson Keisone, 1594: HCA 13/31 fol. 108; R., H., *Newes from the Levane Seas*, 18–19. A different privateering captain's attempt to sell German and Portuguese

prisoners to the "Turks" at Safi was thwarted when his sailors mutinied, "saying . . . that they should sell none here, for if they did it were not for them to go into England again." Peter Brower, 1591: HCA 13/29 fol. 59r.

85. Evan Hugan, 1600: HCA 13/34 fol. 195r; Peter Arents, 1601: HCA 13/35 fol. 108r; Rawliffe Urients, 1602: HCA 13/35 fol. 256r.

86. HCA 13/29 fols. 279v, 296v (Peter Hales) and fol. 283r (William Mulford).

87. Edward Blunt, 1614: HCA 13/98 fol. 241v.

88. All gunners on Spanish ships, Hawkins thought, were foreigners, "for the Spaniards are but indifferently practised in this art." He reported with satisfaction that an English gunner on the Spanish flagship had his head quite blown off in the fight, and he claimed that renegades he had known "lived to be pointed at with detestation, and ended their lives in beggary, void of reputation." Hawkins, *Observations*, 186, 193, 195.

89. HCA 13/34 fols. 84v–86v.

90. Roger Donne, 1602: HCA 13/35 fols. 464v–66.

91. Jonas James, 1602: HCA 13/35 fol. 462v.

92. Jonas James: HCA 13/35 fols. 460v–61r.

93. Andrew Richardson, 1592: HCA 13/35 fols. 462v–63r. If Allyn meant to buy Hare's favor, he was unsuccessful: when Allyn was eventually taken into custody, Hare gave evidence against him, and he was hanged for the murder of John Monie on a spring Saturday in 1604, while a festive crowd watched. See HCA 1/5 fol. 33v, 13/37 fol. 33v.

94. Edward Diaz, 1595: HCA 13/31 fol. 317r.

95. HCA 13/34 fol. 374 (Thomas Flood) and fol. 247r (Christopher Cornelison).

96. HCA 13/29 fols. 219r, 220r (Hendrick Arnold) and fol. 221r (Christian Claison).

97. Arnold: HCA 13/29 fol. 219v.

98. William Mulford, 1592: HCA 13/29 fol. 284r.

99. Arnold: HCA 13/29 fol. 220r.

100. Linschoten, *Discours of Voyages*, 193; Raleigh, *A Report of the Truth*, sig. B4.

101. See Rodger, *Safeguard*, 322.

102. John Cooke's narrative, in Temple, *The World Encompassed*, 158.

103. Michael Lok, "The doinges of Captayne Furbisher," 1581, in Taylor, *Troublesome Voyage*, 3.

104. Cooke's narrative and Fletcher's notes, in Temple, *World Encompassed*, 148–50, 156, 128.

105. Edward Sellman's narrative, in Taylor, *Troublesome Voyage*, 4–5.

106. Fenton's journal, in Taylor, *Troublesome Voyage*, 101; Madox, "Diary," 163, 166.

107. Cooke's narrative, in Temple, *World Encompassed*, 158.

108. Madox, "Diary," 184–85; Walker, "Diary," 313.

109. Walker, "Diary," 328.

110. Madox, "Register" and "Diary," in Donno, *An Elizabethan*, 285, 141.

111. Taylor, *Troublesome Voyage*, 244; Walker, "Diary," 332; Fenton's journal, in Taylor, *Troublesome Voyage*, 144.

112. Fenton's journal and Hawkins's narrative, in Taylor, *Troublesome Voyage*, 147–48, 278.

113. Hakluyt, *Principal Navigations*, 2nd ed., 3:841. For this voyage, see Andrews, "New Light on Hakluyt."

114. John Jane, "Last voyage of Thomas Candish," in Markham, *Voyages and Works of John Davis*, 98.

115. Quinn, *Last Voyage of Thomas Cavendish*, 113, 115, 123, 127.

116. Jane, "Last voyage," in Markham, *Voyages and Works of John Davis*, 127.

117. See for example John Hills, 1601: HCA 13/35 fol. 209r; Nicholas Stephens, 1592: HCA 13/29 fol. 323r; Roger Isaac, 1602: HCA 13/35 fol. 430r.

118. He signed with an initial B. HCA 13/34 fol. 294v.

119. Lawrence Brooke: HCA 13/34 fol. 284r.

120. Richard Philmore: HCA 13/34 fols. 279–80r.

121. Hugh Bonde: HCA 13/34 fols. 334v–35r.

122. Lockyer: HCA 13/34 fol. 295r. See also fol. 341r.

123. John Darracott, 1592: HCA 13/30 fols. 37–39v.

124. Andrews, *Elizabethan Privateering*, 230.

Chapter 2. Renegades and Reprisals

1. Tomkins to Cecil, 22 Sept. 1602: CP 95/108; *CSP Venice* 10: 12 April and 4 Sept. 1603; Chester, 1604: HCA 13/36 fol. 293v.

2. *CSP Venice* 10 passim; Chester, 1604: HCA 13/36 fol. 294r; Tomkins to the Council, [1604], CP 190/27; John Keye, 1607: HCA 13/97 fol. 13v. Notwithstanding Tompkins's protestations, he was eventually caught, imprisoned, and condemned to death, though a royal pardon rescued him from the noose. See HCA 1/6 fol. 169r and *CSP Venice* 12: 4 Nov. 1610.

3. John Martyn to the Council, 26 June 1603, CP 100/136.

4. Before this date, Mediterranean goods bound for England were usually carried in Venetian ships, and direct sea trade between England and Venice appears to have halted entirely between 1566 and 1573. Fusaro, *Political Economies*, 47–8.

5. Fusaro, *Political Economies*, 69, 21; Andrews, *Trade, Plunder and Settlement*, 90–91.

6. See Fusaro, *Political Economies*, 50; Cameron, "Royal Authority Versus Corporate Sovereignty."

7. See, for example, Divitiis, *English Merchants in Seventeenth-Century Italy*, 28–29.

8. Greene, "Beyond the Northern Invasion," 43–46.

9. For these structures, see Panzac, *La caravane maritime*.

10. Even so, friction between British and Ottoman maritime law persisted. Reluctantly and at substantial expense, the Levant Company continued to pay compensation to the Ottoman victims of British privateers in the following century. Talbot, *British-Ottoman Relations*, 182–95.

11. *CSP Venice* 10: 17 Nov. and 4 Dec. 1604.

12. Luther to Staper, SP 99/2 fol. 151; Andrews, "Cecil and Mediterranean Plunder."

13. Edward Watson, 1599: HCA 13/34 fols. 18v–19r; John Morta, 1604: HCA 13/36 fol. 300v.

14. John Muffett, 1595: HCA 13/31 fols. 152v, 185v.

15. The shipmaster sold Pipe's slave at Toulon. Roger Mariner, 1598: HCA 13/33 fol. 42. When merchantmen carried letters of reprisal, sailors might accept somewhat lower monthly wages. John Berry received two shillings less in 1594, for example. HCA 13/31 fol. 222r.

16. John Jackson, 1602: HCA 13/36 fol. 173v; *CSP Venice* 10: 4 Dec. 1604, 29 April 1603. For English depredations on Venetian shipping, see also Tenenti, *Piracy and the Decline of Venice*, chap. 4.

17. "English ships and Venetian galleys," June 1603, CP 102/117.

18. William Browne, 1604: HCA 13/36 fol. 294v; *CSP Venice* 10: 23 Aug. 1603.

19. John Weddell, 1605: HCA 13/37 fol. 207.

20. *CSP Venice* 10: 6 Sept. 1603; John Cotterell to the King, 1608, CP Petitions 895.

21. Ironically, the first Venetian ambassador, Nicolò Molin, was personally robbed by English pirates en route to London. *CSP Venice* 10: 26 May 1604, appendix II, no. 1. For the enforcement of these orders, see the extensive references to the Venetian capture of the English ship *Costly* or *Corseletta* in *CSP Venice* 11.

22. *CSP Venice* 10: 8 March 1607; complaints of the Spanish ambassador and of the States General, 1605, CP 124/155.

23. Council to Winwood, 7 March 1604, BL, Cotton Galba E/I 88; examination of Joseph Tenny, 30 April 1605, CP 110/115; James I, *Proclamations*, no. 50.

24. Fusaro, *Political Economies*, 98–101.

25. See Gyfford to Buckhurst, 28 June 1601, SP 98/1 fols. 187–90; Andrews, "Cecil and Mediterranean Plunder," 520–21; Gyfford to Buckhurst, 1 Sept. 1601, SP 98/1 fol. 217r.

26. Gyfford to Cecil, 13 Oct 1604, SP 98/2 fol. 93.

27. "Memorial of the injuries which the Great Duke hath caused to be done to the English nation," SP98/2 fol. 253r. Gyfford claimed that he showed no colors at Bugia or Algiers. SP 98/2 fol. 93v.

28. Devereux Morgan to Council, 28 April 1604, SP 71/1 fol. 20r; Levant Company to Munn, 2 April 1607, SP 105/110 fol. 7r.

29. See *CSP Venice* 10: 11 May 1604; James I, *Proclamations*, no. 67; SP 98/2 fols. 112r, 115; SP 14/57 fol. 40.

30. *CSP Venice* 10: 10 Aug. 1606; Ciano, "Corsare inglesi."

31. Matthew Cavell and Francis Magner, 1606: HCA 13/38 fols. 45r, 47r–48v.

32. *CSP Venice* 10: 10 Feb., 15 Jan., and 28 June 1606; Wotton to Salisbury, 9 March 1607, SP 99/4 fol. 49v.

33. Wotton to Salisbury, 9 Feb. 1606, SP 99/3 fols. 13–14v; Donati, *Tra inquisizione e gran-ducato*, 37, 52; Magner: HCA 13/38 fol. 47v.

34. HCA 13/38 fols. 46r (Magner) and 44r (Cavell).

35. Cavell: HCA 13/38 fol. 44v.

36. Wotton to Salisbury and to James, both 5 June 1607, SP 99/4 fols. 103r, 100r.

37. White, *Piracy and Law,* 130; Wotton to Salisbury, 20 June 1606, SP 99/3 fol. 116r.

38. *CSP Venice* 11: 11 June 1607; HCA 13/38 fol. 48r.

39. Richard Hey, 1608: HCA 13/39 fol. 128r.

40. Davies, *A True Relation,* sigs. B4v, C1. See also Neri, *Uno schiavo inglese.*

41. Bennassar, "Les chrétiens convertis à l'Islam," 49–50.

42. Sayer, 1613: HCA 13/98 fol. 55v. He was convicted but escaped and soon returned to piracy. See HCA 13/98 fols. 195–97r, 200, 205v–6r.

43. Ward's name was a common one, so it is hard to trace his career before his turn to piracy. An English seaman who met Ward in Tunis reported in 1608 that he had begun his seafaring career as a fisherman and gained promotion during the war with Spain. *CSP Venice* 11: 23 June 1608.

44. Barker, *A True and Certaine Report,* sig. A4v; Senior, "An Investigation," 59; Robert Rickman, 1602: HCA 13/35 fol. 354r.

45. Largueche, "The Mahalla," 110.

46. *CSP Venice* 11: 23 June 1608.

47. De Brèves, *Relation,* 325, 332–33.

48. Wiseman, 1608: HCA 13/39 fol. 147v; Mitton, 1608: HCA 13/39 fol. 226v; Longcastle, 1609: HCA 1/47 fol. 56r.

49. David Thomas, 1603: HCA 13/36 fol. 272r.

50. Michael Darby, 1614: HCA 13/42 fol. 155r; Atkins, 1613: HCA 13/98 fol. 111v.

51. William Isaac, 1611: HCA 13/41 fol. 217v; *CSP Venice* 11: 23 June 1608.

52. Andrew Florey, 1607: HCA 13/97 fol. 88r; Wiseman: HCA 13/39 fol. 148r.

53. *CSP Venice* 11: 23 June 1608; Mitton: HCA 13/39 fol. 225v.

54. De Brèves, *Relation,* 307–8.

55. Foucques claimed in May 1609 that these changes had taken place in the previous three years. Foucques, "Mémoires," 224. Wotton's English informant also reported that Uthman's partnership with Ward was essential to the dey's success: "He began by being a very poor tailor and has grown into an extremely rich and powerful personage through the patronage of certain pirates, especially of Ward." *CSP Venice* 11: 23 June 1608.

56. Tenenti, *Piracy and the Decline of Venice,* 77–78. For Venetian sailors' low pay and consequent reluctance to fight, see De Brèves, *Relation,* 62.

57. Wotton to Salisbury, 10 March 1607, SP 99/4 fol. 48v; *CSP Venice* 11: 5 Nov. 1607.

58. See Gentili, *Hispanicae advocationis,* 112–3; Benton, *Search for Sovereignty,* 126–7.

59. Bromfield, 1608: HCA 13/39 fols. 105v; Durson, 1608: HCA 13/40 fol. 40v.

60. Edmund Willoughby, 1608: HCA 13/39 fol. 59v; Thomas Morse, 1608: HCA 13/39 fol. 66r.

61. HCA 13/39 fol. 94v.

62. Anthony Bullock and Peter Edwards, 1608: HCA 13/39 fols. 70v, 99r.

63. Henry Hough, 1608: HCA 13/39 fol. 96; Bromfield, HCA 13/39 fols. 105r, 110v, 105r.

64. HCA 13/39 fols. 95v (Hough) and 64–67r (Morse); Gentili, *Hispanicae advocationis,* 108.

65. James I, *Proclamations,* no. 93. For disputes about the *Soderina*'s goods, see SP 99/5 fols. 10–13 and 111–12, and many entries in *CSP Venice* 11 and 12.

66. Mitton and Hancock, 1608: HCA 13/39 fols. 228r and 232r.

67. Jasper Tion and Jacob Pountis, 1608: HCA 13/39 fols. 130v, 81r.

68. HCA 13/39 fols. 66v (Morse) and 195v (Hancock).

69. HCA 1/5 fol. 191v; Pepwell to Salisbury, 22 August 1609, SP 63/227 fol. 92.

70. Sherley, "Discours of the Turkes," 10.

71. HCA 13/39 fols. 105r (Bromfield) and 70r (Bullock).

72. See Buti, "Aller en caravane," 10.

73. Sherley, "Discours of the Turkes," 8.

74. Rodger, "Guns and Sails," 86. On the "economical" feeding of Dutch sailors, see Boxer, *Dutch Seaborne Empire,* 67.

75. Thomas Rastell, 1606: HCA 13/38 fol. 35v.

76. When he arrived in Algiers later, however, "he saw not any of the Englishmen misused, saving that now and then the Turks would give them a box on the ear as they met them in the streets." Robert Browne, 1606: HCA 13/38 fol. 146r.

77. Browne, Devereux Morgan, and Rastell, 1606: HCA 13/38 fols. 146r, 109v, and 35v.

78. Philip Dickinson, 1606: HCA 13/38 fol. 41v.

79. HCA 1/5 fol. 137; Morgan, 1606: HCA 13/38 fol. 110r; Senior, "An Investigation," 412.

80. There were six hundred on the *Transporter* alone. Tendering, 1612: HCA 13/42 fol. 53v. For this expulsion and the reception of Morisco refugees in Algiers and Tetouan, see Harvey, *Muslims in Spain,* 291–331; Missoum, "Andalusi Immigration," 341–44; García-Arenal, "The Moriscos in Morocco," 316–23.

81. Tendering: HCA 13/42 fol. 52r.

82. HCA 13/42 fols. 52v (Tendering) and 57v (Ivery).

83. Tendering: HCA 13/42 fol. 52v.

84. HCA 13/42 fols. 47 (Thomas Allen), 53r (Tendering), and 58r (Ivery).

85. Similar "violent dynamics of reciprocity and revenge" produced a shared consensus about Christian and Muslim captives' rights in the Mediterranean. Hershenzon, *The Captive Sea,* 120.

86. *CSP Venice* 11: 18 March and 23 June 1608.

87. Pepwell to Salisbury, 22 August 1609, SP 63/227 fol. 92r.

88. *CSP Venice* 11: 17 and 18 August 1609; Barker, *A True and Certaine Report,* sigs. C3v–C4r.

89. *CSP Venice* 11: 18 July 1609.

90. *CSP Venice* 12: 23 Dec. 1610.

91. Mitton: HCA 13/39 fol. 226v; *CSP Venice* 11: 14 March and 30 May 1609.

92. Matar, *Britain and Barbary,* 6–7.

93. Sylvester Pritchett, 1613: HCA 13/42, fol. 184; Samuel Sotherne, 1613: HCA 13/98 fol. 64v.

94. Godfrey Counsell, 1611: HCA 1/47 fol. 230, also fols. 228v–29r; Foucques, "Mémoires," 225.

95. An account of his death in 1612 was premature. See Daborne, *A Christian Turn'd Turk*.

96. *CSP Venice* 12: 16 Nov. 1610; Lithgow, *Totall Discourse*, 358, 380; George Barefoot or Barker, 1620: HCA 13/43 fol. 109v. For similarly nuanced dynamics, see Graf, *The Sultan's Renegades*, 165.

Chapter 3. Risks and Rewards

1. Lewis Roberts, 1602: HCA 13/35 fols. 436v–37r.

2. HCA 13/35 fols. 431 (Robert Atkinson) and 433v–34v (Sampson Misken).

3. HCA 13/35 fols. 436r (Robert Sexton) and 432r (Atkinson).

4. William Lord, 1602: HCA 13/35 fol. 450v.

5. See for example Rossi, *Insurance in Elizabethan England*.

6. On short voyages sailors were often paid lump sums roughly equivalent to monthly wages. For the value of seamen's wages and victuals in the seventeenth century, see Blakemore, "Pieces of Eight," 1169.

7. Davis, *Rise of English Shipping*, 135, 152.

8. See "Anthony's Account" in Andrews, *Ships, Money and Politics*, 84–105.

9. Boteler, *Six Dialogues*, 84–86.

10. Sharpe, *Britaines Busse*, sig. C2r.

11. HCA 13/39 fols. 247r, 249v, 250v; HCA 13/41 fol. 30v.

12. HCA 13/40 fol. 247v; HCA 13/41 fol. 187r.

13. Davis, *Rise of English Shipping*, 151.

14. Blakemore, "Pieces of Eight," 1174–78.

15. Keeling, "Journal of His Third Voyage," 64.

16. HCA 13/40 fol. 247r; HCA 13/40 fol. 78r.

17. HCA 13/36 fol. 3; HCA 13/38 fols. 200v–201v, 203v–4r.

18. HCA 13/37 fol. 39r; HCA 13/30 fol. 67r.

19. Norwood, *Journal*, 37–38.

20. Baker, 1610: HCA 13/40 fol. 60r; Baker, 1613: HCA 13/42 fols. 211v–14r.

21. For the English law of salvage, see Melikan, "Shippers, Salvors, and Sovereigns"; Steckley, "Origins of Modern Salvage Law."

22. Thomas Ford, 1613: HCA 13/42 fol. 278; John Sone, 1579: HCA 13/23 fol. 317r.

23. Roger Clarck, 1600: HCA 13/34 fol. 188; Skutt, 1580: HCA 13/24 fol. 87r; Davis, *Rise of English Shipping*, 156.

24. Hakluyt, *Principal Navigations*, Glasgow ed., 2:216, 320, 391, 410.

25. "A true declaration of the discovery," 1614: HCA 13/42 fol. 275r. On the movement of expertise across imperial borders, see Kupperman, "The Love-Hate Relationship with Experts"; Polónia, "Portuguese Seafarers."

26. HCA 13/42 fols. 275r, 277v.

27. HCA 13/42 fols. 275r, 338v–39r.

28. HCA 13/42 fols. 276v, 339r.

29. HCA 13/33 fols. 47r (Rowe), 50r (Best), and 42r–46r (Pipe's estate).

30. Andrews, *Spanish Caribbean*, 191.

31. HCA 13/37 fols. 160v (Chambers), 90v (William Revett), and 161r (Chambers).

32. HCA 13/37 fols. 199 (William Squire) and 95v (John Bellman).

33. Thomas Man, 1609: HCA 13/40 fol. 136r. This may be the earliest recorded example of a "round robin," an allegedly mutinous form of petitioning that would be outlawed in 1631. See Andrews, *Ships, Money and Politics*, 63.

34. Andrew Miller, 1609: HCA 13/40 fol. 139v; William Resold, 1610: HCA 13/41 fol. 41r.

35. Silvanus Man, 1604: HCA 13/37 fol. 67v; John Russell, 1608: HCA 13/39 fols. 186v–87v.

36. Thomas Bourne, 1608: HCA 13/39 fols. 182v–83v.

37. HCA 13/39 fols. 185r (Richard Langley) and 187v (Russell).

38. HCA 13/39 fols. 184r (Bourne) and 188v (Walter Whiting).

39. HCA 13/39 fols. 188 (Whiting) and 184v (Bourne).

40. Margaret Man: HCA 13/41 fol. 24. For Halliwood v. Staper in Chancery, see TNA, C 2/Jasl/H25/20.

41. Richard Dixon, 1613: HCA 13/42 fol. 230r.

42. They knew the terms of the charter party because they had taken it out of Okes's chest and copied it in his absence. Dixon: HCA 13/42 fol. 230r; Okes: HCA 13/98 fol. 122r.

43. Dixon: HCA 13/42 fol. 230v; Okes: HCA 13/98 fol. 122v.

44. HCA 13/98 fols. 121v (Okes) and 124v–25r (Walker).

45. Okes: HCA 13/98 fols. 121r, 123.

46. Lancelot Fisher, 1613: HCA 13/42 fol. 228r.

47. Cane, 1614: HCA 13/42 fol. 261v.

48. HCA 13/42 fols. 229v (Fisher) and 262v (Cane).

49. Fisher: HCA 13/42 fol. 229v.

50. Fisher: HCA 13/42 fol. 229v.

51. Lawrence Woodward, 1612 HCA 1/47 fols. 303v–4r, HCA 13/42 fols. 265v–66r.

52. Davis, *Rise of English Shipping*, 141; SP 29/327 fol. 45.

53. Venetian courts were supposed to enforce English maritime custom, but it was understandably difficult for them to know what English custom was. See Fusaro, "Invasion of Northern Litigants," 35–38; Addobatti, "English Seafaring and Wage Litigation," 50–52.

54. *CSP Venice* 9: 15 Jan. 1602. What eighteenth-century historians have called "the well-established Mediterranean maritime custom of allowing corsairs and privateers to search neutral vessels for enemy goods and passengers" would have been considered

rank betrayal by those who paid extra for English security in the early seventeenth century. See Stein, "Passes and Protection," 609.

55. Official plans for the relief of disabled seamen were badly hampered by corruption and only open to those injured in service of the Crown. See Hudson "The Relief of English Disabled Ex-Sailors."

56. *CSP Venice* 10: 15 Jan. 1606.

57. John Browne, 1608: HCA 13/39 fol. 137v.

58. SP 98/2 fol. 119r; Whiting, 1608: HCA 13/39 fol. 144v.

59. Browne: HCA 13/39 fols. 137v–38r.

60. Thomas Hawyes, 1605: HCA 13/37 fol. 202.

61. HCA 13/37 fols. 247r (Foulke Lee), 268r, 269r (Arnold Browne).

62. HCA 13/37 fols. 202v (Hawyes), 240v (Edmund Willoughby), and 286 (Sotherne).

63. Hawyes: HCA 13/37 fol. 203.

64. William Vittrey: HCA 13/40 fol. 256v; Nicholas Butler: HCA 13/41 fol. 33r.

65. Joseph Jackson, 1596: HCA 13/32 fol. 150r.

66. Whiting, 1608: HCA 13/39 fol. 144v.

67. Robert Browne, 1605: HCA 13/37 fols. 226v–27r.

68. James Lile, the master of the *Trial*, had indeed combined trade and piracy in the past, though not on this particular voyage. See Tenenti, *Piracy and the Decline of Venice*, 64.

69. Browne: HCA 13/37 fol. 227r.

70. HCA 13/38 fols. 6r (West) and 7v (Humphrey Goddard).

71. Browne: HCA 13/37 fol. 227; West: HCA 13/38 fol. 6v.

72. Goddard: HCA 13/38 fols. 7v–8r. For the validity of such "confessions under torture" see Gentili, *Hispanicae advocationis*, 115.

73. Wives of the mariners of the *Trial* to the Privy Council, ca. 1607, CP Petitions 434; Alice Lyle and others, widows of those taken in the *Trial* of London, to the Privy Council, CP Petitions 2055.

74. CP Petitions 434; *CSP Venice* 10: 29 March and 30 May 1607.

75. HCA 13/39 fols. 144v (Whiting) and 137v (Browne).

76. Humphrey Aldington, 10 Oct. 1607, SP 98/2 fol. 120. For the Tuscan charges, see *CSP Venice* 11: 24 and 28 March 1608.

77. Henry Pepwell to Salisbury, 29 Nov. 1607, SP 98/2 fol. 121r.

78. Walter Matthew to Salisbury, 14 Dec. 1607, SP 98/2 fols. 124–5r.

79. Jonas Aldrich to Salisbury, 25 May 1608, SP 98/2 fol. 140r; Lesieur to Salisbury, 21 June 1608, SP 98/2 fol. 157r.

80. Davis, "England and the Mediterranean," 12; Earle, *Corsairs of Malta and Barbary*, 39.

81. Coxere, *Adventures by Sea*, 134; Charles II, *Proclamation Touching on the Articles of Peace*; Stein, "Passes and Protection."

82. John Driver, 1614: HCA 1/48 fols. 22v–23r; George Barcfoot, 1620: HCA 13/43 fol. 109; Harris, *Trinity House of Deptford Transactions*, no. 196.

83. "Admirable escape . . . of Nicholas Roberts," *Purchas* 9:311–21.

84. For example Johnson, *Nova Britannia*.

85. "A true reportory of the wracke," *Purchas* 19:28, 38.

86. Quinn, *Roanoke Voyages*, 2:521, 523.

87. Quinn, *Roanoke Voyages*, 2:568.

88. Charles Leigh to Olave Leigh, *Purchas*, 16:318, 322.

89. "The relation of Master John Wilson," *Purchas*, 16:338–51; Nicholl, *An Houre Glasse of Indian Newes*, sigs. B2v, B4.

90. Gorges, "A Briefe Narration," 5.

91. Roger Bamford, 1607: HCA 13/39 fol. 19v. For this abortive venture, see Quinn, *Explorers and Colonies*, 363–81.

92. "Francis Magnel's Relation," in Barbour, *Jamestown Voyages*, 1:151–57; "Examination of Francis Magner," 16 Dec. 1610, SP 14/58 fol. 157.

93. Rodger, "Guns and Sails," 87; Barbour, *Jamestown Voyages*, 1:243.

94. Archer, "Captaine Gosnols Voyage," and Bartholomew Gosnold to Anthony Gosnold, 7 Sept. 1602, in Quinn and Quinn, *New England Voyages*, 135, 210.

95. HCA 13/39 fols. 217v (John Elliott, 1608) and 213r (John Deoman, 1608).

96. Elliot: HCA 13/39 fol. 218r; Quinn and Quinn, *New England Voyages*, 334.

97. "Occurrents in Virginia," *Purchas*, 18:464; Strachey, "A true reportory of the wracke," *Purchas*, 19:50–51.

98. "A note of the orders," in Quinn and Quinn, *New England Voyages*, 394.

99. Barbour, *Jamestown Voyages*, 1:79.

100. Strachey, "A true reportory," *Purchas* 19:51.

101. Bradford, *A Relation or Journall*, 33; "Generall Historie of New-England," in Smith, *Complete Works*, 2:401.

102. James I, *Proclamations*, no. 233.

103. "Generall Historie of the Bermudas," in Smith, *Complete Works*, 2:363–64.

104. *A True Declaration of the Estate of the Colonie in Virginia*, 36–37.

Chapter 4. Piracy and Empire

1. George Percy, "Observations," in *Purchas*, 18:403–7; John Smith, "Proceedings of the English colony in Virginia," in *Complete Works*, 1:224, 230, 243.

2. Jackson, 1613: HCA 13/98 fols. 75v–76r.

3. HCA 13/98: fols. 76r (Jackson), 54r (Isgrave), 54r (Isgrave's brother-in-law Richard Lancaster), and 56v–57r (Newport).

4. HCA 1/6 fols. 107, 126r; HCA 13/98 fol. 58r (Prophett) and 113r (Mitche).

5. HCA 13/98 fol. 113 (Mitche), 190v (Tuching). Prophett may have learned about Mamora from his accomplice Walter Rockwell, who knew it well. See Senior, "An Investigation," 424.

6. SP 14/65 fol. 30. Rediker estimates that there were between one thousand and two thousand Anglo-American pirates active at any one time between 1716 and 1726, a period in which British shipping was vastly greater. Rediker, *Between the Devil*, 256.

7. Rediker, 276; SP 14/65 fol. 30r.

8. Gorges to Salisbury, 5 July 1611, SP14/65 fol. 29; James Paine, 1612: HCA 1/47 fol. 298r.

9. *Lives . . . of the 19 Late Pyrates,* sig. Cv.

10. *Lives . . . of the 19 Late Pyrates,* sig. Bv.

11. *CSP Venice* 11: 23 June 1608; Jeffrey Wiseman, 1608: HCA 13/39 fol. 150r.

12. James Harris, 1609: HCA 1/47 fol. 32; HCA 13/39 fols. 67r (Thomas Morse) and 72v (John Motham).

13. Walter Hancock, 1608: HCA 13/39 fol. 195v; Anthony Wye, 1609: HCA 13/40 fols. 99v–100r.

14. Jennings, 1609: HCA 1/47 fols. 27v–28r.

15. See John Seline, 1600: HCA 13/34 fols. 194v, 194Br, for Sockwell as a piratical Elizabethan privateer, and Lord Saye and Sele to Viscount Cranborne, 20 April 1605, CP 110/99, for his naval command. For Sockwell as a piratical Dutch privateer, see William Adams, 1607: HCA 13/97 fol. 32.

16. Cottington, *True Historicall Discourse,* sig. G1r.

17. HCA 1/47 fols. 45–46r (Grice) and 64r (Burton).

18. The African captives had been sent to Spain, with the merchants held hostage for their ransom. William Penne, 1611: HCA 1/47 fols. 239v–40r; William Paenter, 1614: HCA 13/98 fol. 198v.

19. Paul Goddard, 1611: HCA 1/47 fol. 237v; Simon Tuching, 1614: HCA 13/98 fol. 191r.

20. HCA 13/98 fols. 199r, 191r; Senior, "An Investigation," 413.

21. Penne: HCA 1/47 fol. 240v.

22. See Rediker, *Between the Devil,* 264; HCA 1/47 fols. 305r–8v.

23. Some of Bishop's part may have been shared with his men. James Harris, 1609: HCA 1/47 fol. 61v.

24. Morish, 1612: HCA 1/47 fol. 311r.

25. Appleby, "A Nursery of Pirates," 10, 14, 15; SP 14/53 fol. 148.

26. Bracke, 1609: HCA 1/47 fol. 24. Spere is listed as a pirate in HCA 1/6 part III, 155.

27. Mainwaring, "Of the Beginnings, Practices, and Suppression of Pirates," 41.

28. He later complained that Baugh swindled him out of his rightful share of the plunder. Baker, 1613: HCA 13/42 fol. 213r.

29. HCA 13/98 fols. 199v (Paenter, 1614) and 211 (Jackson, 1614).

30. Keepus, 1613: HCA 13/98 fol. 57.

31. Appleby, "A Nursery of Pirates," 14.

32. HCA 13/98 fols. 7 (Appleyard), 59v (John Neave), and 62v (Thomas Frost).

33. Hunt, 1610: HCA 13/41 fol. 59r.

34. Perse, 1613: HCA 13/98 fol. 149r; Robert Rose, 1611: HCA 1/47 fol. 234v.

35. HCA 13/98 fols. 181r (William Thorne), 191v (Simon Tuching), and 246r (John Walker).

36. Similarly, recruits who joined pirate ships at Munster usually recounted being enticed on board and plied with drink while the ships sailed away. See HCA 1/47 fols. 33r–38v.

37. Forced pirates did indeed mutiny against Captain Christopher Webbe, running the ship ashore near Southampton. See Paul Goddard, 1611: HCA 13/41 fols. 180r–81v.

38. Mainwaring, "Of the Beginnings, Practices, and Suppression of Pirates," 22–23.

39. Trall, 1612: HCA 1/47 fols. 274v–75r; Edward Roberts, 1613: HCA 13/42 fol. 156r.

40. John Jennings, 1614: HCA 13/98 fol. 203r.

41. HCA 1/47 fols. 256v–58r (Wright) and 258v–59r (John Johnson).

42. Mainwaring, "Of the Beginnings, Practices, and Suppression of Pirates," 22–23.

43. Digby, 1613: HCA 13/42 fol. 210v.

44. Hunt, 1610: HCA 13/41 fol. 59r.

45. HCA 13/41 fols. 233r (Harman), 256v (Milton), and 241 (Rickman).

46. Jay, 1613: HCA 13/98 fols. 115r–16r.

47. HCA 13/41 fols. 59 (Hunt), 60v (John Friar), and 61r (John Harman).

48. See HCA 1/47 fols. 223–24r (torture) and 177r (unpaid forced labor).

49. Jennings, 1614: HCA 13/98 fols. 202v–3r.

50. John Raynes, 1614: HCA 13/98 fol. 226r.

51. HCA 13/98 fols. 222 (Hall), 221r (Richard Moaine), and 215v, 216v (Henrick Thomas).

52. Thomas: HCA 13/98 fols. 216v–17v.

53. HCA 13/98 fols. 223r (Hall), 14v (Rochester), 191v (Tuching), and 203r (Jennings).

54. Sayers, 1614: HCA 13/98 fol. 192. For more on pirates' wives in this period, see Appleby, *Women and English Piracy*, 51–85.

55. *Lives . . . of the 19 Late Pyrates*, sig. E2r–v.

56. Wye, 1609: HCA 13/40 fol. 100r; *Lives . . . of the 19 Late Pyrates*, sig. B2v.

57. Senior, *A Nation of Pirates*, 43, 29.

58. Mainwaring was less magnanimous with the Lübeck sailors, seizing their goods and clothing. HCA 13/98 fols. 179v (Marmaduke Neave) and 184r (Joachim Werdeman).

59. Nicholas Yeman, 1613: HCA 13/98 fol. 15v.

60. Jonathan Turner, 1611: HCA 1/47 fol. 233r–34r.

61. There were rumors of a similar rift in the Mediterranean, where Henry Pepwell reported in 1609 that the pirate captain John Kerson of Emden "extremely hated Ward" and was willing to kill him in exchange for a pardon. Pepwell to Salisbury, 22 Aug. 1609, SP 63/227 fol. 92. For Dutch pirates in this period, see Lunsford, *Piracy and Privateering.*

62. Robert Barum, 1611: HCA 13/41 fol. 248r; Bell, 1611: HCA 1/47 fols. 177v–78r.

63. For rescues, see, for example, William Goulde, 1611: HCA 1/47 fol. 224v.

64. HCA 1/47 fols. 263r (Richard Mason), 276v (Beaumont), and 279v (Lewis Davy).

65. Isaack: HCA 13/98 fols. 63r–64r.

66. HCA 13/98 fol. 64r; John Guy to Master John Slany, 29 July 1612, in *Purchas* 19:417. See also Cell, *English Enterprise in Newfoundland*, 68.

67. HCA 13/98 fols. 6v (Cuthbert Appleyard) and 64 (Isaack).

68. Spanish complaints about the "intense" raiding of the Mamora pirates have given Atlantic historians an exaggerated idea of the scope of West Indian piracy. Relying on Spanish sources, Heywood and Thornton mistakenly identify Robert Walsingham as "one of the earliest Bermuda-based privateers," for example, and Hanna also identifies Walsingham as a "Bermudian." Heywood and Thornton, *Central Africans*, 26–27; Hanna, *Pirate Nests*, 74.

69. See John Sears, 1610: HCA 1/47 fol. 118r.

70. Norwood, *Journal*, 57; Lefroy, *Historye of the Bermudaes*, 93–98.

71. Francisco de Angola, 1614: HCA 13/42 fol. 321v. This shipwreck may be the origin of the oral tradition about the arrival of Africans on St. Vincent described in Taylor, *The Black Carib Wars*, 15–17.

72. Lane, *Pillaging the Empire*, 51; Hanna, *Pirate Nests*, 65–66, 60.

73. Even when the pirates did sell their plunder in Ireland, the buyers were sometimes traders who brought it directly to the Mediterranean, not local settlers. Gideon Johnson bought West Indian hides from Captain Saxbridge at Crookhaven and sold them in Venice, for example. Lancelot Fisher, 1613: HCA 13/42 fol. 228.

74. Harrison to the English pirates, 25 July 1614, in Castries, *Sources inédites*, 1st series, Pays-Bas, 2:320–1.

75. These pirates were not necessarily English. *Newes from Mamora*, sig. B3r. See also García-Arenal and Wiegers, *A Man of Three Worlds*, 84–86.

76. A mixed English, Dutch, Scottish, Norwegian, and Moroccan crew sailed out of Salé, was captured by Dutch forces in November 1614 and brought to the Netherlands to face trial and execution. See Lunsford, *Piracy and Privateering*, 121–22.

77. Emmanuel Butta, 1615: HCA 1/48 fols. 67v–68r.

78. *A Fight at Sea*, sigs. A3v, B1v, B2v, A2r.

79. Walsingham, 1618: HCA 1/48 fols. 175v–76r. See also fol. 176r–v for John Lucom's explanation of his service on "Turk" ships.

80. HCA 13/37 fol. 114v; HCA 13/40 fols. 17r and 161v; examination of David Cockburn, 5 July 1625, SP 16/4 fol. 14r.

81. SP 14/149 fol. 35r.

Chapter 5. Sailors and the Company-State

1. Satow, *Voyage to Japan*, 91–92. For the *Mayflower*'s pinnaces, see chapter 3 above.

2. Saris, *Clove* MS, fols. 43v, 56r.

3. Saris, *Clove* MS, fol. 73v. For high numbers of European Christians in Ottoman Red Sea shipping, see Casale, "Ethnic Composition of Ottoman Ships," 130–32.

4. Satow, *Voyage to Japan*, 91–93.

5. Satow, *Voyage to Japan*, 110, 120, 150.

6. Satow, *Voyage to Japan*, 155–57; *Letters Received*, 1:316.

7. Satow, *Voyage to Japan*, 162, 178; *Cal. SP East Indies*, 1513–1616, no. 889.

8. Satow, *Voyage to Japan*, lxvii.

9. Stern, *Company-State*, 6, 93, 87. See also Stern, "Soldier and Citizen"; Hunt, "The 1689 Mughal Siege of Bombay."

10. Stern, *Company-State*, 99, 87.

11. Edmund Barker, "Voyage with Three Tall Ships," 4, 10–11; "Voyage of Benjamin Wood," in *Purchas* 2:289.

12. Israel, *Dutch Primacy in World Trade*, 67–68.

13. Stevens, *Dawn of British Trade*, 8; "The First Voyage," in *Purchas*, 2:400, 403, 435.

14. While the Banda Islands fall within the modern Indonesian province of Maluku, in the early modern period usually only the clove islands of Ternate, Tidore, Makian, Motir, and Bacan were called by the name Molucca Islands. See Villiers, "Trade and Society," 724.

15. Loth, "Armed Incidents and Unpaid Bills," 708–9; Israel, *Dutch Primacy in World Trade*, 72.

16. For Roe's difficult position as the representative of both the Crown and the East India Company, see Mishra, "Diplomacy at the Edge."

17. Digges, *Defence of Trade*, 33.

18. "The First Voyage," in *Purchas*, 2:395–96, 400; Marlowe, "*Hector* Journal," 77, 81.

19. Walter Peyton, *Expedition* MS, 97; *Letters Received*, 3:52.

20. Reid, *Expansion and Crisis*, 86–90; Reid, *Lands below the Winds*, 37–8.

21. Peyton, *Expedition* MS, 22, 34, 48.

22. Peyton, 54, 59.

23. Peyton, 64, 65, 66.

24. Peyton, 67, 69.

25. Peyton, 70, 74.

26. Peyton, 76, 88.

27. Peyton, 92, 93, 96.

28. Jourdain, *Journal*, 303; *Cal. SP East Indies*, 1513–1616, no. 762.

29. Edmund Scot, "Discourse of Java," in *Purchas*, 2:480–81; Thomas Clayborne, "The Second Voyage," in *Purchas*, 2:500; *The Last East-Indian Voyage*, 69.

30. Bernard Couper to Thomas Hide, 1 March 1611, in *Purchas*, 3:79; Digges, *A Defence of Trade*, 24.

31. "The First Voyage," in *Purchas*, 2:403; *A Letter Written to the . . . Governours*, 3.

32. Saris, *Clove* MS, fol. 109v; Peyton, *Expedition* MS, 81; Saris, *Clove* MS, fol. 108v. For alcohol in Southeast Asia, see Reid, *Lands below the Winds*, 39–40.

33. Kayll, *The Trades Increase*, 20. For an overview of these debates, see Mishra, *A Business of State*, 121–44.

34. Digges, *A Defence of Trade*, 28, 32–33; Mun, *A Discourse of Trade*, 35–36, 42.

35. Satow, *Voyage to Japan*, 2.

36. For quarreling officers, see, for example, *Letters Received*, 1:15–16.

37. Henry Middleton's commission, second voyage, in Birdwood and Foster, *Register of Letters*, 53; Millworth's commission, 1614, in *Letters Received*, 3:57; Keeling, "Journal of His Third Voyage," 69.

38. Nicholas Downton, "Journal," in *Purchas*, 3:201; "Unhappy Voyage of the *Union*," in *Purchas*, 3:77.

39. Barbour, *Third Voyage Journals*, 141, 39; Thomas Jones, "Relations," in *Purchas*, 3:67.

40. *Letters Received*, 1:266, 2:176, 1:262, 267.

41. *The Last East-Indian Voyage*, 9.

42. Hearne and Finch, "*Red Dragon* Journal," 187–88; Marlowe, "*Hector* Journal," 99–100.

43. Saris, *Clove* MS, fols. 45v–46v.

44. "Anonymous *Hector* Journal," 58; Keeling, "Journal of His Third Voyage," 69.

45. Keeling, "Journal of His Third Voyage," 63, 73; Saris, *Clove* MS, fol. 44r.

46. "Anonymous *Hector* Journal," 46, 49.

47. Hearne and Finch, "*Red Dragon* Journal," 160; Marlowe, "*Hector* Journal," 89.

48. The documentation of this case is tangled. Cheryl Fury has shown that the trial was recorded in the manuscript journals of John Jourdain and William Revett (BL L/MAR/A /VII fol. 23 and BL Sloane MS 858 fol. 20v) but silently omitted from Sir William Foster's edited version of Jourdain's journal. Robert Coverte's printed account stated that Acton himself was hanged, and that the real culprit had been the ship's Dutch master, Philip de Grove, "a detestable buggerer," making no mention of White or the steward. Possibly Robert Coverte and Nicholas Cober (both described as stewards) were the same person. See Fury, "Accounts of the Sodomy Trial," and Coverte, *A True and Almost Incredible Report*, 68, 19.

49. Jourdain, *Journal*, 79–80.

50. Marlowe, "*Hector* Journal," 98; Saris, *Clove* MS, fols. 21v, 25r; Peyton, *Expedition* MS, 62.

51. Keeling, "Journal of His Third Voyage," 120–21, 162–63; John Hatch, "Relations and Remembrances," in *Purchas*, 4:542.

52. Keeling, "Journal of His Third Voyage," 112.

53. *A True and Large Discourse of the Voyage*, 17.

54. Lantro himself was unchastened. Later in the voyage, when the "master taking some word . . . in evil part, struck the master carpenter a small blow upon the head with the handle of a hammer." Lantro came to his colleague's defense and "wrested the hammer out of the master's hand." When the master struck him in the face, Lantro gave him "a box under the ear." The following day he was ducked three times at the yardarm. Marlowe, "*Hector* Journal," 113–14, 120.

55. *Letters Received*, 6:15–16; *Cal. SP East Indies*, 1617–1621, no. 143; Cocks, *Diary*, 2:175.

56. Standish, "Journall," 120–21.

57. Standish, "Journall," 116, 127.

58. EIC Court Minutes, 17 June 1614, BL IOR/B5 pp. 121–22.

59. Stevens, *Dawn of British Trade*, 130, 70; Foster, *Voyage of Sir Henry Middleton*, 184.

60. EIC Court Minutes, BL IOR/B/3, fol. 33v; Saris, *Clove* MS, fol. 104v. Chaudhuri's early assessment that EIC sailors earned "extremely poor" wages, "about £5 a year," was in error. Chaudhuri, *English East India Company*, 105.

61. Saris, *Clove* MS, fol. 109; EIC Court Minutes, BL IOR/B/5, pp. 7, 30–31.

62. EIC to factors, 19 and 15 March 1610, in Birdwood and Foster, *Register of Letters*, 314, 317.

63. EIC Court Minutes, BL IOR/B/3, fols. 147v, 149v, 159v.

64. See Anthony Cope, 1613: HCA 13/98 fol. 130; Saris, *Clove* MS, fol. 101v.

65. Keeling, "Journal of His Third Voyage," 64. See Polónia, "Portuguese Seafarers," 227–228; Ketting, *Leven, werk en rebellie*, 55.

66. Satow, *Voyage to Japan*, 119–20; Saris, *Clove* MS, fol. 93v; EIC Court Minutes, BL IOR/B/5, pp. 188, 237.

67. Peyton, *Expedition* MS, 100; Keeling, "Journal of His Third Voyage," 162; *Cal. SP East Indies*, 1617–1621, no. 146.

68. *Letters Received*, 6:161.

69. Muqarrab Khan was allegedly looking for novelties to offer to the Mughal emperor. Middleton, "The sixth voyage," and Nicholas Downton, "Journal," in *Purchas*, 3:179, 262; Cocks, *Diary*, 1:291.

70. Keeling, "Journal of His Third Voyage," 102; Peyton, *Expedition* MS, 22, 38

71. *Letters Received*, 5:107, 118.

72. Floris, *His Voyage*, 62; HCA 13/43, fols. 94v (Thomas Hughes) and 124v (John Tucker). In the long run, this private trade may have been a strength: see Erickson, *Between Monopoly and Free Trade*, 13–15.

73. *Letters Received*, 5:118; EIC Court Minutes, BL IOR/B/6 p. 6.

74. Saris, *Clove* MS, fols. 71v, 75v; Standish, "Journall," 149.

75. Cocks, *Diary*, 2:120–21, 181–82, 212.

76. Mishra, *A Business of State*, 179; EIC Court Minutes, BL IOR/B/8, pp. 45–46.

77. *Letters Received*, 2:245.

78. Harris, *Trinity House of Deptford Transactions*, nos. 8, 22.

79. Mishra, *A Business of State*, 215; *Answere to the Hollanders Declaration*.

80. George Jackson, 1620: HCA 13/43 fol. 100v, according to foliation on lower left.

81. HCA 13/43, fols. 102v–3r (Roberts), 94v (Hughes), and 103v (Cook) by lower left foliation.

82. Mishra, "Merchants, Commerce, and the State," 92; SP 14/124 fol. 221.

83. PC 2/31 fol. 611; Harris, *Trinity House of Deptford Transactions*, no. 204.

84. See EIC Court Minutes, BL IOR/B/10, p. 323.

85. Clulow, "Great Help from Japan," 200–201. Very few VOC employees, about 1 percent, were from Great Britain: Ketting, *Leven, werk en rebellie*, 44–47, 272–73.

86. The port official was "a friend" to one of the duelists "because he did instruct him in the building of ships." Floris, *His Voyage*, 125–26, 89.

87. *Letters Received*, 1:304; Best, "Jornall of the Tenth Voyage," 35.

88. Peyton, *Expedition* MS, 36–37; Keeling, "Journal of His Third Voyage," 126.

89. Nicholas Downton, "Journal," in *Purchas*, 3:266; *Letters Received*, 5:147–8.

90. Cocks, *Diary*, 2:204, 205, 207.

91. Saris, *Clove* MS, fol. 39.

92. Foster, *Journal of John Jourdain*, 239n; *Letters Received*, 2:91.

93. *Cal. SP East Indies*, 1513–1616, no. 744; Peyton, *Expedition* MS, 79.

94. Farrington, *English Factory in Japan*, 2:827; Cocks, *Diary*, 2:210.

95. Adams, "William Adams his Voyage," in *Purchas*, 2:330–31, 336.

96. Satow, *Voyage to Japan*, 109.

97. Scot, "Discourse of Java," in *Purchas*, 2:493; Cocks, *Diary*, 1:269, 274.

98. Cocks, *Diary*, 2:120–21 and 181–82, 1:270 and 279.

99. Cocks to Richard Wickham, in Farrington, *English Factory in Japan*, 1:197.

100. Keeling, "Journal of His Third Voyage," 62; *Letters Received*, 2:189–90.

101. *Letters Received*, 5:155–56.

102. *Letters Received*, 2:270 and 3:129.

103. Satow, *Voyage to Japan*, 179; *Letters Received*, 1:204; Cocks, *Diary*, 1:297–300.

104. For the later eighteenth century, see Jaffer, *Lascars and Indian Ocean Seafaring*, 97–126.

105. Saris, *Clove* MS, fol. 60r.

106. Saris, *Clove* MS, fol. 105r.

107. Saris, *Clove* MS, fols. 108r, 110v; Satow, *Voyage to Japan*, 25–26.

108. EIC Court Minutes, BL IOR/B/5 fol. 25.

109. See EIC Court Minutes, BL IOR/B/7 pp. 276, 404; IOR/B/8 p. 202; Sharpe, "Gender at Sea."

110. These efforts to keep low-status British laboring people loyal to the Company were only somewhat successful, and mutiny and desertion plagued its outposts. Hunt, "The 1689 Mughal Siege of Bombay," 153.

Chapter 6. Englishness Abroad

1. "Anonymous *Hector* Journal," 65–66; Barbour, *The Third Voyage Journals*, 244. The performance of these plays is not certain, because Keeling's original journal has been lost and the version published in *Purchas* is highly abbreviated. Two independent nineteenth-century sources reproduce extracts mentioning the plays, however, and they are widely considered to be legitimate.

2. Jourdain, *Journal*, 7.

3. Company officers had not always been so tolerant. In an earlier voyage, the belligerent Henry Middleton seized Khoekhoe cattle after a similar dispute. Violence was not a viable long-term strategy, however, since the Khoekhoe could simply withdraw. Jourdain, *Journal*, 15, 14; *The Last East-Indian Voyage*, 13–14.

4. Jourdain, *Journal*, 15–16; Coverte, *Report*, 5–6.

5. Barker, "A Voyage with Three Tall Ships," 6; Jourdain, *Journal*, 24–26.

6. This was "so thick and muddy" that the Englishmen would not drink it. Coverte, *Report*, 10.

7. Coverte, *Report*, 8; Jones, "Relation of the Fourth Voyage," in *Purchas*, 3:62.

8. Jourdain, *Journal*, 37–38. Thomas Jones, who returned home to England from India in a Portuguese carrack, heard that Churchman later died of the bloody flux in captivity at Mombasa. See *Purchas*, 3:63.

9. Jourdain, *Journal*, 38–39.

10. The children were not mentioned again. They may have died or were set on shore or sold as slaves. Coverte, *Report*, 16; Jourdain, *Journal*, 41–43.

11. Jones, "Relation," in *Purchas*, 3:65; Jourdain, *Journal*, 58, 58n.

12. For his description of Aden, see Jourdain, *Journal*, 74–78.

13. Jourdain, *Journal*, 98–9; Coverte, *Report*, 22.

14. Jourdain, *Journal*, 110, 114; Coverte, *Report*, 23; Jones, "Relation," in *Purchas*, 3:68.

15. Jourdain, *Journal*, 116–18; Coverte, *Report*, 24.

16. Jourdain, *Journal*, 120–23.

17. The Englishmen wanted Sharpeigh to keep the two hundred *reales*, "which he had gathered amongst the company" to buy gifts for the governor at Surat, but according to Jourdain, Sharpeigh inexcusably kept the money for himself. Jourdain, *Journal*, 123–26, 127.

18. Jourdain, *Journal*, 128–31.

19. Jourdain, *Journal*, 132; William Finch, "Observations," in *Purchas*, 4:26.

20. William Nicols, "Report," in *Purchas*, 3:72; Jourdain, *Journal*, 134, 140.

21. Jones, "Relations," in *Purchas*, 3:70–72; Guerreiro, *Relaçam annal*, fol. 22v.

22. The men were accused of spreading rumors about Sir Robert Sherley, an English traveler resident in Persia. See Hugh Lee to Salisbury, 6 July 1611, SP 89/3, fol. 172r.

23. He would be captured by the VOC in 1619, enslaved, and sent to attack the Philippines, never to return. Nicols, "Report," in *Purchas*, 3:72–73; *Answere to the Hollanders Declaration*, sig. Dv.

24. Jourdain, *Journal*, 141; Saris, *Clove* MS, fol. 104v.

25. Coverte, *Report*, 28–31, 35–36.

26. Coverte, *Report*, 37–41; Hawkins, "Relations," in *Purchas*, 3:17.

27. Coverte, *Report*, 41–42.

28. Nicholas Downton, "Journal," in *Purchas*, 3:257.

29. Keeling, "Journal of His Third Voyage," 122; Foster, *Embassy of Sir Thomas Roe*, 2:292.

30. Coverte, *Report*, 5–6.

31. For food and difference, see Suranyi, "Seventeenth-Century English Travel Literature." For the Khoekhoe and European racism, see Merians, *Envisioning the Worst*; Fauvelle-Aymar, *L'invention du Hottentot*; Hudson, " 'Hottentots' and the Evolution of European Racism"; Penn, "Written Culture and the Cape Khoikhoi."

32. See Hubbard, *City Women*, 123.

33. Boonzaier et al., *Cape Herders*, 30–31.

34. *A True and Large Discourse of the Voyage*, 3–4.

35. Marlowe, "*Hector* Journal," 101, 96; Stevens, *Dawn of British Trade*, 105.

36. John Milward (1614), Edward Blitheman (1615), and Walter Peyton (1615) in Raven-Hart, *Before Van Riebeeck*, 70–72.

37. Peyton, *Expedition* MS, 9, 93; Martin Pring, "Brief notes," in *Purchas*, 4:571.

38. Stanley, *Selling Women*, 9, 33–34.

39. See Ingram, *Carnal Knowledge*, 412–13; Hubbard, *City Women*, 88–90.

40. See Stanley, *Selling Women*, 94, 148–49; Drixler, *Mabiki*.

41. Satow, *Voyage to Japan*, 119, 145, 150, 176–77, 182.

42. Cocks to Saris, 10 Dec. 1614, in Farrington, *The English Factory in Japan*, 1:254.

43. Saris, *Voyage to Japan*, 132–33, 153.

44. Cocks, *Diary*, 1:179.

45. See Said, *Orientalism;* Kupperman, *Indians and English;* Matar, *Britain and Barbary.*

46. Maclean, *Looking East*, 21.

47. Historians focused on the close religious and ethnic ties that allowed Indian and Armenian merchants, for example, to maintain the mutual trust necessary to build commercial networks, while economists examined principal-agent problems within trading diasporas, not cross-cultural trade itself. See Curtin, *Cross-Cultural Trade;* Levi, *Indian Diaspora;* Aslanian, *From the Indian Ocean to the Mediterranean;* North, "Institutions, Transaction Costs, and the Rise of Merchant Empires"; Greif, *Institutions and the Path.*

48. See, for example, Trivellato, *Familiarity of Strangers*, chap. 7; Kaiser and Calafat, "The Economy of Ransoming"; Hershenzon, *The Captive Sea*, chap. 5; van Meersbergen, "Dutch and English Approaches to Cross-Cultural Trade."

49. Games, *Web of Empire*, 10.

50. Best, "A true discourse," in Hakluyt, *Principall Navigations*, 2nd ed., 3:59.

51. Best, "A generall and briefe description," in Hakluyt, *Principall Navigations*, 2nd ed., 3:94.

52. Best, "A true discourse," in Hakluyt, *Principall Navigations*, 2nd ed., 3:59.

53. Markham, *Voyages and Works of John Davis*, 7, 18, 36.

54. Best, "A true discourse," in Hakluyt, *Principall Navigations*, 2nd ed., 3:59.

55. Christopher Hall, "The first voyage of M. Martine Frobisher," in Hakluyt, *Principall Navigations*, 1st ed., 621.

56. Markham, *Voyages and Works of John Davis*, 18–20, 23–24.

57. Barbour, *Jamestown Voyages*, 1:90.

58. Marlowe, *Hector* Journal, 85–86.

59. Edward Heynes, "Voyage of the *Anne Royal*," in *Purchas*, 4:554; Mishra, "Diplomacy at the Edge," 11.

60. Hawkins, "Relations," *Purchas*, 3:18–9; *Letters Received*, 3:167–68, 205; *The Last East-Indian Voyage*, 17.

61. Satow, *Voyage to Japan*, 93; *Letters Received*, 1:279–80, 2:298, 5:245

62. Foster, *Voyage of Thomas Best*, 230; Mishra, "Diplomacy at the Edge," 19. See also Clulow, "European Maritime Violence," 75.

63. *Letters Received*, 5:341.

64. "Second voyage of John Davis with Edward Michelborne," in *Purchas*, 2:356, 365.

65. EIC Court Minutes, BL IOR/B/5, p. 136; PC 2/27 fol. 308v; Mishra, *A Business of State*, 159–160.

66. *Letters Received*, 6:174.

67. EIC Court Minutes, BL IOR/B/6 p. 235 (23 Oct. 1618).

68. When Captain Kidd attacked Mughal shipping about eighty years later, Mughal pressure on the East India Company prompted Kidd's trial and execution, and a general crackdown on British Indian Ocean piracy. See Ritchie, *Captain Kidd*.

69. *Letters Received*, 3:292, 5:9.

70. "The first voyage," in *Purchas*, 2:428.

71. Saris, *Clove* MS, fol. 105v; Saris, "Journal," in *Purchas*, 3:407.

72. *Letters Received*, 1:282; Satow, *Voyage to Japan*, 93; Scot, "Discourse of Java," in *Purchas*, 2:456. See also Games, *Inventing the English Massacre*, 15.

73. Clulow, *The Company and the Shogun*, 34–7.

74. Scot, "Discourse of Java," in *Purchas*, 2:452, 456–7.

75. Scot, "Discourse of Java," in *Purchas*, 2:457–58; Games, "Anglo-Dutch Maritime Interactions," 178–9.

76. Peyton, *Expedition* MS, p. 29; Satow, *Voyage to Japan*, 107; Cocks, *Diary*, 2:198.

77. "Voyage of David Middleton" and Saris, "The eighth voyage," in *Purchas* 3:60, 363; Satow, *Voyage to Japan*, 159.

78. Davis, "A brief relation," in *Purchas*, 2:307–9, 311.

79. Shepard, *Meanings of Manhood*, 28, 87–88.

80. Keeling, "Journal," in *Purchas*, 2:532; *The Last East-Indian Voyage*, 54.

81. Cocks, *Diary*, 1:274 and 2:177.

82. Cocks, *Diary*, 2:175, 181; Skinner, *True Relation of the Proceedings*, 26.

83. Emanuel van Meteren, extracts from "History of the Netherlands," in Rye, *England as Seen by Foreigners*, 69–70.

84. G. Reynst to Heren XVII, 26 Oct. 1615, in Coolhaas, *Generale Missiven*, 1:51; J. P. Coen to Heren XVII, 16 Nov. 1621, in Coen, *Bescheiden*, 1:644; Bertrand, *L'histoire à parts égales*, 384.

85. Scot, "Discourse of Java," in *Purchas*, 2:467–8; Das Gupta, "Indian Merchants," 497–98.

86. Clulow, *The Company and the Shogun*, 83; Bertrand, *L'histoire à parts égales*, 180–88; Reid, "Early Southeast Asian Categorizations of Europeans," 271.

87. Jourdain, *Journal*, 99; *Letters Received*, 6:205.

88. Chida-Razvi, "The Perception of Reception," 280.

89. Satow, *Voyage to Japan*, 121. See also Toby, "Japanese Iconographies of Other."

90. Casale, "Ottoman Administration of the Spice Trade," 187; Edward Heynes, "Voyage of the *Anne Royal*," in *Purchas*, 4:555.

91. Sir Henry Middleton, "The sixth voyage," in *Purchas*, 3:136–38, 149.

92. Jourdain, *Journal*, 331–32; Peyton, *Expedition* MS, p. 78.

93. Games, "Anglo-Dutch Maritime Interactions," 182–87; Games, *Inventing the English Massacre*, 24–26.

94. See van Ittersum, "Debating Natural Law in the Banda Islands," for a balanced account.

95. Peyton, *Expedition* MS, p. 78; Thomas Spurway, "A letter," in *Purchas*, 4:517, 520.

96. *Letters Received*, 5:306.

97. Jackson, 1620: HCA 13/43, fols. 98r, 101r, according to foliation on upper right.

98. *Answere to the Hollanders Declaration*, sigs. C2r, D1v, C4r.

Chapter 7. Sailors and the State

1. Rawlins, *Recoverie of a Ship of Bristoll*, sig. B2.

2. Wadsworth, *The English Spanish Pilgrime*, 40; Okeley, *Eben-ezer*, 9.

3. Rawlins, *Recoverie of a Ship of Bristoll*, sig. B4.

4. Hebb, *Piracy and the English Government*, 163.

5. Rawlins, *Recoverie of a Ship of Bristoll*, sig. A2v.

6. For debates about the sovereignty of the seas, see Armitage, *Ideological Origins*, 100–124.

7. Rodger, *Safeguard*, 380, 388–89.

8. Scottish fishermen paid a tax, the assize-herring, suggesting that the fisheries belonged to the Crown, and Dutch fishermen seem to have been forbidden by treaty to fish within view of the Scottish coast. See Dee, *General and Rare Memorials*, 7; Fulton, *Sovereignty of the Sea*, 74–78, 94.

9. Monson, "A Demonstration of the Hollanders increase in shippinge and our decay therein," 1609, SP 14/47 fol. 263r; Hales, "A Declaration," 1609, SP 14/45 fol. 34v; Fulton, *Sovereignty of the Sea*, 146–7.

10. Fulton, *Sovereignty of the Sea*, 185–208.

11. Fulton, *Sovereignty of the Sea*, 159, 171–73.

12. Robert Bertie, Earl of Lindsey, to the King, SP 16/288 fol. 201r. For the shifting geography of the Sea of England, see Fulton, *Sovereignty of the Sea*, 20–21.

13. Davis, *Rise of English Shipping*, 293.

14. Fulton, *Sovereignty of the Sea*, 89–99; SP12/27 fol. 281v.

15. Act 5 Eliz. c. 5; Sgroi, "Piscatorial Politics Revisited."

16. Hitchcock, *A Pollitique Platt*, sig. A1v; Dee, *General and Rare Memorials*, 26.

17. Gentleman, *Englands Way to Win Wealth*, 44; Sharpe, *Britaines Busse;* SP 14/157 fol. 69.

18. Poulsen, "Imitation in European Herring Fisheries," 187, 194.

19. Innis, *Cod Fisheries*, 31–32; Whitbourne, *A Discourse Containing a Loving Invitation*, 45.

20. Quinn, "Newfoundland in the Consciousness of Europe," 310.

21. SP 12/118, fol. 31r.

22. See Cell, *English Enterprise in Newfoundland*, 47; John Marshall, 1609: HCA 13/27 fol. 260.

23. Whitbourne, *Discourse and Discovery of Newfoundland*, 22; Martizano de Aristega, 1596: HCA 13/32 fol. 33.

24. In 1597, French Basque seamen protected their Spanish neighbors against English aggression, while other French Basque ships were directly targeted by privateers on the

pretense they were Spanish. See HCA 13/32 fols. 339 (Francisco de Neava), 366v (Martin de Arisaga), and 368v (William Downe).

25. Polónia, "Portuguese Seafarers," 219–22.

26. Barkham, "Offshore and Distant-Water Fisheries," 242–43.

27. Kayll, *The Trades Increase,* 25; Whitbourne, *Discourse and Discovery of Newfoundland,* 24.

28. Kayll, *The Trades Increase,* 23–26.

29. Two years later, the company did manage to assume the mantle of the common good, on the grounds that only a settled plantation could protect the valuable but vulnerable fisheries from piracy or domination by other European powers. Its victory was fleeting, however, as the colony soon collapsed, its expenses seriously outpacing its revenues. Cell, *English Enterprise in Newfoundland,* 74–75, 78–80.

30. Rodger, *The Command of the Ocean,* 207.

31. *CSP Venice* 10: no. 739.

32. Wotton to Salisbury, 12/22 March 1607, SP 99/4 fols. 59v–60v; Lorimer, *Settlement on the River Amazon,* 147.

33. William Bonner, 1611: HCA 1/47 fol. 196r; *CSP Venice* 12: 9 July 1611.

34. Antoine de Sallettes fled inland but was captured and forced to serve Moulay Zidan before being executed for trying to escape. Castries, *Sources inédites,* 1st series, France, 3:xl–xlvii.

35. Mainwaring, "Of the Beginnings, Practices, and Suppression of Pirates," 11.

36. Nottingham to Salisbury, 17 July 1611, SP 14/65 fol. 59.

37. Senior, "An Investigation," 25, 308.

38. *CSP Venice* 12: 7 July 1611.

39. *CSP Venice* 12: 14 July 1611; SP 84/68 fol. 108. For a detailed account, see Senior, "An Investigation," 292–317.

40. He allegedly extracted such heavy bribes in exchange that "many of the poorer sort . . . complaine[d] that they had as great need to go to sea again to get more, as ever before." William Marlett, 1613: HCA 13/98 fol. 130r.

41. Chichester and Carew to the Council, 29 July 1611, SP 63/231 fol. 164; *CSP Venice* XII, 9 Sept. 1611; Gorges to Salisbury, 4 Jan. 1612, SP 14/68 fol. 7; Senior, "An Investigation," 316.

42. Council to Chichester, 27 Sept. 1612, *CSP Ireland,* 4: no. 525.

43. *CSPD,* James I, 2:206.

44. Mainwaring, "Of the Beginnings, Practices, and Suppression of Pirates," 42, 18–19.

45. George Spencer, 1609: HCA 1/47 fol. 33v; *Lives . . . of the 19 Late Pyrates.*

46. Nighton Filps: HCA 13/98 fol. 210v.

47. John Hoskins, 1613: HCA 13/42 fol. 201v.

48. Pyborne, 1613: HCA 13/42 fols. 203r, 194r.

49. HCA 13/98 fols. 24v (Andrew Fursland), 30r (John Bayly), and 21v (Henry Orenge).

50. Len, 1613: HCA 13/42 fols. 207r–8v.

51. HCA 1/5 fol. 40r; Jourdain, *Journal,* 279, 284.

52. Neve, 1613: HCA 13/98 fol. 58v; *Cal. SP East Indies,* 1617–1621, no. 146.

53. HCA 1/47 fols. 65r (Richard Parker) and 32v (James Harris); HCA 13/43 fols. 62v–64r.

54. HCA 1/5 fols. 73, 91–91c, 116; HCA 13/43 fol. 98v (foliation on lower left).

55. HCA 13/42 fols. 139v–41v (Ingle) and 187r (Stephen Davis); SP 16/135 fol. 118r.

56. Andrews, *Ships, Money and Politics,* 66–68.

57. For a recent account, see Mancall, *Fatal Journey.*

58. Wilson, 1612: HCA 13/42 fol. 9r.

59. These cases were brought in 1608–1609 and 1628–1629. Steckley, "Litigious Mariners," 323, 327–38, 333, 338.

60. Zouch, *The Jurisdiction of the Admiralty,* 151; Exton, *The Maritime Dicaeologie,* 145–6; Wiseman, *The Law of Laws,* 150.

61. SP 16/102 fol. 141r.

62. Quinn, "James I and the Beginnings of Empire," 328.

63. "Virginia and the Indies," ca. 1606, CP 119/149.

64. William Squier and Thomas Tiler to Salisbury, 19/29 March 1606, CP 115/148.

65. Adam Tanner to Salisbury, ca. 1606, CP Petitions 1171.

66. Wives of the Spanish Prisoners to Salisbury, ca. 1606, CP Petitions 425.

67. Philip III to Elda, 18/28 Nov. 1607, SP 94/14 fol. 223.

68. Stoneman, "Voyage of M. Henry Challons," in *Purchas,* 19:289, 291, 292–94.

69. "Virginia and the Indies," ca. 1606, CP 119/149.

70. Davis to Salisbury, 21/31 May 1608, CP 195/10; Cornwallis to Salisbury, 7 July 1608, CP 126/16; SP 94/15 fol. 156r.

71. Council to Sir Thomas Smith, 9 March 1617, PC 2/28 fol. 581r; Council to Zouch, 7 Feb. 1619, SP 14/105 fol. 140.

72. Hebb, *Piracy and the English Government,* 17–20.

73. *CSP Venice* 18: 27 May 1624; White, *Piracy and Law,* 144. Bertons were armed round ships.

74. The following summary of the Mansell expedition is drawn from the detailed account in Hebb, *Piracy and the English Government,* chaps. 2–6.

75. Ford to James I, 24 Feb. 1622, SP 71/1 fol. 40r.

76. Leate to Conway, 3 July 1623, SP 71/1 fols. 44–45.

77. Hebb, *Piracy and the English Government,* chap. 8.

78. SP 16/1 fols. 97r (Thomas Ceely to Council, 18 April 1625) and 98r (examination of William Knight); John Trewinnard to Conway, 7 May 1625, SP 16/2 fol. 78.

79. James Bagg to Buckingham, 18 April 1625, SP 16/1 fol. 100r; examination of William Court, 7 May 1625, SP 16/2 fol. 83r.

80. Blithell and Lins to Council, 19 May 1625, SP 16/2 fol. 150r; examination of David Cockburne, 5 July 1625, SP 16/4 fol. 14r.

81. Harris, *Trinity House of Deptford Transactions,* no. 261.

82. SP 16/5 fols. 38r, 39r.

83. Buckingham to Sir Francis Stewart, 27 June 1625, *CSPD* Charles I, 1:49.

84. SP 71/1 fol. 77; Hebb, *Piracy and the English Government,* 160–61, 210–12.

85. Hebb, *Piracy and the English Government*, 152; SP 105/109 fol. 52r.

86. See Andrews, *Ships, Money and Politics*, chap. 7; Hebb, *Piracy and the English Government*, chap. 11.

87. Hebb, *Piracy and the English Government*, 167–70.

88. Thomas Duffield and Hendrick Henderson, 23 Feb. 1626, HCA 13/45 fols. 200v–201r.

89. Hebb, *Piracy and the English Government*, 157–63.

90. Council to Buckingham, 21 April 1625, SP 16/1 fol. 108r.

91. Pennington to Pembroke, 29 June 1625, SP 16/3 fol. 154.

92. SP 14/214 fol. 113r; SP 16/3 fol. 193r; Rodger, *Safeguard*, 356.

93. Michael Geere to William Geere, 11 Dec. 1625, SP 16/11 fol. 111r; St. Leger to Conway, 29 Dec. 1625, SP 16/12 fol. 139r; Edward Harwood to Dudley Carleton, 3 Jan. 1626, SP 16/18 fol. 14.

94. Edward Cecil to John Coke, 27 Feb. 1626, in Glanville, *Voyage to Cadiz*, xli–xlii.

95. Rodger, *Safeguard*, 501–2; SP 16/23 fol. 190r.

96. Commissioners at Plymouth to the Council, 17 April 1626, SP 16/25 fol. 17; Council to Deputy Lieutenants of Surrey, 29 June 1626, PC 2/33 fol. 368r; note of the demands of the seamen, 19 July 1626, SP 16/31 fol. 154r. See also Rodger, *Safeguard*, 401–3.

97. Pory to Mead, 18 Aug. 1626, in Cockburn, "Letters of Joseph Mead," 421–22.

98. Gyfford to Edward Nicholas, 24 Aug. 1626, SP 16/34 fol. 37. This was the same man who had attempted to burn the galleys in Algiers more than twenty years before, older and presumably wiser.

99. Gell to Mead, 1 Sept. 1626, and Mead to Stuteville, 14 Oct. 1626, in Cockburn, "Letters of Joseph Mead," 437, 493; Charles I, *Proclamations*, no. 54.

100. John Pory, 1 Dec. 1626, in Cockburn, "Letters of Joseph Mead," 581.

101. Watts to Buckingham, 6 Dec. 1626, SP 16/41 fol. 54r; Mead to Stuteville, 26 Jan. 1627, in Cockburn, "Letters of Joseph Mead," 637.

102. SP 16/49 fol. 210r.

103. Mead to Stuteville, 2 and 10 Feb. 1627, in Cockburn, "Letters of Joseph Mead," 647, 641.

104. Mead to Stuteville, 24 March 1627, in Cockburn, "Letters of Joseph Mead," 711; Mervyn to Buckingham, 27 May 1627, SP 16/64 fol. 136v.

105. Apsley to Nicholas, 1 Nov. 1627, SP 16/84 fol. 1r; Mervyn to Nicholas, 23 Dec. 1627, SP 16/87 fol. 54r.

106. PC 2/36 fol. 237v; Watts to Nicholas, SP 16/86 fol. 123r.

107. Watts to Buckingham, 4 Jan. 1628, SP 16/90 fol. 22r; Watts to Nicholas, 11 Jan. 1628, SP 16/90 fol. 79r.

108. Mervyn to Buckingham, 8 Jan. 1628, SP 16/90 fol. 51r; Watts to Nicholas, 15 Jan. 1628, SP 16/90 fol. 124r.

109. Denbigh to Buckingham, 23 March 1628, SP 16/98 fol. 67r; Mervyn to Dorset, 25 Sept. 1629, SP 16/149 fol. 127r.

110. See Palmer to Nicholas, 19 March 1628, SP 16/96 fol. 128r; Coke to Conway, 1 Sept. 1628, SP 16/116 fol. 2r.

111. Council to Denbigh, 29 March 1628, PC 2/38 fol. 53r; also Weddell to Nicholas, 7 April 1628, SP16/100 fol. 82r; Denbigh to Buckingham, 22 June 1628, SP 16/107 fol. 200r.

112. Rodger, *Safeguard*, 370–4; BL Add. MS 35331 fol. 18.

113. 1627 3 Chas. 1 c. 1; Rodger, *Safeguard*, 368–78.

Epilogue

1. Rodger, *Safeguard*, 361. For privateering in the 1620s, see Appleby, "English Privateering."

2. Andrews, *Ships, Money and Politics*, 128–59.

3. Andrews, *Ships, Money and Politics*, 160–83; Hebb, *Piracy and the English Government*, 237–65.

4. Andrews, *Ships, Money and Politics*, 21–23, 74–77.

5. Earle, "English Sailors, 1570–1775," 75–76.

6. See Davis, *Rise of English Shipping*, 135–37.

7. Stein, "Passes and Protection," 607.

8. For impressment, see Rogers, *The Press Gang;* Brunsman, *The Evil Necessity;* Dancy, *The Myth of the Press Gang.*

9. In the reign of Charles II, Rodger finds, "flogging for desertion was regarded as an extreme brutality," but by the late eighteenth century the punishment had become much more commonplace. *The Command of the Ocean*, 133–34, 492–94.

10. See Land, "Customs of the Sea," passim; Sirota, "The Church," 198.

11. Fielding, *A Brief Description*, xv.

12. Earle, "English Sailors, 1570–1775," 77.

13. Christopher, *Slave Ship Sailors*, 26, 97, 205–6.

14. For limits on disciplinary violence, see Earle, *Sailors*, 147–63.

15. Hakluyt, *Principal Navigations*, 1st ed., 3.

16. Jane, "Last voyage of Thomas Candish," in Markham, *Voyages and Works of John Davis*, 106; John Morta, 1604: HCA 13/36 fols. 300v–302r; "The first voyage" and Thomas Clayborne, "The second voyage," in *Purchas*, 2:435, 497.

17. See Markham, *Voyages and Works of John Davis*.

18. Hunt, "Peter Easton"; de Sá, "Knyvett [Knivet], Anthony."

19. See SP 16/5 fol. 70, SP 16/6 fol. 176, SP 16/8 fol. 7.

20. Walsingham was one of the neighbors who rescued Margaret Etheridge from her abusive husband around 1629. See Hubbard, *City Women*, 258, and Walsingham's deposition, LMA DL/C/231 fol. 104r.

BIBLIOGRAPHY

Manuscript and Archival Sources

British Library

Add MS 19276, Walter Peyton's *Expedition* journal, 1614–1617.
ADD MS 35331, Walter Yonge, diary.
IOR/B2-IOR/B/11, East India Company, Court Minutes.
IOR/L/MAR/A/XIV, John Saris's *Clove* journal, 1611–1613.
Lansdowne MS 100/3, John Sarracoll's *Red Dragon* journal, 1586.

Hatfield House Archives

CECIL PAPERS

CP vols. 95, 100, 110, 115, 119, 124, 126, 190, 195.
CP petitions.

Library of Congress

G. R. G. Conway Collection, "Englishmen and the Mexican Inquisition, 1559–1577." Typescript, transcribed from Mexico City, Archivo General de la Nación, Inq. 7. 56.

London Metropolitan Archives

DL/C/230, Diocese of London, Consistory Court. Depositions.
P93/DUN/264, Parish register, St. Dunstan's, Stepney.

The National Archives, Kew

HIGH COURT OF ADMIRALTY

HCA 1/2–1/6. Oyer and Terminer. Indictments etc.
HCA 1/46–1/48. Oyer and Terminer. Examinations of pirates and others.
HCA 13/20–13/46. Instance and Prize Courts. Examinations and answers.
HCA 13/97, 13/98. Oyer and Terminer. Examinations of pirates and others,

PRIVY COUNCIL

PC 2   Registers.

STATE PAPERS

SP 12   State Papers Domestic, Elizabeth I.
SP 14   State Papers Domestic, James I.
SP 16   State Papers Domestic, Charles I.
SP 63   State Papers Ireland.
SP 71   State Papers Foreign, Barbary States.
SP 89   State Papers Foreign, Portugal.
SP 94   State Papers Foreign, Spain.
SP 98   State Papers Foreign, Tuscany.
SP 99   State Papers Foreign, Venice.
SP 105/109–10   Levant Company.

HUNTINGTON LIBRARY

HM 1648, Red Dragon Logbook, 1586–1587.

Published Primary Sources

"The Anonymous *Hector* Journal." In *The Third Voyage Journals: Writing and Performance in the London East India Company, 1607–1610*, edited by Richmond Barbour, 33–74. New York: Palgrave Macmillan, 2009.
An Answere to the Hollanders Declaration, Concerning the Occurrents of the East-India. The First Part. Written by Certaine Marriners, Lately Returned from Thence into England. London, 1622.

Appleby, John C., ed. *A Calendar of Material Relating to Ireland from the High Court of Admiralty Examinations, 1536–1641*. Dublin: Irish Manuscripts Commission, 1992.

Barbour, Philip L., ed. *The Jamestown Voyages under the First Charter, 1606–1609*. . . . 2 vols. London: Hakluyt Society, 1969.

Barbour, Richmond, ed. *The Third Voyage Journals: Writing and Performance in the London East India Company, 1607–1610*. New York: Palgrave Macmillan, 2009.

Barker, Andrew. *A True and Certaine Report of the Beginning, Proceedings, Overthrowes, and Now Present Estate of Captaine Ward and Danseker, the Two Late Famous Pirates from their First Setting Foorth to This Present Time*. London, 1609.

Barker, Edmund. "A Voyage with Three Tall Ships . . . to the East Indies. . . ." Originally published in Hakluyt's *Principall Navigations* (London, 1598–1600). In *The Voyages of Sir James Lancaster to Brazil and the East Indies 1591–1603*, edited by Sir William Foster, 1–21. London: Hakluyt Society, 1940.

Best, Thomas. "A Jornall of the Tenth Voyage. . . ." In *The Voyage of Thomas Best to the East Indies*, edited by Sir William Foster, 1–92. London: Hakluyt Society, 1934.

Birdwood, Sir George, and William Foster, eds. *The Register of Letters &c. of the Governour and Company of Merchants of London Trading into the East Indies, 1600–1619*. London: Bernard Quaritch, 1893.

Boteler, Nathaniel. *Six Dialogues about Sea-Services: Between an High-Admiral and a Captain at Sea*. London, 1685.

Bradford, William. *A Relation or Journall of the Beginnings and Proceedings of the English Plantation Setled at Plimoth in New England*. . . . London, 1622.

Brèves, François Savary de. *Relation des voyages de Monsieur de Brèves, tant en Grèce, Terre Saincte et Aegypte qu'aux royaumes de Tunis et Arger*. . . . Paris, 1628.

Calendar of State Papers Colonial, East Indies, China and Japan, ed. Noel W. Sainsbury. London, 1864–1892. *British History Online* https://www.british-history.ac.uk /search/series/cal-state-papers—colonial—east-indies-china-japan

Calendar of State Papers, Ireland, ed. C. W. Russell and John P. Predergast. London, 1877. *British History Online* https://www.british-history.ac.uk/cal-state-papers /ireland/1611–14

Calendar of State Papers Relating to English Affairs in the Archives of Venice. Vols. 8–12 (ed. Horatio F. Brown), vols. 13–20 (ed. Allen B Hinds). London: 1894–1905. *British History Online* https://www.british-history.ac.uk/search/series/cal-state-papers—venice

Castries, Henry de, ed. *Les sources inédites de l'histoire du Maroc de 1530 à 1845*. 1st series, Dynastie saadienne, 1539–1660. Archives et bibliothèques des Pays-Bas. Vol. 2. Paris: E. Leroux, 1907.

————, ed. *Les sources inédites de l'histoire du Maroc de 1530 à 1845.* 1st series, Dynastie saadienne, 1539–1660. Archives et bibliothèques de France. Vol. 3. Paris: E. Leroux, 1911.

Chamberlain, John. *Letters of John Chamberlain.* Edited by Norman Egbert McClure. Philadelphia: American Philosophical Society, 1939.

Charles I. *Royal Proclamations of King Charles I, 1625–1646.* Edited by James Larkin. Oxford: Clarendon Press, 1983.

Charles II. *A Proclamation Touching on the Articles of Peace with Argiers, Tunis, and Tripoli.* London, 1663.

Cockburn, David Anthony John, ed. "A Critical Edition of the Letters of the Reverend Joseph Mead, 1626–1627, Contained in British Library Harleian MS 390." Ph.D. thesis, University of Cambridge, 1994. https://doi.org/10.17863/CAM.16199

Cocks, Richard. *Diary of Richard Cocks, Cape-Merchant in the English Factory in Japan, 1615–1622.* Edited by Edward Maunde Thompson. 2 vols. London: Hakluyt Society, 1883.

Coen, Jan Pieterzoon. *Jan Pieterszoon Coen: Bescheiden omtrent zijn bedrijf in Indië.* Edited by Herman T. Colenbrander. 6 vols. The Hague: Martinus Nijhoff, 1919–1934.

Coolhaas, W. Ph., ed. *Generale missiven van Gouverneurs-Generaal en raden aan Heren XVII der Oostindische Compagnie.* Part 1. The Hague: Martinus Nijhoff, 1960.

Cottington, R. *A True Historicall Discourse of Muley Hamets Rising to the Three Kingdoms of Moruecos, Fes, and Sus. . . .* London, 1609.

Coverte, Robert. *A True and Almost Incredible Report of an Englishman, that . . . Travelled by Land through Many Unknowne Kingdoms, and Great Cities. . . .* London, 1614.

Coxere, Edward. *Adventures by Sea of Edward Coxere. . . .* Edited by E. H. W. Meyerstein. London: Oxford University Press, 1946.

Daborne, Robert. *A Christian Turn'd Turk, or, The Tragicall Lives and Deaths of the Two Famous Pyrates, Ward and Dansiker.* London, 1612.

Davies, William. *A True Relation of the Travailes and Most Miserable Captivitie of William Davies, Barber-Surgeon of London, under the Duke of Florence. . . .* London, 1614.

Dee, John. *General and Rare Memorials Pertayning to the Perfect Arte of Navigation. . . .* London, 1577.

Digges, Sir Dudley. *The Defence of Trade in a Letter to Sir Thomas Smith Knight, Governor of the East-India Companie, &c. from One of That Society.* London, 1615.

Donno, Elizabeth Story, ed. and trans. *An Elizabethan in 1582: The Diary of Richard Madox, Fellow of All Souls*. London: Hakluyt Society, 1974.

Exton, John. *The Maritime Dicaeologie, or, Sea-Jurisdiction of England*. London, 1664.

Farrington, Anthony, ed. *The English Factory in Japan, 1613–1623*. 2 vols. London: British Library, 1991.

Fielding, Sir John. *A Brief Description of the Cities of London and Westminster*. London, 1776.

A Fight at Sea, Famously Fought by the Dolphin of London Against Five of the Turkes Men of Warre. . . . London, 1617.

Floris, Peter. *Peter Floris, His Voyage to the East Indies in the Globe, 1611–1615: The Contemporary Translation of His Journal*. Edited by W. H. Moreland. London: Hakluyt Society, 1934.

Foucques, Capitaine. "Mémoires portants plusieurs advertissements présentés au roy." In *Archives des voyages; ou, Collection d'anciennes relations inédites ou très-rares, de lettres, mémoires, itinéraires et autres documents relatifs à la géographie et aux voyages*, edited by Henri Ternaux-Compans, vol. 1. Paris: A. Bertrand, 1840.

Foster, Sir William, ed. *The Embassy of Sir Thomas Roe to the Court of the Great Mogul, 1615–1619*. 2 vols. London: Hakluyt Society, 1899.

———, ed. *Letters Received by the East India Company from Its Servants in the East*. 6 vols. London, Sampson Low, Marston, 1892–1902.

———, ed. *The Voyage of Sir Henry Middleton to the Moluccas 1604–1606*. London: Hakluyt Society, 1943.

———, ed. *The Voyages of Sir James Lancaster to Brazil and the East Indies 1591–1603*. London: Hakluyt Society, 1940.

———, ed., *The Voyage of Thomas Best to the East Indies, 1612–1614*. London: Hakluyt Society, 1934.

Gentili, Alberico. *Hispanicae advocationis libri duo*. Translated by Frank Frost Abbott. New York: Oxford University Press, 1921.

Gentleman, Tobias. *Englands Way to Win Wealth, and to Employ Ships and Marriners*. . . . London, 1614.

Glanville, John. *The Voyage to Cadiz in 1625, Being a Journal Written by John Glanville*. . . . Edited by Alexander B. Grosart. Westminster: Camden Society, 1883.

Gorges, Sir Ferdinando. "A Briefe Narration of the Originall Undertakings of the Advancement of Plantations into the Parts of America." In *America Painted to the Life: The True History of the Spaniards Proceedings*. . . . London, 1659.

Guerreiro, Fernão. *Relaçam annal das cousas que fizeram os padres da Companhia de Iesus, nas partes da India Oriental*. . . . Lisbon, 1611.

Hakluyt, Richard. *The Principal Navigations, Voyages, Traffiques and Discoveries of the English Nation.* . . . 1st ed. London, 1589.

———. *The Principal Navigations, Voyages, Traffiques and Discoveries of the English Nation.* . . . 2nd ed. 3 vols. London, 1599–1600.

———. *The Principal Navigations, Voyages, Traffiques & Discoveries of the English Nation.* . . . 12 vols. Glasgow: James MacLehose and Sons, 1903–1905.

Harris, G. G., ed. *Trinity House of Deptford Transactions, 1609–35.* London: London Record Society, 1983.

Hawkins, Sir Richard. *The Observations of Sir Richard Hawkins, Knight, in His Voyage into the South Sea in the Year 1593.* Edited by C. R. Drinkwater Bethune. London: Hakluyt Society, 1847.

Hearne, John, and William Finch. "The *Red Dragon* Journal of John Hearne and William Finch, 8 March 1607 to 19 June 1608." In *The Third Voyage Journals: Writing and Performance in the London East India Company, 1607–1610,* edited by Richmond Barbour. New York: Palgrave Macmillan, 2009.

Hitchcock, Robert. *A Pollitique Platt: for the Honour of the Prince, the Greate Profite of the Publique State, Relief of the Poore, Preservation of the Riche, Reformation of Roges and Idle Persones, and the Wealthe of Thousandes That Knowes Not Howe to Live.* London, 1580.

Hortop, Job. *The Travailes of an English Man: Containing His Sundry Calamities Indured By the Space of Twentie and Odd Yeres in His Absence from His Native Countrie.* . . . London, 1591.

James I. *Royal Proclamations of King James I 1603–1625.* Edited by James Larkin and Paul Hughes. Oxford: Clarendon Press, 1973.

Jobson, Richard. *The Golden Trade: or, A Discovery of the River Gambra, and the Golden Trade of the Aethiopians.* . . . London, 1623.

Johnson, Robert. *Nova Britannia: Offering Most Excellent Fruites by Planting in Virginia.* . . . London, 1609.

Jourdain, John. *The Journal of John Jourdain 1608–1617: Describing His Experiences in Arabia, India, and the Malay Archipelago.* Edited by Sir William Foster. Cambridge: Hakluyt Society, 1905.

Kassell, Lauren, Michael Hawkins, Robert Ralley, John Young, Joanne Edge, Janet Yvonne Martin-Portugues, and Natalie Kaoukji, eds. *The Casebooks of Simon Forman and Richard Napier, 1596–1634: A Digital Edition.* http://casebooks.lib.cam.ac.uk

Kayll, Robert. *The Trades Increase.* London, 1615.

Keeling, Wiliam. "Keeling's Journal of His Third Voyage to East India." In *The East India Company Journals of Captain William Keeling and Master Thomas Bonner,*

1615–1617, ed. Michael Strachan and Boies Penrose. Minneapolis: University of Minnesota Press, 1971.

The Last East-Indian Voyage. Originally published in London, 1606. In *The Voyage of Sir Henry Middleton to the Moluccas, 1604–1606,* edited by Sir William Foster, 1–64. London: Hakluyt Society, 1943.

Lefroy, Sir J. Henry, ed. *The Historye of the Bermudaes or Summer Islands. Edited from a MS. in the Sloane Collection, British Library.* London: Hakluyt Society, 1882.

A Letter Written to the Right Worshipfull the Governours and Assistants of the East Indian Marchants in London. . . . London, 1603.

Linschoten, Jan Huygen van. *John Huighen van Linschoten his Discours of Voyages into the Easte and West Indies.* London, 1598.

Lithgow, William. *The Totall Discourse, of the Rare Adventures, and Painefull Peregrinations of Long Nineteene Yeares Travayles, from Scotland, to the Most Famous Kingdomes in Europe, Asia, and Affrica.* London, 1632.

The Lives, Apprehensions, Arraignments, and Executions, of the 19 Late Pyrates. . . . London, 1609.

Lorimer, Joyce, ed. *English and Irish Settlement on the River Amazon 1550–1646.* London: Hakluyt Society, 1990.

Madox, Richard. "The Diary of Richard Madox." In *An Elizabethan in 1582: The Diary of Richard Madox, Fellow of All Souls,* edited and translated by Elizabeth Story Donno. London: Hakluyt Society, 1974.

Mainwaring, Sir Henry. "Of the Beginnings, Practices, and Suppression of Pirates." In *The Life and Works of Sir Henry Mainwaring,* edited by G. E. Manwaring and W. G. Perrin. Vol. 2. London: Navy Records Society, 1922.

Markham, Albert Hastings, ed. *The Voyages and Works of John Davis the Navigator.* London: Hakluyt Society, 1880.

Marlowe, Anthony. "The *Hector* Journal of Anthony Marlowe, 14 July 1607 to 22 June 1608." In *The Third Voyage Journals: Writing and Performance in the London East India Company, 1607–1610,* edited by Richmond Barbour. New York: Palgrave Macmillan, 2009.

Marsden, Reginald G., ed., *Documents Relating to Law and Custom of the Sea. Volume I: 1205–1648.* London: Navy Records Society, 1916.

———, ed. *Select Pleas in the Court of Admiralty. Volume II: 1547–1602.* London: Selden Society, 1897.

Mun, Thomas. *A Discourse of Trade, from England unto the East-Indies: Answering to Diverse Objections Which Are Usually Made Against the Same.* London, 1621.

Mundy, Peter. *The Travels of Peter Mundy in Europe and Asia, 1608–1667.* Edited by Sir Richard Carnac Temple. Vol. 3. Cambridge: Hakluyt Society, 1919.

Newes from Mamora, or, A Summary Relation Sent to the King of Spaine of the Good Successe of a Voyage: Which It Hath Pleased God to Give in the Taking, and Surprising, of Mamora, a Port in Barbary. . . . London, 1614.

Nicholl, John. *An Houre Glasse of Indian Newes. Or A True and Tragicall Discourse, Shewing the Most Lamentable Miseries, and Distressed Calamities Indured by 67 Englishmen, Which Were Sent for a Supply to the Planting in Guiana in the Yeare 1605.* . . . London, 1607.

Norwood, Richard. *The Journal of Richard Norwood, Surveyor of Bermuda.* New York: Published for the Bermuda historical monuments trust by Scholars facsimiles and reprints, 1945.

Okeley, William. *Eben-ezer, or, A Small Monument of Great Mercy: Appearing in the Miraculous Deliverance of William Okeley.* . . . London, 1675.

Purchas, Samuel. *Hakluytus Posthumus, or, Purchas His Pilgrimes: Contayning a History of the World in Sea Voyages and Lande Travells by Englishmen and Others.* 20 vols. Glasgow: J. MacLehose and Sons, 1905–1907. First published in London, 1625.

———. *Purchas His Pilgrimage. Or Relations of the World and the Religions Observed in All Ages and Places Discovered, From the Creation unto this Present.* London, 1613.

Quinn, David Beers, ed. *The Roanoke Voyages, 1584–1590: Documents to Illustrate the English Voyages to North America under the Patent Granted to Walter Raleigh in 1584.* 2 vols. London: Hakluyt Society, 1955.

———, ed. *The Last Voyage of Thomas Cavendish 1591–1592: The Autograph Manuscript of His Own Account of the Voyage, Written Shortly before His Death, from the Collection of Paul Mellon.* Chicago: Newberry Library, 1975.

Quinn, David Beers, and Alison M. Quinn, eds. *The English New England Voyages 1602–1608.* London: Hakluyt Society, 1983.

R., H. *Newes From the Levane Seas. Describing the Many Perrilous Events of the Most Woorthy Deserving Gentleman, Edward Glenham, Esquire.* London, 1594.

Raleigh, Sir Walter. *Judicious and Select Essayes and Observations by that Renowned and Learned Knight, Sir Walter Raleigh.* . . . London, 1650.

———. *A Report of the Truth of the Fight about the Iles of Açores, This Last Sommer: Betwixt the Revenge, One of Her Majesties Shippes, and an Armada of the King of Spaine.* London, 1591.

Raven-Hart, R., ed., *Before Van Riebeeck: Callers at South Africa from 1488 to 1652.* Cape Town: C. Struik, 1967.

Rawlins, John. *The Famous and Wonderfull Recoverie of a Ship of Bristoll, Called the Exchange, from the Turkish Pirates of Argier.* . . . London, 1622.

Rye, William Benchley, ed. *England as Seen by Foreigners in the Days of Elizabeth and James the First.* . . . London: J. R. Smith, 1865.

Satow, Sir Ernest, ed. *The Voyage of Captain John Saris to Japan, 1613.* London: Hakluyt Society, 1900.

Sharpe, Edward. *Britaines Busse, or a Computation Aswell of the Charge of a Busse or Herring-Fishing Ship: As Also the Gaine and Profit Thereby.* . . . London, 1615.

Sherley, Thomas. "Discours of the Turkes." Edited by E. Denision Ross. In *Camden Miscellany: Volume XVI.* London: Camden Society, 1936.

Skinner, Sir John. *A True Relation of the Unjust, Cruell, and Barbarous Proceedings against the English at Amboyna in the East-Indies.* . . . London, 1624.

Smith, John. *The Complete Works of Captain John Smith.* Edited by Philip L. Barbour. 3 vols. Chapel Hill: Institute of Early American History and Culture, 1986.

Standish, Ralph, and Ralph Croft. "A Journall of the Tenth East Indea Vaige." In *The Voyage of Thomas Best to the East Indies, 1612–1614,* edited by Sir William Foster. London: Hakluyt Society, 1934.

Stevens, Henry, ed. *The Dawn of British Trade to the East Indies as Recorded in the Court Minutes of the East India Company 1599–1603.* London, H. Stevens and Son, 1886.

Taylor, E. G. R., ed. *The Troublesome Voyage of Captain Edward Fenton, 1582–1583.* Cambridge: Hakluyt Society, 1957.

Temple, Sir Richard Carnac, ed. *The World Encompassed and Analogous Contemporary Documents Concerning Sir Francis Drake's Circumnavigation of the World.* New York: Cooper Square, 1969.

A True and Large Discourse of the Voyage of the Whole Fleete of Ships Set South the 20 Aprill 1601. By the Governours and Assistants of the East Indian Marchants in London, to the East Indies. . . . London, 1603.

A True Declaration of the Estate of the Colonie in Virginia. . . . London, 1610.

Wadsworth, James. *The English Spanish Pilgrime. Or, A New Discoverie of Spanish Popery and Jesuiticall Strategems.* . . . London, 1629.

Walker, John. "Diary of John Walker." In *An Elizabethan in 1582: The Diary of Richard Madox, Fellow of All Souls,* edited and translated by Elizabeth Story Donno. London: Hakluyt Society, 1974.

Whitbourne, Richard. *A Discourse and Discovery of New-found-land with Many Reasons to Proove How Worthy and Beneficiall a Plantation May There Be Made, After a Far Better Manner Than Now It Is.* . . . London, 1620.

———. *A Discourse Containing a Loving Invitation Both Honourable, and Profitable to All Such as Shall Be Adventurers, Either in Person, or Purse, for the Advancement of his Majesties Most Hopeful Plantation in the New-found-land, Lately Undertaken.* London, 1622.

Wiseman, John. *The Law of Laws: or, The Excellency of the Civil Law, Above All Humane Laws Whatsoever. Shewing of How Great Use and Necessity the Civil Law is to this Nation.* London, 1657.

Zouch, Richard. *The Jurisdiction of the Admiralty of England Asserted against Sr. Edward Coke's Articuli Admiralitatis.* London, 1663.

Secondary Works

Addobatti, Andrea. "Until the Very Last Nail: English Seafaring and Wage Litigation in Seventeenth-Century Livorno." In *Law, Labour and Empire: Comparative Perspectives on Seafarers, c. 1500–1800*, edited by Maria Fusaro, Bernard Allaire, Richard J. Blakemore, and Tijl Vanneste. New York: Palgrave Macmillan, 2015.

Alsop, J. D. "Tudor Merchant Seafarers in the Early Guinea Trade." In *The Social History of English Seamen, 1485–1649*, edited by Cheryl A. Fury. Rochester: Boydell Press, 2012.

Andrews, Kenneth R. *Elizabethan Privateering: English Privateering during the Spanish War 1585–1603.* Cambridge: Cambridge University Press, 1964.

———. "New Light on Hakluyt." *Mariner's Mirror* 37, no. 4 (1951), 299–308.

———. *Ships, Money and Politics: Seafaring and Naval Enterprise in the Reign of Charles I.* Cambridge: Cambridge University Press, 1991.

———. "Sir Robert Cecil and Mediterranean Plunder." *English History Review* 87, no. 344 (July 1972): 513–32.

———. *The Spanish Caribbean: Trade and Plunder 1530–1630.* New Haven: Yale University Press, 1978.

———. *Trade, Plunder and Settlement: Maritime Enterprise and the Genesis of the British Empire, 1480–1630.* Cambridge: Cambridge University Press, 1984.

Appleby, John C. "English Privateering during the Spanish and French Wars, 1625–1630." Ph.D. thesis, University of Hull, 1983. https://hydra.hull.ac.uk/resources/hull:4669

———. "A Nursery of Pirates: The English Pirate Community in Ireland in the Early Seventeenth Century." *International Journal of Maritime History* 2, no. 1 (1990), 1–27.

———. "War, Politics, and Colonization, 1558–1625." In *The Oxford History of the British Empire. Volume 1. The Origins of Empire: British Overseas Enterprise to the Close of the Seventeenth Century.* Edited by Nicholas Canny. Oxford: Oxford University Press, 1998.

————. *Women and English Piracy, 1540–1720: Partners and Victims of Crime.* Woodbridge, Suffolk: Boydell Press, 2013.

Armitage, David. *The Ideological Origins of the British Empire.* Cambridge: Cambridge University Press, 2000.

Aslanian, Sebouh David. *From the Indian Ocean to the Mediterranean: The Global Trade Networks of Armenian Merchants from New Julfa.* Berkeley: University of California Press, 2011.

Barkham, Michael M. "The Offshore and Distant-Water Fisheries of the Spanish Basques, c. 1500–1650." In *A History of the North Atlantic Fisheries,* edited by David J. Starkey, Jón Th. Thór, and Ingo Heidbrink. Vol. 1. Bremen: Hauschild, 2009.

Beckles, Hilary. *White Servitude and Black Slavery in Barbados, 1627–1715.* Knoxville: University of Tennessee Press, 1989.

Bennassar, Bartolomé. "Les chrétiens convertis à l'Islam: 'Renégats' et leur intégration aux XVIe et XVIIe siècles." *Les cahiers de Tunisie,* 44 nos. 157–58 (1991), 45–53.

Benton, Lauren. *A Search for Sovereignty: Law and Geography in European Empires, 1400–1900.* Cambridge: Cambridge University Press, 2010.

Bertrand, Romain. *L'histoire à parts égales: Récits d'un rencontre Orient-Occident, XVIe– XVIIe siècle.* Paris: Seuil, 2011.

Blakemore, Richard. "The Legal World of English Sailors, c. 1575–1729." In *Law, Labour and Empire: Comparative Perspectives on Seafarers, c. 1500–1800,* edited by Maria Fusaro, Bernard Allaire, Richard J. Blakemore, and Tijl Vanneste. New York: Palgrave Macmillan, 2015.

————. "Pieces of Eight, Pieces of Eight: Seamen's Earnings and the Venture Economy of Early Modern Seafaring." *Economic History Review* 70, no. 4 (November 2017), 1153–84.

Boonzaier, Emily, Penny Berens, Candy Malherbe, and Andy Smith. *The Cape Herders: A History of the Khoikhoi of Southern Africa.* Athens: Ohio University Press, 1996.

Boxer, C. R. *The Dutch Seaborne Empire 1600–1800.* London: Knopf, 1965.

Brennan, Gillian. *Patriotism, Power and Print: National Consciousness in Sixteenth-Century England.* Cambridge: James Clarke, 2003.

Brunsman, Denver. *The Evil Necessity: British Naval Impressment in the Eighteenth-Century Atlantic World.* Charlottesville: University of Virginia Press, 2013.

Burwash, Dorothy. *English Merchant Shipping 1460–1540.* Toronto: University of Toronto Press, 1947.

Buti, Gilbert. "Aller en caravane: Le cabotage lointain en Méditerrannée, XVIIe et XVIII siècles." *Revue d'histoire moderne et contemporaine* 52, no. 1 (January—March 2005), 7–38.

Cameron, Jason. "Royal Authority Versus Corporate Sovereignty: The Levant Company and the Ambiguities of Early Stuart Statecraft." *Seventeenth Century* 32, no. 3 (February 2017), 231–55.

Carey, Daniel, and Claire Jowitt, eds. *Richard Hakluyt and Travel Writing in Early Modern Europe.* Farnham: Ashgate, 2012.

Casale, Giancarlo. "The Ethnic Composition of Ottoman Ships and the 'Rumi Challenge' to Portuguese Identity." *Medieval Encounters* 13, no. 1 (March 2007), 122–44.

———. "The Ottoman Administration of the Spice Trade in the Sixteenth-Century Red Sea and Persian Gulf." *Journal of the Economic and Social History of the Orient* 49, no. 2 (May 2006), 170–98.

Cell, Gillian T. *English Enterprise in Newfoundland 1577–1660.* Toronto: University of Toronto Press, 1969.

Chaudhuri, Kirti N. *The English East India Company: The Study of an Early Joint-Stock Company 1600–1640.* London: Frank Cass, 1965.

———. "The Portuguese Maritime Empire, Trade, and Society in the Indian Ocean during the Sixteenth Century." *Portuguese Studies* 8 (1992), 57–70.

Chida-Razvi, Mehreen M. "The Perception of Reception: The Importance of Sir Thomas Roe at the Mughal Court of Jahangir." *Journal of World History* 25, nos. 2–3 (June/September 2014), 263–84.

Christopher, Emma. *Slave Ship Sailors and Their Captive Cargoes, 1730–1807.* New York: Cambridge University Press, 2006.

Ciano, Cesare. "Corsare inglesi a servizio de Ferdinando I." In *Atti del convegno di studi gli Inglesi a Livorno e all'isola d'Elba: Sec. XVII–XIX.* Livorno, 1980.

Clulow, Adam. *The Company and the Shogun: The Dutch Encounter with Tokugawa Japan.* New York: Columbia University Press, 2014.

———. "European Maritime Violence and Territorial States in Early Modern Asia, 1600-1650." *Itinerario* 33, no. 3 (November 2009), 72–94.

———. " 'Great Help from Japan': The Dutch East India Company's Experiment with Japanese Soldiers." In *The Dutch and English East India Companies: Diplomacy, Trade and Violence in Early Modern Asia,* edited by Adam Clulow and Tristan Mostert. Amsterdam: Amsterdam University Press, 2018.

Colley, Linda. " 'Whose Nation? Class and National Consciousness in Britain 1750–1830." *Past and Present* 113, no. 1 (November 1986), 97–117.

Collinson, Patrick. "This England: Race, Nation, Patriotism." In *This England: Essays on the English Nation and Commonwealth in the Sixteenth Century.* Manchester: Manchester University Press, 2011.

Curtin, Philip. *Cross-Cultural Trade in World History.* Cambridge: Cambridge University Press, 1984.

Dancy, J. Ross. *The Myth of the Press Gang: Volunteers, Impressment and the Naval Manpower Problem in the Late Eighteenth Century.* Rochester: Boydell Press, 2015.

Das Gupta, Ashin. "Indian Merchants and the Western Indian Ocean: The Early Seventeenth Century." *Modern Asian Studies* 19, no. 3 (1985), 481–99.

Davis, Natalie Zemon. *Trickster Travels: A Sixteenth-Century Muslim between Worlds.* New York: Hill and Wang, 2006.

Davis, Ralph. "England and the Mediterranean, 1570–1670." In *Essays in the Economic and Social History of Tudor and Stuart England,* edited by F. J. Fisher. Cambridge University Press, 1961.

———. *The Rise of the English Shipping Industry in the Seventeenth and Eighteenth Centuries.* London: Macmillan, 1962.

Divitiis, Gigliola Pagano de. *English Merchants in Seventeenth-Century Italy.* Cambridge: Cambridge University Press, 1997.

Donati, Barbara. *Tra Inquisizione e Granducato: Storie di Inglesi nella Livorno del primo seicento.* Rome: Storie e Letteratura, 2010.

Drixler, Fabian. *Mabiki: Infanticide and Population Growth in Eastern Japan, 1660–1950.* Berkeley: University of California Press, 2013.

Dursteler, Eric. *Venetians in Constantinople: Nation, Identity, and Coexistence in the Early Modern Mediterranean.* Baltimore: Johns Hopkins University Press, 2006.

Earle, Peter. *Corsairs of Malta and Barbary.* London: Sidgwick and Jackson, 1970.

———. "English Sailors, 1570–1775." In *"Those Emblems of Hell"? European Sailors and the Maritime Labour Market, 1570–1870,* edited by Jaap R. Bruijn, Paul C. van Royen, and Jan Lucassen. Liverpool: Liverpool University Press, 1998.

———. *Sailors: English Merchant Seamen 1650–1775.* London: Methuen, 1998.

Erickson, Emily. *Between Monopoly and Free Trade: The English East India Company, 1600–1757.* Princeton: Princeton University Press, 2014.

Fauvelle-Aymar, François-Xavier. *L'invention du Hottentot: Histoire du regard occidental sur les Khoisan (15e–19e siècles).* Paris: Publications de la Sorbonne, 2002.

Fuchs, Barbara. "An English *Pícaro* in New Spain: Miles Philips and the Framing of National Identity." *CR: The New Centennial Review* 2, no. 1 (Spring 2002), 55–68.

Fuller, Mary C. "Arthur and Amazons: Editing the Fabulous in Hakluyt's *Principal Navigations.*" *Yearbook of English Studies* 41, no. 1 (2011), 173–89.

Fulton, Thomas Wemyss. *Sovereignty of the Sea: An Historical Account of the Claims of England to the Dominant of the British Seas. . . .* London: W. Blackwood, 1911.

Fury, Cheryl A., ed. *The Social History of English Seamen, 1485–1649.* Woodbridge, Suffolk: Boydell Press, 2012.

———. *Tides in the Affairs of Men: The Social History of Elizabethan Seamen 1580–1603.* Westport, Conn.: Greenwood Press, 2002.

———. " 'To Set Down All the Villanie': Accounts of the Sodomy Trial on the Fourth East India Company Voyage (1609)." *Mariner's Mirror* 102, no.1 (January 2016), 74–80.

Fusaro, Maria. "The Invasion of Northern Litigants: English and Dutch Seamen in Mediterranean Courts of Law." In *Law, Labour and Empire: Comparative Perspectives on Seafarers, c. 1500–1800,* edited by Maria Fusaro, Bernard Allaire, Richard J. Blakemore, and Tijl Vanneste. New York: Palgrave Macmillan, 2015.

———. *Political Economies of Empire in the Early Modern Mediterranean: The Decline of Venice and the Rise of England, 1450–1700.* Cambridge: Cambridge University Press, 2015.

Games, Alison. "Anglo-Dutch Maritime Interactions in the East Indies during the Early Seventeenth Century." In *Governing the Sea in the Early Modern Era: Essays in Honor of Robert C. Ritchie,* edited by Peter C. Mancall and Carole Shammas. San Marino, Calif.: Huntington Library, 2014.

———. *Inventing the English Massacre: Amboyna in History and Memory.* Oxford: Oxford University Press, 2020.

———. *The Web of Empire: English Cosmopolitans in an Age of Expansion, 1560–1660.* Oxford: Oxford University Press, 2008.

García-Arenal, Mercedes. "The Moriscos in Morocco: From Granadan Emigration to the Hornacheros of Salé." In *The Expulsion of the Moriscos from Spain: A Mediterranean Diaspora,* edited by Mercedes García-Arenal and Gerard Wiegers, translated by Consuela Lopez-Morillas and Martin Beagles. Leiden: Brill, 2014.

García-Arenal, Mercedes, and Gerard Wiegers. *A Man of Three Worlds: Samuel Pallache, a Moroccan Jew in Catholic and Protestant Europe.* Translated by Martin Beagles. Baltimore: Johns Hopkins University Press, 2003.

Ghobrial, John-Paul. "The Secret Life of Elias of Babylon and the Uses of Global Microhistory." *Past and Present* 222, no. 1 (February 2014), 51–93.

Goetz, Rebecca Anne. "Indian Slavery: An Atlantic and Hemispheric Problem." *History Compass* 14, no. 2 (February 2016), 59–70.

Graf, Tobias P. *The Sultan's Renegades: Christian-European Converts to Islam and the Making of the Ottoman Elite, 1570–1610.* Oxford: Oxford University Press, 2017.

Greene, Molly. "Beyond the Northern Invasion: The Mediterranean in the Seventeenth Century," *Past and Present* 174, no. 1 (February 2002), 42–71.

Greenfeld, Liah. *Nationalism: Five Roads to Modernity.* Cambridge, Mass.: Harvard University Press, 1992.

Greif, Avner. *Institutions and the Path to the Modern Economy: Lessons from Medieval Trade.* Cambridge: Cambridge University Press, 2006.

Haigh, Christopher. *English Reformations: Religion, Politics, and Society under the Tudors.* Oxford: Clarendon Press, 1993.

Hair, P. E. H. and J. D. Alsop. *English Seamen and Traders in Guinea, 1553–1565: The New Evidence of Their Wills.* Lewiston, N.Y.: E. Mellen Press, 1992.

Hanna, Mark. *Pirate Nests and the Rise of the British Empire, 1570–1740.* Chapel Hill: University of North Carolina Press, 2015.

Harvey, L. P. *Muslims in Spain 1500 to 1614.* Chicago: University of Chicago Press, 2005.

Hebb, David Delison. *Piracy and the English Government, 1616–1642.* Aldershot: Scolar Press, 1994.

Helgerson, Richard. *Forms of Nationhood: The Elizabethan Writing of England.* Chicago: University of Chicago Press, 1992.

———. " "I Miles Philips": An Elizabethan Seamen Conscripted by History," *PMLA* 118, no. 3 (May 2003), 573–80.

Hershenzon, Daniel. *The Captive Sea: Slavery, Communication, and Commerce in Early Modern Spain and the Mediterranean.* Philadelphia: University of Pennsylvania Press, 2018.

Heywood, Linda, and John Thornton. *Central Africans, Atlantic Creoles, and the Foundation of the Americas, 1585–1660.* Cambridge: Cambridge University Press, 2007.

Hindle, Steve. *On the Parish? The Micro-Politics of Poor Relief in Rural England c. 1550–1750.* Oxford: Oxford University Press, 2004.

Hubbard, Eleanor. *City Women: Money, Sex, and the Social Order in Early Modern London.* Oxford: Oxford University Press, 2012.

Hudson, Geoffrey L. "The Relief of English Disabled Ex-Sailors." In *The Social History of English Seamen 1485–1649,* edited by Cheryl A. Fury. Woodbridge, Suffolk: Boydell Press, 2012.

Hudson, Nicholas. " 'Hottentots' and the Evolution of European Racism." *Journal of European Studies* 34, no. 4 (December 2004), 308–32.

Hunt, E. "Easton, Peter." In *Dictionary of Canadian Biography,* 1:300–301. Toronto: University of Toronto/Université Laval, 1966.

Hunt, Margaret R. "The 1689 Mughal Siege of East India Company Bombay: Crisis and Historical Erasure." *History Workshop Journal* 84, no. 1 (September 2017), 149–69.

Ingram, Martin. *Carnal Knowledge: Regulating Sex in England 1470–1600*. Cambridge: Cambridge University Press, 2017.

Innis, Harold. *Cod Fisheries: The History of an International Economy*. Toronto: University of Toronto Press, 1954.

Israel, Jonathan. *Dutch Primacy in World Trade 1585–1740*. Oxford: Clarendon Press, 1989.

Ittersum, Martine Julia van. "Debating Natural Law in the Banda Islands: A Case Study in Anglo-Dutch Imperial Competition in the East Indies, 1609–1621." *History of European Ideas* 42, no. 4 (March 2016), 459–501.

Jaffer, Aaron. *Lascars and Indian Ocean Seafaring, 1780–1860: Shipboard Life, Unrest and Mutiny*. Woodbridge, Suffolk: Boydell Press, 2015.

Kaiser, Wolfgang, and Guillaume Calafat. "The Economy of Ransoming in the Early Modern Mediterranean: A Form of Cross-Cultural Trade between Southern Europe and the Maghreb (Sixteenth to Eighteenth Centuries)." In *Religion and Trade: Cross-Cultural Exchanges in World History, 1000–1900*, edited by Francesca Trivellato, Leor Halevi, and Cátia Antunes. Oxford: Oxford University Press, 2014.

Ketting, Herman. *Leven, werk en rebellie aan boord van Oost-Indiëvaarders (1595–1650)*. Amsterdam: Aksant, 2002.

Kidd, Colin. *British Identities before Nationalism: Ethnicity and Nationhood in the Atlantic World, 1600–1800*. Cambridge: Cambridge University Press, 1999.

Kupperman, Karen Ordahl. *Indians and English: Facing Off in Early America*. Ithaca, N.Y.: Cornell University Press, 2000.

———. "The Love-Hate Relationship with Experts in the Early Modern Atlantic." *Early American Studies* 9, no. 2 (Spring 2011), 248–67.

———. *Settling with the Indians: The Meeting of English and Indian Cultures in America, 1580–1640*. Totowa, N.J.: Rowman and Littlefield, 1980.

Land, Isaac. "Customs of the Sea: Flogging, Empire, and the 'True British Seaman' 1770 to 1870," *Interventions: International Journal of Postcolonial Studies* 3, no. 2 (December 2010), 169–85.

Lane, Kris. *Pillaging the Empire: Global Piracy on the High Seas*. 2nd ed. New York: Routledge, 2016.

Largueche, Dalenda. "The Mahalla: The Origins of Beylical Sovereignty in Ottoman Tunisia during the Early Modern Period." Translated by Julia Clancy-Smith and Caroline Audet. *Journal of North African Studies* 6, no. 1 (January 2001), 105–16.

Levi, Scott C. *The Indian Diaspora in Central Asia and its Trade, 1550–1900*. Leiden: Brill, 2001.

Linebaugh, Peter, and Marcus Rediker. *The Many-Headed Hydra: Sailors, Slaves, Commoners, and the Hidden History of the Revolutionary Atlantic.* Boston: Verso, 2000.

Loth, Vincent. "Armed Incidents and Unpaid Bills: Anglo-Dutch Rivalry in the Banda Islands in the Seventeenth Century." *Modern Asian Studies* 29, no. 4 (October 1995), 705–40.

Lunsford, Virginia W. *Piracy and Privateering in the Golden Age Netherlands.* New York: Palgrave Macmillan, 2005.

Maclean, Gerald. *Looking East: English Writing and the Ottoman Empire before 1800.* New York: Palgrave Macmillan, 2007.

Mancall, Peter C. *Fatal Journey: The Final Expedition of Henry Hudson.* New York: Basic Books, 2009.

Mancke, Elizabeth. "Early Modern Expansion and the Politicization of Oceanic Space." *Geographical Review* 89, no. 2 (April 1999), 225–36.

———. "Negotiating an Empire: Britain and Its Overseas Peripheries, c. 1550–1780." In *Negotiated Empires: Centers and Peripheries in the Americas, 1500–1820,* edited by Christine Daniels and Michael V. Kennedy. New York: Routledge, 2002.

Massarella, Derek. *A World Elsewhere: Europe's Encounter with Japan in the Sixteenth and Seventeenth Centuries.* New Haven: Yale University Press, 1990.

Matar, Nabil. *Britain and Barbary, 1589–1689.* Gainesville: University Press of Florida, 2005.

———. "Introduction: England and Mediterranean Captivity, 1577–1704." In *Piracy, Slavery, and Redemption: Barbary Captivity Narratives from Early Modern England,* edited by Daniel Vitkus. New York: Columbia University Press, 2001.

McCormick, Ted. "Population: Modes of Seventeenth-Century Demographic Thought." In *Mercantilism Reimagined: Political Economy in Early Modern Britain and Its Empire,* edited by Philip J. Stern and Carl Wennerlind. Oxford: Oxford University Press, 2014.

McJannet, Linda. "Purchas His Pruning: Refashioning the Ottomans in Seventeenth-Century Travel Narratives." *Huntington Library Quarterly* 74, no. 2 (June 2011), 219–42.

Meersbergen, Guido van. "Dutch and English Approaches to Cross-Cultural Trade in Mughal India and the Problem of Trust, 1600–1630." In *Beyond Empires: Global, Self-Organizing, Cross-Imperial Networks, 1500–1800,* edited by Cátia Antunes and Amélia Polónia. Leiden: Brill, 2016.

Melikan, Rose. "Shippers, Salvors, and Sovereigns: Competing Interests in the Medieval Law of Shipwreck." *Journal of Legal History* 11, no. 2 (September 1990), 163–82.

Merians, Linda E. *Envisioning the Worst: Representations of "Hottentots" in Early-Modern England.* Newark: University of Delaware Press, 2001.

Miller, Joseph C. "The Significance of Drought, Disease and Famine in the Agriculturally Marginal Zones of West-Central Africa." *Journal of African History* 23, no. 1 (January 1982), 17–61.

Mishra, Rupali. *A Business of State: Commerce, Politics, and the Birth of the East India Company.* Cambridge, Mass.: Harvard University Press, 2018.

———. "Diplomacy at the Edge: Split Interests in the Roe Embassy to the Mughal Court." *Journal of British Studies* 53, no. 1 (January 2014), 5–28.

———. "Merchants, Commerce, and the State: The East India Company in Early Stuart England." Ph.D diss., Princeton University, 2010.

Missoum, Sakina. "Andalusi Immigration and Urban Development in Algiers (Sixteenth and Seventeenth Centuries)." In *The Expulsion of the Moriscos from Spain: A Mediterranean Diaspora,* edited by Mercedes García-Arenal and Gerard Wiegers, translated by Consuela Lopez-Morillas and Martin Beagles. Leiden: Brill, 2014.

Morgan, Edmund S. *American Slavery, American Freedom: The Ordeal of Colonial Virginia.* New York: W. W. Norton, 1975.

———. "The First American Boom: Virginia 1618 to 1630." *William and Mary Quarterly* 28, no. 2 (April 1971), 169–98.

Neri, Algerina. *Uno schiavo inglese nella Livorno dei Medici.* Pisa: ETS, 2000.

Newell, Margaret Ellen. *Brethren by Nature: New England Indians, Colonists, and the Origins of American Slavery.* Ithaca, N.Y.: Cornell University Press, 2015.

Newman, Simon P. *A New World of Labor: The Development of Plantation Slavery in the British Atlantic.* Philadelphia: University of Pennsylvania Press, 2013.

North, Douglass C. "Institutions, Transaction Costs, and the Rise of Merchant Empires." In *The Political Economy of Merchant Empires,* edited by James D. Tracy. Cambridge: Cambridge University Press, 1991.

Palmer, Philip. " 'All Suche matters as passed on this vyage': Early English Travel Anthologies and the Case of John Saracoll's Maritime Journal (1586–87)." *Huntington Library Quarterly* 76, no. 3 (September 2013), 325–44.

Panzac, Daniel. *La caravane maritime: Marins européens et marchands ottomans en Méditerranée.* Paris: CNRS, 2004.

Penn, Nigel. "Written Culture and the Cape Khoikhoi: From Travel Writing to Kolb's 'Full Description.' " In *Written Culture in a Colonial Context: Africa and the Americas 1500–1900,* edited by Adrien Delmas and Nigel Penn. Leiden: Brill, 2012.

Polónia, Amélia. "Portuguese Seafarers: Informal Agents of Empire-Building." In *Law, Labour and Empire: Comparative Perspectives on Seafarers, c. 1500–1800,* edited by Maria Fusaro, Bernard Allaire, Richard J. Blakemore, and Tijl Vanneste. New York: Palgrave Macmillan, 2015.

Poulsen, Bo. "Imitation in European Herring Fisheries, c. 1550–1860." *Scandinavian Journal of History* 41, no. 2 (April 2016), 185–207.

Quinn, David B. "James I and the Beginnings of Empire in America." In *Explorers and Colonies: America, 1500–1625*. London: Bloomsbury Academic, 1990.

———. "Newfoundland in the Consciousness of Europe in the Sixteenth and Early Seventeenth Centuries." In *Explorers and Colonies: America, 1500–1625*. London: Bloomsbury Academic, 1990.

Rediker, Marcus. *Between the Devil and the Deep Blue Sea: Merchant Seamen, Pirates, and the Anglo-American Maritime World, 1700–1750*. Cambridge: Cambridge University Press, 1989.

———. *Villains of All Nations: Atlantic Pirates in the Golden Age*. Boston: Verso, 2004.

Reid, Anthony. "Early Southeast Asian Categorizations of Europeans." In *Implicit Understandings: Observing, Reporting, and Reflecting on the Encounters between Europeans and Other Peoples in the Early Modern Era*, edited by Stuart B. Schwartz. Cambridge: Cambridge University Press, 1994.

———. *Southeast Asia in the Age of Commerce: Expansion and Crisis*. New Haven: Yale University Press, 1993.

———. *Southeast Asia in the Age of Commerce: The Lands below the Winds*. New Haven: Yale University Press, 1988.

Ritchie, Robert. *Captain Kidd and the War against the Pirates*. Cambridge, Mass.: Harvard University Press, 1989.

Rodger, N. A. M. *The Command of the Ocean: A Naval History of Britain 1649–1815*. New York: W. W. Norton, 2004.

———. "Guns and Sails in the First Phase of English Colonization, 1500–1650." In *The Oxford History of the British Empire. Volume 1. The Origins of Empire: British Overseas Enterprise to the Close of the Seventeenth Century*. Edited by Nicholas Canny. Oxford: Oxford University Press, 1998.

———. *The Safeguard of the Sea: A Naval History of Britain 660–1649*. New York: W. W. Norton, 1997.

Rogers, Nicholas. *The Press Gang: Naval Impressment and Its Opponents in Georgian Britain*. London: Continuum, 2007.

Rodríguez García, José María. "Signs of the Other in Three Early Modern American Texts: Contexts for 'A Discourse Written by One Miles Philips.' " *Atlantis* 20, no. 2 (December 1998), 193–214.

Rossi, Guido. *Insurance in Elizabethan England: The London Code*. Cambridge: Cambridge University Press, 2016.

Sá, Vivien Kogut Lessa de, ed. *The Admirable Adventures and Strange Fortunes of Master Anthony Knivet.* Cambridge: Cambridge University Press, 2015.

———. "Anthony Knyvett [Knivet], 1577?–1649." *Oxford Dictionary of National Biography.* Article published 11 October 2018. https://doi.org/10.1093/odnb/9780198614128.013.112252

Said, Edward. *Orientalism.* New York: Vintage Books, 1979.

Schwartz, Stuart B. *All Can Be Saved: Religious Tolerance and Salvation in the Iberian Atlantic World.* New Haven: Yale University Press, 2008.

Senior, Clive Malcolm. "An Investigation of the Activities and Importance of English Pirates 1603–1640." Ph.D. thesis, University of Bristol, 1972.

———. *A Nation of Pirates: English Piracy in Its Heyday.* Newton Abbot, Devon: David and Charles, 1976.

Sgroi, R. C. L. "Piscatorial Politics Revisited: The Language of Economic Debate and the Evolution of Fishing Policy in Elizabethan England." *Albion: A Quarterly Journal Concerned with British Studies* 35, no. 1 (Spring 2003), 1–24.

Sharpe, Pamela. "Gender at Sea: Women and the East India Company in Seventeenth-Century London." In *Women, Work and Wages in England, 1600–1850,* edited by K. D. M. Snell, Penelope Lane, and Neil Raven. Woodbridge, Suffolk: Boydell Press, 2004.

Shepard, Alexandra. *Meanings of Manhood in Early Modern England.* Oxford: Oxford University Press, 2006.

Sirota, Brent S. "The Church: Anglicanism and the Nationalization of Maritime Space." In *Mercantilism Reimagined: Political Economy in Early Modern Britain and Europe,* edited by Philip J. Stern and Carl Wennerlind. Oxford: Oxford University Press, 2014.

Stanley, Amy. *Selling Women: Prostitution, Markets, and the Household in Early Modern Japan.* Berkeley: University of California Press, 2012.

Steckley, George. "Litigious Mariners: Wage Cases in the Seventeenth-Century Admiralty Court." *Historical Journal* 42, no. 2 (June 1999), 315–45.

———. "The Seventeenth-Century Origins of Modern Salvage Law." *Journal of Legal History* 35, no. 3 (October 2014), 209–30.

Stein, Tristan. "Passes and Protection in the Making of a British Mediterranean." *Journal of British Studies* 54, no. 3 (July 2015), 602–31.

Stern, Philip J. " 'Bundles of Hyphens': Corporations as Legal Communities in the Early Modern British Empire." In *Legal Pluralism and Empires, 1500–1850,* edited by Lauren Benton and Richard J. Ross. New York: NYU Press, 2013.

———. *The Company-State: Corporate Sovereignty and the Early Modern Foundations of the British Empire in India.* Oxford: Oxford University Press, 2011.

———. "Soldier and Citizen in the Seventeenth-Century English East India Company." *Journal of Early Modern History* 15, nos. 1–2 (January 2011), 83–104.

Subrahmanyam, Sanjay. *Three Ways to Be Alien: Travails and Encounters in the Early Modern World.* Waltham, Mass.: Brandeis University Press, 2011.

Suranyi, Anna. *The Genius of the English Nation: Travel Writing and National Identity in Early Modern England.* Newark: University of Delaware Press, 2008.

———. "Seventeenth-Century English Travel Literature and the Significance of Foreign Foodways." *Food and Foodways* 14, nos. 3–4 (December 2006), 123–149.

Swingen, Abigail L. *Competing Visions of Empire: Labor, Slavery, and the Origins of the British Atlantic Empire.* New Haven: Yale University Press, 2015.

———. "Labor: Employment, Colonial Servitude, and Slavery in the Seventeenth-Century Atlantic." In *Mercantilism Reimagined: Political Economy in Early Modern Britain and Its Empire,* edited by Philip J. Stern and Carl Wennerlind. Oxford: Oxford University Press, 2014.

Talbot, Michael. *British-Ottoman Relations, 1661–1807: Commerce and Diplomatic Practice in Eighteenth-Century Istanbul.* Woodbridge, Suffolk: Boydell Press, 2017.

Taylor, Christopher. *The Black Carib Wars: Freedom, Survival, and the Making of the Garifuna.* Jackson: University Press of Mississippi, 2012.

Tenenti, Alberto. *Piracy and the Decline of Venice 1580–1615.* Translated by Janet and Brian Pullan. Berkeley: University of California Press, 1967.

Thornton, John. "Cannibals, Witches, and Slave Traders in the Atlantic World." *William and Mary Quarterly* 60, no. 2 (April 2003), 273–94.

Toby, Ronald P., "The 'Indianness' of Iberia and Changing Japanese Iconographies of Other." In *Implicit Understandings: Observing, Reporting, and Reflecting on the Encounters between Europeans and Other Peoples in the Early Modern Era,* edited by Stuart B. Schwartz. Cambridge: Cambridge University Press, 1994.

Tomlins, Christopher. *Freedom Bound: Law, Labor, and Civic Identity in Colonizing English America, 1580–1865.* Cambridge: Cambridge University Press, 2010.

Trivellato, Francesca. *The Familiarity of Strangers: the Sephardic Diaspora, Livorno, and Cross-Cultural Trade in the Early Modern Period.* New Haven: Yale University Press, 2009.

Vansina, Jan. "On Ravenstein's Edition of Battell's Adventures in Angola and Loango." *History in Africa* 34 (January 2007), 321–47.

Vickers, Daniel. *Young Men and the Sea: Yankee Seafarers in the Age of Sail.* New Haven: Yale University Press, 2005.

Villiers, John. "Trade and Society in the Banda Islands in the Sixteenth Century." *Modern Asian Studies* 15, no. 4 (October 1981), 723–50.

Waters, David W. *The Art of Navigation in England in Elizabethan and Early Stuart Times.* New Haven: National Maritime Museum, 1958.

Wheat, David. *Atlantic Africa and the Spanish Caribbean, 1570–1640.* Chapel Hill: University of North Carolina Press, 2016.

White, Joshua M. *Piracy and Law in the Ottoman Mediterranean.* Stanford: Stanford University Press, 2018.

Withington, Phil. *The Politics of Commonwealth: Citizens and Freemen in Early Modern England.* Cambridge: Cambridge University Press, 2005.

INDEX

Aceh 168, 171, 173, 230

Acton, William 180–81

Adams, Captain (Virginia Company) 136

Adams, Mary 199

Adams, Robert 183

Adams, William 198–99

Adriatic Sea 72

Aegean Sea 70–71, 91, 108–10, 114

Africa: Alexandria 86–87, 100, 118, Bugia 74, Cabo Blanco 156, Ceuta 148, Gambia River 34–35, Oran 104, Mombasa 210, Malindi 211, São Tomé 69, Senegal 3, 153, 156, Sudan 140, Tripoli 123, 217, Zanzibar 210–11. *See also* Algiers, Cape of Good Hope, Cape Verde Islands, Guinea, Madagascar, Morocco, Sierra Leone, Table Bay, Tunis

Africans: Angolans 36–38, 141, 157–59, enslaved 8, 35–37, 69, 141, 157–59, Imbangala 36–38, Khoekhoe 168, 208–11, 217–19, 233, 302n3, North Africans 51, 74, 78–93, 111, 116–17, 123–25, 139–41, 157, 160–62, 243–44, 263–67, West Africans 33–36, 38–39, 69, 171, 225–26, Zanzibari 210–11

Algiers 93, attacks on English shipping 116–17, 123, 125, 160–61, 263–64, 274, and Dutch captives 17, and Elizabethan privateers 51, and English captives 74, 116, 125, 243–44, 263–65, 274, and English corsairs 72, 78–79, 86, 112, 140, 160–61, and English Crown 264–66, 282n6, English merchant ships calling at 84–91, 111, 114, 123, 291n76, Gyfford's attack on 73–74, 79, 86, 289n27, 309n98, relation to Ottoman Empire 78, 264

Allen, Richard 88–90, 112

Allyn, John 53–54, 287n93

Ambon (Amboyna) 194, 235, 240

Andrews, Kenneth 5, 8–9, 39

Anglo-Spanish War 2, 4, 11, 29, 46–56, 64, 248

animals, eaten 1, 31–34, 134, 194, encountered 30–34, 37, hunted 4, 32–33, 103–4, 209, purchased from coastal people 168, 171, 206, 208–9, 218–19, on shipboard 33, 52, 109, 118, 188, 233

Anne of Denmark, Queen of England 193

Antonison, Lucas 200

Antwerp 4, 66, 168

Appleby, John 9, 144

Appleyard, Cuthbert 104, 144–45

Apsley, Sir Allen 272

Arctic Ocean 23, 103–4, 223–25, 237, 258

Armenians 66, 304n47

arms trade, in Morocco 140–41, with Native Americans 132–33, with pirates and corsairs 84, 119, 141, 154

Asian seamen 173, 201–2, 278

Azores Islands 2, and Anglo-Spanish War 26–27, 46, 50, 56, 62, 127, and English piracy 110, 143, 157, and trade 130

Baffin, William 258

Baffin Island 223

Baker, Thomas 100–101, 143

Banda Islands 166, 169–70, 193, 199, 239–41, 299n14, 305n94, Neira 193–94, 240

Banten 3, 215–16, 228, 239, English mortality 64, 171–74, English trade and diplomacy at 164, 168–69, 186, 198, 227, 230–31, 240

Barbados 7–8, 13

Barbour, Richard 21

Barker, Andrew 78–79

Barry, Lording 253

Basque ships and sailors 66, 103, 150, 157, 250, 306n24

Battell, Andrew 36–38, 285n35

Baugh, William 143, 147, 154–55, 255–57

Benton, Lauren 10

Bermuda 1–2, 4, 11, 126, 133, 136, 158, 298n68

Bernardi, Filippo 110–11, 156, 229

Bertrand, Romain 236

Best, George 223–24

Best, Thomas 104, 183–85, 187, 190, 192, 194–95, 228

Bey, Muhammad, 116–17, 139

Bishop, Richard 80–81, 139, 142, 257, 296n23

Boulton, Nicholas 201–2

boys, abuse of 109, 144, 180, low status of 59, 182, 200, 234, present on shipboard 43, 47–48, 61, 124, 135, 161, 167, and religious conversion 40–41, 144, 239, 265, seen as weak 19, 45–46, spared severe treatment 211, 257, 261, 263

Brazil 39, Englishmen in 34, 36, 43–44, 49, 61, 278, goods from 8, 44, 141, 157

Brewer, John 58

bribery: of officials 82, 88, 97, 144, 256, 265, 307n40, of seamen 54, 85, 97, 119, 151

Bright, Edward 58

Brimstead, Edward 153–54

Bristol: men from 40, 77, 144, ships from 48, 60, 80, 82, 123, 139–40, 149, 152

Bromfield, Richard 83–85

Browne, John 115, 120–21

Buckingham, George Villiers, Duke of 18, 191, 244, 267, 269–74

Bullock, Hugh 117
Burton, Thomas 141
Bylot, Robert 258

Cade, Samuel 80, 139–40, 152, 162
Caesar, Sir Julius 18
Canary Islands 134, 156–57, 208, 268
Cape of Good Hope: East India
    Company ships at 170–71, 178, 200,
    208, 217–19, route to Asia 38, 61, 168
Cape Verde Islands: 2, 31, 105, pirates
    at 156, traders and slavers at 35, 208
captives, English seamen: of Dutch
    pirates 150, 155, in France 71, on
    Malta 109–10, in North Africa 92–93,
    116, 123–25, 139, 202, 243–44, 263–68,
    in Ottoman power 71, 238–39, in
    Portuguese power 3, 36–37, 43–44,
    192–93, in Spanish power 40–42, 106,
    118–20, 260–63, in Tuscany 77–78,
    120–23, of VOC 193–94, 240–41
captives, taken by Englishmen:
    European 44–46, 51–52, Inuit 225,
    Native American 132, 262, Ottoman
    and North African 74, 88–90, 125,
    Sub-Saharan African 33, 35–36, 69,
    158, 210, 218–19, 296n18
Carey, Sir George 47
Caribbean Sea 26–27, 30, 48, 50, 105–6,
    126–29, 158–59, 168, 260–62
carpenters: compensation of 48–49, 98,
    forced into service 92, 157, status on
    shipboard 58, 176, 182, 300n54,
    targeted by privateers 45–46
Catholic League 45, 52
Catholicism 40, 42–43, 78, 129, 165,
    229–30
Cavendish, Thomas 38–39, 43, 49, 206
Cecil, Sir Edward 270
Cecil, Robert, Earl of Salisbury 65, 69,
    120, 122, 136, 260–61, 263

Cecil, William, Baron Burghley 248
Challons, Henry 128
Chambers, Arthur 105–6, 129
Charles I 245, 247, 249, 257, 266–75
Charles II 123
Chesapeake Bay 127, 134
China 2–3, 173, 228, 236
Churchman, Bartholomew 193, 241–42
Churchman, Edward 210, 302n8
citizenship 5–7, 12
civility 35–36, 207, 210, 217, 235, 238
Cleeve, Christopher 106
Clerck (or Clark), William 160
clothing, sailors' own 63, 92, 101, 141,
    150, 179, 194, 238, as gifts 59, 118,
    224, lack of 135, 150, 160, 270, 272,
    as pillage 49, 51, 152, 160, as trade
    goods 99, 141
Cober, Nicholas 180–81, 300n48
Cocks, Richard 165, 188, 190–91,
    197–201, 219–20, 230, 232, 234–35
Coen, Jan Pieterszoon 236
Coke, Sir Edward 247
Coke, Sir John 270
Cole, Alexander 278
Colley, Linda 15
Collins, Edward 118–20
colonies 6–10, 125–35, 138, 144, 158–59,
    166
commonwealth 5–7, 14, 125, 174–75,
    184, 192
Comoro Islands 209–10, 233
consortship 27, 61–63, 96, 106, 115
Constantinople. *See* Istanbul
consuls 67, 74, 84, 89, 110–13, 123, 265
conversion: to Islam 71, 91–92, 144, 202,
    239, 244, 254, 265, to Catholicism 2,
    40–41, 43, 75, 129, 253, to
    "paganism" 221, to Quakerism 123
convicts 7–8, 152, 219. *See also*
    galley-slaves

Coree the Saldanian 218–19

Cornwallis, Sir Charles 263

corsairs: attacks on English ships 16, 23, 77, 92, 109–11, 114–24, 160–61, 263–68, 293n54, Catholic 74, 77, 109–10, 114–15, 117–23, English 16, 22, 67–68, 73–85, 90–93, 107, 139–40, 160–62, Muslim 81, 90–92, 111, 116–17, 123–25, 141, 144, 160–62, 244, 263–68

cotton 8, 69, 83–84

Courthope, Nathaniel 169–70

Coverte, Robert 181, 209–12, 216–17, 300n48

Coxere, Edward 123

Cradell, William 26–28, 62

credit and seamen 28, 99–100, 135, 139, 152, 189, 197, 199, 268

cross-cultural trade and trust 15–16, 69, 85–91, 114–15, 169–70, 206–7, 222–42

Cumberland, Earl of, George Clifford, 39

currants 8, 67, 70, 99, 117, 124, 157

Curtin, Philip 222

damage to cargo 101–2, 191

Danish sailors and shipping 54, 150–51

Danseker, Simon 80, 117

Das Gupta, Ashin 236

Davies, Nevill 263

Davies, William 77–78

Davis, John, of Sandridge 57, 61, 168, 224–25, 228, 233–34, 278

Dee, John 246

Denball, Sampson 81, 92, 113, 161

Denbigh, Earl of, William Feilding 272–73

desertion 12, 59, 97, 259, from corsairs 91, from the East India Company 3, 164–65, 173, 193, 196–97, 302n110, in

the Mediterranean 112–13, from the Navy 79, 140, 270–73

Digby, Thomas 147

Digges, Sir Dudley 170, 173–75

documents: bills of lading 117, 120–21, certificates 84, 146, charter parties 105, 107, 109, 110–11, 293n42, confessions 119, 122, deeds 54, demands 107, 191, passports 71, 129, 250, petitions 61, 71, 113, 119–120, 178, 194, 260, 262–63, 270–71, round robins 107, 271, 293n33, safe-conducts 93, 216

Dodsworth, Thomas 188

dogs, people compared to 50, 55, 59, 87, 215, 217–18, 243, 261, 269

Doughty, Thomas 57–59

Downing, Joshua 108–9, 278

Downton, Nicholas 177

Drake, Arthur 162

Drake, Sir Francis 29, 38, 42, 46, 57–59, 206

Dudley, Sir Robert 72, 168

Dunkirk: privateers 53–54, 94–95, 274, whalers 104

Duppa, James 141

Duppa, Michael 141, 150–51

Dutch people, English attitudes to 55, 150, 193–94, 230–36

Dutch Republic 250, 264, opposition to English piracy 160, 254–56, privateering 35–36, 72, 81, 140, 252, relation to VOC 4, 168, territorial waters 245–48

Dutch Republic, places: Amsterdam 45, 157, Bergen 45, Bremen 56, Delft 45, Enkhuisen 51, Flushing 109, 135, 140, Holland 55–56, 72, 168, 240–41, Middelburg 51, 55, 135, Zeeland 55, 168

Dutch sailors, and herring fishery 245–49, in Admiralty court 19,

51–52, attacked by English privateers 44–46, 51–52, compensation
and discipline 98, 187, 196, on
English ships 55–56, 112, 151, 200–1,
212, expertise of 197, pirates 23, 80,
112, 117, 150, 154–55, 158, 244

Dutch service, English sailors in 55, 72,
80–81, 104, 128, 140, 196, 198–99,
233

Dutch shipping, profitable 30, 86, 98,
248–49, 276, 284n14, English attacks
on 44–45, 51, 55, 153–54, 156–57

dyestuffs: brazilwood 44, 141, cochineal
27, indigo 83–84, 118, 120, 157

dysentery 34, 128, 168, 171–73, 179, 215,
278, 302n8

East India Company 3, 6, 12, 21, 23–24,
28, 64, 163–222, 225–42, 257, 276

Eastland Company 94–97

Easton, Peter 142, 146, 149–50, 153–54,
156–57, 253, 257, 278

Edwards, William 191–92

Eldred, John 105–7

Elizabeth I, and East India Company
168, 231–32, death of 30, 64, 86,
107, diplomacy of 5, 67, 73, 140,
honor of 50–51, investment in maritime enterprise 46, maritime policy
246

Elliott, John 130–31

Emden 44, 81, 297n61

English locations: Barnstaple 63,
Colchester 135, Cornwall 78, 80,
156, 257, 266, Dartmouth 27, 56, 62,
Devon 267, Dover 124–25, 136, 146,
155, 217, the Downs 163, 172,
Gravesend 135, 171, Harwich 150–51,
Ipswich 101, 135, Isles of Scilly 136,
Isle of Wight 270, King's Lynn 136,
Limehouse 53, 151–52, Lundy 142,

Newcastle 143, 250–51, 276,
Portsmouth 130, 230, 272–73,
Ratcliffe 146, 150, 161, 286n81,
Southampton 81, 92, 250, 297n37,
Southwark 18, 80, Stepney 28, 279,
286n81, Topsham 147, Wapping 52,
152, 174, 286n81, 287n93, Weymouth
62, 266, Yarmouth 80, 143. *See also*
Bristol, London, Plymouth

Evans, Christopher 163–65, 196

Exton, John 259

extortion 51, 87, 111, 117–18, 307n40

Fajardo, Don Luis 261–62

families of seamen: abandoned 173,
202, 221, children on shipboard 144,
money sent to 151–52, petitioning for
aid 165, 198, 265, 267, precarity 28,
122, 124, 192, 198, 261–62, 264–65,
travels of 3, 75, 203

Fenton, Edward 31–34, 38, 42, 57–60

Ferdinand I de' Medici 79, attacks on
English ships 77, 121–23, patron of
English corsairs and renegades
73–74, 77, 91, 141, 253, use of
English ships 2, 16, 75–76, 87, 107

Fernandes, Simon 126–27

fish: cod 4, 8, 66, 132, 249–52, herring
69, 98, 118, 141, 245–46, 248–49,
306n8, pilchards 111, 144

fishing, commercial 8, 28–29, 66, 138,
144, 150–51, 156–57, 246, 248–52,
276, for food and recreation 32–33,
134

flags, 213, 231–32, "bloody" 70, different
from sailors' nationality 16, 76, 80,
93, 140, disrespect shown 240, 261,
homage paid 247, identifying ships
16, 74, 121–22, 140, 232, 289n27,
truce 105–6, 210

Fletcher, Francis 42, 58

Florence 73, 77–78, 120–23, 253–54

Floris, Peter 189, 196

food: customary rights 14, 86, 98, 268–69, foreign 31–32, 34, 212–14, 217–18, shortages 129–31, 164, 177, 269, 271–72, theft 131, 180

Foucques, Captain 81, 92, 290n55

France 55, 65, 81, 250, 269, 271, 274–75

Franck, Thomas 141, 145, 154

freight: paid by corsairs 114–15, 117, 152, and sailors' wages 100, 108, 112, 259, for sailors' goods 99, 187

French ports: Bordeaux 28, 104, 262, Dieppe 53, Le Havre 50, 286n82, Île de Rhé 272–73, Marseille 71, 119, 154, La Rochelle 127, 149, Toulon 289n15

French sailors, shipping, and traders: attacked by English ships 45, 51, 65–66, 79–80, 140, 142, 147, 153, 156, Brazil 43, Cape Verde Islands 35, East Indies 228–29, employing Englishmen 53, Newfoundland 249–50, North Africa 51, 84, 86, 91, 141, 244, 264, 267, warships 50–52, 70–71

friendship 41, 43–44. *See also* social networks

Frizell, James 265–66

Frobisher, Martin 57–58, 223–24

Frobisher, Richard 1, 3, 16–17, 163, 233, 282n8

furs 4, 8, 100, 103, 131–32. *See also* hides

galley-slaves: France 71, Ottoman 83, 110, 116, Spain 33, 41, 78, 163, 261, 263, Tuscany 77–8, 122, VOC 241

Games, Alison 3, 223, 239

Gardner, Thomas 115, 120

Garrett, William 88–90

Gates, Sir Thomas 1, 126

Geere, Michael 48, 269

Gentili, Alberico 18, 84

Gentleman, James 138, 150–51

Gentleman, Tobias 248

gift-giving: and foreigners 34, 170, 188, 209–10, 214, 216, 219, 223, 226, 303n17, to friends and family 135, 151–52, by pirates and privateers 54, 83–85, 144, 150–51. *See also* bribery, extortion

Gilbert, Bartholomew 130

Gilbert, Sir Humphrey 249

Glanfield, Toby 81, 92

Glenham (or Glemham), Edward 51

Goddard, Thomas 106

Gorges, Sir Ferdinando 128, 132, 136, 138

Gosnold, Bartholomew 130

Greece 108, 111, Candia 110, Chios 71, 77, 91, Corfu 111, 118, Kastellorizo 87, Milos 70–71, Patras 65, 69. *See also* Zante

Greeks 19, 67, 69, 74, 121

Grenville, Sir Richard 56–57

Grice, Richard 141

Grotius, Hugo 245

Grove, Philip de 181, 212, 215, 300n48

Guernsey 135

Guinea 3, 28, 69, 80, 129, 154, 156, 278

Gujarati shipping, seamen, and merchants 173, 190, 202, 211–12

gunners 48, 52–55, 98, 140, 197–98, 217, 287n88

gunpowder: blowing up ships 53, 74, 95, provision of 108, 168, 228, 252, seized 87, 114, 150, 154, traded 84, 119, 132, 154

Gyfford, Richard 73–74, 79, 86, 88, 271, 309n98

Haggerston, Captain 160

Hakluyt, Richard 20, 38, 278, 285n33

Hales, Sir Nicholas 246

Hall, Richard (London merchant) 105–7, 139–40

Hall, Richard (shipmaster) 150–51

Hamburg 51, 55, 147, 156–57

Hancock, Walter 80, 85

Hanna, Mark 158–59

Hare, John 53–54

Harris, Christopher 182–83

Harris, James 139, 142, 152–53, 256

Harrison, John 160

Havercomb, John 130–31

Hawkins, Sir John 29, 33, 35–36, 40, 46

Hawkins, Sir Richard 32–33, 53

Hawkins, Sir William (Fenton's lieutenant) 57, 59–60

Hawkins, William (at Agra, possibly same man as above) 216, 226

Hawlse, Matthew 60–61

Heath, William 144–45

Hebb, David 264

Henri IV of France 45, 55, 71, 246

Herod, Thomas 197–98

Heywood, Linda 158, 298n68

hides 8, 27, 69, 105–6, 111, 141, 154, 156–57, 298n73

High Court of Admiralty 18–20, 47, 51, 107, 109, 245, 256–60

Hindus 212–14

Hirado 3, 164, 191, 219, 220, 233, 236

Hitchcock, Robert 248

Hoar, William 179

Holliday, William 55–56

honor: of English royalty 50–52, 121, 170, 193, 240–42, 248, 261–62, 264, of the English nation 15–16, 114–15, 122–23, 161, 167, 183–84, 225–29, 237, of seamen 11, 13, 22, 56–58, 138, 143, 165–66, 184, 207, 220, 225, 278

Hood, Thomas 43

Hortop, Job 33, 35–36, 40, 42

Howard, Charles, Earl of Nottingham 18

Howard, Thomas, Earl of Suffolk 26–27

Hudson, Henry 258

Hughes, William 154

humiliation: of the English nation 24, 167, 170, 193, 207, 222, 238–41, 261, and enslavement 77, 122, 243–44, 261

Hunt, Thomas 132, 145, 148–50

Hussey, Thomas 139, 154–55

Iceland 28, 150, 249, 251, Westman Islands 150–51

identities, false 43, 55, 116, 146, 210, 216, 227, 231

impressment of sailors: by foreign princes 74–75, by pirates 145–47, 156, 268, by the state 47, 135, 247, 250, 252, 256, 268, 273, 277

impressment of ships 74, 87, 107–8, 121, 247, 250

indentured servants 6–8, 11, 220, 282n16

India 6, Agra 215–16, 231–32, Calicut 171, Cambay 177, 215, Daman 196–97, Dhabol 236, Goa 170, 192, 215, 227, Jafrabad 184, Mahuva 212, Masulipatnam 215–16, Narasapuram 196. *See also* Surat

Indian Ocean 2–3, 15, 163–204, 206–7, 209–12, 215–17, 226–42, 257, 305n68, Maldives Islands 233–34, Nicobar Islands 168, Seychelles 211

Indigenous peoples, American: Algonquian 4, 8, 12, 131–35, 225, 262–63, Inuit 223–25, Mexico 40, and sailors' trade 4, 128, 132, 158, 223, South America 43–44, 127–28, West Indies 128, 134, 158–59

Inquisition 17, 39–42, 78, 118, 198

instruments, of navigation 70, 133, 189, 244

insurance 86, 96

interloping 104–5, 132, 185, 228, 260. *See also* smuggling

interpreters 19, 116, 201–2, 205, 212–13

Ireland 61, 133, oppression of 129, and pirates 23, 111, 136, 144–45, 147, 157–59, 162, 255–58, 298n73, territorial waters 246, 256, trade 111, 298n73, and war 38, 144. *See also* Munster

Irish sailors and ships 19, 75, 129, 145, 153, 228, 256, 265

Isaac, Roger 140

Isaack, George 156–57

Islam: conversion to 71, 91, 144, 202, 239, 244, 254, 265, in Southeast Asia 230. *See also* Muslims

Istanbul: Ottoman capital 65, 67, 71, 78, 264–65, and trade 75, 85, 108–9, 120–21

Italy, places: Civitavecchia 69, 87, Genoa 2, 83, 110–11, Naples 129, 143, Pisa 74, 121, Rome 78, Sicily 111, 118. *See also* Florence, Tuscany, Venice

Ivery, William 89–90

ivory 35, 69, 156

Ivy, William 55–56

Jahangir 170, 216–17, 226–29, 237

James I 261, and EIC 232, 237, 241–42, and North African corsairs 264–65, and pirates 93, 137, 142–43, 254–55, proclamations 72, 84, 140, 142, and territorial waters 246, 261, 263–64, transition to peace 21, 64, 66, 80

Jamestown 2, 4, 8, 126, 129–35

janissaries 80–81, 87, 91

Japan: Edo 221, 237, EIC and European rivals 183, 199–200, 229–31, 240, English views and vice versa 217, 219–21, 227, 230, 232, 237, European sailors' behavior 3, 16, 164–65, 183, 197–99, 220, 232, 234–35, Nagasaki 164–65, 197, 233, political relations 165, 188, 219, 233, 236–37. *See also* Hirado

Japanese seamen and travelers 43, 200–201, 278

Java: English mortality 173, relations with authorities 16, 202, 236–37, relations with local people 227, 231–32, 236, 240, rivalry with VOC 166, 199, trade 168. *See also* Banten

Jay, William 149

Jennings, John: (pirate captain) 138–41, (merchant shipmaster) 146, 150

Jesuits 215–16, 227, 229–31

Jews 78, English attacks 66, hostile depictions 149, 215, passengers 16, 83, 85, 87, 108, 114, 121, 212–13, trading partners 46, 69, 141, 159

Jobson, Richard 34

Johnson, Anthony 81

Johnson, Gideon 111–12, 298n73

Jolliffe, Edward 145

Jolliffe, William 62–63

Jones, Thomas 210–11, 215, 303n22

Jourdain, John 169, 172–73, 201, 208–15, 237, 239, 300n48

Kayll, Robert 174, 251

Keeling, William 176, 178–79, 181, 187–90, 200, 205, 217, 234

Keepus, John 143–44

Kelly, Captain 160–61

Kerridge, Thomas 189, 227, 231

King, George 180

Knights of St. Stephen 73, 114–15, 121–22

Knivet, Anthony 43–44, 49, 57, 278

Lake, Evan 179–80

Lancaster, Sir James 167–71, 230

Lane, William 27

language barriers 206, 208, 218, 223–26

Lantro, Goodman 182, 300n54

law: evidence 19–20, 121–22, favoring
sailors 245, 252–60, forum shopping
107, 111, 113, 259–60, martial 24,
165, 175, 197, outlaws 76–7, 82, 93,
253, privateering 57, 61–63, proclamations 64, 72, 120, 123, 132, 140,
142, 245, 252, 271, Rolls of
Oléron 29, trade 84, 95–6, 102. *See
also* maritime custom, pardons,
reprisals

Lawse, Abraham 70, 177

Leate, Nicholas 265–66

Leigh, Charles 127–28

Len, Richard 257

Lesieur, Stephen 122

letters of reprisal 5, 28, 47, 64, 69, 106,
286n68

Levant Company 67, 108, 123, 288n10,
and English sailors 16, 22–23,
68–69, 74–77, 82, 84, 88, 93, 114–15,
122–23, 222, 265–67

Lile, Alice 119–20

Lile, James 118–19, 294n68

Linebaugh, Peter 11

lingua francas: French 116, Italian 80,
116, Latin 40, Portuguese 208, 213,
Spanish 205

Linschoten, Jan Huygen van 56

Lisbon 4, 44, 56, 67, 148, 159, English
sailors in 55, 124–25, 192, 215, 263

Lithgow, William 92–93

Livorno: English captives 77, 120–22,
English corsairs 73–78, 82, 91,
English merchant ships 67, 69,
107–8, 113, 118, 143, trade links with
Mamora 137, 141, 143, 155

London 218, dominant port 15, 50, 98,
251, merchants 48, 105, 129, 136,
162–63, politics 66, 71, 77, 123, 241,
sailors' lives 23, 52, 66, 77, 129, 146,
220, 257, sailors' protests 270–73. *See
also* East India Company, High
Court of Admiralty

Longcastle, William 80, 139–40, 152

Lübeck 153, 297n58

Lux, Richard 86–88

Macao 165, 282n8

MacLean, Gerald 222

Madagascar 8, 168, 171, 173, 176, 178,
208, 233

Madox, Richard 31, 34, 38, 42–43,
59–60

Magner, Francis 75–77, 129

Mainwaring, Sir Henry 143, 146–47,
153, 254–57

Malem, William 94–95, 97

Malta 91, 109, 118, 123–24

Mamora: Elizabethan privateers 80,
English and Dutch conflict 154–55,
English captives 80, English pirates
3, 23, 91, 136–38, 140–52, 154–55,
157–62, 253–55, 257, 295n5, 298n68,
Spanish capture 160, 298n75

Man, Silvanus 108–9

Mancke, Elizabeth 9

manhood 79, 114, 138, 224, 233–36, 242,
257. *See also* boys

Manila 165, 240, 286n56

Mansell, Sir Robert 264–65

manufactured goods 117, 128, 141,
188–89, 223. *See also* textiles

maritime custom 118, origins 10–11, 29,
sailors' pay, duties, and rights 14,
18–19, 96, 98, 100–102, 104, 108, 113,
190, 194

Marlett, William 255

Marlowe, Anthony 171, 178, 218, 225–26

marriage 28, 42, 80, 151, 197–99, 202–3, 282n8. *See also* wives

Marshalsea Prison 135–36

Matar, Nabil 90

Matthew, Walter 121–22

Maurits of Orange 72, 231, 240

Mediterranean Sea 22–23, 65–93, 99–100, 102, 104, 107–25, 139–43, 159–61, 263–68

Mellin, William 86–88, 141

Mervyn, Sir Henry 272–73

metals: copper 4, 132, 147, gold 35, 140, 155, iron 69, 86, 111, 128, 149, 218, lead 67, 148, 181, tin 67, 99, 117–18. *See also* silver

Mexico 33, 40–42, 105

Michelborne, Edward 228

Michiel, Maffio 69, 72

Middleton, Sir Henry 176, 178, 188, 190, 202, 228, 238–39

Middleton, Roger 255

Milton, Thomas 148–49

Mitche, Joan 135–36

Mitton, Thomas 80, 84, 91

mixed crews 78, 150–51, 244, 266, 298n76, disloyalty 54–55, 70, 104–5, 112, 200–202, Englishmen on hostile ships 54, 114–15, 160–62, 199, shipboard conflicts 55–56, 74–76, 90–91, 112, 140, 154

Mocha 170, 190, 201–2, 211–12, 238

Molucca Islands 166, 169, 172, 193, 202, 233, 240–41, 299n14, Ternate 234

monarchy 231–32, 240

Monie, John 53, 297n93

monopolies 12–13, 23, 96, 102–4, 131, 169, 185–89, 239–40

Monson, Sir William 246

Morecock, Robert 92

Morgan, Devereux 88

Moriscos 78, 88–90, 111, 141, 151, 263, 266, 291n80

Morocco 136–44, 146, 148–49, 151–52, 154–57, 159–62, 266–68, 275, Fedala 157, Mogador 140, 154, Saadi dynasty 140–41, Safi 63, 140, 155–56, 287n84, Santa Cruz (Agadir) 142, 156, Tetouan 88, 90, 114, 265, 291n80. *See also* Mamora, Salé

Morris, Henry 216

mortality 7, 46, 61, 97–98, 170–74, 269, 272

Motham, James 88–90

Muckell, John 81

Mughal Empire 16, 170, 215–17, 221–22, 226–29, 232, 237

Mun, Thomas 175

Munster, Ireland 142, 144, 159, 254, 256, 297n36, Crookhaven 256,

Muqarrab Khan 188, 227, 301n69

Muscovy 8, 28, 251, Archangel 54

Muscovy Company 28, 53–54, 102–4, 251

Muslims: attacked 74–76, 87, 89, 91, 108–9, 118, corsairs 92–93, 116–17, 123–25, 144, 151, 263–67, and English corsairs 3, 22, 74–76, 78–81, 91–92, 139, 160–62, 244, and English slaves 152, 243–44, 263–67, hostile depictions 149, lascars 201–3, passengers 16, 74, 77, 85–90, 114–15, 120–21, 123, trading partners 15, 51, 83–84, 120–21, 141, 159, 162, 211, 230–33. *See also* Islam, renegades

mutiny 10, 13, 25, 60–61, 78, 112, 181–83, 258, 269

Myagh, Patrick 256

Navigation Acts 14, 277

navy: British naval power 123, Charles I 245, 247, 266–78, Elizabeth 46,

James I 79, 140, 143–44, 160, 252, 254, 257, 264. *See also* impressment

Neve, John 188, 257

Newfoundland 4, 8, 60, 66, 143, 145, 156–58, 266, importance of 249–52

Newport, Christopher 50, 64, 134, 200, 225

Nicholas, Sir Edward 270, 273

Nicholl, John 128

Nicols, William 215–16

Norris, Sir John 46

North Virginia (Maine) 128, 130, 147, 262

North Virginia Company 128, 131, 147

Northwest Passage 224–25, 258, 278

Norway 95, Svalbard 103–4

Norway, John 65–66, 80

Norwood, Richard 100, 159

Okes, William 110–11, 293n42

opium 142, 215

Orenge, Henry 257

Ormuz 191, 238

Ottoman Empire 221, relations 2, 16, 22, 67–68, 74–75, 93, English captives 71, 110, 264–65, Englishmen in Ottoman service 164, 222, Red Sea trade 170, 211, 238

Ottoman Empire, places: Aden 181, 211, 303n12, Aleppo 216, Cyprus 65,74, Damascus 85, Iskenderun 76, 85, 99, 109, Mecca 202, Rhodes 74, Sana'a 211, 238, Sidon 108–9, 114, 120. *See also* Africa, Algiers, Greece, Istanbul, Mocha, Tunis

Ottoman passengers on English ships 85–90, 114–15, 120–21, 123

Ottoman shipping 2, 16, 74–76, 118

Oyapock (Wiapoco) River 28, 127–28

Pacific Ocean 29–30, 38–39, 61, 163

pardons: denied 82, 91, 93, deserters 185, pirates 3, 24, 136–37, 140–41, 154, 157, 160, 245, 252–57, 288n2, 297n61

Parker, John 145, 148–49, 154–55

Parliament 194–95, 252, 260, 273–74, 277

passengers 85, 111, EIC 212–13, safety 22, 83, 85–90, 114–17, 120–21, 123, 149

Pate, William 109, 115

Pecke, Peter 147, 154–55

Pepwell, Henry 85, 197, 200, 228, 298n61

Perfeit, William 184–85

Persia 191, 227, 238, 303n22, Isfahan 227

petitioning 203, captives 71, 119, 261–65, charity 28, 71, 165, 203, for compensation 119–20, 173, 184, 194–95, 260, 270–71, shipboard 61, 113, 178

Peyton, Walter 171–74, 188, 196–98, 219, 239–40

Philip II of Spain 29, 46, 52, 54, 140, 168, 249

Philip, Miles 41–42

Philippines 163, 165, 240, 303n23

Philmore, Richard 62–63

pillage 49, 51–52, 54, 69, 118, 127, 147, and EIC 190, 195, 211

Pinheiro, Emanuel 215

Pipe, Thomas 70, 105, 289n15

Plymouth, England 26, 45, 55, 66, 79–80, 121, 136, 162, 243–44, 266

Plymouth, New England 8, 132

Poland 94, Elbing 94, 99

polyglot seamen 43–44, 80, 122, 165, 198, 201–2

Popham, Sir Francis 130–31

population 6–7, 13, 138, 174–75, 220, 276–77

porcelain 186, 189, 194

Portuguese empire: Brazil and western Africa 34–37, 43, 205, Indian Ocean 3, 166, 169–70, 183–84, 191–92, 196–98, 210, 213–15, 217, 227–29, Madeira 45, 157, São Tomé 69. *See also* Azores

Portuguese sailors and shipping 19, 187, and Elizabethan privateers 11–12, 44, 50, 62, 69, 167, 250, and English pirates 141, 156–57, in English service 126, fishermen 66, 157, 250, slave ships 141, 158

Pory, John 270

Pountis, Jacob and John 83, 85

prayer, 235, before battle 124, 161, 184, Latin 40–41, psalms 213, 230, 235, 244, shipboard 88, 176, 211, 213

principal-agent problem 100–102, 115, 117, 185–90

Pring, Martin 128, 229

Privy Council: appeals to 119 20, 162, 194, 266, maritime policy 246, 252, 263–64, 270, piracy 66, 254–55

Prophett, Jonas 134–36, 143, 152

Protestantism 4, 14–15, 22, 39–43, 78, 153, 277, contrasted with Catholicism 230, Huguenots 269, 272–73, "puritans" 83. *See also* prayer, conversion

providence 102, 124–25, 150, 172, 180–81

public good 6–7, 125, 174–75, 273

Purchas, Samuel 20–21, 36, 38, 125

Pyborne, William 256–57

Ragusa 83, 118

Ragusan ships and sailors 73–74, 86, 91

Raleigh, Sir Walter 9, 45, 56

ransoming: Dunkirkers 95, English pirates 135, Mediterranean 71, 74, 124, 144, 152, 265–67, 296n18. *See also* captives

rape and sexual harassment 151, 180, 227, 234, 238

Rastell, Thomas 189

Rawlins, John 243–44, 265

recreation: gambling 164, 176, games 223–24, hunting 32–34, 224, theater 205–6

Red Sea 164, 190, 201–2, 211, 238, 298n3

Rediker, Marcus 11, 13, 295n6

Reekes, John 89–90

religion 14–15, 39–44, 176, 229–30. *See also* Catholicism, conversion, Islam, prayer, Protestantism, providence

renegades 12, 15, 22, Atlantic and Arctic 53–54, 103–4, 129, with Catholic corsairs 2, 72–78, 114–15, 157, 160, Indian Ocean, Red Sea, Asia 164–65, 196–97, with Muslim corsairs 66, 72, 78–85, 90–93, 117, 153, 160–62, 244, 264–68

reprisals: avenging and deterring abuses 16, 68, 74–76, 86–88, 90, 123, 228–29, 236, privateering 47. *See also* letters of reprisal

Revett, William 211, 215

Reynst, Gerard 236

Rich, Robert, Earl of Warwick 158–59, 229

Richelieu, Cardinal 268

Rickman, Robert 116–17, 149, 161, 194–95

Roan, John 183, 235

Roanoke 126–27, 283n39

Rodger, N. A. M., 9

Roe, Sir Thomas 170, 217, 228, 232, 237, 265

Roope, Gilbert 139, 162, 255

Russell, Sir William 271

Said, Edward 221

Salbank, Joseph 216

Saldania. *See* Table Bay

Salé 141, English pirates 80–81, 92, 160, 162, 298n76, slaving corsairs 124–25, 144, 243, 263, 265–67, 274–75

Salisbury, Earl of. *See* Cecil, Robert, Earl of Salisbury

Sallowes, Allen 103–4

salvage 100–101

Sampson, Captain. *See* Denball, Sampson

Saris, John 163–65, 187, 190, 197, 216, 230, and Asian seamen 201–2, and illness 173–74, 179, in Japan 164, 199, 219–21, 227, 231–32, 237

Savary de Brèves, François 65, 71, 79–81

Savoy, Duke of 157, 160, 229, 253–54, 278

Saxbridge, Tibault 158, 258n73

Sayer, Ambrose 78, 86, 111, 290n42

Scot, Edmund 199, 231–32

Scotland 246, Leith 113, Hebrides 249

Scottish sailors 19, captives 265–66, corsairs 78, 298n76, and Elizabethan privateers 50, on English ships 106, 191, 199, and Muscovy Company 104

Scottish ships 112–13, 153

scurvy 167–68, 170–71, 178–79, 205–6, 208

Selden, John 245

Senior, C. M. 153, 155

Sexton, Robert 94–95

sexual license: in Asia 164–65, 183, 214, 219–21, 227, 232, 234, 238, pirates 81, 151, shipboard 180. *See also* rape

Sharpe, Edward 248–49

Sharpeigh, Alexander 181, 208, 211–15, 303n17

Sherley, Sir Anthony 72

Sherley, Sir Robert 303n22

Sherley, Sir Thomas 85–6

ships: *Affection* 44, *Aid* 58, *Alcedo* 66, 69, *Ambition* 152, *Amy* 150–51, *Angel* 86, *Angola Man* 141, *Anne Royal* (royal) 135, *Ascension* (EIC) 180–81, 208–12, 216–17, *Attendant* (EIC) 193, 240 *Balbiana* 65–66, 257, *Bennett* 146, *Black Eagle* 51, *Blessing* (i) 80, (ii) 88–90, *Blue Sheres* 52, *Brave* 127, *Brown Fish* 45, *Bull* (EIC) 191, *Carnation* 101, *Castor and Pollux* 260, *Centaur* 27, 44, 50, *Clove* (EIC) 163–64, 179, 181, 187, 219–20, 230, 233, *Commongain* 149, *Concord* (i) 130, (ii) 136, 145, 156–57, *Consent* (i) 117, (ii, EIC) 233, *Consolation* 48, *Content* 45, *Cynthia* 99, *Dainty* 50, *Daisy* 3, 145, *Darling* (i) 76, 86–87, (ii, EIC) 172, 197–98, 257, *Defence* 240, *Delight* (i) 60–61, (ii) 124, *Deliverance* 1–2, *Desire* 61, 278, *Diamond* 44, 62–63, *Discovery* (i) 138, (ii) 258, *Dolphin* 161, *Dorothy* (i) 100, (ii) 111–12, *Double Des* 50, *Dragon* (EIC, initially called *Malice Scourge*, also called *Red Dragon*) 168–69, 173, 178–81, 183–87, 196, 205, 218, *Edward Bonaventure* (i) 31, (ii) 167, *Elizabeth* (EIC) 190, *Elizabeth Anne Judith* 93, 123–4, *Esperance* 50, 52, *Expedition* (EIC) 28, 171–72, 181, 189, 200, *Falcon* (i) 102, (ii) 156, *Fox* 45, *Francis* 77, *Friendship* 154, *Galleon Leicester* 32, *Galleon Shute* 49, *George* 81, *Gift* 80, *Gift of God* (i) 100, (ii) 130, (iii) 145, 148–50, *Globe* (EIC) 183, 189, 257, *Golden Dragon* (i) 50, (ii) 142, *Good Hope* (EIC) 181, 209, *Greyhound* 80, *Hare* 51, *Hart* 155, *Hector* (EIC) 163–64, 169, 173, 176, 178, 180–81, ships: (*continued*)

192–93, 196, 205, 218, 230, 278, *Hope* 44, *Hopewell* 86–88, 141, *Hosiander* (EIC) 183–85, 187, 221, *Humphrey Bonaventure* 146, *Husband* 82–86, *Isaac* 86, *Jacob* 156–57, *Jacques* 104, *John and Francis* 86, *Joshua* 108–11, *Lion* 126–27, *Lion Doré* 157, *Lioness* 73, *Lion's Whelp* (royal) 79, 140, *Little John* (i) 26–27, (ii) 143, 158, *Love* 155, *Malice Scourge* (see *Dragon*), *Margaret* 150–52, *Margaret and John* 65, 71, *Marigold* (i) 58, (ii) 145, *Mary* 106, *Mary Anne* 86, 116–17, *Matthew* 121–23, *Mayflower* (i) 105–7, 163, 298n1, (ii) 146, *Merchant Royal* (i) 2, 74–77, 121, (ii) 167, *Mermaid* 104–5, *Michael and Barnard* 94–96, *Michael and John* 48, *Moonshine* 224–25, *Moresini* 70, *Nightingale* 135, *Olive Branch* 128, *Patience* 1–2, *Peppercorn* (EIC) 181–82, 197, *Philip Bonaventure* 136, *Phoenix* (i) 95, (ii) 128, (iii) 153–54, *Princesse* 50, *Prospect* 94, *Prosperous* 259, *Prudence* (i) 62–63, (ii) 63, *Rainbow* 147, *Red Dragon* (see *Dragon*), *Refusal* 50, *Reniera e Soderina* 81–82, 84, 90–91, 139, 291n65, *Report* 104, *Revenge* 56, *Richard* (i) 105–6, (ii) 128–29, 262–63, *Roebuck* 45, 76, 87, *Rose Lion* (i) 54–55, (ii) 101–2, *Salamander* 70–71, *Sampson* (EIC) 240, 257, *Seaflower* 88–90, *Sea Venture* 1–2, 11, 126, *La Señora del Rosario* 44, *Seraphim* 82–5, *Solomon* (i) 151, (ii, EIC) 193, 230, *Sovereign of the Seas* (royal) 245, *Speedwell* (i) 53–54, (ii, royal) 256–57, *St. Jacob* 45, *St. Mary* 55, *Sunshine* 224–25, *Susan* (i) 140, 152, (ii, EIC) 173, *Susan Bonaventure* 110–11, *Susan Constance* 151–52, 160–61, *Swallow* (i) 27, (ii) 133, *Swan* (i) 115, 120, (ii) 156, (iii, EIC) 189, 194, 240, *Thomas* (i) 69, 77, (ii, EIC) 180, *Thomas and William* 121–22, *Thomasine* 157, *Tiger* (i) 55–56, (ii) 123, (iii) 150–51, *Tindealer* 143–44, *Trade's Increase* 172–73, 238, *Transporter* 88–90, *Trial* (i) 87, 118–21, (ii) 129, *Triumph* 114–15, 120–21, 123, *Truelove* 51, *Ulysses* 139–40, 152, *Unicorn* 82, 85, 139, *Union* (EIC) 173, 193, 208–9, *Vanguard* (royal) 271, *Vine* 145, *Wagon* 81, *White Greyhound* 52, *Willing Mind* 156

shipbuilding 30, 86, 129–30, 284n14

shipowners 251, 276, and piracy 66, 86–88, 142–43, 149, privateering 26–27, 474–8, 54–56, 63, 66, and risk 12, 96–97, 102, 109, 110, 115, 121–22, 267, and sailors' compensation 75–76, 100, 107–10, 125, 259–60

Ship Money 267, 275

shipwreck 75, 90, 107, and castaways 1–3, 11, 35, 91, 126, 159, 208, 212–13, 298n7, caused by mortality 173, 193, economic consequences of 28, 97, 100–102, 108, 143, 193

Sicklemore, Thomas 145–46

sickness 44, 46, 57, 108, 122, 167, 214, 269, 272, venereal disease 161, 174. *See also* dysentery, mortality, scurvy

Sierra Leone 30–32, 34, 38–39, 43, 171, 180, 205–6, 225–26

silk 8, 49, 69, 100, 120, 147, 186, 196

silver 26–27, 46, 191, 212

Simnell, John 139, 257

Skevington, Thomas 58–59

slavery in English colonies 8, 13, 158

slaves, English sailors described as: in Livorno 77–78, 122, in the navy 143, 277, in North Africa 87, 91–93, 116, 152, 243, 266, in Ottoman galleys 71,

110, held by pirates 148, 150, held by
VOC 194, 241, in West Indies 261
slave ships 35–36, 69–70, 141, 157,
159–60, 278, 296n18
slave trade: English 34–36, 40, 46, 51,
69–70, 158, Portuguese 34–36, 43,
69. *See also* captives, ransoming
Smith, John (colonial governor) 132, 134
Smith (or Smythe), Sir Thomas 136, 192
smuggling 3, 105–6, 110, 139, 162–63,
187
social mobility 14, 98–99, 138–39
social networks, sailors': with foreign
seamen, renegades, and pirates
53–54, 82–85, 107, 141–42, 148–53,
and trade 99–100, 110, and women
135–36, 151, 220–21. *See also* families,
wives
Sockwell, Thomas 140, 142
Socotra 171, 188, 211–12
Somers Isles Company 158
South America 8, 30, Amazon River 78,
253, Mocha Island 198, Oyapock or
Wiapoco River 28, 127–28, Río de la
Plata 36, Strait of Magellan 38–39,
57, 60, 198, 278. *See also* Brazil
Spaight, Arthur 201
Spain 64, 160, 250, 264, English
subjects working for 53–54, 72, 129,
seizure of English ships 105–6,
118–20, 260–63, trade with 28–29,
46, war with 11, 29, 39, 46–47, 52,
248, 271
Spain, locations: Alicante 90, 111, 113,
Barcelona 69, Cadiz 100, 143–44,
268–70, 282n6, Cartagena 84–85,
111–12, Gibraltar 243, Majorca 73, 99,
Málaga 132, Sanlucar 141, 150,
262–63, Seville 106, 110–11, 141, 159,
263
Spanish Armada 46, 127

Spanish possessions: Ceuta 148, Oran
104, Mamora 160, Naples 129, 143,
Sicily 111, 118–19. *See also* Mexico,
Philippines, West Indies
Spanish sailors and shipping 19, 98,
126, 164, 227, and Dutch warships
72, 80, and Elizabethan warships 11,
27, 39, 44, 46–47, 54–6, 60, 69, 73,
127, 249, English contempt for 197,
262, 287n88, and Jacobean pirates
110, 155–58, 160, 253–54, naval 66,
72, 78, 104, 118, 129
Spere, Isaac 142–43
spices 4, 8, 55, 66, 141, 168–69, 185–87,
239, cinnamon 84, cloves 69, 100,
169, ginger 52, 141, 154, mace 169,
189, nutmeg 70, 169, pepper 35, 100,
147, 168–69, 186–88, 194, 202
Squire, William 261
St. Helena 59, 61, 171–72
St. John, Sir William 256
St. Leger, Sir William 269
Standish, Ralph 183–85
Staper, Richard 69, 108–9, 115
Steckley, George 258–59
Stephenson, Robert 145–47, 257
Stern, Philip 5–6, 165–66
Stoneman, John 262–63
storms 1, 60–61, 97, 100–102, 169, 244,
250
Strachey, William 4, 126, 131
Stuart, Elizabeth, Queen of Bohemia 135
sugar 8, 31, 43–44, 140–41, 147, 152, 154,
156–57, 194
suicide 41, 92, 180, purposefully
blowing up one's ship 53, 56, 95
Sumatra 168, 172, 181, 227
Surat 170–71, 181, 188–90, 227–28, 232,
303n17, and English castaways 208,
211–17, English relations with the
Portuguese 170, 183–85, 192, 196

surgeons 78, 183, 200, 221, 258, and
 pirates 143, 257, trade and investment 48, 100, 188, wounded and
 sick seamen 45, 55, 95, 179

Table Bay 178, 208–9, 217–19, 233, 278
Tanner, Adam 261–62
Taverner, William 139–40
Tendering, Robert 88–90
territorial waters 245–47
textiles, traded: cotton 69, 189, 202,
 linen 39, 70, 99, 147, luxury 49, 66,
 147, silk 69, 100, 120, 147, 186,
 woolen 4, 54, 84, 99, 114, 140
Thirty Years' War 247, 276
Thornton, John 158, 298n68
Thornton, Robert 2, 75–78, 91, 93, 141
Tile, Thomas 261
tobacco 7, 99–100, 110, 141
Tokugawa Ieyasu 198, 237
Tomkins, Thomas 65–66
Tordesillas, Treaty of 105
torture 236, by English privateers
 45–46, of English seamen 41,
 118–21, 150, 154, 180, 226, 263
Totten, John 199
Towerson, Gabriel 187
Townes, Anthony 90
trade, sailors' 13, 24, 52, 99–103, 113,
 128, 131–32, 185–90, 209
Trevor, Richard 259
trials on shipboard 58–59, 180–81, 183
Trinity House of Deptford 28, 49, 107,
 113, 149, 192–95, 266
trust: cross-cultural 16–17, 24, 86–91,
 114, 206–7, 209–11, 221–32, principal-agent problem 96, 117
Tuching, Simon 151–52
Tunis, 123, and attacks on English shipping 92–93, 116–17, 125, 161, 243,
 263–65, English corsairs 3, 17,

65–66, 73, 78–82, 91–93, 139–40,
 160–61, 254, 257, 263, English
 merchant ships 65, 82–86
Tuscany, Grand Duchy of 2, 16, 78,
 120–22, 253, 255. *See also* Ferdinand I

United Provinces. *See* Dutch Republic
Uthman Dey 79–81, 83–84, 91, 139,
 290n55

Venetian ships and sailors 65–66,
 68–70, 80–82, 86, 91, 108
Venice 67, 75, 264, archives 21, and
 English piracy 22, 68–72, 82–84, 93,
 English ships and seamen at 99, 107,
 111–13
Verney, Sir Francis 72
Villefranche 110, 157
Virginia 1–3, 126, 129–32, 134, 138, 158,
 225, 260, and labor 7–9, 11–12
Virginia Company 4, 7, 64, 129,
 131, 136
VOC 166–70, 230–32, 235, 237, Batavia
 170, 236, capture of English seamen
 and ships 189, 193–95, 207, 239–42,
 257, English seamen working for
 198–99, 215, and sailors' working
 conditions 183, 187, 196–97, 200,
 276

wages, sailors': disputes 19–20, 104–5,
 107, 109–13, 120, 125, 191–93, 201,
 258–60, in the navy 270–73, typical
 98, 186, 203
Walker, John (chaplain) 31–32, 34,
 42–43
Walsingham, Robert 2–3, 16–17, 145,
 160–62, 257, 264, 279
Ward, John 66, 78–85, 90–93, 107,
 139–40, 161–62, 257, 290n43, 297n61
Ward, Luke 32, 59

Watts, Sir John: (investor) 26–28, 48, (naval officer, son of previous) 271–72

Waymouth, George 128, 262

West Africa 34–36, 156. *See also* Africa, Guinea, Sierra Leone

West Country 29, 162, 252, 263, 266

West Indies 13, cutting wood 143, 158–59, dangers of capture 105–6, 128, 143–44, 260, Dominica 134, and Elizabethan privateers 27–28, 48, 50, Englishmen Cuba 27, 44, Guadeloupe 134, Hispaniola 100, 105–6, Margarita 261, Mona 134, 167, Nevis 134, Puerto Rico 127–29, Saint Lucia 128, Santo Domingo 106, Trinidad 167, Virgin Islands 134

Westby, Richard 227

whaling 4, 103–4, 132, 250

Wheddon, Jacob 45

Whitbourne, Richard 249, 251

Whitbrook, Hugh 69

White, John 126–27

White, Nicholas 180–81

Whiting, Walter 115, 118, 120

Williams, Richard 40–41

Wilson, Edward 188, 258

Wiseman, John 259

wives and widows of seamen 3, 28, 100, 103, 109, 129, 147, appearing in court 109, connections with piracy 85, 135–36, 151–52, petitioning 28, 119–20, 135–36, 152, 173, 199, 203, 262, 265, 274, 282m8, poverty of 124, 161, 203, 264–65 sailors' obligations to 124, 185, 198–99, 202–3, unfaithful 198

women, on ships 3, 74, 115, 159, 203, 223–24, and sailors' social networks 135–36. *See also* wives and widows

Woodcock, Nicholas 103–4

Wotton, Sir Henry 75–77, 82, 253

Wright, William 146–47

Wye, Anthony 152

Zante 69, 70, 72, 92, 99, 111, 118, 124

Zouch, Richard 259